Second Edition

CRACKS IN THE MELTING POT

Second Edition

CRACKS IN THE MELTING POT

Racism and Discrimination in American History

Melvin Steinfield

Assistant Professor of History
San Diego Mesa College

Glencoe Press
A division of Benziger Bruce & Glencoe, Inc.
New York • Beverly Hills

Glencoe Press
A division of Benziger Bruce & Glencoe, Inc.
8701 Wilshire Boulevard
Beverly Hills, California 90211
Collier-Macmillan Canada, Ltd., Toronto, Canada

Library of Congress catalog card number: 72-86031

First printing, 1973

CONTENTS

Foreword by Senator Mervyn M. Dymally   xi

Preface to the Second Edition   xiii

Preface to the First Edition   xv

General Introduction   xix

PART 1   ESTABLISHING AN ACCURATE PERSPECTIVE   1

Chapter One   Racism and Discrimination in Other Countries   3

Introduction   *3*

Race Relations around the World: "Race Trouble—No U.S. Monopoly," *U.S. News & World Report*   *4*

Racism in Western Civilization: from *Race and Racism*, Pierre Van den Berghe   *16*

A Quarter Century of United Nations Protest in Vain, Don Shannon   *23*

Suggestions for Further Reading   *24*

Chapter Two   Racism and Discrimination in America: A Montage   27

Introduction   *27*

Twenty Examples of American Racism   *28*

Suggestions for Further Reading   *46*

PART 2 RACIST RATIONALIZATIONS FOR TERRITORIAL ACQUISITION   49

Chapter Three   Anti-Indian Policies and Practices   51

Introduction *51*

Early Contacts, from *The American Indian Wars,* John Tebbel and Keith Jennison *53*

The Making of an Indian Warrior, Mingo Chief Logan *57*

All We Want Is to Be Left Alone, Chief Red Jacket *58*

Cherokee Removal, from *Indians of the Americas,* John Collier *61*

Conquest and Control, from *Man's Rise to Civilization as Shown by the Indians of North America from Primeval Times to the Coming of the Industrial State,* Peter Farb *66*

Suggestions for Further Reading *77*

Chapter Four   The Mexican War and Its Aftermath   79

Introduction *79*

"The Mexicans Are Indians!" *New York Evening Post* *82*

Unfit for Liberty, John C. Calhoun *83*

Whig Opposition to the Mexican War, Thomas Corwin *84*

Violence against Mexicans, from "Mexican-American Conflict on the Mining Frontier, 1848-1852," William Robert Kenny *86*

The Aftermath of the Mexican War, from *Mexican Americans and the Administration of Justice in the Southwest,* The U.S. Commission on Civil Rights *94*

Suggestions for Further Reading *102*

**Chapter Five   The Annexation of the
                        Philippines**   **105**

Introduction   *105*

Taking up the White Man's Burden, from *Manifest Destiny and Mission in American History,*
Frederick Merk   *107*

God's Chosen People, Albert Beveridge   *117*

Uplifting Our Little Brown Brothers, William
McKinley   *119*

Justifying Atrocities against Filipinos, Stuart
Creighton Miller   *120*

Brutality Is Advocated by the Press, *San Francisco Argonaut*   *122*

Suggestions for Further Reading   *125*

**PART 3   RACIST ROOTS OF
           ANTI-IMMIGRANT
           DISCRIMINATION**   **127**

**Chapter Six   White Responses to the
                    "Yellow Peril"**   **129**

Introduction   *129*

Anti-Chinese Riots, from *Mountain of Gold,* Betty
Lee Sung   *131*

Mass Expulsion, from *Race and Ethnic Relations,*
Brewton Berry   *135*

Ban the Japs!, from *America's Concentration
Camps,* Allan R. Bosworth   *140*

A Personal Account of the Evacuation and Internment, from *American in Disguise,* Daniel I.
Okimoto   *144*

Suggestions for Further Reading   *151*

**Chapter Seven   Anti-Semitism in
                American Life**   **153**

Introduction *153*

Racism in the Textbooks, from "The Jew in American History," Jerome L. Ruderman *154*

Jews as a Class, from *Discrimination, U.S.A.*, Jacob Javits *158*

Recent Trends, from *The Course of Modern Jewish History*, Howard M. Sachar *163*

Populism and Anti-Semitism, from *The Age of Reform*, Richard Hofstadter *169*

Suggestions for Further Reading *173*

**Chapter Eight   Other Ethnic Minorities:
                Immigration and
                Discrimination**   **175**

Introduction *175*

Ethnic Groups and the Melting Pot, from *Beyond the Melting Pot*, Nathan Glazer and Daniel P. Moynihan *176*

Racism and Nationality, from *Race and Nationality in American Life*, Oscar Handlin *184*

From *The American Irish*, William V. Shannon *187*

Suggestions for Further Reading *195*

**PART 4 BLACK TARGETS OF
          WHITE RACISM**   **197**

Chapter Nine   Racism in the Law   **199**

Introduction *199*

Legal Discrimination and Governmental Racism, from *Black Resistance, White Law: A History of Constitutional Racism in America*, Mary Frances Berry *202*

Northern Segregation before the Civil War, from *The Strange Career of Jim Crow*, C. Vann Woodward *206*

Legal Status after the Civil War, from *Racial and Cultural Minorities: An Analysis of Prejudice and Discrimination*, George Eaton Simpson and J. Milton Yinger *209*

Racial Distinctions in State Law *217*

Suggestions for Further Reading *219*

Chapter Ten   Extralegal Racism, Institutional and Overt **221**

Introduction *221*

The Perpetuation of the Ghetto, from *Apartheid American Style*, John Denton *223*

The Myths of Black History, from "Brainwashing of Black Men's Minds," Nathan Hare *228*

The Not-So-Subtle Put-Down, from *The Black Situation*, Addison Gayle, Jr. *235*

The Boomerang of White Racism, from "Charlie Doesn't Even Know His Daily Racism Is a Sick Joke," Bob Teague *241*

Suggestions for Further Reading *251*

Chapter Eleven   Presidential Racism **253**

Introduction *253*

Our Racist Presidents from Washington to Nixon, Melvin Steinfield *255*

New Freedom and Old Hypocrisy, from "Woodrow Wilson and Federal Segregation," Kathleen Wolgemuth *270*

Suggestions for Further Reading *286*

PART 5   THE FUTURE OF RACISM IN AMERICA **289**

Chapter Twelve   Developments in the 1960's **291**

Introduction *291*

There Is No American Dilemma, from *Crisis in Black and White*, Charles E. Silberman *293*

The Fires of Frustration, John F. Kennedy *299*

Lighting the Candle, Lyndon B. Johnson *304*

Red Power Meets White America: *Proclamation to the Great White Father and All His People,* Indians of all Tribes *311*

Sexism and Racism Linked, from "Why Women's Liberation?" Marlene Dixon *313*

October 1966 Black Panther Party Platform and Program *316*

The Young Lords' 13-Point Program and Platform *319*

Suggestions for Further Reading *323*

Chapter Thirteen   The 1970's and Beyond   325

Introduction *325*

From *Black Rage,* William H. Grier and Price M. Cobbs *326*

Brown Power, from "Insurrection in New Mexico —the Land of Enchantment," Armando Valdez *330*

The New Order, from *Look Out, Whitey! Black Power's Gon' Get Your Mama!,* Julius Lester *339*

Future Trends, from "New Black Directions: A Reappraisal," Eleanor Holmes Norton *344*

Which Way to Attack Racism?, from "Chicanos Divided by Sympathy for Aliens, Fear for Own Jobs," Frank del Olmo *353*

A Symbol of Black Resistance in the 1970's, "Statement to the Court," Angela Y. Davis *357*

The Awakening of Chinatown, from "Let 100 Flowers Bloom," Jeffry Paul Chan *358*

A Ray of Hope in a Modest Dimension?, from "Madison Avenue Minds its P's and Q's" *363*

Suggestions for Further Reading *366*

Index   367

Foreword

When the first edition of *Cracks in the Melting Pot* came out in 1970, I was teaching a course in The Politics of Race at Whittier College, alma mater of Richard M. Nixon. I adopted the book for use in my class.

In the intervening three years, the Nixon record has been one of retreat from the civil rights fight and general inaction in matters requiring vigorous Presidential leadership to combat racism. Thus, I am particularly pleased to see that this revised edition contains an updated treatment of Presidential racism in Chapter 11, as well as numerous other revisions to keep the book relevant to understanding how broad-based and deep-seated the problem of racism in America has become.

This book deserves to be read and thought about by all who wish to comprehend the nature of our most pressing challenge in the field of human relations.

January, 1973   MERVYN M. DYMALLY,
Founder and Co-Chairman,
National Conference
of Black Elected Officials,
and Chairman, Democratic Caucus
of the California Senate

Preface to the Second Edition

As a result of historical developments that have occurred since the appearance of the first edition of this book in January 1970, there has been a growing recognition that racism is as American as violence and cherry pie.

There has also been an increased rejection of the myth of the Melting Pot. Among white Americans, there are now fewer advocates of assimilation by coercion. Among minority Americans, there is more emphasis upon self-determination and pride in the unique life-styles of one's own cultural heritage, as opposed to an imaginary "American" ideal.

Thus, new metaphors are replacing the old Melting Pot. We hear increasingly of the "salad bowl" or the "patchwork quilt," or as Senator Hubert Humphrey put it early in his 1972 campaign for the Democratic Presidential nomination, "a rich tapestry of separate strands woven together."

If the Melting Pot is dead, interest in the history of racism is heightening. This new, revised edition was undertaken to improve and update the coverage of a subject that seems to be gaining student interest in colleges across the country. Among the features of this edition are more information on the Young Lords Party in the Puerto Rican community, expansion of the treatment of Philippine Annexation, significant revision of the chapter on Presidential racism, addition of more timely pieces on the future of racism, and an updating of the bibliographical suggestions at the end of each chapter.

San Diego, California   MELVIN STEINFIELD
January, 1973

Preface to the First Edition

Racism and discrimination are woven intimately into the fabric of American life. They have been from the very beginning. Yet only in the last few years have Americans begun to recognize the full extent to which racism and discrimination have influenced American history. In mid-1968, for example, when the Kerner Commission Report pinpointed white racism as "essentially responsible for the explosive mixture which has been accumulating in our cities since the end of World War II," many Americans still preferred to look with scorn at Australia for its exclusion policies, South Africa for its apartheid practices, or Mississippi for its white-supremacy doctrines and segregation codes. Two years ago, Americans were still looking away from the racism and discrimination in their own midst. Even "liberals" had not yet become completely adjusted to the idea that their commitment and efforts were needed just as much in Berkeley and Chicago as in Selma and Jackson.

Within the past two years, however, the indictment by our contemporaries has been articulated with such frequency, and from so many respectable sources within the establishment, that it may be difficult for the reader of this preface to guess what this book can offer that may be new or worthwhile. The answer is: a broader focus. For, in spite of the flood of books purporting to "tell it like it is" which has inundated trade and textbook markets these past few years, most treatments focus rather narrowly upon a single group, to the exclusion of other victims of white racism and discrimination. While college students today will encounter little difficulty in locating excellent materials on black history, there is still a need for a textbook which presents a broader picture of racism and discrimination in American history.

Although much in this book does deal with the black targets of white racism, considerable space is devoted also to American Indians, Mexican-Americans, Chinese, Japanese, and other ethnic minorities. The user of this text cannot come away from it without an awareness that racism and discrimination have provided rationalizations for territorial acquisition, have influenced immigration laws, have generated presidential utterances and actions, have provoked constitutional crises, have encouraged barbaric brutalities, have created torrents of resentment and rivers of rage, and have brought us to the brink of self-destruction, face-to-face with the gravest challenges to our conscience as well as our survival.

As Americans, we are becoming more honest with ourselves. Less often now do we sneer with self-righteous indignation at discriminatory practices elsewhere. Perhaps we no longer can spare the time, as we grope for solutions to the problems whose seeds go back deep into our history, and whose ripening has reached the point of rot. Perhaps this book will serve as a useful introduction to those neglected aspects of our history which underlie the great domestic crisis we now confront. By understanding the degree to which racism and discrimination have permeated our past, we lay the foundation for acknowledging the deeply-rooted nature of the turmoil of the present.

This book is not a complete history. Rather, it is a simple attempt to provide insightful glimpses of some dramatic and significant examples of racism and discrimination in American history. There are five parts to the book. Part One provides an overview of racism in American life and elsewhere, in order to establish an accurate perspective. Part Two demonstrates some rationalizations for territorial acquisition that have been closely linked to racist attitudes; there are separate chapters in Part Two dealing with American Indians, the Mexican War and Mexican-Americans, and the annexation of the Philippines. Part Three presents evidence of discrimination against immigrant groups, with separate chapters on Chinese and Japanese, Jews, and other ethnic groups. The three chapters of Part Four illustrate legal, extralegal, and presidential racism and discrimination against black Americans. The last section of the book, Part Five, looks at recent developments and focuses upon the major trends that are likely to influence the future in significant ways.

Each chapter opens with a brief introduction by the editor intended to be a helpful summary of background information. Then follow the readings drawn from a variety of primary and secondary sources. At the end of each chapter are suggestions for further reading.

The painful process of selecting a few readings from a huge reservoir of possibilities was eased considerably by the valuable suggestions of several of my colleagues at San Diego Mesa College. Lawrence Schwartz of San Diego City College was especially helpful to me as selections for reprinting were being made. Without question, my deepest obligations are to Robert Guthrie and Burl Hogins of San Diego Mesa College, who were the two consulting editors. From start to finish, their roles were crucial in all stages of the preparation of this book. For encouraging me to develop and to teach courses in the history of racism while this book was being prepared, I am grateful to Gary Monell of San Diego Mesa College and to C. A. "Shelly" Lewis of University Extension, University of California at San Diego.

Finally, I wish to express my appreciation for the patience and understanding exhibited by my wife Dorothy, my son Steven, and my daughter Brenda during the past year. It is to them that this book is dedicated.

And to the dream of a world without racism.

San Diego, California   MELVIN STEINFIELD
January, 1970

General Introduction

This book is about the Melting Pot idea and its relationship to racism and discrimination.

For most of America's history her theoreticians have painted the concept of the Melting Pot in glorious terms. According to this myth, America is the land of freedom, democracy, and golden opportunity in which people of all races, creeds, and colors are accepted on equal terms. Pride in the assimilation of huge numbers of immigrants is a vital companion to the myth of the Melting Pot.

Thus we find J. Hector St. John de Crèvecoeur, in his *Letters from an American Farmer* (1782), boasting about America as the great asylum for refugees from all over the world:

> I could point out to you a family whose grandfather was an Englishman, whose wife was Dutch, whose son married a French woman, and whose present four sons have now four wives of different nations. HE is an American, who leaving behind him all his ancient prejudices and manners, receives new ones from the new mode of life he has embraced, the new government he obeys, and the new rank he holds. He becomes an American by being received in the broad lap of our great ALMA MATER. Here individuals of all nations are melted into a new race of men, whose labors and posterity will one day cause great changes in the world.

Throughout our history, foreigners as well as natives romanticized the vision of harmony that is part of the Melting Pot. President Theodore Roosevelt said: "We Americans are children of the crucible." In 1908 there was even a play by Israel Zangwill, entitled *The Melting Pot,* which shared the attitude of the other prophets of peaceful fusion.

As recently as 1959 the distinguished historian Arthur M. Schlesinger described the Melting Pot as a great American achievement. Writing in the March, 1959, issue of *The Atlantic Monthly,* in an article entitled "Our Ten Contributions to Civilization," he listed the Melting Pot concept as contribution number five: "America has been in the best sense of the term, a Melting Pot, every ingredient adding its particular element of strength."

Schlesinger continued, "Many other peoples, it is true, are also of mixed origin; but the American achievement stands alone in the scale, thoroughness, and rapidity of process and, above all, in the fact that it has been the outcome not of forcible incorporation but of peaceful absorption."

Schlesinger did acknowledge one crack in the Melting Pot: "Our most tragic failure has involved our Negro citizens, now a tenth of our number." That acknowledgment, which was the sole qualification of an otherwise unrestrained enthusiasm, seems to characterize most of the Melting Pot theorists of the twentieth century: America is truly the great Melting Pot, with the possible exception of the Negro, who is on the verge of total acceptance because America's conscience is about to be touched.

In a sense, the monumental study by Gunnar Myrdal in 1942 (*An American Dilemma*) shared the Melting Pot faith implicitly. It is precisely because we do harbor so dearly the goals of assimilation and equality that we found ourselves in a dilemma. In Australia or South Africa, there can be no dilemma, for there is no Melting Pot. But in America the disparities between the "American Creed," as Myrdal labeled it, on the one hand, and the bitter realities of race relations on the other hand, require some sort of reconciliation.

The concept of the American Dream reinforced the American Dilemma and also shared the vision of the Melting Pot. The nature of the American Dream was articulated in memorable phrases by Dr. Martin Luther King in the speech which climaxed the March on Washington on August 28, 1963. That speech was perhaps the last noble expression of hope that the sons of former slaves and the sons of former slave owners would be able to live together in harmony and in a spirit of brotherly love; the historical climate was changing and the fulfillment of the Dream soon appeared less attainable than ever before.

When the civil rights movement shoved the American Dilemma right into our faces and when direct practical confrontations were forced on issues for which Myrdal's book provided merely an intellectual prelude, the days of the Melting Pot were numbered. As the black sense of rejection by white America seemed to be leading to irreversible divisions in American society, a new set of challenges to the Melting Pot concept was being mounted. If white middle-class America was racist through and through and essentially responsible for the ills of our society, then why would anyone want to assimilate into the homogenized sterility of antiseptic WASPdom? A confluence of militant pride accompanied the civil rights movement, and later, the black revolution. Blacks were beginning to reject the Anglo-chosen term "Negro" in favor of "black." Browns registered their protest against Anglo-imposed labels also as they proudly replaced "Mexican-American" with "Chicano." Hippies and Yippies too preferred to live according to their own life-styles. They were not anxious to conform to majority standards. From Indians to women, from homosexuals to Puerto Ricans—many groups were saying *NO* to the Melting Pot. They were all part of a new struggle: the *human* liberation movement.

In the 1960's the Melting Pot was under fire because it had come to symbolize an entire set of values that were themselves being subjected to skeptical scrutiny. As Nathan Glazer and Daniel P. Moynihan pointed out in *Beyond the Melting Pot* (1963), "The point about the Melting Pot . . . is that it did not happen."

Thus, while the Melting Pot was the outspoken goal of much official policy, there have been opponents from the start and American history is replete with instances in which those who have wanted to assimilate have not been permitted to do so. The relationship between these cracks in the Melting Pot and racism and discrimination is a strong one. Every instance of racism or discrimination is a vivid contradition of the myth of the Melting Pot.

The Question of Terminology

There are differences of opinion among scholars regarding the proper use of the terms "racism" and "racist." Many scholars maintain that "racism" should not be applied to events which preceded the formulation of pseudoscientific theories of "race."

According to this interpretation, the Mexican War cannot be considered a racist war because in the 1840's there were no well-developed theories of Mexican racial inferiority. Likewise, Cherokee removal in the 1830's was not a racist act. The development of slavery in America is seen as a variety of English ethnocentrism,* rather than as racism.

While there are those who urge the avoidance of the careless use of the term "racism" because they see distinctions between various kinds of discrimination, there is emerging a broader usage of the term "racism." In the late 1960's "racist," as used conversationally at any rate, applied to overt acts of brutal bigotry and also to the more subtle forms of racism: attitudes rooted in an acceptance of the status quo with respect to segregation and inequality. There is some evidence that this usage of the term "racism" is beginning to be adopted by scholars. For example, Thomas Gossett, in *Race: The History of an Idea in America* (1965) writes:

> What is certain is that the tendency to seize upon physical differences as the badge of innate mental and temperamental differences is not limited to modern times. The racism of ancient history, even though it had no science of biology or anthropology behind it, was real, however difficult it may be for us to judge the extent of its power.

Elsewhere in his book he notes that:

> During the age of exploration, an even more explicit racism developed from the contacts of Europeans with native peoples all over the world. In Spain a debate continued throughout the sixteenth century on the question of whether the Indians in the New World were really men, or whether they were beasts or perhaps beings intermediate between beasts and men.

In his book, *Manifest Destiny and Mission in American History* (1963), the distinguished Professor Emeritus of American History at Harvard University, Frederick Merk, compared the Mexican War and the Spanish-American War and concluded: "As in the 1840's, expansionism synchronized with racism."

---

*See Pierre Van den Berghe's discussion of "Ethnocentrism" in Chapter One.

Before there were explicitly racist theories, there were many references to American Indians as "savages," but the fact remains that historians are frequently cautioned not to apply the term "racism" to pre-Darwinian incidents. The highly respected scholar Arnold Rose wrote an essay entitled "Distortion in the History of American Race Relations" which appeared in his volume, *Assuring Freedom to the Free*, published in 1964. He stated that ". . . the historians have perpetuated the popular southern myth that racism and caste have existed from the first interracial contacts and are endemic to race relations."

It is not the purpose of this book to resolve the questions of terminology discussed briefly in the foregoing paragraphs. It is certainly not the purpose of this book to endorse the concept of "race" and the many myths that usually go along with it. "Race" is an unscientific concept whose careless use is condemned in the scientific world. For example, Ashley Montagu criticizes its use in his highly regarded work, *Man's Most Dangerous Myth: The Fallacy of Race*. L. C. Dunn, Professor of Zoology at Columbia University, has commented that:

> The modern view of race, founded upon the known facts and theories of heredity, leaves the old views of fixed and absolute biological differences among the races of men, and the hierarchy of superior and inferior races founded upon this old view, without scientific justification.*

Professor Dunn concluded: "The persistence of race prejudice where it exists is a cultural acquisition which as we have seen finds no justification in biology."† Finally there can be no doubt about the unscientific nature of "race" if we accept the conclusion of the thirteen-point statement on race entitled "Proposals on the Biological Aspects of Race," which was signed by twenty-two authorities on August 18, 1964:

> The biological data given above stand in open contradiction to the tenets of racism. Racist theories can in no way pretend to have any scientific foundation and the anthropologists should endeavor to prevent the results of their researches from being used in such a biased way that they would serve nonscientific ends.

---

*L. C. Dunn, *Race and Biology* (New York: UNESCO, 1958), p.7.
†*Ibid.*, p. 42.

The Purpose of This Book

It is the purpose of this book to indicate that there have been
and still are many instances of racism and discrimination in
American life. These examples can be construed as cracks in the
Melting Pot. The promise of the Statue of Liberty notwithstanding, there are varying degrees of assimilation into American life.
While Anglos and other immigrants from northern and western
Europe were "melting," blacks were enslaved, sold, denied voting
rights, and lynched; Indians were shoved off the paths of westward expansion and massacred; Chinese and Japanese were excluded or interred; Mexicans were conquered and oppressed, and
other ethnic minorities were victimized to the point that Oscar
Handlin could write, in *Race and Nationality in American Life:*
"Discrimination was the permanent manifestation of the hostilities bred by racism."

In 1973 Americans must realize that the Melting Pot has
just as often been a boiling cauldron of conflict in which the
vehement fury of racism and discrimination has never stopped
bubbling.

PART 1   ESTABLISHING AN ACCURATE PERSPECTIVE

Chapter One

Racism and Discrimination in Other Countries

The fact that some of the most horrifying atrocities took place in Germany is coincidental. In the past they were perpetrated in Egypt, Rome, and Mexico. Any segment of mankind is capable of atrocity when a small band of persecutors rises to pervert, exploit, and enjoy power over those to be persecuted.

—WILLIAM GILLIS, editor,
in Frederick Durrenmatt's, *Suspicion* (1964)

William Gillis was referring to conditions in a dictatorship, but racism and discrimination do not depend exclusively upon dictatorships in order to flourish. There are many examples of racism and discrimination in countries of differing political persuasions, both past and present.

It was in England, not America, that Enoch Powell, the Conservative party former Cabinet Minister, urged Britons to "Keep Britain white" during the mid-1960's.

It was in South Africa, not America, that the body of the black man who was the donor of the heart which went into Dr. Philip Blaiberg's body was carted off, minus his heart, to a segregated black cemetery during the mid-1960's.

It is in South Africa today, not America, where some three million whites maintain a brutal regime with police-state control over twelve million blacks as a matter of official government policy.

It was in Germany, not America, that genocide became the cornerstone of a national policy that resulted in the extermination of six million Jews during the 1930's and 1940's.

So we must not lose perspective. American racism and discrimination are not unique. Because this book focuses upon negative features of American history, we may lose sight of the many admirable aspects of our record. A balanced assessment of America ought to take into consideration the many other patterns in American history, both favorable and unfavorable, which are not the concern of this book.

*Race Relations around the World**

This article surveys the world situation with regard to discrimination against minorities based on color, caste, and creed. It specifies conditions in a variety of countries today and illustrates its main point: other countries have their human relations problems also.

Racial troubles in the United States are world news. Each outbreak in this country sets off clamor everywhere. So much global attention, in fact, is focused on Negro–white tensions in the United States that this point is often overlooked:

Americans are far from alone in facing race problems. Go around the world, and you find deep—often violent—discord, rooted not only in racial antagonism but in differences in religion, language, customs, caste. Prejudice, as it has through the ages, is causing strife in Asia, Africa, Europe—all across the earth. No easy solution is in sight.

One conclusion emerges from a close look at questions of race, color, religious beliefs, and other sources of dissension in countries abroad:

Nowhere else is to be found concern to match that shown by the United States in its efforts to bring about full racial equality—to achieve workable integration in all levels of life.

Members of the international staff of *U.S. News & World Report* were asked to assess color conflicts and other problems

---

*"Race Trouble—No U.S. Monopoly," reprinted from *U.S. News & World Report* (July 8, 1968), pp. 76-80.

of bias or intolerance, worldwide. Their reports follow, area by area.

Asia

In most parts of Asia, prejudices arising from differences in race, color, language, religion, or caste are strong. Day-to-day results of this problem—riots, demonstrations, discrimination, and the like—are often more violent than the racial upheavals which have hit the United States in recent years. Look almost anywhere in Asia, and you see the consequences of these passions.

In India, hardly a week goes by without demonstrations against efforts to impose two or three common languages on a sprawling nation with scores of regional tongues.

The caste system has been outlawed in India. But basic attitudes of most Indians toward the former untouchables have not changed. The millions of untouchables remain economically disenfranchised. They still must endure mistreatment and frequently are victims of mob violence.

An Indian government commission reported earlier this year that "untouchability" is still widely practiced. A nationwide survey showed, the report said, such instances of segregation as these: Former untouchables were not allowed to take water from municipal taps in New Delhi, to ride bicycles in Madras, or to walk with shoes on in Mysore.

Religious strife among Indians has cost countless lives. For example, two decades ago, when India was winning independence from Britain and undergoing partition, the Punjabi outbreak that pitted Muslims, Sikhs, and Hindus against each other killed an estimated three hundred thousand to one million Indians.

Discrimination, as practiced in India and elsewhere in Asia, can be far more severe than anything that Negroes have encountered in the United States.

It is in Communist China that racialism is most virulent. For thousands of years, Chinese were taught that all non-Chinese were barbarians. Communism has not changed this. In fact, Communist leaders have stepped up the centuries-old persecution by the Han, or so-called pure Chinese, of minority peoples in their midst.

Mainland China is home to fifty different ethnic groups. Ever since the Communists won power in 1949, minorities have been special targets for ill treatment. Typically, the Moslems in Chinese Provinces such as Kansu and Sinkiang have had their religious rites banned, their local customs abolished, and their leaders deported.

... Ironically, outside of China, the Chinese themselves are victims of bigotry. There are approximately seventeen million of these "overseas Chinese," most living in Southeast Asia. Economically, they are important far beyond their numbers.

In scores of Asian cities and towns, the Chinese are the dominant small shopkeepers, moneylenders, rice-mill operators, and wholesalers—trades that are wide open to charges of "exploitation" of local people when race passions run high. In Malaysia last year, demonstrations against devaluation of the country's currency turned into anti-Chinese riots.

The "overseas Chinese" are often nearer the top than the bottom of the economic ladder. The fact that this position usually was achieved by working harder and saving more does not spare the Chinese from resentment of the local people.

In the Philippines, segregation into "ghettos" has been a fact of life for Chinese for centuries. Even now, the Chinese are scapegoats, blamed for everything that is wrong from crime to high prices. A law passed in 1954 excluded Chinese from retailing. Another, enacted in 1960, barred them from the rice and corn trade.

... Booming, prosperous Japan is one of the most race-conscious nations in the world. The Japanese treat other Asians with contempt, mistreat the aboriginal Ainus, and even look down on fellow Japanese from the outlying Ryukyu Islands.

Worst off in Japan are the Eta—a Japanese version of untouchables—who are forced to live outside normal society. An estimated three million Eta people live close to a subsistence level in about six thousand special communities which are among the most squalid in the land, frequently without even rudimentary public services.

Next to the Eta, the most obvious victims of discrimination in Japan are Koreans. Nearly seven hundred thousand Koreans live in Japan. Many were forcibly moved in during World War II when Korea was still a Japanese colony. They are treated as second-class citizens, live segregated lives, seldom achieve full rights of citizenship such as access to government-subsidized, low-rent housing. A Korean in Japan has difficulty getting a bank loan or a good job. Some who are university graduates end up in menial work. The stigma is such that a well-known actress sued a Japanese publication for libel because it listed her as a Korean by birth.

. . . Looking at Asia as a whole, some students of social problems say that this part of the world is generally much farther away from resolving its problems of prejudice than is the United States.

Australia

This country has a "white Australia" policy. The rigid immigration laws bar all nonwhites—Negroes and Asians—except a few who possess certain skills the nation needs. Such screening is supported by most Australians. A banker in Sydney expresses a widely held view: "When you look at the race troubles today in the United States and Britain, you don't see much reason for changing the immigration policy."

. . . Only in the last few years has Australia included its black people—the aborigines—in the national census. In themselves, the aborigines present no real problem. There are only about forty-five thousand full-blooded aborigines and about the same number of half-breeds.

You do not see signs of racial discrimination in Australia, because there are very few nonwhites around. Of more than 2.2 million immigrants admitted since World War II, only about nineteen thousand were nonwhite.

There is, however, a tendency on the part of British Australians, who make up the overwhelming majority of the country, to look down their noses at all other groups.

Many Australians, for instance, profess to be amused by Italian immigrants. The "amusement" arises from the large families of the Italians and their clannishness.

. . . The reason why Australia does not have a race problem is that this country, unlike the United States, is no Melting Pot and has no intention of becoming one. An Australian official explains: We want to maintain a homogeneous society, and admission of other races would not contribute to that, because people of all those races could not be assimilated easily."

Despite this, Australians consider themselves quite tolerant. As an illustration of "tolerance," one Australian spoke in a kindly way of the Chinese who live here. They are few in number, but some have been here ever since the gold-rush days of the last century. Said the Australian who wanted to indicate his tolerant attitude: "The Chinese are good citizens. They are clean, keep to themselves and never start any riots. If they kill anybody, it is one of their own and you rarely hear about it."

Africa

Over much of Africa, the problem of race goes far deeper than it does in the United States. There are few race riots in Africa, and there are reasons to explain this.

Take South Africa, where the white population of 3.5 million is outnumbered nearly four to one by nonwhites. The white minority sees to it that physical power is kept in its own hands. There is little the nonwhite can do to express his grievances.

... In South Africa, the power of the government is used to keep the races separate. Even though they are seldom visible, South Africa has its tensions. The real question is whether the solution advanced by the government—complete racial separation —is the answer. Only time will tell.

Rhodesia, another African country ruled by a white minority, has less stringent segregation than South Africa has. But Rhodesia's 230,000 whites have shown in recent elections that they favor more, not less, separation of the races as their own answer to the problem. That is the nub of Rhodesia's dispute with Britain, which led to the Rhodesian declaration of independence.

In Portuguese Africa—Angola, Mozambique and Portuguese Guinea—there are no segregation laws. Whites and blacks are considered equal in the eyes of the law. Racial intermarriage is not uncommon. Residential and social integration can be seen in main towns.

Yet this system has not prevented strife. The Portuguese

are being subjected to warfare by black guerrillas in all three of Portugal's African territories.

... In countries of Africa which are under black rule, there are serious problems involving rival population groups. In tiny Rwanda, for instance, bloody clashes between the Watusi peoples and the Bahutus have taken thousands of lives. Ethnic differences between the Ibos and the Hausa-Fulani peoples of Nigeria contributed to the animosities that led to that country's present civil war.

In the Sudan, tens of thousands of southern blacks have died in the past five years in a civil war with northern Sudanese of lighter complexion. [The] cause of the war was an attempt by the northerners—who are in the majority and control the Sudanese national government—to crush a southern movement for local autonomy.

The southern Sudanese are of the Hamitic race, mostly pagans. The lighter-skinned northern Sudanese are mainly Semitic, Arabic-speaking, and Moslem. The northerners believe the southerners should become integrated with the rest of the country. To the southerners, integration seems more like persecution.

In some black-ruled countries of Africa—such as the Ivory Coast and Kenya—whites are living without difficulty, unimperiled by racial terrorism such as the Mau Maus inflicted upon white settlers in Kenya in years before independence. It must be remembered, however, that where whites are living in countries run by black Africans, they are doing so only by sufferance of the governments.

... Virtually every African country has as official policy the principle of "Africanization." Many countries are willing to tolerate non-Africans only until the black natives are qualified to take over the jobs that whites now hold. It may be a long time, but eventually Africans will replace the white jobholders—and then, presumably, the whites will have to leave.

Middle East

This part of the world has been tormented for centuries by conflict over ethnic, religious, and racial rivalries.

The Arab–Israeli dispute was originally political, not racial.

Arabs objected to establishment of a Jewish state, not to Jews, who are fellow Semites. Bitterness between the two peoples caused by the frequent fighting since 1948 has spilled over into Arab–Jewish relations in general, with constant claims of persecution of Jews in Arab countries and of Arabs in Israel.

. . . Hatred of one Arab faction for another often leads to bloodshed. . . . In the Arab country of Lebanon, rivalry between Moslems and Christians was a main cause of the 1958 insurrection in which casualties numbered in the thousands. The conflict still simmers under the surface. In Yemen, where fighting has gone on for five years between "republican" and "royalist" forces, religious rivalry—one Moslem sect against another—is a basic cause of the civil war.

But it is not always Arab against Arab. In Iraq, a non-Arab mountain people, the Kurds, have been fighting the Arabs who run the country.

Religion creates problems in the Arab world. In Egypt, the small Christian community—mainly Copts—is discriminated against in the vital matter of jobs. In Syria, persecution of a Moslem sect known as Alawites ended only when Alawites got strong representation in the military leadership which holds the reins of power.

Western Europe

Britain suddenly is finding itself forced to move drastically to blunt the threat of widespread racial strife. Stringent controls are being clamped on further immigration of nonwhites from British Commonwealth countries. At the same time, civil rights legislation is being enacted to ease grievances of nonwhites.

Triggering these moves was the racial animosity that burst into the open after Enoch Powell, a Conservative former Cabinet Minister, delivered a "keep Britain white" speech on April 20. In the wake of Mr. Powell's speech, a public-opinion poll showed overwhelming support for measures to cut the inflow of nonwhites and to induce some of the immigrants who are in Britain to go back home.

. . . Britain's race problem is a postwar phenomenon. Since the early 1950's, the nonwhite population has expanded from a handful to just under a million. Discrimination against the new-comers—blacks from the West Indies, Asians from India and Pakistan—has built up steadily. This brought a "black backlash," with immigrants organizing for "militant action."

There is growing alarm among leaders of both major political parties that Britain over the next few years may be plunged into the kind of racial turmoil that has beset the United States.

The worrisome questions now are: Has Britain closed the door to immigration soon enough to cool off white hotheads? Will civil rights laws be effective enough to prevent growth of "black power" extremism among nonwhites?

. . . In West Germany, race no longer creates problems of much importance. For one thing, racists have no particular target now.

The Jewish community, Hitler's target, is now so small that many Germans have never met a Jew. There are fewer than thirty thousand people of the Jewish faith in the country.

Negroes are not numerous. There are about eight thousand African Negroes, including university students and Africans sent to West Germany for vocational training. They have been involved in virtually no racial incidents. The only other Negro group—not large—is made up of "GI babies," offspring of American soldiers and German women. Several thousand have now grown to adulthood.

Life presents difficulties for these German Negroes, who for the most part carry the stigma of illegitimacy and who have been reared in lower-class homes with little opportunity for higher education. But German sociologists say that since the total number of these Negroes is insignificant in relation to the national population, racial prejudice against them has not developed to an important degree.

. . . In Sweden and other Scandinavian countries, there are few colored people. With no racial problem of their own, Scandinavians have been vehement in their attacks on discrimination against Negroes elsewhere. From Sweden, particularly, have come loud declarations in favor of racial equality.

Yet the man in the street in Sweden admits that he dislikes the idea of Swedish girls' marrying Negroes. And one Swedish sociologist says: "Personally, I believe that Sweden would soon be up against some serious racial trouble if five thousand or ten thousand Negroes were brought here as immigrants." In actual practice, immigration to Scandinavian countries by colored people is restricted to "special cases."

... In France, most of its fifty thousand African Negro residents live as second-class citizens. Frenchmen say this has nothing to do with race but is based on their lack of education. "We tend to be snobbish," said one Frenchman, "but not racist."

Holland is one country where racial integration appears to work without friction. Dutch integration, however, does not involve Negroes. Most of the three hundred thousand dark-skinned people who have immigrated to the Netherlands since World War II are Asians from Indonesia, who were given the opportunity to choose Dutch citizenship when Indonesia became independent.

Surveys show that Holland's colored inhabitants are fairly widely dispersed, hold jobs in accordance with their abilities, seldom encounter discrimination in such matters as housing. . . .One reason for this is that the Dutch, from colonial days, have had many people of mixed parentage—Dutch fathers and Indonesian mothers. Another reason is that the Dutch government prepared carefully for the wave of colored immigration that began shortly after World War II and set up machinery to deal with it.

Communist Europe

Communist doctrine preaches brotherhood and equality of all mankind and theoretically provides freedom of religion. But things do not work out that way in practice. Negro students from Africa have complained bitterly about racial antagonism in the Soviet Union—and have, in fact, held protest demonstrations. Cited were attacks by gangs of Russian youths on African students who had danced with Russian girls.

... In Bulgaria, African students asserted that Bulgarian classmates were unwilling to sit next to them, and that the Africans were referred to as "black apes." Africans claim to have been mistreated in Czechoslovakia, as well.

In the past six years, more than one thousand young Africans have quit universities in the Soviet bloc, going to West Germany. Racial reasons are given, in most cases.

Anti-Semitism persists in the Soviet Union. Here is a comment by Dr. Isaac Franck, an American educator, made just after his return from a trip to Russia: "The government-directed program of suppressing and strangulating Jewish religion and cultural life has continued unabated. Added to it is the recent overt manifestation of anti-Semitism. If this process continues for the next decade or two there is a real danger that the three million Jews of the Soviet Union will be a disappearing people."

... In the last two years, Baptists have been extensively persecuted in the Soviet Union. More than two hundred Baptists have been jailed; others have been beaten and tortured by police. Chapels have been confiscated or bulldozed; prayer meetings have been broken up and their participants fined; children have been put forcibly into boarding schools to prevent their parents from giving them a religious upbringing.

Russians account for only about half of the population of the Soviet Union. The other half is made up of more than one hundred nationalities, ethnic groups, and tribes which were subjugated by the Czars and never set free by the Reds. This, in effect, makes the Soviet Union the only large colonial empire remaining in the world today.

... Any manifestation by any of the nationalities—such as the Ukranian, Latvian, and Uzbek "republics"—of an urge toward independence is regarded by the Kremlin as treason and treated as such.

For example, some thirty Ukranian intellectuals and artists were arrested a few years ago. Twenty were tried on charges of "anti-Soviet nationalistic propaganda and agitation." In most cases, the offense consisted of possession of material glorifying the history of the Ukranian nation. The trials resulted in prison sentences of up to six years. Moscow acts quickly and ruthlessly to suppress all forms of action against central authority.

Latin America

Racial discrimination is forbidden by law in much of Latin America, but racial prejudices are strong in many areas. Too, the Negro and the Indian often are set apart by poverty and ignorance.

Throughout South America, most nonwhites are restricted to the lowest types of employment because they lack education. In Brazil, for example, few Negroes are to be found as waiters. The proprietor of a well-known restaurant explains: "I have no race prejudice—it's just that you can't find a Negro who knows how to serve and where to put the forks."

... History shows that Negroes have never prospered in the southern portion of Latin America—and the history books tell in matter-of-fact terms how Indian populations were slaughtered by the Spanish conquerors and mistreated by the European immigrants who followed.

In Chile, a high official once smilingly told a visitor from the United States: "We solved our Indian problem the same way the United States did—we killed most of them and put the rest on reservations."

That attitude now is outmoded, and Chile's government is working hard to integrate the country's three hundred thousand Indians into the economy and into society in general. This is true also in Bolivia, where until 1952 the Indian had no legal rights.

... In Central America, the Indian—whose numbers vary from more than fifty percent of the population in Guatemala to about fifteen percent in Mexico—is at the bottom of the economic ladder. A regional conference on Indian problems held recently in Mexico deplored neglect of the Indians and their exploitation as a poorly paid source of unskilled labor.

There are countries of Latin America in which racial conflict does not involve whites. In Guyana, a major national crisis is threatened by friction between East Indians and Negroes. The East Indians, a numerical majority, support Communist leader Cheddi Jagan for racial reasons. Negroes support the present Prime Minister, Forbes Burnham, a Negro. There is widespread fear that general elections ... will spark a violent racial struggle.

Dominicans, colored themselves, are traditional enemies of the Haitians, their neighbors on the island of Hispaniola.

Even in Cuba, where Castro has attempted to wipe out segregation and bring Negroes into his Communist government, racial tensions are still found. An illustration: The extremist American Negro agitator Robert Williams, who spent years in Cuba broadcasting antiwhite speeches to the United States, finally moved on to Red China, complaining that the Castro Government was "prowhite."

. . . On islands of the Caribbean, a racial showdown took place long ago when Negro slaves won freedom from their Danish, British, Dutch, and French masters and achieved economic, political, and social rights. With Negroes and mulattoes constituting ninety percent of the overall population, rigid segregation is a thing of the past. But hatreds exist, with dominant economic and political groups—regardless of skin color—as targets. A saying often heard in the Caribbean is that "the black man with money and position is whiter than the white man or lighter-skinned man."

Canada

Although it is often held up by its own leaders as a model of tolerance, Canada has a growing racial problem of potentially explosive proportions. Warnings are heard that major conflict may be coming between whites and the Indian and Métis populations in dozens of western Canadian communities.

. . . Advocates of "red power" are cropping up, exhorting the four hundred thousand Indians and Métis to fight against discrimination and poverty. The Métis are a French-Indian mixture, descendants of French trappers and Indian women. There are two hundred thousand of them, chiefly in the northern prairie towns. They do not get the government aid that goes to Indians living on tribal reserves. It is estimated that forty percent of the Métis are unemployed, most have incomes of less than one thousand dollars a year, and that twenty-four percent are functionally illiterate.

In northern Ontario, in Alberta, and in British Columbia, Indians and Métis have staged protest marches. In some parts of northern Ontario there have been clashes between whites and protesting Indians. Dr. Howard Adams of the University of Saskatchewan, a Métis, is quoted in a recent newspaper account of the "red power" movement as saying: "Don't ask if there will be racial violence. There already is—against us. Now the question is whether we will fight back."

Says Duke Redbird, an Indian living in Toronto: "There are

terrible things happening every day to Indians in Canada. There are many, many communities like powder kegs, ready to blow up."

From a British Columbian Indian who traveled in the United States to study black power methods: "Canadians look across the border and say it can't happen here—but what is going on down there is what happens when people have nothing to lose. And a lot of us here have nothing to lose."

> Summing it all up, a look around the world shows this:
> —The problem of racial strife is by no means confined to the United States. Countries in every part of the earth have conflicts that grow out of differences in race, color or religion.
> —One big contrast is that the United States—though often criticized by nations which have not solved their own problems of prejudice and violence—is acting on a scale unmatched anywhere in efforts to achieve solution of its racial troubles.

*Racism in Western Civilization**

Van den Berghe discusses several important issues in this concise excerpt from his book. He distinguishes between racism and ethnocentrism, discusses the causes of racism, and outlines a social explanation for the origin of Western racism, which he considers the most severe kind of racism in the world.

It is important to stress that racism, unlike ethnocentrism, is not a universal phenomenon. Members of all human societies have a fairly good opinion of themselves compared with members of other societies, but this good opinion is frequently based on claims to cultural superiority. Man's claims to excellence are usually narcissistically based on his own creations. Only a few human groups have deemed themselves superior because of the contents of their gonads. Of course, racist cultures have also

---

*From pp. 12–18 of *Race and Racism* by Pierre Van den Berghe, © Copyright John Wiley and Sons; New York, 1967.

been ethnocentric, and some peoples have held the theory that their cultures were superior because of their superior genetic pool. But the reverse is not true: many, indeed most, societies have exhibited ethnocentrism without racism.

On the other hand, the contention that racism is a unique invention of the nineteenth-century western Europe culture and its colonial offshoots in the Americas, Australia, Africa, and Asia is also untrue. Racism, as might be expected of such a crude idea, has been independently discovered and rediscovered by various peoples at various times in history. For example, in the traditional kingdoms of Rwanda and Burundi in the Great Lakes area of central Africa, the Tutsi aristocracy (about fifteen percent of the population) ruled over the Hutu majority and a small group of Twa. The three groups are physically distinguishable: the Twa are a Pygmoid group of shorter stature and somewhat lighter complexion than the Negroid Hutu; the Tutsi, although as dark as the Hutu, are by far the tallest group and have distinctly non-Negroid features. Of course, miscegenation over three centuries of Tutsi domination has somewhat blurred these physical distinctions, but, nevertheless, physical characteristics, notably height, play a prominent role in the Tutsi claim to superiority and political domination.

The Muslin emirates of northern Nigeria, where a Fulani aristocracy conquered the local Hausa in the first decade of the nineteenth century, provide another illustration of non-Western racism, albeit only a mild manifestation. Thus M. G. Smith writes about one of the vassal states of Sokoto in northern Nigeria:

> In Zaria also, social significance is given to color distinctions; value is placed on lightness of skin as an attribute of beauty, and as a racial character, and a host of qualitative terms reflect this interest, such as *ja-jawur* (light-copper skin), *baki* (dark), *baki kirim* or *baki swal* (real black), and so forth. The Fulani rules of Zaria distinguish on racial grounds between themselves and their Hausa subjects, stressing such features as skin color, hair, and facial form, and also make similar distinctions among themselves, since past miscegenation has produced wide physical differences among them.[1]

---

[1] *Plural Society in the British West Indies*, p. 132.

Allowing, then, for the independent discovery of racism in a number of societies, it remains true that the Western strain of the virus has eclipsed all others in importance. Through the colonial expansion of Europe racism spread widely over the world. Apart from its geographical spread, no other brand of racism has developed such a flourishing mythology and ideology. In folklore, as well as in literature and science, racism became a deeply ingrained component of the Western Weltanschauung. Western racism had its poets like Kipling, its philosophers like Gobineau and Chamberlain, its statesmen like Hitler, Theodore Roosevelt, and Verwoerd; this is a record not even remotely approached in either scope or complexity by any other cultural tradition. Therefore ... we shall concentrate on Western racism.

Let us ask again the question of the origin of racism in the specific context of the Western tradition. Two major ways of answering the question are in terms of necessary antecedent conditions and efficient causes. The most important necessary (but not sufficient) condition for the rise of racism is the presence in sufficient numbers of two or more groups that look different enough so that at least some of their members can be readily classifiable. In addition to their physical differences, these groups also have to be culturally different (at least when they first met) and in a position of institutionalized inequality for the idea of inherent racial differences to take root. It seems that only when group differences in race overlap at least partly with dissimilarities in status and culture are these two sets of differences held to be causally related to one another.

These conditions are most clearly met when groups come into contact through migration, of which the most common types are the following:

1. Military conquest in which the victor (often in numerical minority) establishes his political and economic domination over an indigenous group (e.g., European powers in tropical Africa, starting in the 1870's.)

2. Gradual frontier expansion of one group which pushes back and exterminates the native population (e.g., European expansion in North America or Australia), as contrasted with the "dominating symbiosis" of type 1.

3. Involuntary migration in which a slave or inden-
tured alien group is introduced into a country to constitute a servile caste (e.g., the slave regimes of the United
States, Brazil, and the West Indies).

4. Voluntary migration when alien groups move into
the host country to seek political protection or economic
opportunities (e.g., Puerto Rican, Mexican, or Cuban immigration to the United States mainland or West Indian
immigration into Britain).

These various forms of migration, singly or in combination,
account for most of the interracial societies created by Western
powers and indeed probably also for most non-Western societies
in which racism is present. However, the migration (whether
peaceful or military, voluntary or involuntary) of culturally and
physically different groups does not tell the whole story. Indeed,
there have been many cases in which these conditions were met
but in which racism did not develop. This is true despite the fact
that such pluralistic societies are often rigidly stratified and characterized by acute ethnic competition and conflict. Thus, for
example, the Spanish conquest of the New World, brutal as it was,
gave rise to only a mild form of racism toward Indians, although
religious bigotry and ethnocentricism were dominant traits of the
Spanish outlook. Similarly, the Aryan invasion of India, although
it probably marked the beginnings of the Hindu caste system, does
not appear to have brought about racism. Some scholars argue
that mild racism exists in India and underlies the origin of the
caste system. *Varna* (the broad division into four groups of castes:
Brahmin, Kshatriya, Vaisya, and Sudra) literally means "color";
Hinduism uses the same kind of color symbolism as the Judeo-
Christian tradition, associating evil with black and good with
white; and there is a mild esthetic preference for lighter skin in
modern Indian culture. But this is very much of a limiting case.

Given the necessary and facilitating conditions for the development of racism, what are the efficient causes of it? It seems
probable that in each historical case in which racism appeared its
causal antecedents have been different. Here, I shall try to answer
the question only with reference to Western racism, a difficult
enough problem in itself. A number of fragmentary answers have

been advanced by various social scientists, most of them ascribing causal priority according to their theoretical predilection. Thus to a psychologist the ultimate source or "seat" of racism is personality, and causation must be sought in terms of the dynamics of frustration and aggression, or the "authoritarian personality." ... [However,] our primary concern at present is with the *social* level of explanation.

Vulgar Marxism has a monocausal theory on the origin of racism: racism is part of the bourgeois ideology designed especially to rationalize the exploitation of nonwhite peoples of the world during the imperialistic phase of capitalism. Racist ideology thus becomes simply an epiphenomenon symptomatic of slavery and colonial exploitation. In the modern American context, vulgar Marxists have interpreted racism as a capitalist device to divide the working class into two hostile segments for better control. Others, more inclined to assign causal priority to the realm of ideas, trace the origins of racism to the current of social Darwinism and the reaction against eighteenth-century environmentalism.

Western racism is a fairly well-defined historical phenomenon, characteristic of a distinct epoch; it came of age in the third or fourth decade of the nineteenth century, achieved its golden age approximately between 1880 and 1920, and has since entered its period of decline, although, of course, its lingering remains are likely to be with us at least for the next three or four decades. To be sure, racist ideas were occasionally expressed in the eighteenth century and even before. Thus Thomas Jefferson wrote in his *Notes on Virginia* (1782) : "This unfortunate difference of color, and perhaps of faculty, is a powerful obstacle to the emancipation of these people [i.e., Negroes]." In various places Jefferson described Negroes in the following terms: "In music they are more generally gifted than the whites." "They seem to require less sleep." "They secrete less by the kidneys, and more by the glands of the skin, which gives them a very strong and disagreeable odor." Even the Spanish of the sixteenth and seventeenth centuries, who have a reputation for lack of racism, did exhibit it in mild form, but it was almost invariably intertwined with, and secondary to, ethnocentrism.

The era of the Enlightenment which immediately preceded

the growth of racism was strongly environmentalist (i.e., the belief was that both the physical and social environment determined human behavior to a greater extent than heredity), and Jefferson himself never resolved this intellectual dilemma to his satisfaction. He continuously wavered between racist and social "explanations" of group differences. Racist thinking in the Anglo-Saxon world, in Germany, and to a lesser extent in other European countries was in the ascendancy in the 1830's and 1840's; throughout the second half of the century it retained the status of a firmly established, respectable orthodoxy, and it received the accolade of science, both natural and social, in the United States, Canada, Britain, Australia, Germany, and to some degree in the Low Countries and France. Two great classes of racist literature are Arthur de Gobineau's *Essai sur l'Inégalité des Races Humaines,* published in 1853–1855, and in 1911, Houston Stuart Chamberlain's *The Foundations of [the] Nineteenth Century.* Lesser luminaries like Adolph Hitler and Theodore Roosevelt also penned substantial contributions to the field, but, unlike their armchair predecessors, applied their ideas with a considerable degree of success.

Any social explanation of the genesis of Western racism must, I believe, take three main factors into account.

1. Racism was congruent with prevailing forms of capitalist exploitation, notably with slavery in the New World and incipient colonial expansion in Africa. There is no question that the desire to rationalize exploitation of non-European peoples fostered the elaboration of a complex ideology of paternalism and racism, with its familiar themes of grown-up childishness, civilizing mission, atavistic savagery, and arrested evolution. However, any simple, direct, causal relationship that makes racism an epiphenomenal derivative of the system of production is unsatisfactory. European chattel slavery antedated the development of racist thinking; it was not until the nineteenth century that racism became a well-defined ideology distinguishable from ethnocentrism. Of course, the dehumanizing effect of slavery on both slave and owner facilitated the view of the Negro as a beast of burden without culture, and racism was a convenient rationalization for both slavery and colonialism. Yet both slavery and colonialism existed, as far as we know, without an appreciable amount of racism; therefore

racism cannot be accounted for purely as a consequence of slavery and colonialism.

2. Racism was congruent with the new Darwinian current of thought in the biological sciences.[2] Notions of stages of evolution, survival of the fittest, hereditary determinism, and near constancy of the gene pool (except for rare mutations) were all eagerly applied to *Homo sapiens* and adopted by the bourgeois social science of the late nineteenth century, represented by such figures as Herbert Spencer and William Graham Sumner. Social Darwinism and organicism (i.e., the notion that society is analogous to biological organisms) also dovetailed with the economic liberalism of the early nineteenth century. Although John Stuart Mill and other early liberals were explicitly antiracists, laissez faire was later reinterpreted as a mandate not to interfere with any form of human inequality and suffering. The poor were poor because they were biologically inferior; Negroes were slaves as a result of natural selection which had found the best place for them. Thus philanthropy, abolitionism, or any other attempt to interfere with "nature" could only debilitate the superior race by favoring inferior people (who already had the nasty habit of reproducing like rabbits, perhaps to compensate for their deservedly high mortality rate).

3. The egalitarian and libertarian ideas of the Enlightenment spread by the American and French Revolutions conflicted, of course, with racism, but they also paradoxically contributed to its development. Faced with the blatant contradiction between the treatment of slaves and colonial peoples and the official rhetoric of freedom and equality, Europeans and white North Americans began to dichotomize humanity between men and submen (or the "civilized" and the "savages"). The scope of applicability of the egalitarian ideals was restricted to "the people," that is, the whites, and there resulted what I have called *"Herrenvolk* democracies"—regimes such as those of the United States or South Africa that are democratic for the master race but tyrannical for the subordinate groups.[3] The desire to preserve both the profit-

---

[2] Cf. Richard Hofstadter, *Social Darwinism in American Thought* (New York: George Braziller, Inc. 1959).

[3] I dealt with this concept of *Herrenvolk* democracy and egalitarianism in my book, *South Africa, a Study in Conflict.*

able forms of discrimination and exploitation and the democratic ideology made it necessary to deny humanity to the oppressed groups. It is only an apparent paradox that the lot of the slave has typically been better in aristocratic societies (like colonial Latin America or many traditional African kingdoms that practiced domestic slavery) than in *Herrenvolk* democracies like the United States.

A Quarter Century of United Nations Protest in Vain*

Except for some token changes in the field of international sports competition, the repressive apartheid policy of the South African government is becoming more, rather than less entrenched. The following news report cites the discouragement of renowned leaders in the fight against discrimination.

United Nations: Opponents of South Africa's apartheid policy marked the International Day of the Elimination of Racial Discrimination Tuesday with confessions of failure outside the area of international sports.

The sixteen-nation special committee on apartheid chose the day, anniversary of the 1960 Sharpeville massacre in which sixty-nine demonstrators were killed by South African police, to begin a two-day seminar on how to strengthen their campaign for reform. Most of the participants agreed with U.N. Secretary General Kurt Waldheim that "regrettably, there has been little progress."

Waldheim traveled to South Africa earlier this month to discuss with officials there the future of the disputed territory of South-West Africa, ruled by Pretoria in defiance of the United Nations. In his statement, he appealed to the white government to "chart a new course which would enable that country to play its rightful role in Africa and in the United Nations."

---

*Don Shannon, "Apartheid Opponents Confess to Failure," *Los Angeles Times*, March 22, 1972, Part I, p. 20. Copyright 1972, *Los Angeles Times*. Reprinted by permission.

Somalia's Abdulrahim Abbry Farah, president of the anti-apartheid group, welcomed nongovernment representatives to the meeting and warned that strong political and economic forces support the South African status quo. "We must also face the fact that twenty-five years of United Nations protest has not stopped the increasingly severe application of apartheid and its entrenchment by all the forces of a militant police state," Farah said. The exception, the Somalian added, is sports, where boycotts of all white South African rugby and cricket teams in Britain and other Commonwealth nations have caused cancellation of international matches and sometimes modification of South African policy.

But Asst. Bishop C. Edward Crowther of the Episcopal diocese of California warned that some gestures towards sports desegregation are deceptive. South Africa's invitation to Evonne Goolagong, an Australian aborigine, to play in racially mixed tournaments was meaningless, he said, because she appeared only before segregated spectators.

Ambassador Mikhail D. Polyanichko of the Ukraine urged a halt in the flow of both arms and investment to South Africa, mostly from the United States and its North Atlantic allies.

Several U.S. clergymen called for a ban on U.S. investment, and the Rev. Ralph David Abernathy of the Southern Christian Leadership Conference attacked the Polaroid Corporation for its publicized program of equal pay for black and white employes in South Africa. "If Polaroid was really interested in African reform it would insist that the African majority get the right to vote and travel," he said.

Suggestions for Further Reading

1. Milton L. Barron (ed.), *Minorities in a Changing World* (New York: Alfred A. Knopf, 1967).

2. Carl N. Degler, *Neither Black Nor White* (New York: Macmillan, 1971).

    A historical comparison of slavery and race relations in Brazil and the United States.

3. E. Franklin Frazier, *Race and Culture Contacts in the Modern World* (Boston: Beacon Press, 1957).

    This study of the varieties of race–culture situations is particularly good for establishing an understanding of the social organizations which have been created to accommodate peoples with different racial and cultural backgrounds in other countries. Frazier comes up with such interesting generalizations as: "Where assimilation does not occur, nationalistic movements tend to arise."

4. Thomas F. Gossett, *Race: the History of an Idea in America* (New York: Schocken Books, 1965).

    Chapter 1 in this book presents an overview of race theories in other countries up to the time of the Spanish explorations of the New World. Racism, it is pointed out, existed in other countries long before the colonization of America. Gossett's discussion of the term "racism" in this chapter is worth consulting.

5. George D. Kelsey, *Racism and the Christian Understanding of Man* (New York: Charles Scribner's Sons, 1965).

6. Arnold M. Rose and Caroline B. Rose, *Minority Problems* (New York: Harper & Row, 1965).

7. Arthur M. Schlesinger, "Our Ten Contributions to Civilization," *Atlantic Monthly* (March 1959).

Chapter Two

Racism and Discrimination in America: A Montage

We can give a rosy, romantic picture of the American past and the American present, thereby convincing no one and fooling no one but ourselves. Or we can face the issues squarely and unequivocally, telling our students the truth about ourselves and about themselves, relying on the inescapable fact that truth is virtue in itself and that like virtue it has its own reward.

—JOHN HOPE FRANKLIN,
The American Teacher

Statistical data and scholarly studies can provide a rational understanding of the scope as well as the depth of racism and discrimination in American history. The human side of racism is vividly conveyed by concrete examples that show feelings and emotions.

This chapter consists of brief flashes that reveal the emotional agony of being a victim of racism. There is no particular significance to the sequence in which they are arranged. It is a montage that reaches into the conscience of this nation.

In 1712, South Carolina passed "An Act for the better ordering and governing of Negroes and Slaves," two sections of which are presented below. This document became a prototype for southern slave codes in the decades which followed.

WHEREAS, the plantations and estates of this Province cannot be well and sufficiently managed and brought into use, without the labor and service of negroes and other slaves; and forasmuch as the said negroes and other slaves brought unto the people of this Province for that purpose, are of barbarous, wild, savage natures, and such as renders them wholly unqualified to be governed by the laws, customs, and practices of this Province, but that it is absolutely necessary, that such other constitutions, laws, and orders, should in this Province be made and enacted, for the good regulating and ordering of them, as may restrain the disorders, rapines, and inhumanity, to which they are naturally prone and inclined, and may also tend to the safety and security of the people of this Province and their estates; to which purpose,

I. *Be it therefore enacted* . . . That all negroes, mulatoes, m[e]stizoes, or Indians, which at any time heretofore have been sold, or now are held or taken to be, or hereafter shall be bought and sold for slaves, are hereby declared slaves; and they, and their children, are hereby made and declared slaves, to all intents and purposes; excepting all such negroes, mulatoes, m[e]stizoes, or Indians, which heretofore have been, or hereafter shall be, for some particular merit, made and declared free . . . and also, excepting all such negroes, mulatoes, m[e]stizos, or Indians, as can prove they ought not to be sold for slaves. . . .

II. And for the better ordering and governing of negroes and all other slaves in this Province, *Be it enacted* . . . That no master, mistress, overseer, or other person whatsoever, that hath the care and charge of any negro or slave, shall give their negroes and other slaves leave, on Sundays, hollidays [*sic*], or any other time, to go out of their plantations, except such negro or other slave as usually wait upon them at home or abroad, or wearing a livery; . . . and every person who shall not (when in his power) apprehend every negro or other slave which he shall see out of his master's plantation, without leave as aforesaid, and after apprehended, shall neglect to punish him by moderate whipping, shall forfeit twenty shillings, . . . and that no slave may make further or other use of any one ticket than was intended by him that granted the same, every ticket shall particularly mention the name of every slave employed in the particular business, and to what place they are sent, and what time they return; and if any person shall presume to give any negro or slave a ticket in the name of his master or mistress, without his or her consent such person so doing shall forfeit the sum of twenty shillings; ... And for the better security of all such persons that shall endeavor to take any runaway, or shall examine any slave for his ticket, passing to and from his master's plantation, it is hereby declared lawful for any white person to beat, maim, or assault, and if such negro or slave cannot otherwise be taken, to kill him, who shall refuse to shew [*sic*] his ticket, or, by running away or resistance, shall endeavor to avoid being apprehended or taken.

Racism for many Americans still conjures up images of black-white relations, to the exclusion of many other groups. One of these groups, regularly labelled by a catch-all phrase, is the American Indian. In the following paragraph, from an important Indian author's book, we see the resentment this has bred.

The Kerner Report seriously announces that society is splitting into two separate and unequal societies. This report is premised on the idea that at one time society was a monolith of opportunity and brotherhood. It overlooks the fact that blacks and whites have never shared one society. But more important, it overlooks the fact that tribalistic people and individualistic people have never shared anything in common. American society has always been divided into the mainstream white and black Americans who shared integrationist philosophies and the Indians, Mexicans, Jews, and ethnic concentrations who stubbornly held traditions and customs brought over from the old country. These are the *others* so casually mentioned when social problems are discussed.*

---

*From Vine Deloria, Jr., *We Talk, You Listen: New Tribes, New Turf* (New York: Macmillan, 1970), p. 89.

One of the major themes of this book is that there is an intimate connection between racism and expansionism. The following excerpt articulates this theme in an unequivocal way.

. . . The history of American expansionism is directly linked to American racism. Almost every instance of armed intervention has been undertaken against a colored people including Latin Americans. If United States foreign policy is examined together with domestic policy, the theme of racism emerges more clearly. Zion in the Wilderness, Manifest Destiny, The American Mission, The American Century, all represent visions of a white America that rules the world; dreams for an empire. . . .

So, when the Black Panthers, the Brown Berets, or the Red Guard talk of forging an alliance with the Third World and colored people all over the world, they are expressing an awareness of the basic facts of American history as well as its present state. Africans and Latin Americans, Asians and Indians, have been *the losers,* oppressed people, in all their contacts with white Americans, at home and abroad. . . . The massacre of Vietnamese women and children at My Lai by American soldiers is only a modern version of the massacre of Indian women and children by American soldiers at Wounded Knee. . . . American expansionism is inextricably linked to American racism.*

In 1970 all was not well in San Francisco's Chinatown. The following piece enumerates some of the problems.

It has only been within the past few years, however, that San Franciscans have begun to acknowledge what should have been obvious long before—that San Francisco's Chinatown, the largest Chinese community outside of Asia and a principal tourist attraction of that city—is in fact a ghetto troubled by formidable economic, educational, social and medical problems. . . .

The great majority of the overcrowded apartments and rooming houses are substandard. The tuberculosis rate is the highest in the city. The suicide rate is three times the national average. Mental illness is a major problem. In the alleys, there

---

*From Paul Jacobs and Saul Landau, *To Serve the Devil,* Vol. I, *Natives and Slaves* (New York: Random House, 1971), pp. 317–320.

are some 150 sweatshops where 3,000 women sew garments for low wages. In the restaurants, men make in the neighborhood of $200 a month for a ten-hour day, six days a week.*

Frederick Douglass was never one to mince words; he said what was on his mind. In 1852 he delivered a now-famous Fourth of July oration that included the following paragraphs.

What, to the American slave, is your Fourth of July? I answer; a day that reveals to him, more than all other days in the year, the gross injustice and cruelty to which he is the constant victim. To him, your celebration is a sham; your boasted liberty, an unholy license; your national greatness, swelling vanity; your sounds of rejoicing are empty and heartless; your denunciation of tyrants, brass fronted impudence; your shouts of liberty and equality, hollow mockery; your prayers and hymns, your sermons and thanksgivings, with all your religious parade and solemnity, are, to Him, mere bombast, fraud, deception, impiety, and hypocrisy—a thin veil to cover up crimes which would disgrace a nation of savages. There is not a nation on the earth guilty of practices more shocking and bloody than are the people of the United States, at this very hour.

Go where you may, search where you will, roam through all the monarchies and despotisms of the Old World, travel through South America, search out every abuse, and when you have found the last, lay your facts by the side of the everyday practices of this nation, and you will say with me, that, for revolting barbarity and shameless hypocrisy, America reigns without a rival.†

Those who believe that Americans can obtain justice in the courts should read the following excerpt from the trial of a Mexican-American youth.

---

*From Kenneth Lamott, "The Awakening of Chinatown," *Los Angeles Times, West Magazine,* January 4, 1970, pp. 7–14.

†From Frederick Douglass, "The Meaning of July Fourth for the Negro," speech given at Rochester, New York, July 5, 1852. Reprinted from Philip S. Foner, ed., *The Life and Writings of Frederick Douglass.*

JUVENILE DIVISION
HONORABLE GERALD S. CHARGIN,

Judge   Courtroom No. 1

In the Matter of
    PAUL PETE CASILLAS, JR.,
        a minor.

No. 40331

STATEMENTS OF THE COURT
San Jose, California   September 2, 1969

APPEARANCES:
For the Minor:

FRED LUCERO, ESQ.
Deputy Public Defender

For the Probation Department:

WILLIAM TAPOGNA, ESQ.
Court Probation Officer

Official Court Reporter:

SUSAN K. STRAHM, C.S.R.

The Court: There is some indication that you more or less didn't think that it was against the law or was improper. Haven't you had any moral training? Have you and your family gone to church?

The Minor: Yes, sir.

The Court: Don't you know that things like this are terribly wrong? This is one of the worst crimes that a person can commit. I just get so disgusted that I just figure what is the use? You are just an animal. You are lower than an animal. Even animals don't do that. You are pretty low.

I don't know why your parents haven't been able to teach you anything or train you. Mexican people, after thirteen years of age, it's perfectly all right to go out and act like an animal. It's not even right to do that to a stranger, let alone a member of your own family. I don't have much hope for you. You will probably end up in State's Prison before you are twenty-five, and that's where you belong, anyhow. There is nothing much you can do.

I think you haven't got any moral principles. You won't acquire anything. Your parents won't teach you what is right or wrong and won't watch out.

Apparently, your sister is pregnant; is that right?

The Minor's Father, Mr. Casillas: Yes.

The Court: It's a fine situation. How old is she?

The Minor's Mother, Mrs. Casillas: Fifteen.

The Court: Well, probably she will have a half a dozen children and three or four marriages before she is eighteen.

The County will have to take care of you. You are no particular good to anybody. We ought to send you out of the country—send you back to Mexico. You belong in prison for the rest of your life for doing things of this kind. You ought to commit suicide. That's what I think of people of this kind. You are lower than animals and haven't the right to live in organized society—just miserable, lousy, rotten people.

There is nothing we can do with you. You expect the County to take care of you. Maybe Hitler was right. The animals in our society probably ought to be destroyed because they have no right to live among human beings. If you refuse to act like a human being, then, you don't belong among the society of human beings.

Mr. Lucero: Your Honor, I don't think I can sit here and listen to that sort of thing.

The Court: You are going to have to listen to it because I consider this a very vulgar, rotten human being.

Mr. Lucero: The Court is indicting the whole Mexican group.

The Court: When they are ten or twelve years of age, going out and having intercourse with anybody without any moral training—they don't even understand the Ten Commandments. That's all. Apparently, they don't want to.

So if you want to act like that, the County has a system of taking care of them. They don't care about that. They have no personal self-respect.

Mr. Lucero: The Court ought to look at this youngster and deal with this youngster's case.

The Court: All right. That's what I am going to do. The family should be able to control this boy and the young girl.

Mr. Lucero: What appalls me is that the Court is saying that Hitler was right in genocide.

The Court: What are we going to do with the mad dogs of our society? Either we have to kill them or send them to an institution or place them out of the hands of good people because that's the theory—one of the theories of punishment is if they get to the position that they want to act like mad dogs, then, we have to separate them from our society.

Well, I will go along with the recommendation. You will learn in time or else you will have to pay for the penalty with the law because the law grinds slowly but exceedingly well. If you are going to be a law violator—you have to make up your mind whether you are going to observe the law or not. If you can't observe the law, then, you have to be put away.

STATE OF CALIFORNIA
} ss
COUNTY OF SANTA CLARA

I, SUSAN K. STRAHM, do hereby certify that the foregoing is a true and correct transcript of the *statements of the court* had in the within-entitled action taken on the 2nd day of September, 1969; that I reported the same in stenotype, being the qualified and acting Official Court Reporter of the Superior Court of the State of California, in and for the County of Santa Clara, appointed to said Court, and thereafter had the same transcribed into typewriting as herein appears.

Dated: This 8th day of September, 1969.

SUSAN K. STRAHM, C.S.R.

When Democratic party leader Stephen Douglas made the follow-ing statements at Galesburg, Illinois, in 1858, he was the senator from Illinois campaigning for reelection against Abraham Lincoln, the Re-publican candidate. In this portion of the famed Lincoln-Douglas debates, Douglas was not announcing a new doctrine. He was merely restating in his own words what Chief Justice Roger Taney had written in the Dred Scott decision one year earlier:

In the opinion of the court, the legislation and histories of the times, and the language used in the Declaration of Independence, show, that neither the class of persons who have been imported as slaves, nor their descendants, whether they had become free or not, were then acknowl-edged as a part of the people, nor intended to be included in the general words used in that memorable instrument.

The majority of Illinois voters favored Douglas' view and he was reappointed to the United States Senate that fall.

The signers of the Declaration of Independence never dreamed of the negro when they were writing that document. They referred to white men, to men of European birth and Euro-pean descent, when they declared the equality of all men. I see a gentleman there in the crowd shaking his head. Let me remind him that when Thomas Jefferson wrote that document he was the owner, and so continued until his death, of a large number of slaves. Did he intend to say in that Declaration that his negro slaves, which he held and treated as property, were created his equals by Divine law, and that he was violating the law of God every day of his life by holding them as slaves? It must be borne in mind that when that Declaration was put forth every one of the thirteen colonies were slave-holding colonies, and every man who signed that instrument represented a slaveholding constituency. Recollect, also, that no one of them emancipated his slaves, much less put them on an equality with himself, after he signed the Declaration. On the contrary, they all continued to hold their negroes as slaves during the revolutionary war. Now, do you be-lieve—are you willing to have it said—that every man who signed the Declaration of Independence declared the negro his equal, and then was hypocrite enough to continue to hold him as a slave, in violation of what he believed to be the divine law? And yet when you say that the Declaration of Independence includes the negro, you charge the signers of it with hypocrisy.

I say to you, frankly, that in my opinion this government was made by our fathers on the white basis. It was made by white men for the benefit of white men and their posterity forever, and was intended to be administered by white men in all time to come.

The following article of the constitution of the state of California was repealed in 1952, after being in effect since 1879.

Article XIX
Chinese

SECTION 1. The legislature shall prescribe all necessary regulations for the protection of the state, and the counties, cities, and towns thereof, from the burdens and evils arising from the presence of aliens who are or may become vagrants, paupers, mendicants, criminals, or invalids afflicted with contagious or infectious diseases, and from aliens otherwise dangerous or detrimental to the well-being or peace of the state, and to impose conditions upon which such persons may reside in the state, and to provide the means and mode of their removal from the state, upon failure or refusal to comply with such conditions; provided, that nothing contained in this section shall be construed to impair or limit the power of the legislature to pass such police laws or other regulations as it may deem necessary.

SECTION 2. No corporation now existing or hereafter formed under the laws of this state shall, after the adoption of this Constitution, employ, directly or indirectly, in any capacity, any Chinese or Mongolian. The legislature shall pass such laws as may be necessary to enforce this provision.

SECTION 3. No Chinese shall be employed on any state, county, municipal, or other public work, except in punishment for crime.

SECTION 4. The presence of foreigners ineligible to become citizens of the United States is declared to be dangerous to the well-being of the state, and the legislature shall discourage their immigration by all the means within its power. Asiatic coolieism is a form of human slavery, and is forever prohibited in this state, and all contracts for coolie labor shall be void. All companies or corporations, whether formed in this country or any foreign country, for the importation of such labor, shall be subject to such penalties as the legislature may prescribe. The legislature shall delegate all necessary power to the incorporated cities and towns of this state for the removal of Chinese without the limits of such cities and towns, or for their location within prescribed portions of those limits, and it shall also provide the necessary legislation to prohibit the introduction into this state of Chinese after the adoption of this Constitution. This section shall be enforced by appropriate legislation.

The following comments, made in 1906, remained true of professional baseball until Jackie Robinson was signed by the Brooklyn Dodgers in 1947.

In no other profession has the color line been drawn more rigidly than in baseball. Colored players are not only barred from white clubs; at times exhibition games are cancelled for no other reason than objections raised by a southern player. These southerners are, as a rule, fine players; and managers refuse to book colored teams rather than lose their services.

The colored player suffers great inconveniences while traveling. All hotels are generally filled from garret to cellar when they strike a town. It is a common occurrence for them to arrive in a city late at night and to walk around for several hours before finding a lodging.

The situation is far different today than it was in the 1870's, when colored players were accommodated in the best hotels in the country. The cause of this change is no doubt the sad condition of things from a racial standpoint today. The color question is uppermost in the minds of Americans at the present time.

The average pay of colored players is $466 a year, compared to an average of $2,000 for white major leaguers and $571 for white minor leaguers. The disparity in salaries is enormous when it is apparent that many colored stars would be playing in the majors but for the color line.

　　　　　　—SOL WHITE, *History of Colored Baseball* (1906)

The following excerpt is from the autobiographical Narrative of the Life of Frederick Douglass, an American Slave, *published in 1845.*

I have had two masters. My first master's name was Anthony. I do not remember his first name. He was generally called Captain Anthony—a title which, I presume, he acquired by sailing a craft on the Chesapeake Bay. He was not considered a rich slaveholder. He owned two or three farms, and about thirty slaves. His farms and slaves were under the care of an overseer. The overseer's name was Plummer. Mr. Plummer was a miserable drunkard, a profane swearer, and a savage monster. He always went armed with a cowskin and a heavy cudgel. I have known him to cut and slash the women's heads so horribly, that even master would be enraged at his cruelty, and would threaten to whip him if he did not mind himself. Master, however, was not a humane slaveholder. It required extraordinary barbarity on the part of an overseer to affect him. He was a cruel man, hardened by a long life of slaveholding. He would at times seem to take great pleasure in whipping a slave. I have often been awakened at the dawn of a day by the most heart-rending shrieks of an own aunt of mine, whom he used to tie up to a joist, and whip upon her naked back till she was literally covered with blood. No words, no tears, no prayers, from his gory victim, seemed to move his iron heart from its bloody purpose. The louder she screamed, the harder he whipped; and where the blood ran fastest, there he whipped longest. He would whip her to make her scream, and whip her to make her hush; and not until overcome by fatigue, would he cease to swing the blood-clotted cowskin. I remember the first time I ever witnessed this horrible exhibition. I was quite a child, but I will remember it. I never shall forget it whilst I remember anything. It was the first of a long series of such outrages, of which I was doomed to be a witness and a participant. It struck me with awful force. It was the blood-stained gate, the entrance to the hell of slavery, through which I was about to pass. It was a most terrible spectacle. I wish I could commit to paper the feelings with which I beheld it.

This occurrence took place very soon after I went to live with my old master, and under the following circumstances. Aunt Hester went out one night—where or for what I do not know—and happened to be absent when my master desired her presence. He had ordered her not to go out evenings, and warned her that she must never let him catch her in company with a young man, who was paying attention to her belonging to Colonel Lloyd. The young man's name was Ned Roberts, generally called Lloyd's Ned. Why master was so careful of her, may be safely left to conjecture. She was a woman of noble form, and of graceful proportions, having very few equals, and fewer superiors, in personal appearance, among the colored or white women of our neighborhood.

Aunt Hester had not only disobeyed his orders in going out, but had been found in company with Lloyd's Ned; which circumstance, I found, from what he said while whipping her, was the chief offence. Had he been a man of pure morals himself, he might have been thought interested in protecting the innocence of my aunt; but those who knew him will not suspect him of any such virtue. Before he commenced whipping Aunt Hester, he took her into the kitchen, and stripped her from neck to waist, leaving her neck, shoulders, and back entirely naked. He then told her to cross her hands, calling her at the same time a d——d b——h. After crossing her hands, he tied them with a strong rope, and led her to a stool under a large hook in the joist, put in for the purpose. He made her get upon the stool, and tied her hands to the hook. She now stood fair for his infernal purpose. Her arms were stretched up at their full length, so that she stood upon the ends of her toes. He then said to her, "Now you d——d b——h, I'll learn you how to disobey my orders!" and after rolling up his sleeves, he commenced to lay on the heavy cowskin, and soon the warm, red blood (amid heart-rending shrieks from her, and horrid oaths from him) came dripping to the floor. I was so terrifiied and horror stricken at the sight, that I hid myself in a closet, and dared not venture out till long after the bloody transaction was over. I expected it would be my turn next. It was all new to me. I had never seen anything like it before. I had always lived with my grandmother on the outskirts of the plantation, where she was put to raise the children of the younger women. I had therefore been, until now, out of the way of the bloody scenes that often occurred on the plantation.

The table and graph which follow, and the newspaper accounts which accompany them, indicate the extent and nature of lynchings. This was only the most obvious variety of terrorism directed at Negroes in the South.

LYNCHINGS BY STATES AND
RACE 1882–1962

State	Whites	Negroes	Total	State	Whites	Negroes	Total
Alabama	48	299	347	New Mexico	33	3	36
Arizona	31	0	31	New York	1	1	2
Arkansas	58	226	284	North			
California	41	2	43	Carolina	15	85	100
Colorado	66	2	68	North			
Delaware	0	1	1	Dakota	13	3	16
Florida	25	257	282	Ohio	10	16	26
Georgia	39	491	530	Oklahoma	82	40	122
Idaho	20	0	20	Oregon	20	1	21
Illinois	15	19	34	Pennsylvania	2	6	8
Indiana	33	14	47	South			
Iowa	17	2	19	Carolina	4	156	160
Kansas	35	19	54	South			
Kentucky	63	142	205	Dakota	27	0	27
Lousiana	56	335	391	Tennessee	47	204	251
Maryland	2	27	29	Texas	141	352	493
Michigan	7	1	8	Utah	6	2	8
Minnesota	5	4	9	Vermont	1	0	1
Mississippi	40	538	578	Virginia	17	83	100
Missouri	53	69	122	Washington	25	1	26
Montana	82	2	84	West Virginia	20	28	48
Nebraska	52	5	57	Wisconsin	6	0	6
Nevada	6	0	6	Wyoming	30	5	35
New Jersey	0	1	1	TOTAL	1,294	3,442	4,736

MOULTRIE, Ga., July 15, 1921—From ... (the) scene of the recent burning of a negro named John Henry Williams, the *Eagle* has obtained the following account by an eyewitness:

"There are many things about the Williams burning more disgraceful than have been published. A sick woman and her child, who had nothing to do with the matter, were beaten into insensibility and left to die because of hoodlumism of the mob. Colored churches were burned, colored farmers chased from their homes.

"Williams was brought from Moultrie on Friday night by sheriffs from fifty counties. Saturday court was called. Not a single colored person was allowed nearer than a block of the courthouse. The trial took half an hour. Then Williams, surrounded by fifty sheriffs armed with machine guns, started out of the courthouse door toward the jail.

"Immediately a cracker by the name of Ken Murphy gave the Confederate yell: 'Whoo—whoo—let's get the nigger!' Simultaneously 500 poor pecks rushed the armed sheriffs, who made no resistance whatsoever. They tore the negro's clothing off before he was placed in a waiting automobile. This was done in broad daylight. The negro was unsexed, as usual, and made to eat a portion

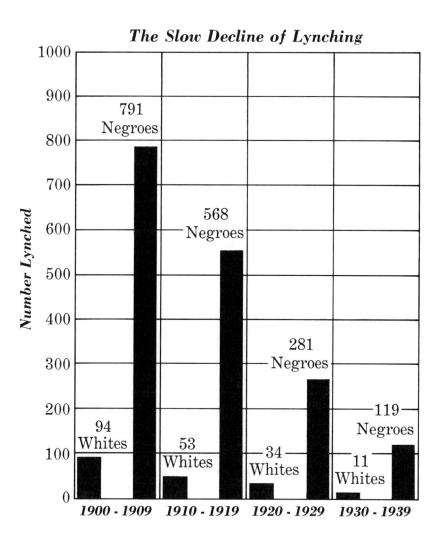

The Slow Decline of Lynching

of his anatomy which had been cut away. Another portion was sent by parcel post to Governor Dorsey, whom the people of this section hate bitterly.

"The negro was taken to a grove, where each one of more than 500 people, in Ku Klux ceremonial, had placed a pine knot around a stump, making a pyramid to the height of ten feet. The negro was chained to the stump and asked if he had anything to say. Castrated and in indescribable torture, the negro asked for a cigarette, lit it, and blew the smoke in the face of his tormentors.

"The pyre was lit and a hundred men and women, old and young, grandmothers among them, joined hands and danced around the negro while he burned, and began to sing 'Nearer My God to Thee'."

—Reported in *The Washington Eagle* (July 16, 1921)

OSCEOLA, Ark., June 2, 1926—Albert Blades, 22-year-old negro, was hanged and burned for allegedly attacking a small white girl. Doctors examined the child today and said that she had not been attacked. It appears that the child had merely been startled by Blades while she was playing.

—Reported in *The St. Louis Argus* (June 8, 1926)

MILLEDGEVILLE, Ga., February 16, 1923—Fingers and ears of two negroes who were lynched near this city last week are now on display in a large bottle filled with alcohol on the counter of the town drug store. An inscription near the bottle says:

"What's left of the niggers that shot a white man."

Lindsey B. Gilmore, a white grocer, was shot when he took after two negroes, unidentified, who were caught stealing cheese and cash from Gilmore's store. A number of witnesses have stated that in the chase Gilmore was shot by a local officer whose aim was faulty.

—Reported in *The Chicago Defender* (February 17, 1923)

COLUMBIA, Mo., April 19, 1923—A mob of 500—consisting mainly of university students—lynched James T. Scott, a negro janitor at the University of Missouri, who was accused of attempting to assault the daughter of the head of the German department. . . . His neck snapped audibly.

—Reported in *The New York World* (April 20, 1923)

A famous white comedian recalls his feelings about a black friend. *

W. C. Fields, no mean pantomimist himself, once said: "Bert Williams is the funniest man I ever saw—the saddest man I ever knew." He was also the most sensitive. The problems of his people weighed heavily on him. Even in his happy moments—and we had many together—I sensed a deep strain of melancholy in him. Once in awhile, it slipped out. The poignancy of those rare remarks stayed with me always. One New Year's Eve, after the show, most of the cast headed for parties. Bert and I had arranged to see the new year in together at the hotel where he was permitted to live providing he used the back elevator. I was to pick up a turkey we had ordered from a nearby restaurant. As we started out the stage door, I said, "See you at the hotel, okay?"

"Okay," Bert replied, "I'm on my way to the back elevator." This was the first hint of bitterness I'd ever heard from my "turn-thine-other-cheek" friend. Painfully aware that no words could help his hurt, I said nothing. We stood for a moment in understanding silence. Then Bert added, "It wouldn't be so bad, Eddie, if I didn't still hear the applause ringing in my ears."*

The following narrative is presented as typical of the petty indignities to which Negroes are exposed as a matter of practice in many areas.

I was a proud and happy child—all hair and legs, my cousin Early B. used to say—and an only child, although not blessed with the privilege of having my own way. One afternoon shortly after my seventh birthday, my mother called me in from play.

"I'm not feeling well," she said. "You'll have to go to the market and get the meat for dinner."

I was thrilled with such an important errand. I put on one of my prettiest dresses and my mother brushed my hair. She gave me a dollar and instructions to get a pound of center-cut pork chops. I skipped happily all the way to the market.

When I entered the market, there were several white adults

---

*From "Bert Williams—the Best Teacher I Ever Had," by Eddie Cantor. Originally published in *Ebony*, June, 1958. Reprinted from *White on Black* (Chicago: Johnson Publishing Co., 1963).

waiting to be served. When the butcher had finished with them, I gave him my order. More white adults entered. The butcher turned from me and took their orders. I was a little annoyed but felt since they were grownups it was all right. While he was waiting on the adults, a little white girl came in and we talked while we waited.

The butcher finished with the adults, looked down at us and asked, "What do you want, little girl?" I smiled and said, "I told you before, a pound of center-cut pork chops." He snarled, "I'm not talking to you," and again asked the white girl what she wanted. She also want a pound of center-cut pork chops.

"Please may I have my meat?" I said, as the little girl left. The butcher took my dollar from the counter, reached into the showcase, got a handful of fat chops and wrapped them up. Thrusting the package at me, he said, "Niggers have to wait till I wait on the white people. Now take your meat and get out of here!" I ran all the way home crying.

When I reached the house, my mother asked what had happened. I started pulling her toward the door, telling her what the butcher had said. I opened the meat and showed it to her. "It's fat, Mother. Let's take it back."

"Oh, Lord, I knew I shouldn't have sent her. Stop crying now, the meat isn't so bad."

"But it is. Why can't we take it back?"

"Go on out on the porch and wait for Daddy." As she turned from me, her eyes were filling with tears.

When I saw Daddy approaching, I ran to him crying. He lifted me in his arms and smiled. "Now, what's wrong?" When I told him, his smile faded.

"And if we don't hurry, the market will be closed," I finished.

"We'll talk about it after dinner, sweetheart." I could feel his muscles tighten as he carried me into the house.

Dinner was distressingly silent. Afterward my parents went into the bedroom and talked. My mother came out and told me my father wanted to see me. I ran into the bedroom. Daddy sat there, looking at me for a long time. Several times he tried to speak, but the words just wouldn't come. I stood there, looking at him and wondering why he was acting so strangely. Finally he stood up and the words began tumbling from him. Much of what he said I did not understand. To my seven-year-old mind he explained as best he could that a Negro had no rights that a white man respected.

He dropped to his knees in front of me, placed his hands on my shoulder, and began shaking me and shouting.

"Can't you understand what I've been saying?" he demanded. "There's nothing I can do! If I went down to the market I would only cause trouble for my family."

As I looked at my daddy sitting by me with tears in his eyes, I blurted out innocently, "Daddy, are you afraid?"

He sprang to his feet in an anger I had never seen before. "Hell, no! I'm not afraid for myself; I'm not afraid to die. I could go down to that market and tear him limb from limb with my bare hands, but I'm afraid for you and your mother."

That night when I knelt to pray, instead of my usual prayers, I found myself praying that the butcher would die. After that night we never mentioned him again.*

The following is from a recent article which claims that the racist character of American society is an effective bar to any hope of integration.

America has always been a separatist society. Whether by slave code, the lash, the lynch mob, Jim Crow laws or subtle, covert discrimination, white separatism has held the black man apart from full and equal participation in this society. The traditional wisdom has been that Americans, when challenged with their democratic credo, would ultimately resolve their "dilemma" in favor of fairness. The Movement provided just such a challenge— it dared white America to be what it said it already was. In the wake of the disillusionment and despair that followed the fragmentation of the Movement, America has been forced to acknowledge the truth about itself—it is racist.†

---

*From Daisy Bates, *The Long Shadow of Little Rock* (New York: 1962). Reprinted by permission David McKay Company, Inc.

†Haywood Burns, "Equal—But Separate?" *Civil Liberties*, No. 260, February 1969, p. 13.

Suggestions for Further Reading

1. David D. Anderson and Robert L. Wright (eds.), *The Dark and Tangled Path: Race in America* (Boston: Houghton Mifflin, 1971).

   A collection of documents that shows attitudes toward black, red, and yellow Americans, from first encounters to the present. Draws heavily from American literature.

2. Leonard Dinnerstein and Frederic Cople Jaher (eds.), *The Aliens: A History of Ethnic Minorities in America* (New York: Appleton-Century-Crofts, 1970).

   Fifteen ethnic groups are treated in twenty-three articles.

3. Stanley Feldstein, *The Poisoned Tongue: A Documentary History of American Racism and Prejudice* (New York: William Morrow, 1972).

4. Dick Gregory, *No More Lies: The Myth and the Reality of American History* (New York: Harper & Row, 1971).

   Famous as a comedian and a civil rights activist, Gregory blends humor with hard-hitting truth as he attacks more than a dozen myths of American history.

5. Paul Jacobs and Saul Landau (eds.), *To Serve the Devil*, 2 vols. (New York: Random House, 1971).

   Analysis, with much documentary support, of American racial history.

6. Louis L. Knowles and Kenneth Prewitt (eds.), *Institutional Racism in America* (Englewood Cliffs, N.J.: Prentice-Hall, 1969).

7. Gustavus Myers, *History of Bigotry in the United States*, edited and revised by Henry M. Christman (New York: Capricorn Books, 1960).

8. Gary Nash and Richard Weiss (eds.), *The Great Fear: Race in the Mind of America* (New York: Holt, Rinehart and Winston, 1970).

Nine analytical essays about white racial attitudes from colonial times to the present. Of special interest is the essay by Stanley Coben, "The Failure of the Melting Pot."

9. Barry Schwartz and Robert Disch (eds.), *White Racism: Its History, Pathology, and Practice* (New York: Dell Publishing, 1970).

PART 2   RACIST RATIONALIZATIONS FOR TERRITORIAL ACQUISITION

Chapter Three

Anti-Indian Policies and Practices

All the nonwhite minorities in American California suffered from various kinds of unjust discrimination, but the mistreatment of the Indians began earliest and was far the worst. Between 1846 and 1900 about one-tenth of the California Indians were victims of outright genocide, while disease and starvation killed many more. In California, as in other parts of the United States, the history of American treatment of the Indians in the nineteenth century was too often a sickening record of racist murder and sanctimonious fraud.

—WALTON BEAN, *California, an Interpretive History* (1968)

From their earliest contacts with white men four hundred years ago to the present day, American Indians have been the victims of a persistent greed for land and an implicit racism which were revealed in a variety of ways. Indians have been lied to, cheated, herded away from their lands like so many cattle, manipulated, brutalized, and decimated. If some managed to survive physical annihilation, they still had to beat back attempts to rob them of their dignity as a people.

Under the pretense of equipping them for assimilation, they have been uprooted from their ancient lands and relocated under military supervision in extensive efforts to remove them as far as possible from the mainstream of American life. Nearly four hundred treaties with Indians were broken by the American government before the present century. Wave after wave of western pioneers (and a sizable number of government agents) took advantage of many opportunities to undermine peaceful relations. Even parcels of land to which Indians had been consigned in the belief that the acreage was valueless were not immune from further encroachments if something valuable was discovered there later on.

Not just the Indians' land and the minerals it contained, but their means of livelihood as well, were the objects of the white man's greed. In 1865 approximately fifteen million head of buffalo —a major source of Indian livelihood—roamed the Great Plains. When buffalo hunting became a white man's sport, railroad expeditions were organized for the luxurious pleasure of white Americans. By 1885 buffalo were nearly extinct. The lack of concern about the consequences of these pastimes for Indian rights or Indian survival characterized the dominant attitude toward Indian culture.

Often the justification for this sustained program of genocide was racist, although there were numerous other factors which played a role. Indians were at best savages, perhaps even subhuman animals. They had no rights worth enumerating in the Constitution. Moreover, subjugation of a native population by an expansionist power was not unique. Americans were simply following the traditions of Western ethnocentrism and racism to justify their plans for territorial acquisition.

Some of the most vivid expressions of white racism are part of the official record of Indian relations. Consider the significance of the following statement which was made by Commissioner W. A. Jones in the *Annual Report of the Commissioner of Indian Affairs for 1903:*

> It is probably true that the majority of our wild Indians have no inherited tendencies whatever toward morality or chastity, according to an enlightened standard. Chastity and morality among them must come from education and contact with the better element of the whites.

Three-quarters of a century before Indian Commissioner Jones was spouting off his racist notions, President Andrew Jackson stood firm in his refusal to enforce a Supreme Court decision which upheld Cherokee Indian rights in Georgia. The subsequent shocking mistreatment of the tribe which was being denied its rights by an American President revealed the extent to which the majority of Americans were willing to look the other way while bigotry prevailed.

Surely here was one crack in the Melting Pot that would not be easily ignored when Americans began to inspect the Melting Pot with two open eyes. In the late 1960's, when the Melting Pot myth was being challenged, Indian grievances were entering the field of majority awareness.

The seizure of Alcatraz, bumper stickers such as CUSTER HAD IT COMING, books such as *Bury My Heart at Wounded Knee* and *Custer Died For Your Sins,* expressions such as "Uncle Tomahawk" (which corresponded to Tio Taco and Uncle Tom), and a general thrust toward Red Power helped America begin to examine its past and present treatment of the original Native Americans. Although it was small comfort, one indication that a new awareness was beginning to creep into governmental circles was Secretary of the Interior Walter Hickel's testimony before a Senate subcommittee in September of 1970: "When the Indian complains that 'White man speaks with forked tongue,' there often is more truth than poetry in his words."

Hickel said that the federal government's obligation to protect American Indians' rights often loses out to covetous ambitions within in the same government toward Indian lands and waters.

These developments are treated in Part 5.

*Early Contacts**

The authors describe the earliest contacts between Indians and European explorers. They find that in practically every instance the Indians welcomed the newcomers, but were repaid with rapine and destruction. The arrival of the Spanish explorers marked the beginning of a four-hundred-year war between red men and white men.

Before the white man came, the vast, magnificent, and comparatively empty region that is now the United States was inhabited by one million Indians, organized into six hundred distinct societies and scattered from the desolate ice wastes of the Far

*From pp. 1–5 *The American Indian Wars* by John Tebbel and Keith Jennison. Copyright © 1960 by John Tebbel and Keith Jennison. By Permission of Harper and Row, Publishers.

North to the hot swamps of the South; from the great forest of the East to the plains, deserts, and mountains of the West. These Indian societies existed in balance with themselves and with nature, a balance achieved through ages of development from Neolithic or Paleolithic time, when Indians first began to populate the continent.

The impact of white conquest on this culture was immediately abrasive and ultimately disastrous. After four centuries of nearly continuous warfare—roughly 1500 to 1900—the Indians were reduced numerically to less than four hundred thousand. Their lands gone, they were confined for the most part to reservations in western United States, the victims of discriminatory laws enacted by white bigots and of governmental neglect and mismanagement of their affairs—not to mention the cupidity of land-hungry business interests deriving their support from the United States Senate.

Yet what the Indians gave up, slowly and bitterly, was only material. As one of their best historians, John Collier, points out, they were never successfully enslaved by their conquerors.

> and even, to the end, [there was] no yielding by the Indians to anything but the sheer fact of being physically overwhelmed . . . Indian social individuality held its own, and even deepened its consciousness of itself. Is it to be wondered at that the Indians north of the Rio Grande have always awakened a strange yet intimate excitement in the white man's soul? They speak to us from out of our long foregone home, and what hears them is the changeless, eternal part of us, imprisoned and immured by our social epoch even as the Indian societies were imprisoned and immured by us in the century behind. . . .

Thus the Indian lost his substance but saved his soul. The permanent damage was done by his conquerors to themselves. In the four-century great war of their conquest, they wrote a page in their history so black it can never be expunged. The conquest itself may be explained by the inexorable march of history, but the manner of its accomplishment cannot be excused. From the first atrocities of the Spanish, French, and English explorers and colonizers to the final, frightful massacre of Indian women and children at Wounded Knee in 1890, the white man's war against the red man is a record to match in savagery, if not in scope, anything the refinements of twentieth-century civilized warfare have produced.

One of the objects of those who first came to explore the continent that would stand forth to the world as a symbol of liberty was to take Indian slaves—either as curiosities, evidences of successful exploration, or as recruits for the mines of Europe.

Such was the result of one of the first recorded meetings between European explorer and Indian. Gaspar Corte Real (or Cortereal), a Portuguese from the Azores, came to the bleak northern reaches of North America in 1500 and again in 1501. On one of these expeditions he abducted fifty-seven (or sixty, depending on the source) Indians whom he intended to sell into slavery. This high purpose was largely frustrated on the voyage home when his vessel sank in a storm, carrying to horrible death all but seven of the Indian captives, [the rest of whom] had been chained in the hold. These seven reached Portugal safely in another ship, and their surviving captors reported themselves so pleased with the hospitality the unsuspecting savages had shown them that they named the Indians' native land Labrador, meaning "the place with an abundance of labor material."

Equally instructive is the narrative left to us by Giovanni da Verrazano (or Verrazzano), a Florentine navigator sent out from Dieppe near the end of 1523 by Francis I, King of France, to find a westward passage to Cathay. Driven back to Brittany by storms, he set out again with only one of his original four caravels, the *Dauphine*, and on March 7, 1524, hove to in the vicinity of what is now Wilmington, North Carolina.

The Indians who watched one of Verrazano's small boats come ashore fled in terror at their first sight of white men, but soon returned in wonder and admiration to help them land, offering their friendship by signs.

A few days later, needing water as he cruised northward along the coast, Verrazano sent another boat ashore, but the surf was too high for a landing. Again a small party of wandering Indians had come down to the beach. Taking some beads and trinkets for them, a daring young sailor jumped over and began to swim ashore. Fear overtook him as he neared land. He flung his gifts at the waiting savages and tried to swim back to the boat, but the heavy surf picked him up and tossed him on the beach into the arms of his prospective hosts.

The more the young sailor cried out in terror, the more the Indians yelled back at him to assure him of their friendship. But as he watched them make a leaping fire on the beach, he shrieked anew, convinced they were going to eat him. When he realized they were only trying to warm him and dry his clothes, he recovered his wits enough to make it known he wanted to swim back to his boat. The Indians led him down to the water, so the narrative goes, "with great love, clapping him fast about, with many embracings." They watched until he was safely aboard the *Dauphine*.

Such kindness, apparently, was lost on Verrazano and his men. Going ashore again somewhere in Virginia or Maryland, they discovered a somewhat less confident reception committee— an old woman, a young girl, and a few children, huddled together terrified in the tall grass near the beach. With calculated brutality, they first won the confidence of these innocents, then abducted one of the children as a trophy of the chase. They would have taken the good-looking young squaw, too, for their later pleasure, but she screamed loudly enough to frighten them away.

After exploring the Bay of New York, Verrazano went on up the Long Island coast, past Block Island, and into what was probably Newport Harbor. There he was well received by two ornately clad chiefs, surrounded by their warriors—so much like a European court that Verrazano called them "kings" in his narrative. He refers also to the "queen" and her "maids," whom the chiefs prudently kept out of reach of the white men in a separate canoe.

At this point the hospitality of the New World ended. When he came to New England, Verrazano found the natives as forbidding as the coastline. As the historian Francis Parkman puts it, in his dryly ironic fashion: "Perhaps some plundering straggler from the fishing-banks, some man-stealer like the Portuguese Cortereal, or some kidnapper of children and ravisher of squaws like themselves, had warned the denizens of the woods to beware of the worshippers of Christ." These Indians would do no more than let down furs on a hook from the forbidding cliffs over the water, hauling up fishhooks, knives, and steel in return, after which they saluted their visitors with indelicate gestures and noises. When the Frenchmen tried to go ashore, they gave them a sterner salute with arrows.

That was the last Verrazano's men and the Indians saw of each other. The *Dauphine* went as far north as Newfoundland, and then returned home. Of the several reports concerning the Italian navigator's death, it would be poetic justice if one could accept the story that he went on another voyage and was killed and eaten by Indians while his own men looked on; but history authenticates that he was hanged as a pirate in 1527.

These early meetings between white men and red, as the first explorers nibbled at the fringes of the new continent, were only mild foretastes of what was to come. The Indians had welcomed the newcomers, with few exceptions, and they had been repaid with rapine and abduction. But these incidents had been so widely scattered up and down the far reaches of the coast that there was yet no organized hostility on the part of the natives. That was inspired first by those notorious masters of deceit and cruelty, the Spanish adventurers, whose bloody history below the Rio Grande is familiar to everyone today but in the early 1500's had not yet reached the ears of the unsuspecting savages in Florida, Georgia, and farther inland along the Gulf Coast, where the Spaniards began to penetrate in their feverish search for gold. With these sanguinary episodes, the Four Hundred Years' War truly began.

*The Making of an Indian Warrior**

Chief Logan explains to Lord Dunsmore why he made war upon the whites. This personal testimony was re-enacted countless times as the open and sharing spirit of the Indians was preyed upon and exploited by whites.

My cabin since first I made one of my own has ever been open to any white man who wanted shelter. My spoils of hunting, since first I began to range these woods, have ever freely imparted to appease his hunger and clothe his nakedness. *But what have I seen? What?* But that at my return at night and laden with spoil my numerous family lie bleeding on the ground by the hands of those who had found my little hut a certain refuge from the inclement storm—who had eaten my food and covered themselves with my skins. *What have I seen? What?* But that those dear little mouths for which I had sweated the livelong day when I returned at eve to fill them had not one word to thank me for my toil.

---

*Mingo Chief Logan, quoted in Paul Jacobs and Saul Landau, *To Serve the Devil*, vol. I (New York: Random House, 1971).

What could I resolve upon? My blood boiled within me and my heart leapt up to my mouth. Nevertheless, I bid my tomahawk be quiet and lie at rest for that war because I thought the great men of your country sent them not to do it. Not long afterwards, some of your men invited our tribe to cross the river and bring their venison with them. They, unsuspicious of design, came as they had been invited. The white men then made them drop, killed them, and turned their knives even against the women. Was not my sister among them? Was she not scalped by the hands of that man whom she had taught how to escape his enemies when they were scenting out his track? What could I resolve upon? My blood now boiled thrice hotter than before and thrice again my heart leapt up to my mouth. No longer did I bid my tomahawk be quiet and lie at rest for that war; because I no longer thought the men of your country sent them not to do it. I sprang from my cabin to avenge their blood; which I have fully done this war by shedding yours from your coldest to your hottest sun. Thus revenged, I am now for peace and have advised most of my countrymen to be so too. Nay, what is more I have offered and still offer myself as a victim, being ready to die, if their good require it.

Think not that I am afraid to die; for I have no relations left to mourn for me. Logan's blood runs in no veins but these. I would not turn my heel to escape death; for I have neither wife, nor child, nor sister to howl for me when I am gone.

*All We Want Is to Be Left Alone**

White conquerors were not content to steal the Indians' land and take advantage of the good-natured cooperation of Indian nations and individuals; they often tried to convert them to Christianity. After listening to a missionary, the Seneca Chief Red Jacket gives an eloquent reply.

Friend and brother, it was the will of the Great Spirit that we should meet together this day. He orders all things, and he has given us a fine day for our council. He has taken his garment from

---

*Chief Red Jacket, Speech to Missionaries at a Council at Buffalo, New York, 1805, quoted in Margot Astrov, *American Indian Prose and Poetry* (New York: Capricorn, 1962).

before the sun, and caused it to shine with brightness upon us; our eyes are opened, that we see clearly; our ears are unstopped, that we have been able to hear distinctly the words that you have spoken; for all these favors we thank the Great Spirit, and him only.

Brother, this council fire was kindled by you; it was at your request that we came together at this time; we have listened with attention to what you have said; you requested us to speak our minds freely; this gives us great joy, for we now consider that we stand upright before you, and can speak what we think; all have heard your voice, and all speak to you as one man; our minds are agreed.

Brother, you say you want an answer to your talk before you leave this place. It is right you should have one, as you are a great distance from home, and we do not wish to detain you; but we will first look back a little, and tell you what our fathers have told us, and what we have heard from the white people.

Brother, listen to what we say. There was a time when our forefathers owned this great island. Their seats extended from the rising to the setting sun. The Great Spirit had made it for the use of the Indians. He had created the buffalo, the deer, and other animals for food. He made the bear and the beaver, and their skins served us for clothing. He had scattered them over the country, and taught us how to take them. He had caused the earth to produce corn for bread. All this he had done for his red children because he loved them. If we had any disputes about hunting grounds, they were generally settled without the shedding of much blood: but an evil day came upon us; your forefathers crossed the great waters and landed on this island. Their numbers were small; they found friends, not enemies; they told us they had fled from their own country for fear of wicked men, and come here to enjoy their religion. They asked for a small seat; we took pity on them, granted their request, and they sat down among us; we gave them corn and meat; they gave us poison in return. The white people had now found our country, tidings were carried back, and more came among us; yet we did not fear them, we took them to be friends; they called us brothers; we believed them and gave them a larger seat. At length their number had greatly increased; they wanted more land; they wanted our country. Our eyes were opened, and our minds became uneasy. Wars took place; Indians were hired to fight against Indians, and many of our people were destroyed. They also brought strong liquors among us: it was strong and powerful, and has slain thousands.

Brother, our seats were once large, and yours were very small; you have now become a great people, and we have scarcely left a place to spread our blankets; you have got our country, but are not satisfied; you want to force your religion upon us.

Brother, continue to listen. You say that you are sent to instruct us how to worship the Great Spirit agreeably to his mind, and if we do not take hold of the religion which you white people teach, we shall be unhappy hereafter; you say that you are right, and we are lost; how do we know this to be true? We understand that your religion is written in a book; if it was intended for us as well as you, why has not the Great Spirit given it to us, and not only to us, but why did he not give to our forefathers the knowledge of that book, with the means of understanding it rightly? We only know what you tell us about it; how shall we know when to believe, being so often deceived by the white people?

Brother, you say there is but one way to worship and serve the Great Spirit; if there is but one religion, why do you white people differ so much about it? Why do not all agree, as you can all read the book?

Brother, we do not understand these things; we are told that your religion was given to your forefathers, and has been handed down from father to son. We also have a religion which was given to our forefathers, and has been handed down to us their children. We worship that way. It teacheth us to be thankful for all the favors we receive; to love each other, and to be united. We never quarrel about religion.

Brother, the Great Spirit has made us all; but he has made a great difference between his white and red children; he has given us a different complexion, and different customs; to you he has given the arts: to these he has not opened our eyes; we know these things to be true. Since he has made so great a difference between us in other things, why may we not conclude that he has given us a different religion according to our understanding: the Great Spirit does right; he knows what is best for his children; we are satisfied.

Brother, we do not wish to destroy your religion, or take it from you; we only want to enjoy our own.

Brother, you say you have not come to get our land or our money, but to enlighten our minds. I will now tell you that I have been at your meetings, and saw you collecting money from the meeting. I cannot tell what this money was intended for, but suppose it was for your minister, and if we should conform to your way of thinking, perhaps you may want some from us.

Brother, we are told that you have been preaching to white people in this place; these people are our neighbors, we are acquainted with them; we will wait a little while and see what effect your preaching has upon them. If we find it does them good, makes them honest, and less disposed to cheat Indians, we will then consider again what you have said.

Brother, you have now heard the answer to your talk, and this is all we have to say at present. As we are going to part, we will come and take you by the hand, and hope the Great Spirit will protect you on your journey, and return you safe to your friends.*

Cherokee Removal†

John Collier served as United States Commissioner of Indian Affairs from 1933 to 1945. In this passage from his authoritative book, which won the Anisfield-Wolf Award in 1948, he tells the infamous story of Chief Justice John Marshall, President Jackson, the Cherokee removal, and the "trail of tears." He cites this as a sample of typical American policy toward Indians.

---

*Originally taken from Samuel G. Drake, *Biography and History of the Indians of North America*, pp. 594 ff. This speech, says Drake, may be taken as genuine, at least as nearly so as the Indian language in which it was delivered can be translated, for Red Jacket would not speak in English, although he understood it. After the Seneca chief had finished his speech, he and others drew near the missionary to take him by the hand; but he would not receive them, and, hastily rising from his seat, said "that there was no fellowship between the religion of God and the works of the devil, therefore, could not join hands with them." The Indians withdrew—politely smiling.

†From *Indians of the Americas* by John Collier. Copyright, 1947, by John Collier. Reprinted by permission of The New American Library, Inc., New York.

More than any other tribe, the Cherokee Nation furnished the crystallizing thread of the United States government policy and action in Indian affairs. The Cherokees were the largest of the Iroquoian tribes; but they never joined the Confederacy, and we never think of them as being Iroquois. In the years before Great Britain's power ended, the British Crown had intervened repeatedly to check the seizure of Cherokee lands by the "borderers." Thus it came about that in the war of the Revolution the Cherokees allied themselves with the British.

Not until 1794 did they stop fighting. The treaty which they then made with the United States was kept by them as a sacred thing.

The Cherokees met every test of peacefulness, of practicality, of Christian profession and conduct, of industry and productiveness, of out-going friendliness to the whites, of "progress" in domestic order and in education. They even offered little resistance to marriages between young men of the whites and their young girls. One of their great men, whom we know as Sequoia, and whom we have idealized, invented an alphabet considered second only to our European system in the various schemes of symbolic thought representation, and the tribe quickly became literate in our European sense. The Cherokees wrote a constitution of the American white man's kind. They established a legislature, a judiciary, and an executive branch. A free press and public schools were set up. Again and again the tribe surrendered great areas of its treaty-held land. Over and over again, however hard pressed, it kept the faith.

Yet, in the years that followed, the treaty was breached both in the letter and in the spirit by the United States over and over again. And it is clear that nothing the Indians could have been or not been, could have done or not done, would have changed the white man's heart and will. The remnant of their lands included seven million àcres, mostly mountain country in the region where Georgia, North Carolina, and Tennessee converge, what is now called the highland country. The Cherokees had to be removed even from these last fastnesses.

In 1828 Andrew Jackson was elected president. He was a "borderer" and had been a famous Indian fighter. Immediately he put through Congress an act called the Indian Removal Act which placed in his own hands the task of leading or driving all Indian tribes to some place west of the Mississippi River. At about the same time gold was discovered in the Cherokee country. The Georgia Legislature passed an act annexing—confiscating—all Cherokee lands within the state, declaring all laws of the Cherokee Nation to be null and void, and forbidding Indians to testify in any state court against white men. The Cherokee lands were distributed to whites through a lottery system.

In 1830, through John Ross, its chief, the tribe vainly appealed to President Jackson. Then it appealed to the Supreme Court. The Court refused to take jurisdiction; the tribe, it ruled, was not a foreign nation. "If it be true," said the Court, "that the Cherokee Nation has rights, this is not the tribunal in which these rights are to be asserted. If it be true that wrongs have been inflicted, and that still greater are to be apprehended, this is not the tribunal which can redress the past or prevent the future."

The conscience of the Court was troubled by this Pilate-like decision. Two years later, it had an opportunity to reconsider. Three white missionaries refused to swear the oath of allegiance to Georgia while resident in the defined country of the Cherokee Nation. They were arrested, chained together, and forced to walk twenty-one miles behind a wagon to jail. Two Methodist preachers intervened against the brutality; they were chained with the others and thrown into jail with them. The missionaries were tried and sentenced to four years' hard labor in the state penitentiary. The case came up before the Supreme Court, and the Court, in effect reversing itself, ruled that Indian tribes or nations

> had always been considered as distinct, independent, political communities, retaining their original natural rights . . . and the settled doctrine of the law of nations is, that a weaker power does not surrender its independence—its right to self-government—by associating with a stronger, and taking its protection.
>
> The Cherokee Nation, then, is a distinct community, occupying its own territory, with boundaries accurately described in which the laws of Georgia can have no force, and which the citizens of Georgia have no right to enter, but with the assent of the Cherokees themselves, or in conformity with treaties, and with the acts of Congress.

President Jackson retorted to the Court: "John Marshall (the Chief Justice) has rendered [made] his decision; now let them enforce it."

So Georgia, and the whole of the federal government apart from the helpless Court, continued their policies toward the Cherokees. The whites could prospect for gold anywhere, the Indians not at all, though the land was their own. The President's commissioners harried some of the Cherokees into signing a treaty giving up the seven million acres still theirs for 4.5 million dollars which would be deposited "to their credit" in the United States Treasury. The leaders and people had been immovable, but in an arranged meeting attended by some four hundred of the tribe's seventeen thousand members, the fictional treaty was extorted. The Senate quickly ratified this "treaty."

Three years passed and the Cherokees were still upon their land. Then came General Winfield Scott with seven thousand troops and a nonmilitary rabble of followers to invade the Cherokee domain. Cherokee men, women, and children were seized wherever found and without notice removed to concentration camps. Livestock, household goods, farm implements, everything went to the white camp followers; the homes usually were burned. After this the long trek to Arkansas in mid-winter was begun. An eyewitness in Kentucky reported:

> Even aged females, apparently nearly ready to drop into the grave, were traveling with heavy burdens attached to their backs, sometimes on frozen ground and sometimes on muddy streets, with no covering for their feet.

Of about fourteen thousand who were herded onto this "trail of tears," as it came to be called, four thousand died on the way. While a hundred Cherokees a day were perishing of exhaustion and cold on that dreadful road, President Van Buren on December 3, 1838 addressed Congress: "The measures [for Cherokee removal] authorized by Congress at its last session have had the happiest effects. . . . The Cherokees have emigrated without any apparent reluctance." The financial costs of the trail of tears were charged by the government against the funds credited to the tribe pursuant to the fraudulent treaty.

As the final company of the Cherokees started on the long trail, their leaders held the last council they would ever hold on their home ground. They adopted a resolution which ought to be remembered forever. They did not ask pity for their people, because they knew there would be no pity, and asking pity was never the Indian's way. They did not reproach or condemn Georgia or the United States government. They did not quote John Marshall's decision, since that decision, for them, had been written on water. To the violated treaties and fraudulent treaties they made no reference; for they had now learned that which General Francis C. Walker was to phrase immortally when, in 1871, writing as Commissioner of Indian Affairs, he described the white man's view concerning honor toward Indians: "When dealing with savage men, as with savage beasts, no question of national honor can arise. Whether to fight, to run away, or to employ a ruse, is solely a question of expediency." Their treaties, the Cherokees had learned, had been "ruses" of the white man. So the resolution, passed in what then seemed to be their final hour, was addressed to no man, and leaned on no consideration, except the principle of justice which they believed was undying:

> The title of the Cherokee people to their lands is the most ancient, pure and absolute known to man; its date is beyond the reach of human record; its validity confirmed by possession and enjoyment antecedent to all pretense of claim by any portion of the human race.
>
> The free consent of the Cherokee people is indispensable to a valid transfer of the Cherokee title. The Cherokee people have neither by themselves nor their representatives given such consent. It follows that the original title and ownership of lands still rests in the Cherokee nation, unimpaired and absolute. The Cherokee people have existed as a distinct national community for a period extending into antiquity beyond the dates and records and memory of man. These attributes have never been relinquished by the Cherokee people, and cannot be dissolved by the expulsion of the Nation from its territory by the power of the United States government.

That was all. Then these men of true greatness, through fraud and violence stripped of everything, set forth on the bitter trail to a place which was to be no lasting home.

To this point the Cherokee narrative, with changes only of detail, is the narrative of all the tribes east of the Mississippi from 1800 to 1840. All, within varied but always amply structured and consecutive societies, held anciently owned lands under treaty guarantees. Always, the treaties were nakedly violated by the United States, or changed or nullified through statute or proclamation, or whittled down or annulled through fraudulent deals by commissioners.

*Conquest and Control**

The present-day situation of the American Indians is discussed against the background of several centuries of outrageous treatment. Besides condemning the mistreatment which Indians have been made to endure, it contains suggestions for ending the miserable circumstances in which most Indians find themselves today. This article appeared just three weeks before the election of Richard Nixon to the Presidency in 1968.

The quadrennial elections never fail to evoke compassion for "the Vanishing Americans," and this year the tragicomedy is again being played with style. "The poor Indian" is once more the theme of position papers and convention planks. As it did four years ago, the Administration has sent a message to Congress that repeats the aspirations of the Great White Father for his red children; better education, better housing, better health care, better job training. (Since "better" is a relative word, the Great White Father has pinpointed exactly how much "better" he has in mind; a mere twelve percent increase from last year's incredibly low, fantastically mismanaged budget.) Politicians of both parties are making their usual salutes to the "progress" of the red man in adapting to a white world. Vice President Humphrey states that tuberculosis among Indians declined fifty-five percent since 1955— but he neglects to add the fact that the Indian death rate from

---

*Excerpted in part from the book *Man's Rise to Civilization as Shown by the Indians of North America from Primeval Times to the Coming of the Industrial State,* by Peter Farb. Copyright ©, 1968 by Peter Farb. This article originally appeared in *The Saturday Review.* Published by E. P. Dutton & Company, Inc. and used with their permission.

tuberculosis is still seven times that of the American population as a whole. Perhaps the last politically motivated obeisance to the red man was Senator Robert F. Kennedy's inquiry, just before his assassination, into the shame of Indian education.

The facts about Indian life today assuredly are bleak enough without election-year dramatization. Some 400,000 of the total 550,000 Indians in the United States live on approximately two hundred reservations in twenty-six states. The reservations exist as poverty-stricken islands surrounded by an ocean of American bounty. The Indians are generally despised by whites; they are in ill health both physically and mentally, almost without political power, inarticulate in their attempts to win respect for their heritage. The amazing thing is not that they have managed to survive at all, but that they still possess patience about the white man's latest aspirations for them this election year. They hang on to a little piece of the future, but every year their grip slips a bit more. For this is their life today:

Housing: About ninety percent of Indians live in tin-roofed shacks, leaky adobe huts, brush shelters, and even abandoned automobiles. Approximately sixty percent of Indians still haul their drinking water, frequently from more than a mile away and often from contaminated sources.

Income and jobs: Indian unemployment ranges between forty and seventy-five percent in comparison with about four percent for the nation as a whole. On one reservation in Utah, I visited this summer, less than twenty-five percent of the eligible work force had jobs—and most of these were employed by their own tribal organization. The average red family lives on $30 a week, while average white and black families earn at least $130 a week.

Health: The average age of death for an Indian today is forty-three years, for a white sixty-eight years. Death from dysentery is forty times greater among Indians than whites; influenza and pneumonia death rates are twice as high; middle-ear infections are so widespread that on some reservations a quarter of the children have suffered permanent hearing loss. Trachoma, an infectious eye disease that often causes blindness, is virtually nonexistent in the United States—except on the reservations. A survey made a few years ago on the San Carlos Apache Reservation in Arizona showed that sixty-one percent of the children between the ages of five and eighteen were afflicted. .

Education: Indian education is the worst of any minority group. The Indian completes about five years of schooling—whereas all other Americans average 11.2 years. It is not only the quantity of education the Indian is deprived of but the quality, for the saddest fact of all is that the longer he stays in school, the farther behind his achievement falls in comparison with white children.

In Idaho's Blackfoot school district, for example, three-fourths of the students in the elementary school are Indian, yet every teacher is white. Speaking any Indian language is prohibited and nothing is taught of Indian culture. In the last few years there have been nearly fifteen suicides by the school children. One out of every five junior-high students was found to be sniffing glue. When Senator Robert Kennedy visited the district this past spring, he asked the principal whether Indian culture and traditions were taught. He was informed, "There isn't any history to this tribe"—although the grandfathers of these children had played an important role in the history of the West. When the Senator asked if there were any books in the library where the children could read about Indian culture, he was shown *Captive of the Delawares,* which had a picture on the cover of a white child being scalped by an Indian.

The Indian can probably survive the bad housing, lack of jobs, dismal health conditions, and poor education—but not the implication that he is irrelevant to American culture. For once the Indians are deprived of the last bit of the culture that has sustained them, they will disappear into the faceless American poor. Yet, the United States Bureau of Indian Affairs was founded a century ago with the stated aim to alienate Indian children "from their native culture and language so they could take their place in modern society—and that has remained an implied aim to this day. A white policy has stripped the Indian of his identity and made him embarrassed about his rich oral culture, his customs and traditions, his native foods and dress. A white education system has turned out imitation whites who succumb to the bleakness of reservation life and the prejudice around them.

"The American Indian today is about to go over the brink—not only of poverty and prejudice, but of moral collapse," says

William Byler, executive director of the Association on American Indian Affairs. The Indian has learned that no one wants to listen or to understand when he speaks his thoughts about his own future. He is bewildered by the capricious policies handed down in Washington—first telling him to leave the reservation and get jobs in the cities, next telling him to stay on the reservation and bring industry to it. Some politicians tell him that he is a child who must be protected by the kindly White Father—and other politicians tell him that he is man enough to be cast adrift to sink or swim in the capitalist tide. The result of such confusion is widespread apathy among Indians. They find it difficult to act in concert with other Indians because whites deliberately ripped apart the intricate web of their social and political relationships.

The present plight of the red man is an indication of exactly how far he has fallen from his state of Noble Savage in little more than 450 years. At first, the newly discovered Indians were greatly respected and admired. Columbus brought home six Indians to show Queen Isabella and, dressed in full regalia, they quickly became the curiosities of Spain. Sir Walter Raleigh brought back Indians also and a craze swept Elizabethan England. Shakespeare complained about it in *The Tempest:* "They will not give a doit [a small coin equal to about half a farthing] to relieve a lame beggar; they will lay out ten to see a dead Indian." The French philosopher Michel de Montaigne talked with Indians who had been brought to the French Court and concluded that the Noble Savage had been found, for the Indian "hath no kind of traffic, no knowledge of letters, no intelligence of numbers, no name of magistrate, nor of politics, no use of services, of riches, or of poverty. . . . The very words that import a lie, falsehood, treason, covetousness, envy, detraction, were not heard among them."

The Noble Savage captivated Europe, but the colonists felt differently about living with red men. When Columbus discovered the Arawak Indians, who inhabited the Caribbean Islands, he described them as "a loving people, without covetousness. . . . Their speech is the sweetest and gentlest in the world." But in their haste to exploit the abundance of the Americas, the Spaniards set the loving and gentle Arawak to labor in mines and on plantations. Whole Arawak villages disappeared due to slavery, disease, warfare, and flight to escape the Spaniards. As a result, the native population of Haiti, for example, declined from an estimated two hundred thousand in 1492 to twenty-nine thousand only twenty-two years later.

The Puritans in New England were not immediately presented with an Indian problem, for diseases introduced by trading ships along the Atlantic Coast had badly decimated the red population. Yet, the Puritans failed miserably in their dealings with even the remnant Indians. They insisted upon a high standard of religious devotion that the Indians were unable or unwilling to give. The Puritans lacked any way to integrate the Indians into their theocracy, for they did not indulge in wholesale baptisms (as they charged the French did), nor were any Puritans specifically assigned to missionary tasks.

In 1637, a party of Puritans surrounded the Pequot Indian village and set fire to it after these Indians had resisted settlement of whites in the Connecticut Valley. About five hundred Indians were burned to death or shot while trying to escape; the woods were then combed for any Pequots who had managed to survive, and these were sold into slavery. The whites devoutly offered up thanks to God that they had lost only two men; when the Puritan divine Cotton Mather heard about the raid, he was grateful to the Lord that "on this day we have sent six hundred heathen souls to hell."

The Indian came to be regarded as a stubborn animal that refused to acknowledge the obvious blessings of white civilization. Hugh Henry Brackenridge, a modest literary figure of the young nation, expressed the changed attitude when he wrote in 1782 of ". . . the animals, vulgarly called Indians." Rousseau's Noble Savage was laid to rest officially in 1790 when John Adams stated: "I am not of Rousseau's opinions. His notions of the purity of morals in savage nations and the earliest ages of civilized nations are mere chimeras." Even that man of enlightened homilies, Benjamin Franklin, observed that rum should be regarded as an agent of Providence "to extirpate these savages in order to make room for the cultivators of the earth."

After the War of 1812, the young United States had no further need for Indian allies against the British, and, as a result, the fortunes of the Indians declined rapidly. Pressure increased to get the Indians off the lands the whites had appropriated from them and, in 1830, Congress passed the Removal Act, which gave the President the right to extirpate all Indians who had managed to survive east of the Mississippi River. It was estimated that the whole job might be done economically at no more than five hundred thousand dollars—the cost to be kept low by persuasion, promises, threats, and the bribery of Indian leaders. When United States Supreme Court Justice John Marshall ruled in favor of the Cherokee Indians in a case with wide implications for preventing removal, President Andrew Jackson is said to have remarked: "John Marshall has made his decision, now let him enforce it."

During the next ten years, almost all the Indians were cleared from the East. Some, such as the Chickasaw and Choctaw and Cherokee, went resignedly. The Seminole actively resisted and retreated into the Florida swamps, where they stubbornly held off the United States Army. The Seminole Wars lasted from 1835 to 1842 and cost the United States some fifteen hundred soldiers and an estimated twenty million dollars (about forty times what Jackson had estimated it would cost to remove all Indians). Many of the Iroquois found sanctuary in Canada. The Sac and Fox made a desperate stand in Illinois against overwhelming numbers of whites, but ultimately their survivors were forced to move, as were the Ottawa, Potawatomi, Wyandot, Shawnee, Kickapoo, Winnebago, Delaware, Peoria, Miami, and many others who are remembered now only in the name of some town, lake, county, or state.

Alexis de Tocqueville, who examined the young United States with the perceptive eye and wrote it all down in his *Democracy in America,* was in Memphis on an unusually cold day when he saw a ragged party of Choctaw, part of the docile thousands who had reluctantly agreed to be transported to the new lands in the West. He wrote:

> The Indians had their families with them, and they brought in their train the wounded and the sick, with children newly born and old men upon the verge of death. . . . I saw them embark to pass the mighty river, and never will that solemn spectacle fade from my remembrance. No cry, no sob, was heard among the assembled crowd; all was silent. Their calamities were of ancient date, and they knew them to be irremediable.

De Tocqueville described with restrained outrage how the Indians were sent westward by government agents: ". . . half-convinced and half-compelled, they go to inhabit new deserts, where the importunate whites will not let them remain ten years in peace. In this manner do the Americans obtain, at a very low price, whole provinces, which the richest sovereigns in Europe could not purchase." He reported that a scant 6,273 Indians still survived in the thirteen original states.

The experience of the Indians west of the Mississippi River was only a sad, monotonous duplication of what had happened east of it—warfare, broken treaties, expropriation of land, rebellion, and ultimately defeat. No sooner were the eastern Indians dropped down on the plains and prairies than the United States discovered the resources in the West, and miners and settlers were on the move. Emigrant trains rumbled westward, and once again the aim of the frontiersman was to get the Indian out of the way.

The "final extermination" was hastened by epidemics that swept the West and sapped the Indians' power to resist. A mere hundred Mandan out of a population of sixteen hundred survived a smallpox epidemic (they are extinct today); the same epidemic, spreading westward, reduced the total number of Blackfoot Indians by about half. The majority of Kiowa and Comanche Indians were victims of cholera. The Indians undoubtedly would have been crushed by whites in any event, but the spread of diseases made the job easier.

Up to 1868, nearly four hundred treaties had been signed by the United States government with various Indian groups, and scarcely a one had remained unbroken. The Indians were promised new lands, then moved off them to some other place. They were shifted about again and again, as many as five or six times. All of which led the Sioux chief Spotted Tail to ask wearily: "Why does not the Great White Father put his red children on wheels, so he can move them as he will?"

In the last decades of the last century the Indians finally realized that these treaties were real estate deals designed to separate them from their lands. Indians and whites skirmished and then fought openly with ferocity and barbarity on both sides.

Group by group, the Indians rose in rebellion only to be crushed—the southern Plains tribes in 1874, the Sioux in 1876, the Nez Percé in 1877, the Ute in 1879, and the Apache throughout much of the 1880's, until Geronimo finally surrendered with his remnant band of thirty-six survivors. The massacre of more than three hundred Sioux, mostly women and children and old people, at Wounded Knee, South Dakota, in 1890 marked the end of Indian resistance to white authority.

Humanitarians who attempted to ease the defeat of the Indians felt that the remnant populations should be given the dignity of private property. As a result, Senator Henry L. Dawes of Massachusetts sponsored the Allotment Act of 1887 to salvage some land for the Indians who otherwise might lose everything to voracious whites. When President Grover Cleveland signed the act, he stated that the "hunger and thirst of the white man for the Indian's land is almost equal to his hunger and thirst after righteousness."

The act provided that after every Indian had been allotted land, the remainder would be put up for sale to the public. But the loopholes with which the act was punctured made it an efficient instrument for separating the Indians from this land. The plunder was carried on with remarkable order. The first lands to go to whites were the richest—bottomlands in river valleys or fertile grasslands. Next went the slightly less desirable lands, such as those that had to be cleared before they could produce a crop. Then the marginal lands were taken, and so on, until the Indian had left to him only desert that no white considered worth the trouble to take. Between the passage of the Allotment Act in 1887 and a New Deal investigation in 1934, the Indians had been reduced to only 56 million acres out of the meager 138 million acres that had been allotted them—and every single acre of the 56 million was adjudged by soil conservationists to be eroded. At the same time that the Indians were being systematically relieved of their lands, their birth rate rose higher than the mortality rate, and so there were more and more Indians on less and less land. The Indians did what they had always done: They shared the little they had and went hungry together.

The victory over the Noble Savage—reduced in numbers, deprived of land, broken in spirit, isolated on wasteland reservations

—was complete except for one final indignity. That was to Americanize the Indian, to eliminate his last faint recollection of his ancient traditions—in short, to exterminate the culture along with the Indians. There was not much culture left to eradicate, but at last zealous whites found something. Orders went out from Washington that all male Indians must cut their hair short, even though many Indians believed that long hair had supernatural significance. The Indians refused, and the battle was joined. Army reinforcements were sent to the reservations to carry out the order, and in some cases Indians had to be shackled before they submitted.

Most of the attention of the Americanizers, though, was concentrated on the Indian children, who were snatched from their families and shipped off to boarding schools far from their homes. The children usually were kept at school for eight years, during which time they were not permitted to see their parents, relatives, or friends. Anything Indian—dress, language, religious practices, even outlook on life—was uncompromisingly prohibited. Ostensibly educated, articulate in the English language, wearing store-bought clothes, and with their hair short and their emotionalism muted, the boarding-school graduates were sent out either to make their way in a white world that did not want them, or to return as strangers to their reservation. The Indian had simply failed to melt into the great American Melting Pot.

He had been remade in the white man's image and then cast adrift or else safely bottled up on reservations. Yet is is apparent to any objective observer that the Indian problem still nags at the American conscience. It seems that whites, both land-hungry settlers and humanitarians, have tried every possible variation in the treatment of the Indian. What, then, is the solution?

Many people concerned about the American Indian are coming to believe that we should simply stop offering the Indian pat solutions. Everything has been tried. The Indians have been herded from reservation to reservation, switched from hunting to agriculture or from agriculture to hunting, moved to cities to work in factories or told instead to make room for factories on their reservations. Indians exist today as the most manipulated people on earth—and yet our Indian policy has produced only failure after failure.

We have never recognized the Indian as someone who has his own historical rights to live and to act as an Indian within the framework of what remains of his culture. It is time that Washington allowed Indians on their own reservations to make their own decisions about their futures. Instead of dismantling the reservations, as some land-hungry congressmen propose, let us begin by dismantling the United States Bureau of Indian Affairs. Indians directly concerned, and many impartial observers of the Indian scene as well, regard BIA as incredibly inefficient and unresponsive to the needs of modern Indians. Most BIA personnel still operate with the nineteenth-century attitudes of the Indian fighters and still regard the Indian as childlike wards of the federal government. BIA is distrusted, and even hated, by most Indians.

A model for a new Indian–government relationship already exists and has been tested successfully for thirty-five years—the United States Soil Conservation Service. SCS is a service agency that provides farmers, ranchers, and timber growers with technical assistance that aids them in deriving the most benefits from various federal and state programs. But the actual policymaking and coordination of the work of many experts are firmly in the hands of some three thousand soil conservation districts across the nation. Each district is a legal entity whose locally elected boards have the authority to work out constructive plans for their individual problems.

With such a new Indian–government relationship, the sprawling federal programs in education, housing, employment, and so forth would be coordinated by local people who would adapt the programs to local need. With such a plan, it would be possible to take away the education responsibilities from BIA and place them in the Office of Education; the employment problems of Indians could be better handled by the Department of Labor; a start in decentralization has already been made in taking many health services away from BIA and having them carried on by the Public Health Service. Taking the human resource problems out of BIA leaves it free to concentrate on the land resource, a responsibility for which the United States Department of the Interior, of which it is a part, has a long history of competence.

But will the Indian be willing to participate in administering his own future? Promising indications that he will exist on many reservations. The Sioux of South Dakota, as just one example, impressed me this summer by their aggressive concern for taking what is best from American society while holding on to what remains of their own traditions. They are working hard to get the most benefits from the existing federal programs in health, education, welfare, employment, and housing while at the same time seeking to make their voices heard. Among other things, they have organized voter registration drives and elected Indians to school boards for the first time in history.

Clearly, it is time we stopped regarding Indians as living museum pieces with no relevance to America today. Their past and their future, for better or for worse, are intertwined with ours.

Suggestions for Further Reading

1. Ralph K. Andrist, *The Long Death: The Last Days of the Plains Indians* (New York: Collier Books, 1968).

   This is a detailed study of the final years of the Plains Indians, 1840–1890.

2. Merrill D. Beal, *I Will Fight No More Forever: Chief Joseph and the Nez Perce War* (Seattle: University of Washington Press, 1963).

3. Dee Brown, *Bury My Heart at Wounded Knee: An Indian History of the American West* (New York: Holt, Rinehart, and Winston, 1971).

4. Edgar S. Cahn (ed.), *Our Brother's Keeper: The Indian in White America* (Washington: New Community Press, 1969).

5. Jeanette Henry, *Textbooks and the American Indian,* ed. Rupert Costo (Indian Historical Press, Inc., 1970).

   A study of over 300 textbooks used in public schools and Bureau of Indian Affairs schools. Reveals countless omissions and distortions of American Indian history in the typical texts that are commonly used.

6. Vine Deloria, Jr., *Custer Died For Your Sins: An Indian Manifesto* (New York: Macmillan, 1969).

7. Jack D. Forbes (ed.), *The Indian in America's Past* (Englewood Cliffs, N.J.: Prentice-Hall, Inc., 1964).

   A series of short quotes by contemporaries effectively communicates the racist attitudes which undergirded so many of the American dealings with Indians.

8. William T. Hagan, *American Indians* (Chicago: University of Chicago Press, 1961).

   Indian–white relations are summarized.

9. Reginald Horsman, *Expansion and American Indian Policy, 1783–1812* (East Lansing: Michigan State University, 1967).

The author treats the period between two wars against England.

10. Alvin M. Josephy, *The Patriot Chiefs: A Chronicle of American Indian Resistance* (New York: Viking, 1969).

11. Stuart Levine and Nancy O. Lurie (eds.), *The American Indian Today* (Baltimore: Penguin, 1970).

12. Edward H. Spicer, *A Short History of the Indians of the United States* (New York: Van Nostrand, 1969).
    This is a history followed by documents.

13. Stan Steiner, *The New Indians* (New York: Harper & Row, 1968).

14. Wilcomb Washburn (ed.), *The Indian and the White Man* (Garden City, N.Y.: Doubleday & Company, Inc., 1964).
    This general anthology presents a documentary history of Indian–white relations.

Chapter Four

The Mexican War and Its Aftermath

*The Americans had always devoutly believed
that the superiority of their institutions, government, and mode of life would eventually spread,
by inspiration and imitation, to less fortunate,
less happy peoples. That devout belief now took
a new phase: it was perhaps the American destiny to spread our free and admirable institutions by action as well as by example, by occupying territory as well as by practicing virtue.*
—BERNARD DE VOTO, *The Year
of Decision: 1846* (1943)

During the 1840's the sentiment for expansion was uncontrolled. In the election of 1844 the key issue was expansion. One
of the campaign slogans was "Fifty-four Forty or Fight," a reference
to American claims in the disputed Oregon country. Another issue
was the annexation of Texas, which had been debated since 1836,
when the Republic of Texas was established against the wishes of
Mexico. The Mexican government had stated that United States
annexation of Texas would be tantamount to a declaration of war.
From the Mexican point of view, the Americans in Texas had violated both the spirit and the letter of the rules under which they
had been invited to settle in Mexican-owned Texas after Mexico
declared its independence from Spain in 1821. One example of

American violation of Mexican law was the fact that there were several thousand Negro slaves in Texas in 1835, yet Mexico had outlawed slavery in 1829.

Polk's election in 1844 was a mandate for annexation of Texas and a prelude to vigorous pursuit of territorial claims in the Oregon country and in the Southwest. Because expansion involved the use of force against another people, it required some sort of rationalization. After all, Americans were too idealistic to sanction the use of raw power in the blood-and-iron sense of Bismarckian *Realpolitik.** For Americans, a clear conscience was desirable when pursuing acquisitive goals. Just as the Puritan ethic authorized a religiously intense pursuit of wealth, the concepts of Manifest Destiny and Anglo-Saxon superiority and mission encouraged a zealous pursuit of territorial gains. Though many scholars would refrain from labeling the Mexican War a racist war, it is quite reasonable to point out that the belief in white racial superiority was partly responsible for the nature of the justification of the war. Of course, there were other causes unrelated to the Anglo-Saxon mission to civilize the world.

Paradoxically, the belief in the superiority of American institutions (and the implied assumption of racial inferiority of Mexicans) functioned as a restraint upon territorial acquisition. Because the Mexicans were viewed as inferior or unworthy of the Melting Pot, they were regarded as unassimilable elements that should therefore not be subjugated. The fear existed that this alien race would cause much difficulty if they had to be part of America. Sparsely populated regions could be annexed with a minimum of difficulty, according to this view, because Americans could populate them easily and become the dominant group. But the densely settled sections of southern Mexico were not desirable because there were too many Mexicans already living there. Mexicans were regarded with the same scorn as Indians and were often equated with them.

Slavery was an important issue at the time and it tied in with

---

*Otto von Bismarck, the "iron chancellor" of Prussia, was a dominant power in European politics between 1862 and 1890. His forceful and unsentimental policies were instrumental in provoking the Franco-Prussian War of 1870, which forged the final link of German unification.

the Mexican War. Northern Whigs* like Abraham Lincoln, and other northerners like Henry Thoreau, expressed strong opposition to the American involvement in the Mexican War. Lincoln introduced his famous "spot resolutions," demanding to know the exact spot on which the Mexicans were alleged by President Polk to have intruded into American territory. Thoreau refused to pay his poll tax, and preferred jail, because he did not wish to support a war that would add more slave territory to the United States. Others felt that the war was inconsistent with our democratic ideals because we were directing aggressive energies toward a weaker, but morally correct, power. Americans had no right to conquer Mexican land on the flimsy pretexts which President Polk manufactured, critics were saying. From the speeches and writings of contemporaries, we can see examples of the breakdown of the Melting Pot. For, while the critics reechoed the theory of the Melting Pot, they condemned its violations in their own time.

What of the bitter legacy of the Mexican War? The attitudes which fostered the war were reinforced by the American victory. Before the war Mexicans were suspected of inferiority. The war confirmed this suspicion. For more than one hundred years after the Treaty of Guadalupe-Hidalgo, Mexicans and Mexican-Americans were to experience a wide variety of discriminatory practices and policies, which they fought in a variety of ways. Their problems and their struggles remained outside the pale of majority awareness until recent exposures of their plight, their protests, and their achievements.

From the government plunder of their land in the 1840's, through the Zoot-Suit riots in the 1940's, to the grape-strikers' grievances Mexican-Americans have had to cope with considerable hostility from the Anglo majority—which earned its nickname, "the colossus of the North," through its use of raw power tactics. Traditionally oblivious to the mistreatment of this forgotten minority, Americans today are awakening from their complacent siesta. The original Americans, peoples such as the Indians and the Mexicans, are at last being acknowledged as the frequent victims of

---

*The Whig Party was the second of the two major parties in America in the 1840's. It was organized in 1834, and ran candidates for the Presidency in every election from 1836 to 1852. It captured the Presidency twice, in 1840 and in 1848.

American racism and discrimination.

The success of the grape strike and boycott led by Cesar Chavez and the Farmworkers Union, the prolonged trials of Reies Tijerina on the issue of New Mexico rights of Chicanos, the new Chicano studies programs at colleges and in high schools, the Denver Crusade for Justice led by Rodolfo "Corky" Gonzalez, the student organizations such as MECHA, the Chicano press, the East Los Angeles protests and demonstrations and the murder of newsman Ruben Salazar by Los Angeles police: these are only some of the more dramatic recent developments that have focused attention upon the Mexican victims of the gringo conquest and occupation. Some of these are treated in Part 5.

"The Mexicans Are Indians!"

The New York Evening Post *editorial which follows was published on December 24, 1847. There is very little evidence that the Christmas spirit had infected its editor.*

The Mexicans are *Indians*—Aboriginal Indians. Such Indians as Cortés conquered three thousand [three hundred] years ago, only rendered a little more mischievous by a bastard civilization. The infusion of European blood whatever it is, and that, too, infused in a highly *illegitimate* way, is not enough, as we see, to affect the character of the people. They do not possess the elements of an *independent* national existence. The Aborigines of this country have not attempted, and cannot attempt to exist *independently* along side of us. Providence has so ordained it, and it is folly not to recognize the fact. The Mexicans are *Aboriginal Indians,* and they must share the destiny of their race.

Now we ask whether any man can coolly contemplate the idea of recalling our troops from the territory we at present occupy, from Mexico . . . and thus, by one stroke of a secretary's pen, reconsign this beautiful country to the custody of the ignorant cowards and profligate ruffians who have ruled it for the last twenty-five years? Why, humanity cries out against it. Civilization, Christianity, protest against this reflux of the tide of barbarism and anarchy.

How we are to maintain our control over the Country—on what terms, under what contingencies—is a matter of detail, and subject to future events; but we do not believe there lives the American, with a true understanding of this country's interests and duties, who, *if he had the power,* would deliberately surrender Mexico to the *uncontrolled* dominion of the mongrel barbarisms, who, for a quarter of a century, have degraded and oppressed her. . . .

No party in this country contemplates the dismemberment of Mexico proper, or the annexation of any portion of her population to our own. It would be a disastrous event for the whole confederacy. But we owe it as a duty to ourselves and the general cause of freedom, to keep our flag flying . . . till the progress of time, and the silent effect of our presence, our customs, our busy commerce, our active intelligence, our press, shall have breathed a new life into this unfortunate country, and we have some security that she will not be a curse to herself and to her neighbors.

Unfit for Liberty

Senator John C. Calhoun, one of the foremost spokesmen of the antebellum South, warned in his Senate speech of January 4, 1848, against the dangers of incorporating Mexico.

We have never dreamt of incorporating into our Union any but the Caucasian race—the free white race. To incorporate Mexico, would be the very first instance of the kind, of incorporating an Indian race; for more than half of the Mexicans are Indians, and the other is composed chiefly of mixed tribes. I protest against such a union as that! Ours, sir, is the government of a white race. The greatest misfortunes of Spanish America are to be traced to the fatal error of placing these colored races on an equality with the white race. That error destroyed the social arrangement which formed the basis of society. The Portuguese and ourselves have escaped—the Portuguese at least to some extent—and we are the only people on this continent which had made revolutions without being followed by anarchy. And yet it is professed, and talked about, to erect these Mexicans into a territorial government, and

place them on an equality with the people of the United States. I
protest utterly against such a project. . . .

But . . . suppose all these difficulties removed; suppose these
people attached to our Union, and desirous of incorporating with
us, ought we to bring them in? Are they fit to be connected with
us? Are they fit for self-government and for governing you? Are
you, any of you, willing that your states should be governed by
these twenty-odd Mexican states, with a population of about only
one million of your blood, and two or three million of mixed blood
better informed—all the rest pure Indians, a mixed blood equally
ignorant and unfit for liberty, impure races, not as good as the
Cherokees or Choctaws?

We make a great mistake, sir, when we suppose that all people are capable of self-government. We are anxious to force free
government on all; and I see that it has been urged in a very
respectable quarter, that it is the mission of this country to spread
civil and religious liberty over all the world, and especially over
this continent. It is a great mistake. None but people advanced
to a very high state of moral and intellectual improvement are
capable, in a civilized state, of maintaining free government; and
among those who are so purified, very few, indeed, have had the
good fortune of forming a constitution capable of endurance. It is
a remarkable fact in the history of man, that scarcely ever have
free popular institutions been formed by wisdom alone that have
endured. . . .

It is a very difficult task to make a constitution to last, though
it may be supposed by some that they can be made to order, and
furnished at the shortest notice. Sir, this admirable Constitution
of our own was the result of a fortunate combination of circumstances. It was superior to the wisdom of the men who made it.

Whig Opposition to the Mexican War

*On February 11, 1847, Thomas Corwin, a Whig senator from Ohio,
delivered before the Senate a condemnation of American aggression
against Mexico. The following excerpt from his speech betrayed the
true American motivation: territorial aggrandizement.*

Mr. President:

I . . . beg the indulgence of the Senate to some reflections on
the particular bill now under consideration. I voted for a bill somewhat like the present at the last session—our army was then in

the neighborhood of our line. I then hoped that the President did sincerely desire a peace. Our army had not then penetrated far into Mexico, and I did hope, that with the two millions then proposed, we might get peace, and avoid the slaughter, the shame, the crime, of an aggressive, unprovoked war. But now you have overrun half of Mexico—you have exasperated and irritated her people —you claim indemnity for all expenses incurred in doing this mischief, and boldly ask her to give up New Mexico and California; and, as a bribe to her patriotism, seizing on her property, you offer three millions to pay the soldiers she has called out to repel your invasion, on condition that she will give up to you at least one-third of her whole territory. . . .

What is the territory, Mr. President, which you propose to wrest from Mexico? It is consecrated to the heart of the Mexican by many a well-fought battle with his old Castilian master. His Bunker Hills, and Saratogas, and Yorktowns, are there! The Mexican can say, "There I bled for liberty! And shall I surrender that consecrated home of my affections to the Anglo-Saxon invaders? What do they want with it? They have Texas already. They have possessed themselves of the territory between the Nueces and the Rio Grande. What else do they want? To what shall I point my children as memorials of that independence which I bequeath to them when those battlefields shall have passed from my possession?"

Sir, had one come and demanded Bunker Hill of the people of Massachusetts, had England's Lion ever showed himself there, is there a man over thirteen and under ninety who would not have been ready to meet him? Is there a river on this continent that would not have run red with blood? Is there a field but would have been piled high with the unburied bones of slaughtered Americans before these consecrated battlefields of liberty should have been wrested from us? But this same American goes into a sister republic and says to poor, weak Mexico, "Give up your territory, you are unworthy to possess it; I have got one-half already, and all I ask of you is to give up the other!" England might as well, in the circumstances I have described, have come and demanded of us, "Give up the Atlantic slope—give up this trifling territory from the Allegheny Mountains to the sea; it is only from Maine to St. Mary's—only about one-third of your republic, and the least interesting portion of it." What would be the response? They would say, "We must give this up to John Bull." Why? "He wants room." The senator from Michigan says he must have this. Why, my worthy Christian brothers, on what principle of justice? "I want room!"

Sir, look at this pretence of want of room. With twenty million people, you have about one thousand million acres of land, inviting settlement by every conceivable argument, bringing them down to a quarter of a dollar an acre, and allowing every man to squat where he pleases. But the senator from Michigan says we will be two hundred millions in a few years, and we want room. If I were a Mexican I would tell you, "Have you not room in your own country to bury your dead men? If you come into mine, we will greet you with bloody hands, and welcome you to hospitable graves."

"Why," says the chairman of this Committee on Foreign Relations, "it is the most reasonable thing in the world! We ought to have the Bay of San Francisco." Why? "Because it is the best harbor on the Pacific!"

*Violence against Mexicans**

From this description of the first four years after the Treaty of Guadalupe-Hidalgo one wonders whether another treaty was not needed to settle the differences in California.

Antiforeign feelings were translated into concrete action early in the history of the gold rush. One of the early sites of antiforeign agitation was the Mokelumne River. Throughout 1849 there were a great many South Americans and Europeans at work in the mining camps of that region. The American miners collected together and elected an "alcalde" whose first duty it was to warn the foreign population that they were trespassing on territory that did not belong to them and "... That they must leave, or as we say here 'Vamous'."[1]

A poem published in the *Sonora Herald* on August 21, 1850,

---

*"Mexican-American Conflict on the Mining Frontier, 1848–1852," *Journal of the West*, Vol. VI, No. 4 (October, 1967). By William Robert Kenny, Professor of History, South Dakota State University.

[1] Kirkpatrick (Manuscript Diary in the Bancroft Library, University of California, Berkeley), October 14, 1849.

aptly illustrates the pointed dislike of Mexicans. Entitled "The Great Greaser Extermination Meeting" the first and last stanzas read:

> In Sonora, one hot and sultry day
> Many people had gathered together
> They were bound to drive the Greasers away
> And they cared not a d——n for the weather.
>
> .   .   .   .
>
> And I hope coming folks will take warning
> And choose (if they would their property save)
> *Some American place to be born in.*

The *Sonora Herald,* which published this bit of "poetry" worried about the effect all this sort of thing would have on business. And with good reason. The Mexicans, as a group, were very free with their money.

Walter Colton warned his fellow nationals: "To drive them (the Mexicans) out of California, or interdict their operations, is to abstract that amount of labor from the mines, and curtail proportionably the proceeds." If Americans would be happier to see the gold remain buried in the mountains and river banks of the Sierra foothills, then by all means the Sonorians should be driven from the mines. But if what was wanted was to have gold "stamped into eagles and incorporated into our national currency," then the presence of a large foreign population of skilled and experienced miners was eminently desirable. Colton was a voice in the wilderness![2]

The manuscript diaries of forty-niners constitute the best original source material for the history of life in the gold fields of California and in virtually every instance they note the outbreaks of violence between the foreign and American population. John Hovey, who camped on the banks of the Calaveras River, got up one morning in December, 1849, and turned out armed and equipped, as the local alcalde had ordered, for military duty. He was one of a group who drove about one hundred Mexicans out of the region. No one was killed. But Hovey's outfit was able to capture some prisoners. They drove the dejected Mexicans

---

[2] *Three Years in California* (October 13, 1848), p. 368.

down to the Iowa Log Cabins and fined them one ounce of gold
dust apiece. The event took place on December 14, 1849. The
next day's entry in his diary includes the revealing statement:
"This morning all those concerned went before the alcalde and
received our share of the spoils which we obtained from the Mexicans in the shape of fines."[3]

The manuscript diary of John Hovey includes one of the
saddest incidents in the violent relationship between South Americans and Americans. A report reached his camp on the Calaveras that some Chileans had descended on a nearby camp and
murdered three American miners. A great commotion resulted
and Hovey and his companions armed themselves to the teeth. As
the story developed, it appears that a small group of Chileans
were given a writ to serve on several Americans who were charged
with having stolen fifteen thousand dollars worth of gold dust
from some Chilean miners. A fight resulted from the attempt to
serve the writ and three Americans were killed. This news spread
all over the mining region as a murderous attack on American
miners. American miners met at various places and passed resolutions in which they swore to "shoot down every one of them on
the road." These events were included under Hovey's entry for
December 28, 184[9]. On January 2, 1850, he records that the
Chileans had been captured, "tried," and convicted. The punishment varied as some were decided to be merely the servants of
others and acting under orders. The "peons" were whipped but
the three leaders were sentenced to death. As Hovey tells it:
"... one of the leaders had a little sick boy in one of the tents;
think of that little boy's feelings, when his father enters and tells
him he's come to see him for the last time ... the little fellow ...
sobbed as though he would break his heart and to think he's left
alone in a foreign land sick." The father was led out, his arms
tied behind him, and blindfolded. Hovey says he made a confession of guilt, and when the handkerchief was dropped the entire
group "was sent into eternity."[4]

Some of these events reached the newspapers. The incident

---

[3] John Hovey (Manuscript Diary in the Huntington Library, San
Marino, California), December 14, 15, 1849.

[4] John Hovey (Manuscript Diary), sometime between December 28,
1849, and January 4, 1850.

of the Chileans serving the writ on the American miners appeared in the *Alta California* [a San Francisco newspaper], January 5, 1850. By this time, however, the size of the Chilean party had grown to two hundred men and it was these two hundred that had attacked a tiny American group of only twenty miners. When the Chileans were finally captured they were ordered to walk to Stockton for trial. However ". . . it was rumored in town yesterday evening that the eleven Chilean prisoners, unable from exhaustion to proceed to the Calaveras, were hung upon the road."⁵ There is no sure way of knowing precisely what happened. But it is known that throughout the Calaveras diggings, Chileans were extremely unpopular and most of them left the region altogether. On February 9, 1850, the *Alta* stated: "There are now no more Chileans in the region."

Inequality before the laws is, indeed, one of the worst manifestations of nativism and this was exhibited with a rigid consistency from 1848 throughout the period of the gold rush. Open violence and lynch law also appeared in the relationships between foreigners and Americans, Mexicans being the usual victims. On the morning of July 10, 1850, to cite an example, four Americans made an appearance in Sonora with four captives, three Mexicans and one Indian. The four were charged with the brutal murder of two Americans at Green Flat Diggings, about eight miles from Sonora. When the men appeared in town a large crowd collected around them, and when an account of the murder was given, a tremendous uproar was heard from the crowd. The sheriff and other officers of the court tried to maintain some kind of order. Judge Barry arraigned the prisoners, whereupon a ". . . scene of unparalleled tumult and confusion took place." Cries of "String 'em up," were heard and echoed on every side. The mob rushed into the courtroom armed with ropes in which nooses had already been tied. The sheriff and other officers were overpowered and the prisoners were successfully captured by the mob. Just before the prisoners were captured by the mob, reliable witnesses had testified to the fact that: "Having heard that a murder had been committed at Green Flat Diggings, they had proceeded to that place and found the prisoners in the act of burning the tent and

---

⁵ *Alta California,* January 5, 1850.

bodies of two men." The defense explained that it was the custom of the countrymen of the prisoners to burn the dead and that the bodies in dispute had been dead for several days, had begun to decay, and they had been in the act of disposing of the corpses according to custom.

The trial turned into a riot during which several Mexicans were shot, one by a man who proclaimed that he did it "on general principles." After the smoke cleared, a trial was finally held during which it was found there was not sufficient evidence to convict the unfortunate Mexicans and they were released.

Incidents of these types occur again and again in the manuscript literature of the times until they jade the researcher. Josiah Royce is perhaps best quoted for a final word: "The fearful blindness of the early behavior of the Americans in California toward foreigners is something almost unintelligible."

Whatever the Americans did in the history of their contact with the Latin races in the mines, the history of the Foreign Miners' Tax looms up as the one overwhelmingly important event. This did more, probably, than any other thing, to set the foreign population against the American miner. Neither group really ever got over the effect of this law.

The *Alta California* reported on April 22, 1850, that a bill had been introduced into the California Senate at San Jose by State Senator Thomas Jefferson Green for the better regulation of the foreign mining population of California. The bill passed both houses of the state legislature and the approval of the governor was secured. The terms of the bill were simple and clear-cut: each and every foreigner in the mining country was ordered to take out a license to mine. This license cost twenty dollars and had to be renewed each month. If any foreigner refused to pay the required amount, the sheriff was instructed to organize a posse of reliable American citizens and forcefully stop his mining activities. Tax collectors were to be appointed by the governor and were to receive two dollars for each license issued.

The immediate reaction of the *Alta* was to comment dryly:

> In many instances it will be merely legalizing the most desperate attacks upon portions of the foreign population, and although a small amount of revenue may probably be derived from this

source, it will not be sufficient to counterbalance the many bad effects which will arise from the operation of the act.

The American mining population was, of course, delighted. The business community, however, was undecided; and many of the newspapers, especially in distant San Francisco, were openly hostile to the act from its conception.

Josiah Royce, whose analysis of California in the years of the gold rush was especially acute, considered the Foreign Miners' Tax as one of the most disastrous pieces of legislation ever passed, as it tended to " . . . discourage decent foreigners from visiting California, and to convert into rogues all honest foreigners who might come."[6]

The *Stockton Times* analyzed the Foreign Miners' Tax from an interesting angle. Looking at the provisions regarding the fee which the tax collectors were supposed to receive for their labors, the *Times* came up with some interesting statistics. Estimating the foreign population in the mines of Tuolumne County at ten thousand—a low estimate—and given a tax of twenty dollars a month per head ". . . we have an income from public lands placed at private disposal of a state or territory of two hundred thousand dollars per month, or nearly two and a half million per annum, from one county alone." And if this did not appear a ridiculously large sum, consider the tax collector's profit. "Again, the collector, I understand, has a commission of three dollars on each license. This is a monthly income of $30,000, or an annual income of $360,000." The commission was actually two dollars per license, but it is clear what the *Times* was driving at.[7]

Few miners could afford to pay twenty dollars a month for the privilege of toiling in the riverbeds of Sierra Nevada streams. Average earning of miners in 1850 would amount to no more than eighty dollars a month, and the outlandish cost of food and supplies could hardly permit the sacrifice of twenty-five percent of their income. The tax proved ruinous; the only alternative,

---

[6] Josiah Royce, *California*, pp. 282–83.
[7] *Stockton Times*, May 25, 1850.

in the long run, was for the foreign population to leave the gold fields.

Charles Plummer recorded in his diary the shocked reaction of the foreign population in the Sonora region, which was largely Mexican—the mass meetings, the petitions sent to the governor, the arrival of the hated tax collectors, the violence, and the final decision to leave. He noted on May 20, 1850: "The foreigners are leaving fast."[8] Armed groups of American miners roamed the countryside terrorizing the foreign population. Walter Murray described one group of American miners from Mormon Gulch who organized themselves into a little "army," marched into Sonora, stopping frequently at the saloons to get "liquored up." The reaction of the Mexican and Chilean population is significant.[9]

> . . . as we marched along, what a scene of confusion and terror marked our way. Mexicans, Chileans, men, women, and children, were packed up and moving, bag and baggage. Tents were being pulled down, houses and hovels gutted of their contents; mules, horses and burros were being hastily packed, while crowds upon crowds were already in full retreat. What could have been the object of our assembly, except as a demonstration of power and determination, I know not; but if intended as an engine of terror, it certainly had its desired effect, for it could be seen painted upon every countenance and impelling every movement of the affrighted population . . .

By August, 1850, the *Sonora Herald* noted a "lull in the . . . social atmosphere," and noted that ". . . the commercial interests of the country have been suffering to the amount of $10,000 per day." Sonora was reported to have invested in the supply needs of miners about $350,000 and a fund was hastily collected among the businessmen to test the legality of the Foreign Miners' Tax. But the damage had already been done. The *Alta California* commented in March, 1851, that the Southern Mines had suffered a "stunning blow" and that "Stockton was knocked completely

---

[8] Charles Plummer (Manuscript Diary in the Huntington Library, San Marino, California), May 19, 1850.

[9] Lang, Tuolumne County, p. 44; *San Jose Pioneer and Historical Review,* August 11, 1877.

on the head." Mexicans and Chileans had left by the thousands with no apparent desire to return since the new laws had given their tormentors legal justification for their oppressions. Already, by March, 1851, the *Alta* observed that the tax law had cost the state millions of dollars in lost business.

A certain William Hooper, from Stockton, wrote to the *Alta California* in a letter dated March 5, 1851, suggesting the possibility of lynching the tax collectors if they did not leave the mines. "If the collection of this tax is persisted in, the business of this place will be ruined, and its effect will also be felt in your city (San Francisco)."

The merchants were interested in one thing only—their profits—and if the Foreign Miners' Tax stood in their way it would have to go. In March, 1851, the original Foreign Miners' Tax was repealed and replaced by a fee of twenty dollars per year required to be paid by any foreigner who wished to carry on mining operations in California. The *Alta,* which had opposed the measure from the very beginning, expressed great pleasure with the repeal, declaring the original tax "unjust, impolitic, and opposed to every principle of our free institutions. . . ." Noting the tens of thousands of men who came to California from Mexico, Peru, and Chile, the *Alta* hastened to point out that they dug more gold and spent it more freely than did the American miners. "They usually expended nearly all of their gold. . . . Even those who occasionally left for their homes, generally purchased a good stock of various articles before leaving." [10]

Even the *Sonora Herald,* the mouthpiece of the nativist point of view, approved the repeal measure. "So far, so good. That bill was in all respects objectionable." The *Herald* suggested, further, that the tax be altered to one dollar a month, collected solely by county agents. No doubt this was to keep the loot closer at home! And what is perhaps the most revealing statement of all, the *Herald* predicted that ". . . . it would not, as last year, be demanded solely from Mexicans." [11]

There is little doubt that the Mexican was the especial object of the Foreign Miners' Tax. Constituting as he did the bulk of

---

[10] *Alta California,* March 7, 1851.
[11] *Sonora Herald,* March 22, 1851.

the foreign population in the southern mining region of the California gold rush, the Mexican was consistently the object of hatred and scorn. The Foreign Miners' Tax was the culmination of the antipathy directed toward the Mexican miner and provided the cloak of legality for the deprivations to which he had been subjected since 1848.

Repeal of the Foreign Miners' Tax did not have the desired effect of returning the Mexicans to the gold fields. In 1852, Tuolumne County realized only slightly over two thousand dollars from the tax on foreign miners.[12] The boom days of the Sonora-Columbia mining region were rapidly fading into the past. In 1859 the *California Chronicle* reported that the largest recent collection of the Foreign Miners' Tax had taken place during the previous week, a sum amounting to eighteen hundred dollars for the entire state.[13]

*The Aftermath of the Mexican War**

The letter of transmittal and the Conclusion and Findings of this 1970 Civil Rights Commission Report to the President and Congress reveal shocking failures and injustices in the treatment of Chicanos today. From the Mexican War to the present, they have not been included in the Melting Pot.

Letter of Transmittal

THE U.S. COMMISSION ON CIVIL RIGHTS
Washington, D.C., March 1970

THE PRESIDENT
THE PRESIDENT OF THE SENATE
THE SPEAKER OF THE HOUSE OF REPRESENTATIVES
SIRS:

The Commission on Civil Rights presents this report to you pursuant to Public Law 85–315 as amended.

---

[12]*Columbia Gazette*, April 23, 1853.

[13]*California Chronicle*, October 8, 1859.

*United States Commission on Civil Rights, *Mexican Americans and the Administration of Justice in the Southwest*, March 1970, United States Government Printing Office.

Under authority vested in this Commission by the Civil Rights Act of 1957 as amended, we have appraised allegations that American citizens of Mexican descent in five Southwestern States are being denied equal protection of the law in the administration of justice. We have found, through extensive field investigations during 1967 and 1968, three State Advisory Committee meetings in 1968, and a Commission hearing in 1968, all in that section of the country, that there is widespread evidence that equal protection of the law in the administration of justice is being withheld from Mexican-Americans.

Our investigations reveal that Mexican-American citizens are subject to unduly harsh treatment by law enforcement officers, that they are often arrested on insufficient grounds, receive physical and verbal abuse, and penalties which are disproportionately severe. We have found them to be deprived of proper use of bail and of adequate representation by counsel. They are substantially underrepresented on grand and petit juries and excluded from full participation in law enforcement agencies, especially in supervisory positions.

Our research has disclosed that the inability to communicate between Spanish-speaking American citizens and English-speaking officials has complicated the problem of administering justice equitably.

We urge your consideration of the facts presented and of the recommendations for corrective action in order to assure that all citizens enjoy equal protection as guaranteed by the Constitution of the United States.

Respectfully yours,

> REV. THEODORE M. HESBURGH, *C.S.C. Chairman.*
> STEPHEN HORN, *Vice Chairman.*
> FRANKIE M. FREEMAN
> HECTOR P. GARCIA, M.D.*
> MAURICE B. MITCHELL
> ROBERT S. RANKIN
>
> HOWARD A. GLICKSTEIN, *Staff Director.*
>
> *No longer member of the Commission

Conclusion

This report paints a bleak picture of the relationship between Mexican Americans in the Southwest and the agencies which administer justice in those States. The attitude of Mexican Americans toward the institutions responsible for the administration of justice—the police, the courts, and related agencies—is distrustful, fearful, and hostile. Police departments, courts, the law itself are viewed as Anglo institutions in which Mexican Americans have no stake and from which they do not expect fair treatment.

The Commission found that the attitudes of Mexican Americans are based, at least in part, on the actual experience of injustice. Contacts with police represent the most common encounters with the law for the average citizen. There is evidence of police misconduct against Mexican Americans. In the Southwest, as throughout the Nation, remedies for police misconduct are inadequate.

Acts of police misconduct result in mounting suspicion and incite incidents of resistance to officers. These are followed by police retaliation, which results in escalating hostilities.

The jury system is also not free from bias against Mexican Americans. At times, bail is set discriminatorily and inequalities in the availability of counsel lead to other injustices in trial and sentencing. Skilled interpreters, sensitive to the culture and background of Mexican Americans, are rare in areas of the Southwest where Mexican Americans predominate. Finally, Mexican Americans have been excluded from full participation in many of the institutions which administer justice in the Southwest. Mexican Americans are underrepresented in employment in police departments, State prosecutor's offices, courts, and other official agencies. Consequently, these agencies tend to show a lack of knowledge about and understanding of the cultural background of Mexican Americans.

The Commission recognizes that individual law enforcement officers and court officers have made positive efforts to improve the administration of justice in their communities. The fact, however, that Mexican Americans see justice being administered unevenly throughout the Southwest tends to weaken their confidence in an otherwise fair system. In addition, the absence of impartial tribunals in which claims of mistreatment can be litigated to a conclusion accepted by all sides tends to breed further distrust and cynicism.

This report is not intended to burden the agencies of justice with responsibilities which lie with society as a whole. The police and the courts cannot resolve the problems of poverty and of alienation which play a large part in the incidence of crime which they attempt to control; and the police and the courts often treat legitimate demands for reform with hostility because society as a whole refuses to see them as justified. The Commission recognizes that the job of law enforcement is extremely difficult. Nevertheless, it finds no justification for illegal or unconstitutional action by the very persons who are responsible for the enforcement of the law.

This report shows that Mexican Americans believe that they are subjected to such treatment again and again because of their ethnic background. Moreover, their complaints bear striking similarities to those of other minority groups which have been documented in earlier Commission studies of the administration of justice. The inequalities suffered by black Americans and Indians described in the Commission's 1961 "Justice" report and its 1965 "Law Enforcement" report, are of a similar nature. Consequently, the Commission's recommendations in this report are designed to be sufficiently broad to be applicable to all minority groups.

The essence of this situation is summed up in the words of a Mexican American participant in the California State Advisory Committee meeting, who said: "I think that my race has contributed to this country with pride, honor, dignity, and we deserve to be treated as citizens today, tomorrow, and every day of our lives. I think it is the duty of our Government to guarantee the equality that we have earned."

Findings

1. Police misconduct

There is evidence of widespread patterns of police misconduct against Mexican Americans in the Southwest. Such patterns include:

(a) incidents of excessive police violence against Mexican Americans;

(b) discriminatory treatment of juveniles by law enforcement officers;

(c) discourtesy toward Mexican Americans;

(d) discriminatory enforcement of motor vehicle ordinances;

(e) excessive use of arrests for "investigation" and of "stop and frisk";

(f) interference with attempts to rehabilitate narcotics addicts.

2. Inadequate protection

Complaints also were heard that police protection in Mexican American neighborhoods was inadequate in comparison to that in other neighborhoods.

3. Interference with Mexican American organizational efforts

In several instances law enforcement officers interfered with Mexican American organizational efforts aimed at improving the conditions of Mexican Americans in the Southwest.

4. Inadequacy of local remedies for police malpractice

Remedies for police malpractice in the Southwest are inadequate:

(a) in most Southwestern cities the only places where individuals can file complaints against the police are the police departments themselves. Internal grievance procedures did not result in adequate remedies for police malpractice;

(b) some cities in the Southwest have established independent or quasi-independent police review boards but these have not provided effective relief to complainants;

(c) civil litigation by Mexican Americans against police officers accused of civil rights violations is infrequent;

(d) there are few instances of successful local prosecutions of police officers for unlawful acts toward Mexican Americans;

(e) there have been instances of retaliation against Mexican Americans who complained about law enforcement officers to the local police department or to the FBI.

5. *Federal remedies*

(a) Agents of the Federal Bureau of Investigation have often failed to interview important witnesses in cases of alleged violation of 18 U.S.C. 242 or interviewed such witnesses in a perfunctory and hostile manner.

(b) More aggressive efforts to implement 18 U.S.C. 242 by the Department of Justice are needed.

6. *Underrepresentation of Mexican Americans on juries*

There is serious and widespread underrepresentation of Mexican Americans on grand and petit State juries in the Southwest;

(a) neither lack of knowledge of the English language nor low-incomes of Mexican Americans can explain the wide disparities between the Mexican American percentage of the population and their representation on juries;

(b) judges or jury commissioners frequently do not make affirmative efforts to obtain a representative cross section of the community for jury service;

(c) the peremptory challenge is used frequently both by prosecutors and defendants' lawyers to remove Mexican Americans from petit jury venires.

The underrepresentation of Mexican Americans on grand and petit juries results in distrust by Mexican Americans of the impartiality of verdicts.

7. *Bail*

Local officials in the Southwest abuse their discretion:

(a) in setting excessive bail to punish Mexican Americans rather than to guarantee their appearance for trial;

(b) in failing to give Mexican American defendants an opportunity to be released until long after they were taken into custody;

(c) by applying unduly rigid standards for release of Mexican Americans on their own recognizance where such release is authorized.

In many parts of the Southwest, Mexican American defendants are hindered in their attempts to gain release from

custody before trial because they cannot afford the cost of bail
under the traditional bail system.

8. *Counsel*

There are serious gaps in legal representation for Mexican
Americans in the Southwest:

(a) the lack of appointed counsel in misdemeanor cases
results in serious injustices to indigent Mexican American defendants;

(b) even in felony cases, where counsel must be provided
for indigent defendants, there were many complaints that appointed counsel often was inadequate;

(c) where public defender's offices are available to indigent
criminal defendants, they frequently did not have enough lawyers
or other staff members to adequately represent all their clients,
many of whom are Mexican Americans;

(d) in parts of the Southwest there are not enough attorneys to provide legal assistance to indigent Mexican Americans
involved in civil matters;

(e) many lawyers in the Southwest will not handle cases
for Mexican American plaintiffs or defendants because they are
"controversial" or not sufficiently rewarding financially;

(f) despite the enormous need for lawyers fluent in Spanish
and willing to handle cases for Mexican American clients, there
are very few Mexican American lawyers in the Southwest.

9. *Attitudes toward the courts*

Mexican Americans in the Southwest distrust the courts
and think they are insensitive to their background, culture, and
language. The alienation of Mexican Americans from the courts
and the traditional Anglo-American legal system is particularly
pronounced in northern New Mexico.

10. *Language disability*

Many Mexican Americans in the Southwest have a language
disability that seriously interferes with their relations with
agencies and individuals responsible for the administration of
justice:

(a) there are instances where the inability to communicate
with police officers has resulted in the unnecessary aggravation

of routine situations and has created serious law enforcement problems;

(b) Mexican Americans are disadvantaged in criminal cases because they cannot understand the charges against them nor the proceedings in the courtroom;

(c) in many cases Mexican American plaintiffs or defendants have difficulty communicating with their lawyers, which hampers preparation of their cases;

(d) language disability also adversely affects the relations of some Mexican Americans with probation and parole officers.

11. Interpreters

Interpreters are not readily available in many Southwestern courtrooms:

(a) in the lower courts, when interpreters were made available, they are often untrained and unqualified;

(b) in the higher courts, where qualified interpreters were more readily available, there has been criticism of the standards of their selection and training and skills.

12. Employment by law enforcement agencies

Employment of Mexican Americans by law enforcement agencies throughout the five Southwestern States does not reflect the population patterns of these areas:

(a) neither police departments, sheriffs' offices, nor State law enforcement agencies employ Mexican Americans in significant numbers;

(b) State and local law enforcement agencies in the Southwest do not have programs of affirmative recruitment which would attract more Mexican American employees;

(c) failure to employ more Mexican Americans creates problems in law enforcement, including problems in police-community relations.

13. Courts and prosecutors

Other agencies in charge of the administration of justice—courts, district attorneys' offices, and the Department of Justice—also have significantly fewer Mexican American employees than the proportion of Mexican Americans in the general population.

Suggestions for Further Reading

1. Patricia Bell Blawis, *Tijerina and the Land Grants: Mexican Americans in Struggle for their Heritage* (New York: International Publishers, 1971).

2. Mark Day, *Forty Acres: Cesar Chavez and the Farm Workers* (New York: Praeger, 1971).

   This book, written by a participant in the movement, contains an introduction by Cesar Chavez.

3. *El Plan de Santa Barbara* (Oakland, Ca.: La Causa Publications, 1969).

   A comprehensive outline of a Chicano plan for higher education, including curriculum, degree programs, bibliography.

4. Ernesto Galarza, *Merchants of Labor: The Mexican Bracero Story* (Santa Barbara, Ca.: McNally & Loftin, 1964).

   Although eighty percent of Mexican-Americans are urbanized, a significant percentage of migrant farm workers in the Southwest are Mexican-Americans or Mexican immigrants who are permitted to work in the United States as *braceros*. This book presents a sympathetic picture of their plight.

5. Ed Ludwig and James Santibanez, *The Chicanos: Mexican American Voices* (Baltimore: Penguin, 1971).

   An outstanding anthology of Chicano writings, including pieces by Cesar Chavez, Reies Lopez Tijerina, Raymond Barrio, Luis Valdez, and others.

6. Carey McWilliams, *North From Mexico: The Spanish-Speaking People of the United States* (New York: Greenwood Press, 1968).

   Among the outstanding features of this much-quoted study is the account of the Zoot-suit riots in June, 1943, and of the role of the press in whipping up sentiment against Mexican-Americans.

7. Wayne Moquin (ed.), *Documentary History of the Mexican American* (New York: Praeger, 1971).

8. Armin Rappaport (ed.), *The War with Mexico: Why Did It Happen?* (Skokie, Ill.: Rand McNally & Company, 1964).

This useful little book presents the issues and interpretations of the war in the words of contemporaries.

9. Ramon Eduardo Ruiz (ed.), *The Mexican War* (New York: Holt, Rinehart and Winston, 1963).

Because this book contains interpretations of the war by scholars representing five different schools of thought, it makes a logical choice to serve as a companion volume to Rappaport, above.

10. Julian Samora, *Los Mojados: The Wetback Story* (Notre Dame: University of Notre Dame Press, 1971).

Chapter Five

The Annexation of the Philippines

We will not renounce our part in the mission of our race, trustee, under God, of the civilization of the world.

—SENATOR ALBERT BEVERIDGE
(January 9, 1900)

Some scholars have recommended caution in applying the term "racist" to such events as the Cherokee removal and the Mexican War because those events occurred prior to the development of full-fledged theories of racial superiority. This caution need not be observed when studying the question of Philippine annexation.

In 1898 the United States engaged in war with Spain, ostensibly to help the Cubans throw off the yoke of their Spanish colonial oppressors. After a single engagement at Manila, the American fleet under Dewey annihilated the Spanish fleet. The Rough Riders under Theodore Roosevelt also had fantastic success on Cuban soil. It was, as Secretary of State John Hay wrote to Theodore Roosevelt, "a splendid little war." Spain was defeated in a few months.

With the Spanish-American War over, America was presented with the opportunity to annex the territory and population of the Philippine Islands, several thousand miles across the Pacific Ocean. But how could one possibly justify replacing Spanish domination with American domination? American ingenuity, good old Yankee know-how, found a way. The answer was to be found in the generous nature of a superior, civilized people who had only the best of intentions toward "our little brown brothers," as we affectionately called the Filipinos. We could not permit Spain to regain its imperialistic control over the Filipino population. Therefore, it was our duty to uplift this people which was "unfit for self-government," as President McKinley so conveniently phrased it.

Consequently, the decision was reached to annex the Philippines. This decision was denounced by Emilio Aguinaldo and his rebel forces who regarded America's action as a betrayal of the American promise of independence. It took the United States two years of brutal warfare to capture Aguinaldo and subdue the Filipino rebellion against American rule.

In two important ways the arguments advanced in the Mexican War were reappearing at the turn of the century. Philippine annexation was justified in part by appealing to "the White Man's burden"* and other racist catchwords. As in the Mexican War, the sense of American mission figured prominently in the Philippine annexation, but this time social Darwinism† added an unmistakable racist flavor to the rationalizations for territorial acquisition in the 1890's. For example, President McKinley's Secretary of War, Elihu Root, stated in a speech at Canton, Ohio, on October 24, 1900: "The testimony is absolutely overwhelming that the people inhabiting the Philippine Archipelago are incapable of self-government. ..." Also reminiscent of the Mexican War was the restraint imposed

------

*Rudyard Kipling's poem, which first appeared in February, 1899, became a catch-phrase for Western imperialists almost immediately after it was published. The first verse is:

Take up the White Man's burden—
Send forth the best ye breed—
Go, bind your sons to exile
To serve your captives' need;
To wait, in heavy harness,
On fluttered folk and wild;
Your new-caught sullen peoples,
Half devil and half child.

†In the late nineteenth century the concept of struggle and survival of the fittest that had come to be associated with Darwin's theory of evolution was being applied to areas of human competition also, particularly politics and economics. Racist theories were reinforced by the picture of nature as a tooth-and-claw, life-or-death struggle, with the superior species—or individual or race—emerging as the victor. Social Darwinism had wide application. It was used to justify international power politics and the success of capitalist entrepreneurs, industrialists, and business tycoons.

by the knowledge that the Filipinos were undesirables. Like the Mexicans fifty years before, they were not considered worthy of the Melting Pot. William Allen White, in an editorial in his Emporia (Kan.) Daily Gazette on February 23, 1898, commented thusly:

> A war with Spain over anything would be beneath the dignity of the United States. A gentleman cannot strike a sore-eyed, mangy, leprous beggar, no matter what provocation he may have. As between Cuba and Spain there is little choice. Both crowds are yellow-legged, garlic-eating, dagger-sticking, treacherous crowds. A mixture of Guinea, Indian, and Dago. One crowd is as bad as the other. It is folly to spill good Saxon blood for that kind of vermin.

A final unpleasant note about American–Filipino relations: Filipinos who came to America encountered much discrimination. "No Filipinos Wanted" was a common sign on the West Coast. Filipinos who remained in their homeland were just as unhappy with American oppression after the Spanish-American War as they had been with Spanish oppression before the war. Cubans and Puerto Ricans, who also ended up under American control as a result of this war, were not pleased by their new oppressors, either.

*Taking up the White Man's Burden**

The racist roots of the Philippine Annexation are explored in this article; in dealing with the dual effects of racism on expansionism, it also draws parallels with the Mexican War.

The appearance of a demand for overseas colonies coincided in time with a revival of racism in the United States. As in the 1840's, expansionism synchronized with racism. In each period the postulates were the superiority of the Anglo-Saxon peoples over all others and the obligation of the superiors to give leadership to the inferiors. In the 1840's, racism had crossed party lines. But it had infected the anti-expansionist Whigs more than it had the Democrats. In the 1880's and 1890's it was especially virulent among Republicans, the party of expansionists.

---

*From *Manifest Destiny and Mission in American History*, by Frederick Merk. © Copyright 1963 by Frederick Merk. Reprinted by permission of Alfred A. Knopf, Inc.

It has been felt by some historians that the dual concept of racial superiority of Anglo-Saxons and leadership owed to racial inferiors was a basic force in generating expansionism in the 1890's. The concept is said to have been fathered by a number of prominent authors in the 1880's and to have gained wide acceptance. The authors especially named as such intellectual progenitors of imperialism in the 1890's are John Fiske, Josiah Strong, and John W. Burgess. Their alleged role is of such significance as to require a closer examination than it has yet had.

John Fiske was a philosopher, historian, and free-lance writer, distinguished for his range and felicity in dealing with history especially. In 1885 he published in *Harper's New Monthly Magazine* an article that was part of a lecture printed in full in the same year in a book.[1] In it he gave a graphic account of the disorders produced in Europe in early times by successive waves of Germanic, Mongolian, and Mohammedan invaders, and the gradual return to order thereafter. The race which led in the return was the Anglo-Saxon. One means it used was the concept of representative government, a major gift to the world. The race possessed physical as well as intellectual powers, as exhibited in the Old World and the New, especially fecundity and enterprise. The fecundity was so marvelous that the day was near when four-fifths of mankind would trace their pedigree to English forebears and the language of man would be the language of Shakespeare. Evidence of high talent on the American side was the development of the principle of federalism in the American Constitution. This seemed to Fiske as great a contribution, especially in its promise for the future, as representative government. The author was a racist, unquestionably, though not in the narrowest sense. The term "Anglo-Saxon" seemed to him to be a slovenly colloquialism. Anglo-Saxons were the various racial elements that had flowed into the Melting Pot of the United States.

But racism was not carried in the article to any anticipated conclusion of expansionism. The central theme of the author was world federalism. The article was an early formulation of that

---

[1] *Harper's New Monthly Magazine,* LXX (1885), 578–90; John Fiske, *American Political Ideas* (New York, 1885), pp. 101–52. The lectures were originally given in England in 1880.

concept as a means to future peace. It bore the arresting title "Manifest Destiny," but this was used as a foil, merely, for the bigger concept. Actually it was derisive of Manifest Destiny in the sense in which the term had been used in the 1840's. It devoted some paragraphs to poking fun at the idea of a United States extending from pole to pole. But these paragraphs had been omitted, for reasons of space, from the article in magazine form. Mankind, as a whole, Fiske thought, will ultimately form one huge federation in which peoples will manage their local affairs in independence, but will submit issues of international import to the decision of a central tribunal supported by the public opinion of the human race. Only then will it become possible soberly to speak of a "United States" stretching from pole to pole. Here was the antithesis of any concept of Anglo-Saxonism blossoming into expansionism, though portions of the article sounded otherwise. These portions were later excerpted by historians and created confusion in the thinking of uninformed readers.

Another writer listed among race propagandists was Reverend Josiah Strong. He was a Congregational pastor especially interested in "home missions" in the United States. In 1885 he wrote for the American Home Missionary Society a work entitled *Our Country,* in which he appealed for funds to evangelize the United States. The theme of his work was the perils to the Protestant way of life found in the United States, which needed to be met and overcome. The perils, described chapter by chapter, were excessive immigration from Europe, Roman Catholicism, Rum, Tobacco, Mormonism, Socialism, improperly used wealth, the City, etc., etc. They added up to a dismal total. Chapter Thirteen, strategically placed just before the final one appealing for money, was more hopeful. Anglo-Saxonism, if preserved, would save the world. The author knew well the Darwinian concept of survival of the fittest and entirely agreed with it. He knew, also, John Fiske's concept of Anglo-Saxon superiority, with which he likewise agreed, though he maintained that he himself had given it to the world some years before. To him, the Anglo-Saxon race meant all who could speak English. He believed the race was being prepared by Providence to spread the tenets of Protestant Christianity. It was being prepared for the final competition of the races.

If I read not amiss, this powerful race will move down upon Mexico, down upon Central and South America, out upon the islands of the sea, over upon Africa and beyond. And can any one doubt that the result of this competition of races will be the "survival of the fittest"?

Strong spelled out in detail the method of the competition. No war to exterminate the inferior races would be necessary. The feeblest of them would be wiped out mercifully, merely by the diseases of, and contacts with, a higher civilization, for which they were unprepared. Races of marked inferiority are intended to be precursors merely of the superior. They are voices crying in the wilderness: "Prepare ye the way of the Lord!" Races, somewhat stronger, will simply be submerged. Decay already is far along in their superstitions and creeds. The dead crust of fossil faiths— Catholic, Mohammedan, Jew, Buddhist, and Brahmin—is being shattered. The pieces left in the process will be assimilated or simply neutralized by the strong Anglo-Saxons. The plan of God is to weaken weaklings and supplant them with better and finer materials.[2]

Ideas of racial superiority were entertained, also, by John W. Burgess, a professor of political science at Columbia University. He was more broad-minded than Fiske or Strong. He was willing to include all Teutonic peoples among those possessing genius for political organization. He had been trained as a student in Germany and was, not unnaturally, desirous of including Teutons in the charmed circle. In 1890 he published a work, *Political Science and Comparative Constitutional Law,* in which he went so far as to admit that Aryans generally had talents. But still, the Teutonic nations had shown genius above all others in developing solutions to problems of modern political organization.[3]

From writings such as these the conclusion has been reached that a causal relationship existed between the racism of the decade 1885–95 and the imperialism of the late 1890's, that racism was the climate in which imperialism flourished. Whether it did flourish then, whether it attained full growth prior to, during, or after

---

[2] Josiah Strong, *Our Country* (New York, 1885), chap. xiii.

[3] John W. Burgess, *Political Science and Comparative Constitutional Law,* I (Boston, 1890), 4, 37–45.

the war with Spain in 1898–9, are questions left relatively un-explored. They deserve to be fully explored.[4]

In the late 1880's and early 1890's Americans were much concerned about their deepening economic depression, its causes, distressing effects, and cures. Political parties were likewise concerned about them. They had widely diverse views, but they agreed in one respect—that any cures to be applied should be home cures, not overseas ones. The Populists, in their famous platform of 1892, recommended among other things free and unlimited coinage of silver at a ratio of sixteen to one, public ownership and operation of railroads, graduated income taxes, postal savings banks, an eight-hour working day, and restriction of undesirable immigration. The Democrats recommended such measures as the coinage of silver and gold without discrimination between them, tariffs for revenue, and the defeat of the "force bills" Lodge was proposing to coerce the South. Republicans recommended protective tariffs, bimetallism, and more stringent laws to exclude criminals, paupers, and contract labor. No party recommended overseas expansion as a restorative or cure. A possible exception in 1892 was a Republican proposal of "achievement of Manifest Destiny in its broadest sense," which was in no way defined, however, and probably meant to innocent readers almost nothing at all.

In the presidential campaign of 1896 problems of domestic politics were still predominant. Free silver was the central issue. The Democrats, merged now with the Populists, recommended free and unlimited coinage of silver at the ratio of sixteen to one. The Republicans opposed it. The Republicans finally said something on the subject of expansionism. They looked forward to the "ultimate union of all English-speaking parts of the continent by the free consent of its inhabitants," the "free consent" indicating, perhaps, that this was not considered a quick relief for the nation's ills. They thought, also, that the Hawaiian Islands should be "controlled" by the United States, that a Nicaraguan canal should be built and operated by the United States, and that the Danish West Indies should be secured for a much-needed naval station.[5] This

---

[4] Pratt, *Expansionists of 1898*, chap. 1; Richard Hofstadter: *Social Darwinism in American Thought* (rev. ed.; New York, 1959), chap. ix.

[5] Stanwood, *History of the Presidency*, I, chaps. xxx, xxxi.

reflected the views of Lodge, who had been chairman of the platform committee.

Racism bubbled up a little in these platforms. It undoubtedly was present in public opinion in the 1890's, as it had been in the 1840's. It reflected fear of competition with immigrants from southeastern Europe for jobs that were hard to find, and fear, also, regarding the dwindling of desirable free public lands. It could not be proclaimed too loudly at election time, and lurked, in platforms, behind such phrases as "criminal, pauper, and contract immigration," "dumping ground for the known criminals and professional paupers of Europe," and "alien ownership of land."

In the 1890's new theories concerning the advance or retardation of races were being developed by anthropologists. One was set forth by Franz Boaz in 1894, that any superiority held by some races in cultural matters was a product of accidents of history and opportunity rather than of innate capacity.[6] This had been suspected by many people earlier. Carl Schurz, for instance, had believed, already in the 1870's, that Indians could be regenerated and assimilated, if their tribalism were broken up. The Dawes Act of 1887 had been based on such premises. Some Republicans thought well of the possibilities of regenerating the Negro. Democrats were divided on that issue. In the big northern cities Democrats found virtue in racial tolerance. But southern Democrats considered Negroes innately inferior. However, southern Democrats were not imperialists in the 1890's, and were certainly not interested in redeeming inferior races in the Pacific Islands.

Confusion of thought on the racial issue was revealed in the 1890's by Republican politicians. In the 1896 platform, for instance, they expressed unwillingness to have the mixed races of Mexico and Central America in the temple of freedom. They thought only the English-speaking peoples of North America ought to be admitted. Yet, in the same breath they proposed to "control" the brown and yellow races of the Hawaiian Islands.

On the other hand, objections on precisely racial grounds

---

[6] Franz Boaz, "Human Faculty as Determined by Race," *Proceedings,* American Association for the Advancement of Science, XLIII (1894), 301–27. For a general survey, see William Stanton, *The Leopard's Spots* (Chicago, 1960).

were raised by Carl Schurz to annexing the Hawaiian Islands. Himself of foreign birth and confident that European immigrants flowing into the United States could be assimilated, he drew the line at Orientals, especially mixed Orientals such as the Hawaiians. In 1893 he wrote an article on the Hawaiian issue for *Harper's* in which he declared:

> Their population, according to the census of 1890, consists of 34,436 natives, 6,186 half-castes, 7,495 born in Hawaii of foreign parents, 15, 301 Chinese, 12,360 Japanese, 8,602 Portuguese, 1,928 Americans . . . and other foreigners. If there ever was a population unfit to constitute a state of the American Union, it is this.[7]

On other grounds than race Schurz deemed Hawaiians ineligible for admission to the Union. They lived in the tropics, and the tropics do not produce democracy. Also, they were isolated in tight communities on their islands and, therefore, hard to assimilate. Foreign territories should be annexed only if their inhabitants could be admitted as states to the Union at no distant day on an equal footing with the older states. To do otherwise would be to undermine the foundations of the Union.

Schurz had like objections to annexing Cuba. Cubans were comparable to Mexicans. Schurz referred ironically to a speech made by Seward in 1868 in which the Secretary had predicted that "in twenty years the city of Mexico would be the capital of the United States." Schurz thought our politics would certainly become "Mexicanized" if that prediction ever materialized.

Even Theodore Roosevelt had racial qualms about expanding over tropical areas. In 1894 he reviewed, in the *Sewanee Review,* a work by an Englishman, Charles F. Pearson, who was a pessimist on the subject of expanding over the tropics. Pearson believed that "higher races" simply could not get established in the tropics. Only in the temperate zones did they do well. White peoples who moved into tropical or subtropical areas were inevitably absorbed and vanished. Roosevelt fully agreed with such views. He believed replacement of the tropical peoples by peoples of the temperate zone impossible. Tropical peoples throw off the

---

[7] Carl Schurz, "Manifest Destiny," *Harper's New Monthly Magazine,* LXXXVII (1893), 737 ff.

yoke of their conquerors and become independent in any case. A
northern race can maintain a hold in the tropics only by a complete
renewal of its pure blood every generation. Surely this was no
hopeful prospect for taking over Hawaii. And yet the distinguished reviewer thought very favorably, if his private corre-
spondence of that period reflected his opinions, of taking over
Hawaii.[8]

As late as June 1898, Richard F. Pettigrew, of South Dakota,
in similar terms declared tropical peoples unsuitable for admission
to the Union. In a clash in the Senate over the annexation of
Hawaii, he declared:

> The founders of this government—recognizing the difficulty
> of maintaining as a unit a republic of extensive proportions—in-
> augurated the federal system, a union of sovereign states, hoping
> thereby to extend self-government over vast areas and to maintain
> therein the purity of republican principles—each state . . . of neces-
> sity containing a population . . . of men capable of governing them-
> selves. Therefore the founders . . . made it an unwritten law that
> no area should be brought within the bounds of the republic which
> did not, and could not, sustain a race equipped in all essentials for
> the maintenance of free civilization and capable of upholding within
> its boundaries a republican form of government. . . . Therefore, if
> we adopt the policy of acquiring tropical countries, where republics
> cannot live, we overturn the theory upon which this government is
> established.[9]

Republicans of this school were reasserting, strangely enough,
Calhounism.

Objection by Republicans to incorporating distant Orientals
into the Union was so common, and a desire to give them racial
leadership so uncommon, prior to the war with Spain, that a question concerning even Fiske, Strong, and Burgess arises. Were
those writers aware of preparing the way for imperialism? In
the case of Fiske the answer is clear. At the outbreak of the war
with Spain, he was an anti-imperialist. He became converted to

---

[8] *Sewanee Review*, II (1893–94), 353 ff.; Elting E. Morison (ed.),
Letters of Theodore Roosevelt (8 vols., Cambridge, 1951–54), Vols. I, II.

[9] *Cong. Record*, 55 Cong., 2 Sess., 6228 (June 22, 1898).

imperialism during the war, perhaps by forces unleashed in the war, though whence his "second thoughts" came he did not make evident.[10] Burgess was a vehement anti-imperialist throughout the war. He fell into the depths of despondency and despair over the course the war took. He thought he had been utterly mis-understood if any of his students believed he had, in insidious form, been teaching them imperialism. He specifically singled out Theodore Roosevelt for disapproval. He considered the imperial-ism generated by the war a disaster to American political civiliza-tion, and for some time after the war adhered to that view.[11]

As for the Reverend Josiah Strong, he had dealt in his book primarily with problems on the home front. His one chapter describing Anglo-Saxon superiority and its relationship to a vast world front was thrown in for inspirational purposes. He doubt-less had vague hopes that the future would open a wider world front to Protestant missionaries. In 1900 he published another book, entitled *Expansion Under New World Conditions,* in which he acclaimed the outcome of the war with Spain. He chided oppo-nents of imperialism as blind and mistaken, even if well-inten-tioned. He thought the common view, that no government can rightfully be established for a people except by their consent, outworn. Without any difficulty at all he could see a providential meaning in the circumstance that with no design on our part, we had become a power in Asia. The Anglo-Saxon race had been created, he thought, to assure freedom to Asia as against the tyranny of the Slav. The practical advantages of the new Asiatic front—rich markets, naval power, coaling stations, and so on—he described with a realism and with a wealth of detail that would have done credit to Mahan. He had learned of them from Mahan, whose utterances, he thought, exhibited "the insight of the philos-opher and the wisdom of the statesman." [12] He especially wel-

---

[10] Milton Berman, *John Fiske* (Cambridge, 1961), pp. 251–52.

[11] Jurgen F. H. Herbst, "Nineteenth-Century German Scholarship in America" (Ph.D. thesis, Harvard University, 1958), p. 166.

[12] Josiah Strong, *Expansion under New World Conditions* (New York, 1900), p. 261. Mahan was a thoroughgoing racist. He believed in-competent and inferior races would go down, and ever have gone down, before the persistent impact of the superior. Mahan, *The Interests of America in Sea Power,* p. 166.

comed the opening of new fields in the Orient for Protestant missionaries. In its inclusiveness of national interests to be served and in its fervor, the book was a powerful presentation of missionary expansionism.

But it is Strong's 1885 book and its impact on public opinion which are the immediate subjects of this inquiry. Its sale was considerable, as those who emphasize its significance all point out. The sale seems to have been principally in evangelical circles. Reviews of it appeared almost exclusively in such journals. They were favorable to the book on the whole, if not always enthusiastic. None of them consulted in this study mentioned the chapter on Anglo-Saxon race superiority and its relationship to the salvation of the world.[13] In that chapter Strong was endorsing Darwinian concepts that were not always greeted with applause in evangelical circles. Missionary-minded Americans of that era seemed generally to feel that the heathen should be strengthened by bringing them the Protestant gospel, not that they should be replaced with finer materials. Among Roman Catholics, little in the book could have had much appeal. In secular journals the work received scant notice. The one secular review found of it was in the New York *Nation*. It was devastating. It dealt solely with the chapters on the perils overhanging the homeland. The chapter on Anglo-Saxon superiority and world leadership was utterly ignored.[14]

Racism in a nation is a complex phenomenon. It varies from section to section, from party to party, and from stratum to stratum in society. If it is alleged to have contributed to imperialism and the allegation is to be tested at all levels, the complexities become bewildering. If such a hypothesis relates to a period when interest in imperialism is marginal everywhere, as it was in the 1880's and early 1890's, and when the nation is in a state of profound peace, a judgment by the historian that such a contribution was made is an act of faith rather than an act of weighing evidence. When a neighboring people, known to Americans for gen-

---

[13] Reviews in evangelical journals which seem to be typical are in *Christian Union*, August 19, 1886; *Zion's Herald,* May 19, 1886; *Presbyterian Review*, July, 1886, p. 584; *Congregationalist* (Boston), February 18, 1886; *Advance* (Chicago), March 18, 1886. The *Baptist Review* and the *American Church Review* took no notice of the book.

[14] *Nation* (New York), September 30, 1886.

erations, as Mexicans had been in 1846, becomes the subject of expansionist discussion and arouses an overwhelming racial objection to having them in the Union, as it did in 1848, is it likely that an Oriental people, inhabiting islands halfway across the Pacific, were the subject of a desire in the 1890's to give them race leadership by annexation? Is it not likely that racism, prior to the war with Spain, was a deterrent to imperialism rather than a stimulant of it?

God's Chosen People

Albert Beveridge's speech of September 16, 1898, was made two months before he was elected United States senator from Indiana. The following excerpt is thoroughly laden with ideas of Anglo-Saxon superiority.

The march of the flag! In 1789 the flag of the Republic waved over four million souls in thirteen states, and this a savage territory which stretched to the Mississippi, to Canada, to the Floridas. The timid minds of that day said that no new territory was needed, and for the hour they were right. But under the lead of Jefferson we acquired the territory which sweeps from the Mississippi to the mountains, from Texas to the British possessions, and the march of the flag began. The infidels to the gospel of liberty raved, but the flag swept on. The title to that noble land out of which Oregon, Washington, Idaho, and Montana have been carved was uncertain. Jefferson obeyed the Anglo-Saxon impulse within him and another empire was added to the Republic and the march of the flag went on. Those who deny the power of free institutions to expand urged every argument, and more, that we hear today, but the march of the flag went on. A screen of land from New Orleans to Florida shut us from the gulf, and over this and the everglade peninsula waved the saffron flag of Spain. Andrew Jackson seized both, the American people stood at his back; and under Monroe the Floridas came under the dominion of the Republic, and the march of the flag went on. The Cassandras prophesied every prophecy of despair we hear today, but the march of the flag went on. Then Texas responded to the bugle calls of liberty and the march of the flag went on. And at last we waged war with Mexico and the flag swept over the Southwest, over peerless California, past the gate of gold to Oregon on the north, and from ocean to ocean its folds of glory blazed. And now, obeying the same voice that Jefferson, Jackson, [and] Seward heard and obeyed, Grant and Harrison heard and obeyed, William McKinley plants the flag over the islands of the sea, and the march of the flag goes on.

Distance and oceans are no longer arguments. The fact that all the territory our fathers bought and seized is contiguous is no longer argument. In 1819 Florida was further from New York than P[ue]rto Rico is from Chicago today; Texas further from Washington in 1845 than Hawaii is from Boston in 1898; California more inaccessible in 1847 than the Philippines are now. Gibraltar is further from London than Havana is from Washington; Melbourne is further from Liverpool than Manila is from San Francisco. The ocean does not separate us from the lands of our duty and desire—the ocean to join us, a river never to be dredged, a canal never to be repaired. Steam joins us; electricity joins us—the very elements are in league with our destiny. Cuba not contiguous! P[ue]rto Rico not contiguous! Hawaii and the Philippines not contiguous! Our navy will make them contiguous. Dewey and Sampson and Schley have made them contiguous and American speed, American guns, American heart and brain and nerve will keep them contiguous forever.

But there is a difference. We did not need the western Mississippi valley when we acquired it, nor Florida, nor Texas, nor California, nor the royal provinces of the far Northwest. We had no emigrants to people this vast wilderness, no money to develop it, even no highways to cover it. No trade awaited us in its savage fastnesses. Our productions were not greater than our internal trade. There was not one reason for the land lust of our statesmen from Jefferson to Harrison other than the prophet and the Saxon within them. But today we are raising more than we can use. Therefore, we must find new markets for our produce, new occupation for our capital, new work for our labor. And so, while we did not need the territory taken during the past century at the time it was acquired, we do need what we have taken in 1898, and we need it now. Think of the thousands of Americans who will invade the Philippines when a liberal government shall establish order and equity there. Think of the hundreds of thousands of Americans who will build a soap-and-water, common-school civilization of energy and industry in Cuba, when a government of law replaces the double reign of anarchy and tyranny. Think of the prosperous millions that empress of islands will support when, obedient to the law of political gravitation, her people ask for the highest honor liberty can bestow—the sacred order of the stars and stripes, the citizenship of the great Republic!

. . . .

Fellow Americans, we are God's chosen people. Yonder at Bunker Hill and Yorktown His providence was above us. At New Orleans and on ensanguined seas His hand sustained us. Abraham Lincoln was His minister; and His was the altar of freedom the boys in blue set up on a hundred smoking battlefields. His power directed Dewey in the east, and He delivered the Spanish fleet into our hands on Liberty's natal day as He delivered the elder armada into the hands of our English sires two centuries ago. His great purposes are revealed in the progress of the flag, which surpasses the intentions of congresses and cabinets, and leads us, like a holier pillar of cloud by day and pillar of fire by night, into situations unforeseen by finite wisdom and duties unexpected by the unprophetic heart of selfishness. The American people cannot use a dishonest medium of exchange; it is ours to set the world its example of right and honor. We cannot fly from our world of duties; it is ours to execute the purpose of a fate that has driven us to be greater than our small intentions. We cannot retreat from any soil where Providence has unfurled our banner; it is ours to save that soil for liberty and civilization. For liberty and civilization and God's promises fulfilled, the flag must henceforth be the symbol and the sign of all mankind.

. . . .

Uplifting Our Little Brown Brothers

President McKinley's explanation to a group of Methodist ministers of the reasons he decided to proceed with Philippine annexation contained at least two strong indications that racism was involved. This explanation came after the annexation of the Philippines.

I went down on my knees and prayed God Almighty for light and guidance more than one night. And one night late it came to me this way—I don't know how it was, but it came: (1) That we could not give them back to Spain—that would be cowardly and dishonorable; (2) that we could not turn them over to France or Germany;—our commercial rivals in the Orient—that would be bad business and discreditable; (3) that we could not leave them to themselves—they were unfit for self-government —and they would soon have anarchy and misrule over there worse than Spain's was; and (4) that there was nothing left for us to do but to take them all, and to educate the Filipinos, and uplift and civilize and Christianize them, and by God's grace do the very best we could by them, as our fellow men for whom Christ also died. And then I went to bed and went to sleep and slept soundly.

*Justifying Atrocities against Filipinos**

The following article presents a concise discussion of America's goals and tactics in the Philippines in the first few years of the twentieth century.

Seventy years ago, the United States fought a protracted and bloody war of counterinsurgency in the Philippines. Circumstantial evidence suggests the possibility that Americans initiated the fighting in 1899, only two days before the Senate was to ratify the treaty with Spain, in order to stampede recalcitrant legislators who were balking over the controversial provision to annex the Philippines.

Once the fighting erupted outside Manila, Maj. Gen. Elwell S. Otis assured the American public that the Filipino nationalist forces of Emilio Aguinaldo would be wiped out in a matter of weeks, a sanguine prediction he continually reiterated with each demand for more troops. Newspapers openly accused Otis of

---

*From Stuart Creighton Miller, "Making War in Asia—in 1900," *The New York Times*, March 20, 1971. © 1971 by The New York Times Company. Reprinted by permission.

inflating enemy body counts while concealing American losses. The general returned a hero to Washington in 1900, and all doubts were washed away in a sea of toasts and patriotic testimony. Once home, Otis exchanged his sword for a pen with which to attack the peace movement for encouraging the Filipinos to continue fighting, long after they were obviously defeated.

The highly respected Republican Senator from Massachusetts, George F. Hoar, became the leading dove, and was in the awkward position of challenging the legality of a war sponsored by his own party. Other distinguished Americans joined him, and university campuses from Ann Arbor to Cambridge hosted peace rallies at which this "inhuman war of extermination" was denounced by professors, who evoked public cries of "treason" for describing the Stars and Stripes as "an emblem of tyranny and butchery in the Philippines."

In spite of the Army's heavy-handed attempts at censorship, correspondents were able to corroborate suppressed rumors of American atrocities in the Philippines: civilians were being slaughtered, herded into concentration camps, tortured to extract information and confessions, and shot as hostages. As frustration mounted in our generals, they began to repeat the tragic errors of their Spanish predecessors.

When denial was no longer viable the atrocities were attributed to our native allies, the Macabebes, a despised group who once served Spain. Euphemisms were invented to mitigate the practices: "relocation camps of instruction and sanitation" were designed to protect the natives from "Aguinaldo's enslavement." Hence the "water cure," a favorite means of torture that often proved fatal, was never used, sometimes resorted to by our native allies, or was described as "merely an unpleasant experience" for the victim. But first prize must go to President McKinley who described the process of subjugating the Filipinos as "benign assimilation."

As the credibility gap widened, unorthodox tactics were justified on the grounds that the *insurrectos* were not revolutionaries, but "bandits" who wore no distinguishing uniforms and blended into the peasantry after ambushing and booby-trapping our troops. For our generals, who cut their military teeth on Indian wars, the ultimate justification was racism. As biologically inferior and treacherous savages, the Filipinos did not rate con-

ventional modes of warfare. Maj. Gen. Adna R. Chaffee cautioned
reporters not to wax sentimental over the shooting of a few "goo
goos," as our troops called the natives.

A government attempt to demonstrate that flagrant violations did not go unpunished backfired when it was learned that
the murder of a Filipino cost one officer a modest fine and the loss
of thirty-five places on the promotion list. The sensational atrocity
trial of a Marine major hurt the Administration more when the
defense contended that he was simply following Brig. Gen. Jacob
H. Smith's orders to take no prisoners, shoot all males over the
age of ten, and make the island of Samar "a howling wilderness"
in retaliation for the bloody ambush of an American company.
Smith's subsequent court-martial led to a reprimand and early
retirement for him and for the Army's Chief of Staff.

By 1902 Americans had had their fill of atrocities and were
eager to sweep the dirt under the rug. The *New York Times*
thanked *Harper's* for "sanely" pointing out that the use of torture
and the shooting of hostages were humane practices in that they
shortened the war and saved lives. Teddy Roosevelt still insisted
that Americans were fighting in the Philippines "for the triumph
of civilization over forces which stand for the black chaos of savagery and barbarism."

The heavy cost of the war—in lives, emotional and political
divisiveness and a tarnished national honor—should have sobered
America sufficiently to question permanently the efficacy of military intervention to frustrate nationalistic aspirations.

*Brutality Is Advocated by the Press**

In 1902 the San Francisco Argonaut *defended the atrocities by
American soldiers who were suppressing the Filipino rebellion against
American takeover of their land. The basis for the apology is racist:
"They are indolent . . . savages."*

There has been too much hypocrisy about this Philippine
business—too much snivel—too much cant. Let us all be frank.

----

*Quoted in Paul Jacobs and Saul Landau, *To Serve the Devil*, vol.
II (New York: Random House, 1971).

We do not want the Filipinos.
We want the Philippines.

All of our troubles in this annexation matter have been caused by the presence in the Philippine Islands of the Filipinos. Were it not for them, the Treaty of Paris would have been an excellent thing; the purchase of the archipelago for twenty millions of dollars would have been cheap. The islands are enormously rich; they abound in dense forests of valuable hardwood timber; they contain mines of the precious metals; their fertile lands will produce immense crops of sugar cane, rice, and tobacco. Touched by the wand of American enterprise, fertilized with American capital, these islands would speedily become richer than Golconda was of old.

But unfortunately, they are infested by Filipinos. There are many millions of them there, and it is to be feared that their extinction will be slow. Still, every man who believes in developing the islands must admit that it cannot be done successfully while the Filipinos are there. They are indolent. They raise only enough food to live on; they don't care to make money; and they occupy land which might be utilized to much better advantage by Americans. Therefore the more of them killed, the better.

It seems harsh. But they must yield before the superior race, and the American syndicate. How shortsighted, then, to check the army in its warfare upon these savages; particularly when the army is merely carrying out its orders and the duly expressed wishes of the American people, as shown through their elections and their representatives.

Doubtless, many of the excellent gentlemen now in Congress would repudiate these sentiments as brutal. But we are only saying what they are doing. We believe in stripping all hypocritical verbiage from national declarations, and telling the truth simply and boldly. We repeat—the American people, after thought and deliberation, have shown their wishes. *They do not want the Filipinos. They want the Philippines.*

It is no one party, no one class, that is responsible for our Philippine policy. It is the people of the United States. The Democratic Party shares equally the responsibility with the Republican Party. The Democratic Party voted for the war with Spain. Had it opposed the fifty-million [arms] appropriation, the war could not have taken place. The Democrats advocate the purchase of the Philippines. For a time, the confirmation of the Philippine treaty was in doubt. It was the direct personal lobbying of William J. Bryan with the Democratic Senators which led to the confirmation of the Philippine purchase, and which also led to the present bloody war. Mr. Bryan said at the time that he advocated the confirmation of the treaty in order to put "the Republicans into a hole." He has certainly put his country into a hole. Is he proud of his work?

We are all responsible. You, reader, are responsible. If you are a Republican, your party has made this action part of its national policy. If you are a Democrat, your party, by its vote in the House of Representatives, made the war possible, and by its vote in the Senate turned the scales for the purchase of the Philippines.

But if we, the people of the United States, are responsible for the Philippine campaign, the American army is not. The army is only seventy thousand out of seventy million. The army did not ask to go there. It was sent. It has fought for four years under tropic suns and torrential rains, in pestilential jungles and miasmatic swamps, patiently bearing the burdens placed upon it by the home country, and with few laurels to be gained as a result of hard and dangerous duty. Nearly every general officer returning from the Philippines has returned to either a wrecked reputation, newspaper odium, or public depreciation. Look at Merritt, Otis, Merriam, MacArthur, Funston. The best treatment that any of them has received is not to be abused. And yet, with these melancholy examples before them, our army toils on uncomplainingly doing its duty.

The army did not bring on the war. We civilians did it. The army is only doing our bidding as faithful servants of their country. And now that they have shown a perfectly human tendency to fight the devil with fire, we must not repudiate their actions, for their actions are our own. They are receiving the fire of the enemy from the front. It is shameful that there should be a fire upon them from the rear.

Suggestions for Further Reading

1. Robert L. Beisner, *Twelve against Empire: The Anti-Imperialists, 1898–1900* (New York: McGraw-Hill, 1968).

   A study of the opposition to Philippine acquisition.

2. L. C. Vann Woodward, *The Strange Career of Jim Crow* (New York: Oxford University Press, 1966).

   An excellent discussion of the implications of the new imperialism for Southern race policies begins on page 72. Woodward shows how the racism which justified Philippine annexation for Northern expansionists redounded to the benefit of Southern white supremacists. Since racial superiority could be used to support domination of "our little brown brothers," why not those in the deep South?

3. The Young Lords Party and Michael Abramson, *Palante: Young Lords Party* (New York: McGraw-Hill, 1971).

   Pages 60–68 contain a discussion of Puerto Rican acquisition in the context of Philippine Annexation. Expansion and colonialism are linked to racism in this important book by Puerto Rican activists.

PART 3 RACIST ROOTS OF ANTI-IMMIGRANT DISCRIMINATION

Chapter Six

White Responses to the "Yellow Peril"

The opposition to Chinese immigration was in the first place almost purely southern, and arose from the antagonism of men accustomed to regard themselves as masters toward races to which there attached any suspicion of servitude. To work at all was a sad coming down for them, but to work beside a pigtail, whom even a wild Indian despised was abasement intolerable.

—HUBERT H. BANCROFT,
History of California (1890)

On the basis of their skin color and other "race-related" superficial features which serve to distinguish them from the Anglo-Saxon physical stereotype, Chinese and Japanese in America have been subjected to a long catalog of racist experiences. Fears of "coolie-labor" competition, mob ravages of Chinese sections of town, exclusion laws, court decisions, concentration camps, and constitutional provisions—the list is long and the message is crisp: neither Chinese nor Japanese have fit conveniently into the WASP mold. Immigrants from the Orient have been punished for not wanting to assimilate at the same time they were punished for trying to assimilate. The most elemental civil rights were denied them until very recently in our history.

Even in a nation which deliberately whitewashes its racist history, certain glaring anomalies have filtered out to the general public. Thus most Americans do know something about the Gentlemen's Agreement in 1907 and the relocation camps in 1942. But the whole story of anti-Oriental racism is not a matter of common knowledge. The concentration camps were not just a single error, but were rather the culmination of a half-century of hatred between Americans, especially those in California, and Japanese.

The Chinese experienced an even longer history of anti-Oriental racism in this country. This was particularly true in California. For example, in *People* v. *Hall,* in 1854, the Chief Justice of the California Supreme Court, Hugh C. Murray, declared the Chinese to be legally Indians, since both were presumed to have descended from the same Asiatic ancestor. In practice, this prohibited the Chinese from testifying in court against a white man because in 1850 a California state law forbade Negroes and Indians from testifying in court for or against a white man. In 1863 the ban was removed for Negroes, but not until 1872 was it removed for Indians and Chinese.

How many Americans are aware that in *Gong Lum* v. *Rice,* in 1927, the United States Supreme Court upheld the right of local school districts to compel Chinese students to attend Negro schools out of their immediate neighborhood instead of white schools in their own neighborhoods?

How many Americans know that Article XIX of the California Constitution, which was in effect from 1879 to 1952, prohibited corporations from hiring Chinese and prohibited the hiring of Chinese on "any state, county, municipal, or other public work, except in punishment for crime"? Antimiscegenation* statutes similar to those directed against white–Negro intermarriages specify "Chinese" or "Mongolian" or "Oriental" in several states.

The concept of "Yellow Peril" symbolized the white racist response to Oriental immigrants. It revealed another crack in the Melting Pot. For the new militancy of Asian-Americans in the 1970's, see Part 5.

---

*Miscegenation refers to interbreeding of different races.

Anti-Chinese Riots*

Anti-Chinese riots are enumerated in this summary of late nine-teenth-century racist rampages.

In this explosive social, economic, and political climate, the heavy concentration of Chinese in California made them a convenient scapegoat for the relief of pent-up frustrations and emotions. In 1870 there were sixty-three thousand Chinese in the United States, ninety-nine percent of whom were on the West Coast. Every tenth person in California in 1860 was Chinese. Their large numbers, their physical differences, the retention of their national dress, the custom of wearing their hair in pigtails, their habits and traditions, so incomprehensible to the Occidental mind, made them an easy target to spot.

When employment with the railroad ceased, the Chinese sought work in the mines, on the farms, in land reclamation, in domestic service, and in the cigar and woolen factories. These were jobs which the white man scorned, for the white man was looking for a quick bonanza. Nevertheless, they were jobs that gave the Chinese employment while the white man was out of work.

So whereas the Chinese had been praised for their industry, their honesty, their thrift, and their peaceful ways, they were now charged with being debased and servile coolies, clannish, dangerous, deceitful, and vicious. They were accused of being contract laborers, although there was not a shred of evidence to show that the Chinese were anything but Argonauts† of a different skin coloring. Degenerate traits were ascribed to them, in direct contradiction of the praises heaped upon them a few years earlier. The workingmen accused them of undermining the white man's standard of living. It was alleged they would work for less because they subsisted on next to nothing. The word was spread that the land and rail companies hired Chinese instead

---

*Reprinted by permission of The Macmillan Company from *Mountain of Gold* by Betty Lee Sung. Copyright © by Betty Lee Sung 1967.

†A term used to denote persons who went to California in 1849 in search of gold. From the Greek legend of Jason and the Argonauts who sought the Golden Fleece.

of white men because the Chinese accepted employment at any price. Yet the books kept by Charles Crocker of the Central Pacific showed that white men were paid at the rate of thirty-five dollars per month plus keep, and the Chinese were paid thirty-five dollars per month without keep, mainly because the Chinese preferred cooking their own food.

The charge of accepting slave wages was shortly disproved after the exclusion laws took effect. The drastic curtailment in immigration brought about a shortage of Chinese laborers. Quick to take advantage of the situation, Chinese laborers demanded and got higher wages for their services—this in spite of a surplus in white labor.

However, reason and fact could not prevail. Elmer Clarence Sandmeyer wrote: ['] . . . there would have been a depression in the 1870's if the entire population had been made up of lineal descendants of George Washington. . . . If the Chinese in California were white people, being in all other respects what they are, I do not believe that the complaints and warfare against them would have existed to any considerable extent.[']¹ But once the charges were made, they spread like a prairie fire, fanned red-hot by Denis Kearney.*

Kearney invariably began his speeches with an attack upon the monopolies—the rich, huge corporate enterprises. He pointed out their owners' ornate mansions on Nob Hill and blamed these moguls for the plight of the workingmen. He accused the Chinese of working hand-in-hand with monopolies, of accepting slave wages, and of robbing the white man of his job. His wrath was directed against both the Chinese and the land and rail monopolies, but the latter were powerful, impregnable, organized, while the Chinese were docile, eager to avoid conflict, and ineffectual in court because their testimony could not be accepted as evidence. Kearney's speeches always ended with the slogan, "The Chinese must go!" So the blame fell upon the Chinese, and thus supplied

---

¹ Elmer Clarence Sandmeyer, *The Anti-Chinese Movement in California* (Urbana, Ill.: University of Illinois Press, 1939), p. 88. [Sandmeyer was quoting Senator Morton. See the previous selection by McWilliams, which contains more of the original Morton quote.]

*The California labor agitator who organized the Workingmen's Party.

with a hate object, the frenzied, incited mob would dash off to another orgy of attacks upon the defenseless Chinese.

During this period, the Chinese were stoned and robbed, assaulted and murdered. Hoodlums would organize attacks against the Chinese camps as sport, for they knew the Chinese could not obtain redress.

In the spring of 1876, the Chinese were driven from small towns and camps, their quarters burned. Some Chinese were killed or injured. In June of 1876, a violent attack was made upon them at Truckee.

In 1877, employers of Chinese labor in Chico received threatening letters. In March of that year, six tenant farmers were attacked and five killed. The murderer who was caught confessed to being under orders from the Workingmen's Party.

In July 1877, a great riot broke loose. Twenty-five wash houses were burned, and there followed an outbreak of riots. For months afterwards, no Chinese was safe on the streets. Arson and personal abuse spread to adjacent counties. Chinese laundries were burned, and when occupants tried to escape, they were shot or left to die in flaming buildings.

In 1878, the entire Chinese population of Truckee was rounded up and driven from town.

In 1885, the infamous massacre of twenty-eight Chinese in Rock Springs, Wyoming, occurred. Many others were wounded and hundreds were driven from their homes.

In 1886, Log Cabin, Oregon, was the scene of another brutal massacre.

Professor Mary Coolidge wrote: "During the years of Kearneyism, it is a wonder that any Chinese remained alive in the United States."

Murdering Chinese became such a commonplace occurrence that the newspapers seldom bothered to print the stories. Police officials winked at the attacks, and politicians all but incited more of the same. There were thousands of cases of murder, robbery, and assault, but in only two or three instances were the guilty brought to justice.

If murders were commonplace, the indignities, abuse, brutalities, and injustices practiced against the Chinese were outrageous. An old-timer told of the indignities he suffered at the hands of drunken white men:

Every Saturday night, we never knew whether we would live to see the light of day. We operated a laundry near a mining camp. Saturday was the night for the miners to get drunk. They would force their way into our shop, wrest the clean white bundles from the shelves and trample the shirts which we so laboriously finished. If the shirts were torn, we were forced to pay for the damages. One night, one of the miners hit his face against the flat side of an iron. He went away, but we knew that our lives were now in danger so we fled, leaving all of our possessions and money behind. The miner came back with a mob who ransacked our shop, robbed us of the $360 that was our combined savings and set fire to the laundry. We were lucky to escape with our lives, so we came east.

Whereas most Chinese had gone straight to San Francisco upon their arrival in the United States, they now began to disperse. Some had already gone north to work on the Northern Pacific and Canadian Pacific Railroads. Others sought work in the silver and coal mines of Nevada, Oregon, Wyoming, and Colorado. But prejudice and hatred confronted them everywhere. The anti-Chinese sentiments had spread like a cancerous growth to other parts of the West.

On February 11, 1870, a joint resolution passed the legislature of the territory of Colorado, affirming the desirability of Chinese immigration.

The preamble stated that the immigration of Chinese labor to Colorado was calculated to hasten the development and early prosperity of the territory by supplying the demand for cheap labor. It was, therefore, resolved that such immigration should be encouraged by legislation that would guarantee the immigrants security of their persons and property.[2]

Ten years later, the seeds of hatred sprouted in Colorado. Anti-Chinese feelings reached their pitch in Denver for the November elections, and these feelings soon gave way to open violence.

There were two versions to the story of how one riot started. The *Rocky Mountain News* version was that a Chinese laundryman charged ten cents more than a white customer was willing

---

[2]"The Chinese in Colorado," *Colorado Magazine* (October, 1952), p. 273.

to pay. An argument ensued, whereupon the Chinese slapped the white man in the face with a knife. The injured man ran into the streets and a crowd gathered, so the Chinese fired a gun into the crowd.

The other version was revealed in a government publication as a result of an investigation to determine if indemnity was due the Chinese. The riots, said the government publication, began when a game of chance between two Chinese was broken up by a couple of drunken white men. Both versions then agreed about the crowd that gathered.

Because only fifteen policemen were on the Denver force, the mayor called out the fire department, promising the crowd a drenching if they did not disperse. The crowd became so angry that they began a destructive rampage lasting throughout the night. Every Chinese laundry, business, and home was destroyed. The mayor, with his pitiful law-enforcement staff, was helpless. An appeal was made to the governor for help. A light artillery battery and the governor's guards were dispatched to Denver. The Chinese were rounded up and locked in jail for their own safety. One Chinese was killed and several white men wounded, but the homes and property of the Chinese were completely destroyed.

*Mass Expulsion**

This brief survey of the Japanese in America focuses upon the concentration camps, or "relocation centers," in which more than 110,-000 Americans of Japanese ancestry were incarcerated after they were forcibly evacuated from their homes in 1942. Although the action was upheld at the time by the United States Supreme Court as a necessary wartime security measure, it is now perceived as simply another chapter in the long conflict between whites and Japanese.

The Japanese are among the most recent immigrants to enter the United States. For a long time Japan was opposed to its citizens leaving their own country. Prior to 1854 emigration was a crime punishable by death, and the construction of ocean-going

―――――――

*From Brewton Berry, *Race and Ethnic Relations,* © Copyright Houghton, Mifflin Company (Boston: 1965).

vessels was forbidden by imperial decree. Then an occasional shipwrecked sailor or a stowaway found his way to these shores. Their numbers were negligible, however, for there were only 55 Japanese here in 1870, and 148 in 1880. But the Hawaiian Sugar Planters' Association, in 1884, prevailed upon the Japanese authorities to reverse their traditional opposition to emigration, and immediately the numbers of Japanese in other countries began to swell. They went to Hawaii in droves, and many came to Canada, the United States, and South America. There were 2,039 here in 1890; and in the first decade of the present century some 55,000 arrived from Japan, and another 37,000 from Hawaii.

They were never warmly received in the United States, even though their labor was needed in the West where they settled. At the time they began to arrive in large numbers, Japan was emerging as a world power; and many Californians regarded the Japanese immigration as the spearhead of invasion. An anti-Japanese meeting was held in San Francisco on May 7, 1900; and in 1905 the Hearst newspapers launched a major attack upon them. Various repressive and discriminatory measures were adopted. In 1907 President Roosevelt, by executive order, stopped Japanese immigration from Hawaii, Canada, and Mexico; and he negotiated the famous Gentlemen's Agreement with the Japanese government, putting an end to immigration from that source, except for the so-called "picture brides." These measures, however, did little to halt the tide of anti-Japanese prejudice. Hostile bills and resolutions were introduced in a number of state legislatures; California placed restrictions upon ownership of land by Japanese, and several other states followed her example. The culmination of the struggle came in 1924, when Congress passed a law barring the immigration of persons "ineligible for citizenship," which was intended, and interpreted, as a blow to the Japanese.

The Japanese have never been one of our large minorities, being greatly outnumbered by the Negro, Jewish, Mexican, and even the Indian groups. On the eve of World War II there were only 126,947 in the continental United States, two-thirds of whom, by virtue of their having been born on American soil, were citizens. They were concentrated, however, and this was a factor contributing to the misfortune they later suffered. At the outbreak of the war, forty-three percent of those gainfully employed

were in agriculture, more particularly in the production of vege-
tables and fruits for the local urban markets; twenty-three percent
were engaged in the wholesale and retail trade, chiefly the distribution of Japanese-grown products; seventeen percent were
employed in service industries—domestic service, cleaning and
dyeing, and the operation of hotels, barber shops, and restaurants;
and others owned stores or were engaged in the professions. In
these latter areas, as a result of discrimination and boycotts, the
patrons and clients were chiefly Japanese.

The attack upon Pearl Harbor gave the anti-Japanese forces
their great opportunity. They began to clamor for expulsion.
The Hearst newspapers took up the cry. Rumors of espionage and
sabotage began to circulate, entirely without foundation in fact,
for Japanese-Americans, both in Hawaii and in the United States,
have a clear record on that score. Lobbyists went to work, and
West Coast representatives in Congress recommended to the
President "the immediate evacuation of all persons of Japanese
lineage." Accordingly, the War Department was authorized in an
executive order to set up military areas and to exclude from such
areas any persons regarded as dangerous. Mr. Stimson, Secretary
of War, delegated this authority to General J. L. DeWitt, who
was commanding officer of the Western Defense Command.

The naive racial beliefs and prejudices of General DeWitt
are clearly manifested in his various public utterances, reports,
and his testimony before congressional committees. Said he, "The
Japanese race is an enemy race and while many second and third
generation Japanese born on United States soil, possessed of
United States citizenship, have become 'Americanized,' the racial
strains are undiluted." And he declared before the House Naval
Affairs Subcommittee that Japanese-Americans "are a dangerous
element, whether loyal or not. There is no way to determine their
loyalty. . . . It makes no difference whether he is an American;
theoretically he is still a Japanese, and you can't change him. . . .
You can't change him by giving him a piece of paper."

In a series of orders General DeWitt called for the evacuation
of all persons of Japanese ancestry from the area of the West
Coast. President Roosevelt, realizing that some agency other
than the army would be needed to perform the task of removal,
created the War Relocation Authority. At the outset, evacuation
was on a voluntary basis and some ten thousand did depart. But

it took money to leave, which many of them did not have; and those who did move suffered many unpleasant experiences. Many of them had substantial investments and businesses, and they could not bring themselves to believe that their rights as American citizens would be so lightly dismissed. The policy of voluntary evacuation, therefore, gave no promise of succeeding, and a shift to compulsory evacuation was made.

On the date fixed by the army all persons of Japanese lineage reported to control stations, whence they were escorted to improvised assembly centers—race tracks, fair grounds, parks, and pavilions. Within about four months more than one hundred thousand persons had been transferred to these centers and placed under guard. Next they were moved to the relocation camps, of which there were ten, situated in Utah, Arizona, California, Idaho, Wyoming, Colorado, and Arkansas. Here, housed in barracks and surrounded by barbed wire, the inmates carried on as best they could. Attempts were made to estimate the loyalty of the Japanese, and those found disloyal were shipped away to the camp at Tule Lake in California. As a matter of fact, the overwhelming majority of them gave every evidence of loyalty, and even most of those who, on the basis of tests, were classified as disloyal hardly deserved that stigma.[1]

Originally it was intended that these camps would become actual relocation centers, but the Japanese did not remain there long. Employers needed labor to meet the manpower shortage, and the evacuees were issued work permits and were assisted in finding jobs in various parts of the country outside the prohibited zone. Students were granted leave to attend college and high schools. Though the evacuees had been declared "ineligible for military service," this decision was rescinded in 1943, and thousands entered the army, where they distinguished themselves for their valor and where their knowledge of the Japanese language enabled them to play an indispensable role in the war as interpreters and intelligence officers. In 1944 the ban on their returning to the Pacific Coast was lifted; and in March, 1946, the last relocation center was closed. Many of the Japanese have returned

---

[1] G. Eleanor Kimble, "The 'Disloyal' at Tule Lake," *Common Ground*, Vol. VI, No. 2 (1946), pp. 74–81.

to their former homes, but large numbers of them have chosen to settle in other states, and start new lives.[2]

This mass expulsion of the Japanese from the West Coast has been called "our worst wartime mistake." In the first place, the necessity for their removal for reasons of national security had no basis in fact. There were enemy aliens of German and Italian extraction in the country at the same time who were not subjected to such treatment. While there were dangerous and disloyal persons among the Japanese, these were well known to the authorities, who had been checking on them for years, and they were promptly arrested at the beginning of the war. Other suspicious ones were under constant surveillance. General DeWitt's defense of his action, which he based upon "military necessity," "the threat of sabotage," [and] "the necessity of protecting the Japanese from the violence of mobs," is supported neither by reason, fact, nor subsequent developments.

In the second place, the injustice inflicted upon these hundred thousand persons was colossal. Neither the army nor the WRA was in a position to act as custodian for the property of the Japanese, who had to move with haste and who suffered great losses in the process. Radios and refrigerators were sold for a pittance, and cars were disposed of for a fraction of their value.[3] No estimate can be placed upon the intangible losses which the Japanese suffered—the businesses and professions, products of years of effort, which were wiped out, and the humiliation and shock which expulsion gave to their pride and status.

Finally, this treatment of persons holding American citizenship presents a threat to certain basic principles of our society. It involved a sweeping deprivation of citizens of their civil rights, and it was done on a racial basis. It dealt a blow to the sacred principle that men are presumed innocent until they are proved guilty, that all citizens stand on an equal footing before the law, regardless of race, color, or previous condition of servitude; and

---

[2] The social and economic losses suffered by the Japanese-Americans are documented convincingly in L. Bloom and Ruth Riemer, *Removal and Return.*

[3] B. Smith, "The Great American Swindle," *Common Ground,* Vol. VII, No. 2 (1947), pp. 34–38; "Legalized Blackmail," *Common Ground,* Vol. VIII, No. 2 (1948), pp. 34–36.

it came dangerously near upsetting the traditional principle of the subordination of the military to the civil authority. Eugene V. Rostow, Professor of Law at Yale University, gives the following estimate of the gravity of the affair:

> The original program of relocation was an injustice, in no way required or justified by the circumstances of the war. But the Supreme Court, in three extraordinary decisions, has upheld its main features as constitutional. This fact converts a piece of wartime folly into national policy—a permanent part of the law—a doctrine enlarging the power of the military in relation to civil authority. . . . As Mr. Justice Jackson has said, the principle of these decisions 'lies about like a loaded weapon ready for the hand of any authority that can bring forward a plausible claim of an urgent need.' All in all, the case of the Japanese-Americans is the worst blow our liberties have sustained in many years. Unless repudiated, it may support devastating and unforeseen social and political conflicts.[4]

*Ban the Japs!**

This excerpt presents a list of organizations which gave support to the campaign against Japanese-Americans in the 1940's. Included in the list are such organizations as the Oriental Exclusion League and the Ban the Japs Committee, as well as labor unions and veterans' organizations.

A detailed account of Japanese troubles on the West Coast would overflow a five-foot shelf. It is enough to say that in the spring of 1942, West Coast officials and the West Coast public had been conditioned for the drastic step of the evacuation, whether the Japanese were ready for it, or not.

---

[4]"Our Worst Wartime Mistake," *Harper's Magazine,* Vol. CXCI, No. 1144 (September, 1945), p. 194.

*Reprinted from *America's Concentration Camps* by Allan R. Bosworth, by permission of W. W. Norton and Company, Inc. Copyright © 1967 by Allan Bosworth.

It is not possible to say how much the West Coast attitudes contributed to the attack on Pearl Harbor and Tokyo's embarkation upon war in general. It is inarguable, however, that the Japanese were a proud and very capable race, with an ancient culture, and that the time was long past when one nation could insult another nation with impunity. Indeed, some of the discriminatory acts on the West Coast had threatened to bring on war much earlier. The 1906 San Francisco segregated school law, for instance, aroused great resentment in Tokyo, and was called "a wicked absurdity" by President Theodore Roosevelt in his annual message to Congress. Thomas A. Bailey quoted the President as telling his son, Kermit, "The infernal fools in California . . . insult the Japanese recklessly, and in the event of war it will be the nation as a whole that will pay the consequences."[1]

The school measure led directly to the Gentlemen's Agreement of 1907, by which the United States government limited emigration from Japan. This stirred up ill feeling because similarly limited quotas were not applied to European nations. California acted independently in 1913, with its Alien Land Law; Washington and Oregon followed suit. The *Hartford* [Connecticut] *Times* editorialized that "of the two it might be cheaper to go to war with California than with Japan."[2]

In 1923, Californians formed a congressional steering committee, opened a Washington office under V. S. McClatchy, and were active in obtaining passage of the Exclusion Act, which shut off immigration entirely. Again Japan felt insulted; again there was talk of war.

Much of this was probably emotional. Japan did not want to lose her people and made emigration difficult. But having the gates closed to Japanese was another matter. It called for face saving.

When war finally came, the pressure groups in California had been generally inactive for a decade, but they had not been disbanded. The following list includes some of the organizations that gave varying degrees of support to the campaign to evacuate or permanently get rid of the Japanese. Some were common to

---

[1] Theodore Roosevelt to his son, Kermit. Cited in Morton Grodzins, *Americans Betrayed* (Chicago: University of Chicago Press, 1949), p. 6.

[2] *Ibid.* Citing Syngman Rhee, *Japan Inside Out.*

the entire West Coast. The names are not in any way presented in the order of their importance:

Political groups: These included officeholders and office seekers, municipal, county, state, and federal. In California, 1942 was election year.

Oriental Exclusion League: In 1908, this group had claimed 110,000 members. It was exceptionally active in 1924.

Joint Immigration Committee: The McClatchy organization which supplanted the Oriental Exclusion League. Formed "temporarily" in 1923, it was active until at least 1941. It had been made up originally of representatives from the American Legion, the State Grange, the Federation of Labor, and the Native Sons of the Golden West.

Labor unions: Various and many.

Native Sons and Daughters of the Golden West: a social order, a lodge, a transplanted people's attempt to create a blue-blooded aristocracy out of the mere fact of California birth. It brought loud guffaws from those not eligible, and an irreverent wag wrote:

> The miners came in forty-nine,
> The whores in fifty-one;
> The two soon got together,
> And produced the Native Son.

The American Legion: The veterans who had fought to save democracy got off the track and dealt democracy some hard blows. The Legion canceled charters of posts made up of Japanese Americans who also fought for this country in 1917. Individual Legion councils and posts on the West Coast submitted more than thirty resolutions aimed at evacuating the Japanese. About half of these were worded so similarly as to suggest a directed pattern. Seconding many of the Legion's policies were some units of:

United Spanish War Veterans: who forgot that seven Japanese went down with the "Maine" and have their names inscribed at Arlington.

Disabled American Veterans: who would soon see hundreds of Nisei being disabled in Italy, France, and the Pacific.

Military Order of the Purple Heart: which later would have to acknowledge that the highest percentage of Purple Hearts ever won by any United States Army outfit was won by the Nisei of the 442nd Regimental Combat Team.

Veterans of Foreign Wars: who overlooked the fact that a considerable number of Nisei were already eligible to join their group.

There were others:

The Associated Farmers: composed of the big and corporate farmers, this group was especially active in the Central California Valley near Fresno and around Salinas.

California Farm Bureau Federation: which may owe its origin to the fact that in 1940 Japanese operated 5,135 farms in California, covering 226,094 acres. The average farm was valued at $16,300; the Japanese farms, usually much smaller, were valued at an average of $12,800. They grew forty-two percent of the state's commercial truck crops.

Western Growers' Protective Association: which apparently protected only Caucasions.

Grower-Shipper Vegetable Association of Central California: which did the same.

Los Angeles Chamber of Commerce: One of the most successful promotional enterprises in the world, it ultimately allowed racial bias to enter a program that had very ably plugged climate, economic growth, the movie industry, and the Los Angeles Harbor.

Clubs: Many and various. It is not meant to suggest that they were following any line laid down by their national organizations, but local groups of Lions Club, Elks Clubs, and—in California—Townsend Clubs went on record against the Japanese. Later, there were a number of "Ban the Japs Committees," "Anti-Japanese Leagues," "California Preservation League," "American Leagues," and the like. The "American Leagues" had nothing to do with baseball, but were designed to keep the Japanese from coming back to California at the end of the evacuation. Most bitterly active of all in this fight were the various Japanese Exclusion Leagues, formed all up and down the West Coast. With a membership consisting principally of farmers, these groups fought to keep the Japanese from returning and claiming their former lands.

A Personal Account of the Evacuation and Internment*

The following account of evacuation and imprisonment in the concentration camps is taken from an autobiography published in 1971. It provides some understanding of the emotional impact upon the victims of white racism, an impact that tends to be lost in the statistics of the two preceding selections.

In late August of 1942, under close military surveillance, the Okimoto family filed out of the sequestered compounds of Santa Anita Assembly Center, part of a large group of persons obediently boarding a nonscheduled train ready for a one-way trip to the wilderness of Arizona. After the last passenger stepped in, guards locked the doors and windows and the "Oriental Express" belched out black smoke as it rumbled toward Poston, Arizona, the largest of ten relocation centers scattered in seven states. Behind them the makeshift evacuation center was torn down even more rapidly than it had gone up, and passed into the pages of American history, forever a national disgrace.

The trip was long and monotonous; inside the crowded train it was painfully hot. The windows had been sealed tightly to prevent escape. The Okimoto baby, barely two weeks old, had trouble breathing and as the hours dragged on he appeared more dead than alive. Frantic, Kirie hurried through the train until she found a medical unit. They had an oxygen tent, and in this the child passed the remainder of the trip. Anguished thoughts ran through Kirie's mind that perhaps this "mistake" was not destined to live very long. Inside the plastic tent the child cried out incessantly. But the sound of screams growing more and more insistent was welcomed by the mother as a sign that he was still very much alive and that breathing was becoming easier. While in the oxygen tent the child contracted pneumonia, but it at least kept him alive.

Poston was a rude shock to many of the evacuees, whose sensitivities to the nuances of nature had been conditioned by the

---

*From Daniel I. Okimoto, "Exiles in the Promised Land," in *American in Disguise* (New York and Tokyo: Walker/Weatherhill, 1971).

green hills, verdant valleys, and richly flowering landscape of the West Coast. Poston stood on a sere desert plain through which the Colorado River snakes its way. In the same state that boasts the majesty of the Grand Canyon, Poston could claim little to redeem its existence: it was a wilderness of cactus and sweltering heat where dust storms swirled through at blinding speeds. On moonlit, still nights coyotes howled plaintively in the distance and even sagebrush hurried on through, as if the desolation were too great to endure.

On this flatland a vast area had been enclosed by barbed-wire fence. This was to be the home of most of the large, dispossessed band of Japanese for the duration of the war. The enclosure was divided into three distinct camps, each of which was subdivided into blocks where long, narrow barracks, each roughly one hundred feet by twenty-five, stretched out in neat, orderly lines, separated occasionally by firebreaks. The barracks were partitioned into four sections, each occupied by a family or group. The living quarters, measuring twenty-five by twenty-five feet, were uniformly drab, furnished only with straw mattresses; accessories such as shelves, closets, chairs, tables, and bookcases had to be built by the occupants themselves. The gray, tar-papered buildings within the demarcated zone, watched from lookout posts by green-garbed guards armed with rifles and machine guns, reflected the style of life within them: austere, barren, caged. To call these quarters a relocation center, as the government did, was plainly a euphemism. Internment camp—or if one chooses to be more descriptive, concentration or prisoner-of-war camp—came closer to capturing the essence of what Poston and similar centers represented.

Superficially at least, life within the camps went on as if little were out of the ordinary. There were no mass murders, no Auschwitz-like atrocities, no tortures; nor were there riots, rebellions, or sit-down strikes by the captives except at Tule Lake where people desiring repatriation and loyalty suspects had been placed. Neither was there any real resistance or nihilistic slothfulness; true to ethnic form, a strong sense of community helped the Japanese make the best of a bad situation.

The 20,000 internees at Poston went about their occupations with exemplary orderliness and purpose. Farmers grew food, carpenters repaired buildings, teachers ran classes, and doctors attended the sick. The area within the perimeter of the fences represented a self-sufficient community which for three years was the only world that existed for its inhabitants. It would have been difficult, judging from the prosaic pace of life inside, to suspect that outside the most devastating war in human history was being waged, and that the world of the camp and the world of war were somehow linked.

At Poston the Okimotos threw themselves busily into church work. On weekdays, after sending the older children off to school, they studied the Bible and meditated for the rest of the morning, then called on members of the congregation; on Sundays they conducted church services. Certainly for them internment did not seriously warp the routine of their daily lives or impair the effectiveness of their calling.

Before evacuation the Okimotos had lived in a church parsonage, owning no land and having very few personal belongings; they consequently sustained almost no financial loss by the change. Indeed, they may well have been among those few whose material livelihood actually improved as a result of internment. In San Diego, their home before the war, they collectively earned a salary of around $110 monthly; only careful spending enabled them to feed, clothe, and educate three growing children. In camp the family was fed in the communal dining halls and housed in the barracks. Unpalatable as both food and lodging seemed at times, there was nonetheless no lack of nutrition, and the rent was unbeatable.

Camp life also placed the missionary couple squarely in the midst of those people they had crossed the Pacific to serve. There could not have been a better opportunity to mingle with immigrants and their children; some of the friends made during the three years were among the closest they ever had. In camp they widened immensely their circle of acquaintances, deepened their own understanding of Japanese-American society, and in the process sharpened their effectiveness as ministers.

But even for the Okimotos—whose adjustment to Poston was probably among the least painful—internment still constituted in human and spiritual terms an ugly interlude. The three older children recall only too clearly the bafflement and fear they felt when they were jerked out of their playgrounds, marched onto trains by rifle-bearing soldiers, and interned in the middle of the desert with a colony of Japanese captives. No explanation for the federal action could be given to children in terms that were readily understandable. They could make no sense of the forced separation from their playmates. Nor could their minds grasp the reasoning that said their loyalties were to Japan rather than America. One child had never seen the country and the other two were too young to remember Japan.

Since they had done no wrong, the only way they could possibly interpret internment was to assume that they were being punished for being Japanese. Every Japanese, after all, was supposed to be bad; as they and their parents were Japanese, they too had to be locked up in concentration camps. The result of this assumption was that they grew to despise the Japanese part of themselves and to feel ashamed for being somehow related to a people who would dare strike so underhandedly at Americans. The psychological wounds went deep, leaving permanent scars that caused them to feel apologetic for their ethnicity. They were estranged from the mainstream of American life for some time. Even for the youngest child, spending the first three years of his life behind barbed-wire fences exclusively among his racial kind probably affected not only his basic feeling of trust but also in subtle, subconscious ways shaped what were to become his adult attitudes and whole sense of selfhood.

Even though on the surface activity went on as normal, the emotional substance of the lives of the interned was grotesquely distorted. Everything was rigidly regimented and monotonous: the same buildings, always the familiar surroundings, set hours for meals, regular routines, prescribed procedures, the next day the same as the one before. Daily existence was devoid of the pleasure of surprise; the greatest excitement each day—for some the only thing to look forward to—was mail delivery. A sense of ennui hung oppressively in the air. At times Rev. and Mrs. Okimoto felt envy for the coyotes calling in the distance, for at least they were not caged.

The Japanese in camps lived a life which, despite its material security and apparent normalcy, was fundamentally inhuman. Without freedom the years of confinement were largely wasted, barren, and spiritually brutal. Under these circumstances it is hardly surprising that unforeseen tensions invaded the lives of many inhabitants. The Okimotos' usual pattern of living was radically changed when the entire family was squeezed together in the same small room, separated only by a thin wall from the occupants of the neighboring unit. There everything a family said or did could be overheard and the most important question in life came to be: how much longer would one be trapped in the desert prison. Underlying tensions occasionally erupted into heated quarrels, emotional arguments, and petty bickering over trivia, straining relationships in the usually close Okimoto household.

It was hard for someone as proud as Tameichi to accept the armed patrols, the authoritarian commands, and the sense of helplessness without feeling deeply resentful. It was particularly frustrating that he, who had so firmly rejected Japanese militarism, should be held accountable for it in the United States. The sense of injustice was driven home when the government handed down a loyalty oath which he, like all Japanese over seventeen, either had to sign or face the Tule Lake camp and ultimate deportation. The coercion was humiliating evidence that by virtue of his race he was considered a traitor and a subversive, unless he swore in writing otherwise.

Tameichi managed largely to suppress his feelings at the time. Afterwards he blotted many of the most grating episodes out of his consciousness, seldom bringing the subject of internment up in conversation. But Poston came back to him periodically during sleep. Twenty-five years later Tameichi still would toss violently in his sleep and scream, "Let me out! Let me out of this concentration camp!" or, "We can't let them do this to us. We have our rights and we've got to stand up for them!"

But of the 117,000 Japanese interned, the hardest hit may have been those nisei, numerically two-thirds of the evacuated population, who were in their late adolescence and early adulthood. For them, incarceration meant at best an interruption of their college education and at worst an abrupt termination of it. College was for them not only an opportunity to deepen their understanding of life but also an indispensable means of acquiring specific vocational skills. The internment deprived this group of the freedom to choose its own careers. Many who aspired to better jobs were forced into gardening or garage work.

Most nisei nonetheless begged for a chance to prove their loyalty by serving in the armed forces. The federal government, however, classified all nisei as enemy aliens in June 1942, barring them from military service. The Japanese-American Citizens League (JACL) protested this measure and fought vigorously to have it changed. But JACL objections went unheeded until the shortage of manpower for the war became apparent. As the death tolls rose, it was decided finally to bestow upon Japanese-Americans the privilege of volunteering for "their country." In a statement that now sounds almost deliberately tongue-in-cheek, President Roosevelt said, "No loyal citizen of the United States should be denied the democratic right to exercise the responsibilities of his citizenship regardless of his ancestry." Spelled out concretely, this generous statement meant that nisei were to have the "democratic right" to die for the United States even if they were deprived of the equally basic right to live normally within its constitutional laws.

The choice put before the twenty-year-old Japanese-American was simple: either stay behind barbed wire for an indefinite period of time or go out into the battlefronts to fight for the country that had imprisoned him. Many of the nisei already in the services prior to Pearl Harbor had been hastily moved into innocuous, nonsecurity jobs or summarily discharged and placed in internment camps. Some had even been jailed on suspicion of treason and detained in military prisons on no more evidence than that of ancestry.

When interned nisei asked whether risking their lives would facilitate the release of their families, the government's answer was an unequivocal no. Nevertheless a large number of Japanese-Americans volunteered for the army. During the war a total of 25,778 Japanese-Americans served: 13,528 from the mainland and 12,240 from Hawaii. On January 20, 1944, with manpower exceedingly low, a draft call went out for all eligible nisei, many of whom were still in concentration camps. Out of those who had been locked up for over two years, only 300 refused to be inducted.

In the army the nisei were segregated in separate units, presumably to avoid problems that might arise in integrated groups. When nisei forces, like the 442nd Infantry Combat Team and the 100th Infantry Battalion, reached the European front, little question remained of their loyalties. Once in action these soldiers joined the ranks of the most decorated in the annals of U.S. military history. Their daring and heroism are legendary: in the Italian campaign alone the 100th Battalion won more than 1,000 Purple Hearts, eleven Distinguished Service Crosses, forty-four Silver Stars, thirty-one Bronze Stars, and three Legion of Merit Ribbons. It took immense violence and wartime valor and a staggering toll of over 9,000 casualties to do it, but the nisei fighters eventually won grudging acknowledgment of their loyalty from even the most hard-bitten racist skeptics.

Suggestions for Further Reading

1. Ping Chiu, *Chinese Labor in California, 1850–1880* (Madison State Historical Society of Wisconsin, 1963).

2. Mary Roberts Coolidge, *Chinese Immigration* (New York: Arno Press, 1969).

   This classic study was originally published in 1909.

3. Robert E. Cushman and Robert F. Cushman, *Cases in Constitutional Law* (New York: Appleton-Century-Crofts, Inc. 1952).

   This sourcebook contains explanations of and judicial opinions rendered in connection with cases in which Chinese and Japanese rights were being adjudicated. The removal of the Japanese in 1942 was upheld as constitutional by the United States Supreme Court in *Korematsu* v. *United States,* which is discussed on pages 128 ff.

4. Roger Daniels, *The Politics of Prejudice: The Anti-Japanese Movement in California and the Struggle for Japanese Exclusion* (Berkeley: University of California Publications in History, 1962).

5. Roger Daniels and Harry H. L. Kitano, *American Racism: Exploration of the Nature of Prejudice* (Englewood Cliffs, N.J.: Prentice-Hall, 1970).

   Among other features, contains several documents showing racism against Oriental-Americans.

6. Stuart Creighton Miller, *The Unwelcome Immigrant: The American Image of the Chinese, 1785–1882* (University of Colorado Press, 1969).

   Illustrates the fact that anti-Chinese attitudes were nationwide, not just confined to California.

Chapter Seven

Anti-Semitism in American Life

We Jews are standing now between outbreaks of open violence, as we stood between the various Crusades, as we stood between vampire trials and Black Death accusations, as we stood between the Count Rindfleisch campaign and the Hussite wars, as we stood between the Chmielnicki bloodbath and the Russian pogroms, as we stood between the Rumanian barbarism and the Nazi holocaust.

—DAGOBERT D. RUNES, *The War Against the Jew* (1968)

Dagobert Runes' belief that American Jews are just as vulnerable as ever to anti-Semitic rampages is a reflection of the dominant Jewish fear stemming from their role as the perennial scapegoat. Many American Jews feel that they are only a few steps removed from Negroes, Puerto Ricans, Indians, Mexican-Americans, and other ethnic minorities that happen presently to be a little lower in the pecking order of discrimination. Much of Jewish civil rights activism on behalf of other groups is really self-defense, for "When one man's rights are threatened, no man's rights are safe."

Periodically, studies are conducted which confirm Dr. Runes' belief. In 1969, for instance, the 63rd Annual Meeting of the American Jewish Committee heard its vice-president reveal preliminary findings which indicate that many errors, omissions, and misconceptions about American Jews are contained in junior high school textbooks. Some books foster outright prejudice. Also in 1969, the 56th Annual Meeting of the Anti-Defamation League of B'nai B'rith discussed a major study of contemporary anti-Semitism in the United States which was conducted by the Survey Research Center of the University of California. The study found "a sizable reservoir of anti-Semitic beliefs and stereotypes, wide acceptance of social club discrimination, and substantial susceptibility to political anti-Semitism."

"What is a Jew?" is a question that has produced some fascinating and confusing answers. Is he a member of a religious group? A nationality? An ethnic group? Is the Jew a member of a "race"? The Jewish experience in America has been influenced partly by the crystallization of a vague collection of myths and half-truths. Like the Indian, he is not Christian; like the eastern European and Oriental, he is not Anglo-Saxon. Politically, he is suspected of unhealthy affinities with radical movements; occupationally, he is caricatured as some sort of unscrupulous animal. The image of the Jew simply does not meld well with the Anglo-Saxon society.

Although Jewish contributions to American life are disproportionately large, Jews do not enjoy complete acceptance in this country. Perhaps it goes too far to attribute anti-Semitism in America to racism, but the fact that many bigots regard Jews as an inferior race does account for the nature of much anti-Semitic rhetoric.

Outsiders are convenient scapegoats. In America Jews are outsiders in more ways than one. They represent another imperfection in the Melting Pot.

*Racism in the Textbooks**

The omissions and distortions of history that have plagued minority groups are perpetuated most often by the textbooks used in schools. In the following article, the author discusses some of the particulars of this problem as it relates to the usual treatment of the role of Jews in American history.

---

*Jerome L. Ruderman, "The Jew in American History." Reprinted from the February 1972 issue of the *ADL* Bulletin, national publication of the Anti-Defamation League of B'nai B'rith.

In 1947, the Anti-Defamation League and the American Council on Education's Committee on the Study of Teaching Materials in Intergroup Relations published cooperatively a study entitled "Intergroup Relations in Teaching Materials." In 1961, ADL published a study on the treatment of minorities in secondary school textbooks. Last year, a similar ADL study reported that the treatment of Jews, though somewhat improved in the intervening ten years, is still inadequate.

The deficiencies of current textbooks with regard to Jews include: omission, indiscriminate identification of Jews, mere listing of Jewish contributions, and perpetuation of stereotypes which portray the Jews as a homogenous people or as a people inordinately subject to persecution and suffering.

The most obvious shortcoming is that of omission. But in attempting to redress the imbalance, some texts indiscriminately identify every individual who was a Jew as such, even though it may be irrelevant to an understanding of the man, his career, or his role in American history. Ethnic identification of an individual is desirable only when it is pertinent to the point under discussion. It is as important to discuss the failure of Jews to participate in colonial politics because of civil restrictions against them, as it is to applaud the patriotism of Haym Salomon during the Revolution. But merely listing a number of Jewish contributors for whatever purpose is of little value.

Topics in American Jewish history should be included in textbooks if, and only if, they illuminate developments and trends in American history generally. If this criterion were adopted, the treatment of minorities would cease to be an act of piety or a mere listing of contributions. Minority history would take its rightful place as one element capable of illuminating major trends, concepts, or processes in the social studies.

In the colonial and early national period, a number of themes suggest themselves. Before there were very many Jews in America, there was already a Hebrew presence in the form of the Old Testament. Judaism's legacy of monotheism, justice and morality are totally ignored in many American history texts, yet they were the basis of the Puritan theocracy and of early legal codes in Massachusetts as well as the close alliance of Church and State which characterized the government of the Bay Colony. The Puritans believed they had a covenant with God, as had the Israelites of the Old Testament. The exodus from Egypt in search of the Promised Land was taken as the prototype of that later exodus which brought the Pilgrims to the New World. The pious Quaker who inscribed on the Liberty Bell the famous words from Leviticus, Chapter 25, Verse 10, "Proclaim liberty throughout the land to all the inhabitants thereof," knew whereof he wrote. The Biblical emphasis on the supremacy of the Divine Law, was a valuable tool in the hands of people who were in revolt against the Crown of England.

The reception which the earliest Jews received in America was mixed and suggests a theme which continued well into the nineteenth century—that America has not always been a land of religious tolerance and equality. Separation of Church and State had to be achieved; it was not always there. Jews were welcomed in liberal colonies, such as Rhode Island, Pennsylvania, Georgia and South Carolina, which were not founded on exclusive adherence to one church. But they were excluded from those colonies that were. Zealous Massachusetts, for example, had no meaningful Jewish community before the Revolutionary War.

New Amsterdam reflects a compromise between both extremes, as Jews were compelled to struggle against local intolerance for almost every right granted them. Textbooks certainly ought not to present this as the struggle of the Jews, alone, but rather as the struggle of minorities among whom there were Jews, Quakers, Catholics, Lutherans and others.

The theme of religious intolerance can be further developed. The First Amendment to the Constitution which mandates religious liberty and prohibits the establishment of religion had its roots in the religious conflicts and persecution of dissidents which at times characterized Colonial life. Only three Jews were ever elected to any Continental assemblies or congresses. The Jewish experience in early America with its dual quality of acceptance and exclusion, as was true of other minorities also, helps to illustrate this theme.

During the era of the Revolutionary War, though numerically few, Jews were becoming visible. They participated in, fought in, and died in the same battles and campaigns as did other

Americans. There were Jewish Loyalists and there were Jewish Radicals. There was, even at this early date, no such thing as a typical American Jew. Some were ridden out of town by angry mobs, others were lauded for heroism in the Continental Army.

The next major topic that might be fruitfully incorporated into general accounts of American history, is the German Jewish migration of the mid-nineteenth century, which easily lends itself to a continuation of the themes of immigration and pluralism and also suggests the theme of America as a land of opportunity. In 1840, there were perhaps 15,000 Jews in America, mainly of Spanish and Portuguese origin. By 1880, the number had risen to 250,000, swelled by substantial numbers of Jewish immigrants from Germany.

The history of the German Jews may have possibilities in studying the larger scene—that of American economic development. These immigrants were, for the most part, quite poor. A few, however, managed to found what have since become some of the largest department stores in America. Examples are Altman's, Bloomingdale's, Macy's and Gimbel's. This achievement is not at all mysterious and helps to illustrate one facet of the development of American capitalism. When the history of these retail enterprises is studied, the picture that emerges is as follows. Many German Jewish immigrants to America became peddlers. After accumulating a bare minimum of capital, they became shopkeepers. The modern department store developed from these humble beginnings.

The Jewish community epitomizes the zeal with which groups in America have founded private, voluntary organizations, and the German Jewish immigrants largely inaugurated this development within the American Jewish community. Many of the congregations, schools, hospitals, free loan societies and defense organizations were founded by German Jewish immigrants or their immediate descendants. In some ways these institutions have served as models for other ethnic groups.

The Jewish population in America between 1880 and 1920 grew from a mere 250,000 to 3,500,000. The increase is accounted for largely by the immigration to America of 2,000,000 Jewish refugees from Russia and other parts of East Central Europe. The Eastern European Jews, unlike the German Jews before them, had few peddlers. The majority sought employment in shops and factories. The Russian Jewish immigrant settled in New York and a few other large Eastern cities and entered the needle trades in substantial numbers. The Jewish experience at this point offers material to illustrate two more important developments in modern American history—the process of urbanization and the development of the trade union movement, both of which illustrate the interaction between the resources an immigrant brings with him and the requirements and opportunities of his new environment.

I do not propose that these are the only opportunities suggested by American Jewish historical material, nor do I for one moment suggest that these themes and movements are to be illustrated by reference to the Jewish experience exclusively. On the contrary, it is because Jews have shared these experiences with many other groups and with the larger society that they have a valid place in the textbooks of American history.

*Jews as a Class**

The United States senator from New York points out the furor which accompanied General Grant's anti-Semitic decree. There is also some discussion of the twentieth-century scene.

As a result of Civil War tensions, discrimination against Jews, which had always persisted on a religious basis, now took on economic and social patterns. Several incidents during the war itself attracted nationwide attention. One issue arose in 1861 over the appointment of a Jewish chaplain to the armed forces. Although there were many thousands of Jewish servicemen in the Union ranks, the application was denied on the grounds that the act of Congress required chaplains to be "of a Christian denomination." Strong protests were registered from various parts

---

*From *Discrimination, U.S.A.,* © 1960, by Jacob Javits. Reprinted by permission of Harcourt, Brace & World, Inc.

of the country, but it took the personal intervention of President Abraham Lincoln himself to settle the problem amicably and satisfactorily. Subsequently, Lincoln appointed several rabbis as army chaplains.[1]

A much greater storm of controversy and protest was created when General Ulysses S. Grant issued General Orders No. 11, expelling "the Jews as a class" within twenty-four hours from the Department of Tennessee under his command. Despite the war in 1862, considerable trade was being carried on legally in the sale of Confederate cotton, which the northern industries needed, for gold, which the South needed. Many soldiers as well as civilians were involved in this speculation, which the military leaders vigorously opposed. Grant had made several efforts to stop it, and his previously issued instructions indicate that he blamed Jewish traders exclusively.[2]

Grant never explained his General Orders, in spite of considerable pressure. It created extreme hardships and aroused a furor across the country because of its sweeping anti-Jewish prejudice. The General Orders were issued on December 17, 1862, and revoked on direct command from President Lincoln by General in Chief of the Army Henry W. Halleck on January 4, 1863.

The controversy was revived in the presidential campaign of 1868, and several Jewish supporters of General Grant defended him against the charge of prejudice. During his term in office, General Grant never showed any sign of prejudice, and appointed Jews to high as well as minor offices on their merits. The fact that one of the leaders of the Confederacy was Judah P. Benjamin, himself Jewish, provided an easy way to defame all Jews in the South as well as in the North. He became the butt of many jokes, derogatory cartoons, and newspaper reports. Allegations that Jews controlled the money of the country by speculating in gold, and were seeking to control its economy, were made in some of the most respectable newspapers of the time. Jews were held to be responsible for every ill—for high prices, for shortages, for inflation, and for many of the problems of the country produced

---

[1] Bertram W. Korn, *American Jewry and the Civil War* (1951), pp. 56 ff.

[2] *Ibid*, pp. 121 ff.

by the war. In the Union Army and in the Army of the Confederacy, Jewish officers suffered because of the fact that they
were Jewish. The multiplicity of anti-Semitic incidents during
the war, however, should not obscure the fact that Jews were only
one of the many scapegoats who were blamed for wartime evils
and hardships.[3]

There had been earlier anti-Semitic episodes involving men
like Mordecai Manuel Noah and Commodore Uriah P. Levy, but
the wartime anti-Semitism brought aroused awareness to American Jews for the first time that this evil could exist in the United
States. It led to the establishment of the Board of American
Israelites to help combat anti-Semitism. But, most important, it
also led to the realization among some Jews that civil rights could
not be denied to any one group, such as Negroes, without affecting
the rights of all other groups.

Most intense interest was aroused in the summer of 1877
when Joseph Seligman, a prominent New York banker and a man
who had rendered distinguished service in helping the North
finance the Civil War, was refused accommodations for himself
and his family at the Grand Union Hotel in Saratoga Springs,
New York. Seligman's custom had been to spend his vacations
at this hotel for many years prior to this incident. In 1877, however, the hotel had been sold to Judge Henry Hilton, a prominent
New York political figure, and A. T. Stewart, a New York department store merchant and himself an Irish immigrant. Like Seligman, Stewart had come to the United States penniless, and
subsequently had risen to a position of wealth and prominence.

It was Judge Hilton, with Stewart's acquiescence, who actually issued the order denying Seligman accommodations at the
hotel. Indignation over the occurrence was widespread, and many
articles were written and sermons preached on this subject. The
fact that a man of such national prominence as Joseph Seligman
had been the victim of this kind of discrimination aroused the
indignation of Oliver Wendell Holmes, Henry Ward Beecher, Mark

---

[3] *Ibid*, pp. 158 ff.

Twain, and many others.[1] Today more than half our states have enacted public accommodation statutes which would prohibit such discrimination.

The Seligman case had its counterpart in many other areas of America's social life, and exposed a pattern of discrimination against Jews which still persists in some quarters. It is interesting to note that the large immigration from the 1880's to 1910 was not responsible for the outbreak of anti-Semitism, although agitators exploited the alien customs and mannerisms of the immigrants. Most Americans looked upon the newcomers with sympathy, and sincerely tried to be helpful in making it possible for them to become settled and productive Americans. Here, too, is an object lesson in how to deal better with the immigration of Puerto Ricans and Negroes to the great cities of the North.

Anti-Semitism did not become a serious danger to American liberty until the second decade of the twentieth century. Three outstanding instances highlight its rise as a social evil. The first was the lynching of Leo Frank in August, 1913, by a Georgia mob. Frank was a graduate of Cornell University and part owner and manager of a pencil factory in Marietta, Georgia. He was accused of assaulting and killing a fourteen-year-old girl who worked in the factory, and his trial was made the subject of the most vicious anti-Semitic propaganda ever heard in America up to that time. The unfortunate man, beaten by other prisoners, was taken from the prison hospital by a mob and hanged. Frank's innocence was established by careful investigation, but in the heated period of his trial, the sensational charges and the violence of language— and action—shocked the world.[5]

The aftermath of the First World War likewise saw widespread incidence of anti-Semitism. The revival of the Ku Klux Klan with its anti-Catholic, anti-Jewish prejudices was responsible in part, but perhaps most damaging was the vicious anti-Semitic campaign waged by Henry Ford through his newspaper, the

---

[1] Lee M. Friedman, *Jewish Pioneers and Patriots* (1942), pp. 271–77.

[5] Anita Libman Lebeson, *Pilgrim People* (1950) p. 397.

Dearborn Independent. For over seven years, beginning in 1920, this paper carried on a relentless campaign against Jews, in which it publicized numerous slanders and scurrilities. Among them was the *Protocols of the Elders of Zion,* a notorious forgery which British, Russian, and German anti-Semites had used extensively. Jews had to expose this fabricated document and formally deny its lies. Henry Ford, after being sued for libel, made a complete retraction and apologized for the false accusations made in his newspaper.[6] His heirs, led by Edsel and Henry Ford II, have shown their outstanding patriotism and freedom from any vestige of prejudice in countless outstanding public services, which have helped to bring about greater respect and justice for minorities in our country.

In the 1930's, under the impact of the rise of Hitlerism in Germany and the economic depression in the United States, anti-Semitism reached a frightening peak of virulence. Its manifestations touched every avenue of American activity and affected Jews in all walks of life. New barriers against Jews were raised in employment, housing, education, and social relations. A whole new breed of hatemongers was developed on the American scene who thrived on the spread of hate propaganda against Jews, then later against Catholics, Negroes, and other minority groups.

From 1933 onward, the word "Jew" appeared with increasing frequency—in the American press, over the radio, and on the speaker's platform. German propaganda had succeeded in making the United States more "Jew-conscious" than it had ever been. The radio sermons and publications of Father Charles E. Coughlin in 1939 whipped up emotions to fever pitch. Anti-Semitic groups multiplied all over the country, and the demagogues had a field day. Anti-Semitism became a factor in the American political scene, and there were dramatic scenes of attack and denunciation on the floor of Congress.[7]

But Americans reacted strongly against this uncontrolled outburst of bigotry and prejudice. Responsible American leaders issued sharp warnings against the consequences of hate-mongering, and the good sense of the American people quickly asserted itself. They realized that these evils were being spread deliberately by the Nazis and by their agents in this country as a means

---

[6] *Ibid,* pp. 385–86.

[7] *American Jewish Yearbook,* XLII, 284–90.

of dividing and weakening our country. This led to the rapid decline of the anti-Semitic groups and the recognition that the fight against religious and racial prejudice and discrimination affected not only specific minority groups but the whole national interest.

Neither racial prejudice nor anti-Semitism or other religious bias has ever been considered a respectable activity in the United States. More recently, the hate movements which have fed on the emotions aroused by the movement to desegregate have ebbed and flowed but have not been able to find a fixed place in the American body politic. Bigotry—organized and unorganized— has always been something of which the people were ashamed and which was indulged in surreptitiously when it could not be suppressed entirely. Our country's political maturity and its rise to the leadership of the free world have intensified the fight against bigotry and the manifestations of discrimination wherever they may appear. In our history, we have tried in many ways to overcome this weakness in our democracy, and there may be no one formula which can cure it. But it is a fact that our country has fought and generally overcome much of the grave prejudice against Quakers, Catholics, Jews, and other religious noncon- formists; against Irishmen, Poles, Chinese, Japanese, Greeks, Italians, Levantines, and others of different national origins. It is still fighting serious prejudice against Negroes, Indians, and those of Puerto Rican and Mexican extraction. That fight will go on until all Americans enjoy equally the opportunities and re- sponsibilities of our democracy without regard to race, creed, or national origin. This is the assurance of our freedom: that the denial of equality of opportunity will not be accepted as the norm in fact or in law.

*Recent Trends**

Beginning with the late nineteenth century, the author discusses var- ious examples of anti-Semitism, including Henry Ford's Dearborn Inde- pendent *and the* Protocols of the Elders of Zion. *Sachar takes us up through the 1950's, relating anti-Semitism to racist currents of the time.*

---

*Reprinted by permission of The World Publishing Company from *The Course of Modern Jewish History* by Howard M. Sachar. Copyright © 1958 by Howard M. Sachar.

   As late as 1880 it did not appear as if the American-Jewish community needed to give more than nominal attention to the problem of anti-Semitism. It was true that a distorted image of Jews existed in many American minds—the image of the German-Jewish peddler with the thick accent, hooked nose, and derby hat. But such a stereotype seemed hardly more offensive than the stage symbol of the drunken Irishman, the chicken-pilfering Negro, or the parsimonious Yankee. The caricature became somewhat less casual a decade later, in the era of the greenback and free silver movements, and the agrarian Populist revolt. During the 1890's the hated money changer, the manipulator of hard currencies, was often associated with such prominent Jewish financiers as the Levis, the Montefiores, the Rothschilds—or, in America, the Belmonts and the Lehmans. The hard-pressed Protestant farmer did not find it difficult to believe that the Jews were members of a "great international conspiracy" to prevent cheap money from reaching the market, and to keep American farm families in chronic debt. When men like Governor Tom Watson of Georgia and William Jennings Bryan of Nebraska drew attention to the "mysterious, invisible money powers" of the world, they unwittingly lent credence to the emergent Jewish stereotype of a "Shylock" or "octopus" of the world's finances. *Caesar's Column,* a Utopian novel written in 1890 by the Populist Ignatius Donnelly, painted a vivid picture of the future domination of Europe by "the Israelites, the great money-getters of the world who rose from dealers in old clothes and peddlers of hats to merchants, to bankers, to princes." The novel's ominous reference to "international Judaism" was lent verification, in some minds, by the Zionist Congress in Basel in 1897.

   Yet the attitude toward the Jews of most Americans was, at the worst, merely vague suspicion; men like Donnelly still spoke primarily for the lunatic fringe of American life. The first serious change came with the spectacular growth of America's cities after the turn of the century. The rise of the American "Mammon" was a terrifying phenomenon for southern and midwestern farmers, people who found their credit and markets, their very livelihoods, governed by far-off metropolises. Bryan expressed their fear in his description of "Babylon the great, the mother of the harlots and of the abominations of the earth . . . drunken with the blood of the saints, and with the blood of the martyrs of Jesus." The cities were filled with more than harlots and dance halls, however, more than bankers and creditors. After 1900 they were filled with foreigners, with immigrants speaking strange tongues, worshiping the Pope in cathedrals, or denying the Trinity in synagogues. In time, it was primarily the Jew whom rural Americans identified with the city. Returning to the United States in 1907, as civilized and cultivated a person as Henry James could profess shock at the "Hebrew conquest of New York," which, he insisted, was transforming that city into a "new Jerusalem." To rural Americans, every Jewish storekeeper was the advance guard of the new commercial civilization, and bore the standard of the dread forces that threatened their security.

This suspicion was buttressed by a recrudescent race doctrine which made its appearance in the United States early in the twentieth century: the theory that men were divided into biological breeds, each incapable of "wholesome" fusion with the other. In the South the doctrine had long been applied to Negroes, and on the Pacific Coast to Orientals; and now, for the first time, it was applied to the "alien" Slavic-Jewish-Italian "islands" in the East. Prescott Hall and William Z. Ripley professed grave concern that the "Anglo-Saxon breed" was about to be inundated by the "hordes" of the big cities. Their fears were given even more "respectable" literary formulation when the writings of Count de Gobineau and Houston Stewart Chamberlain began to reach the United States. By 1914 increasing numbers of Americans were conditioned to the view that the Jews were as a race apart, members of the "Semitic" as distinguished from the "Aryan" race. Even such distinguished intellectuals as John R. Commons, Edward A. Ross, and Henry Pratt Fairchild misapplied sociological and anthropological terminology to urge that society be structured along sound "eugenic" lines; in this manner, they explained, Anglo-Saxons would avoid admixture with "inferior" breeds. The weird pseudoscience of eugenics was widely popularized by Alfred P. Schultz's *Race or Mongrel?* (1908), and Madison Grant's *The Passing of the Great Race* (1916)—two of the most colorful and effective apologias for Anglo-Saxon superiority. By 1920 an influential minority of Americans had swallowed whole the notion that the "great American race" was in danger of permanent contamination by Negroes, Latins, Slavs, and Jews.

These racist fantasies were intensified by the isolationism and xenophobia that followed the First World War. The high tariffs, the virulent nationalism, the rejuvenated religious fun-

damentalism of the 1920's, the revival of Ku Klux Klan terroriza-
tion in Catholic and Jewish neighborhoods of the South and
Midwest—all were merely the outward manifestations of a deeply
rooted fear of contamination by alien ideas. Certainly the most
sinister of those imported ideas was "bolshevism"—or "anarchism"
or "syndicalism": they were all of a piece in the mind of the typical
provincial American. "Once lead this people into war," Woodrow
Wilson had predicted, "and they'll forget there ever was such a
thing as tolerance." Wilson's attorney-general, A. Mitchell Palmer,
now proceeded to justify this prediction by conducting a series of
lawless raids on private houses and labor headquarters, rounding
up thousands of aliens, holding them incommunicado, and subject-
ing them to drumhead interrogations. Even the courts bowed
before the wind, construing the wartime Espionage and Sedition
Acts with inflexible harshness. It was the age of the Sacco-Van-
zetti case, of an unreasoning fear of radicalism, of antipathy to
foreigners, and especially of antipathy to Jews, who, after all,
came from the land of the Bolshevik Revolution, and who were
hardly conservative in their own political and economic orientation.

Into all of these combustible elements there was now dropped
an evil little pamphlet which had originally been circulated
throughout Eastern Europe and Germany as a calculated means
of promoting Jew-hatred. The *Protocols of the Elders of Zion*
first appeared in 1905, as an addendum to a hopelessly confused
religious tract written by Serge Nilus, a czarist civil servant.
According to Nilus, the wise men of Zion had entered into a
"secret" plot to enslave the Christian world. The leaders of the
Jewish world government, who were variously identified as the
chiefs of the twelve tribes of Israel and the leaders of world Zion-
ism, planned to employ the institutions of liberalism and socialism
to ensnare and befuddle the simple-minded "goyim." In the event
of discovery, the Jewish elders apparently had made plans for
blowing up all the capitals of Europe. The implication was plain:
that resistance to liberalism and socialism was vital if the world
was to be rescued from a malevolent Jewish conspiracy.

In 1921 the London *Times* exposed the *Protocols* as a crude
forgery of a lampoon on Napoleon III, written as far back as 1864.
Notwithstanding the exposure, it was in the interest of reaction-

aries everywhere to promote the circulation of the Nilus pamphlet. In the United States, Boris Brasol, a czarist *émigré*, persuaded a group of American business leaders, among them the motor magnate Henry Ford, to publicize the *Protocols*. Ford was a capable enough manufacturer; but his understanding of world affairs was astonishingly limited, and even more profoundly illiberal and bigoted. For several years his private newspaper, the *Dearborn Independent*, quoted liberally from the *Protocols*, and issued repeated warnings against the "Jewish menace." Not until 1927, when a Jewish attorney, Aaron Sapiro, brought a libel suit against the *Dearborn Independent*, did Ford repudiate his anti-Semitism and issue a public apology.

The confluence of all these factors—American provincialism, rural suspicion of the cities, the eugenics theory, the fear of alien radicalism, even, perhaps, the *Protocols of the Elders of Zion*— had its cumulative impact. It was felt not simply in the steady growth of the Ku Klux Klan, nor even in the anti-immigration legislation of 1921 and 1924 which closed America's doors to the fugitives of southeastern Europe; it was felt, too, in the adoption of nationwide Jewish "quotas" by colleges and professional societies. In 1922 President Abbott Lawrence Lowell of Harvard gave these quotas "respectability" when he sought openly to introduce them at his own institution. Similarly, medical and law schools began limiting the admission of Jews to a small fractional percentage of the total enrollment. Eventually employment agencies and large corporations adopted the same practice. Soon the exclusionist policy was extended into the field of housing. Through voluntary covenants of real estate owners, large areas of many cities were abruptly closed to persons of "Hebrew descent."

During the depression period, anti-Semitism proved to be a ready-made defense for some of the bigoted vested interests that feared "that man" Franklin Roosevelt's sweeping social reforms. A number of demagogic politicians, most of them the hired spokesmen for large industrial concerns, stigmatized the New Deal as the "Jew Deal," and identified trade unionism with "Jewish bolshevism." Scores of organizations—the Silver Shirts, the Khaki Shirts, the Militant Christian Patriots, the Green Mountain Boys, and others—many of them creations of cranks and rabble-rousers, but some of them financed by well-known corporations, drenched the United States with an avalanche of appeals to racial and religious hate. Fingers were pointed at the unusual numbers of Jews in Washington, and especially the Jews close to Roosevelt. Even such respected figures as Theodore Dreiser, Representative Louis T. McFadden of Pennsylvania, the eloquent Catholic priest Father Charles Coughlin of Detroit, and the national hero Charles Lindbergh attacked the Jews variously as radicals, international bankers, Reds, materialists, or warmongers.

During the late 1930's American anti-Semitism was given further direction and financial support by Nazi Germany. Hitler's most dependable agents in this campaign were German-Americans, many of them recent immigrants to the United States, veterans of the kaiser's army, and now ardent partisans of the Third Reich. The Nazi propaganda bureau supplied them with organizational leadership, funds, and endless quantities of uniforms, insignia, and propaganda literature. In 1934 many of America's German culture *vereins* were reorganized and centralized in the German-American Bund. Under the successive leadership of Heinz Spanknoebel, Fritz Gissible, Fritz Kuhn, and Wilhelm Kunze, the Bund set about popularizing the doctrine of Hitler's New Order. Of course, anti-Semitism was the most convenient propaganda device of all. The Nazis contributed large sums of money to nativist "hate" groups. They shrilled their anti-Semitic slogans at mass meetings in Madison Square Garden and at the Philadelphia Municipal Stadium. Anti-Semitic literature was distributed to the American team as it departed for the Berlin Olympic Games in 1936. German-born professors frequently served as Nazi agents on university campuses.

Despite the many sewers from which the filth flowed, it is doubtful if the systematic "hate" campaign made a significant impact except on those who were already inclined to anti-Semitism. For the most part, the coverage given by the American press to Nazi barbarism in Europe effectively counteracted the efforts of paid German propagandists in America. It was, in fact, the appropriation of the anti-Semitic movement by the Nazi which ultimately doomed organized Jew-hatred in the United States. When American went to war against Hitler, anti-Semitism at last became clearly identified in the public mind with an alien and subversive ideology. After 1945, organized American anti-Semitism made little significant headway. For one thing, the economic boom of the postwar era left few racial tensions for hate groups to exploit. Most Americans, too, were deeply moved by the courageous struggle of the Jews, as "underdogs," to win statehood for themselves in Israel. They were impressed by Israeli military valor, and by the new Israeli Republic's devotion to the democratic way of life. Moreover, the rise of a Jewish sovereign state endowed the Jews with standing in the eyes of the Christian world; they were no longer "gypsies," begging crumbs of hospitality from others. The B'nai B'rith Anti-Defamation League was able to report, in 1950, that anti-Semitism in America had fallen to an "all-time" low. Yet it is doubtful if Jew-hatred, even at its peak, was ever a major threat to the essential security of the Jewish community in the United States. The problem was rather one of Jewish social acceptance—the opportunity of Jews to gain entrance to colleges, legal and professional societies, restricted areas of employment, exclusive neighborhoods. These were unfortunate survivals which were not to be easily eliminated even with the lifting of depression or the termination of war. But they were mainly in the category of irritants. They were not really an overwhelming menace to the security of the American-Jewish community.

*Populism and Anti-Semitism**

Anti-Semitic rhetoric of Populist spokesmen is exposed in this selection which draws some careful distinctions in terminology.

One feature of the Populist conspiracy theory that has been generally overlooked is its frequent link with a kind of rhetorical anti-Semitism. The slight current of anti-Semitism that existed in the United States before the 1890's had been associated with

*From *The Age of Reform*, by Richard Hofstadter. © Copyright 1955 by Richard Hofstadter. Reprinted by permission of Alfred A. Knopf, Inc.

problems of money and credit.[1] During the closing years of the
century it grew noticeably.[2] While the jocose and rather heavy-
handed anti-Semitism that can be found in Henry Adam's letters
of the 1890's shows that this prejudice existed outside Populist
literature, it was chiefly Populist writers who expressed that
identification of the Jew with the usurer and the "international
gold ring" which was the central theme of the American anti-
Semitism of the age. The omnipresent symbol of Shylock can
hardly be taken in itself as evidence of anti-Semitism, but the
frequent references to the House of Rothschild make it clear that
for many silverites the Jew was an organic part of the conspiracy
theory of history. Coin Harvey's Baron Rothe was clearly meant
to be Rothschild; his Rogasner (Ernest Seyd?) was a dark figure
out of the coarsest anti-Semitic tradition. "You are very wise in
your way," Rogasner is told at the climax of the tale, "the commercial way, inbred through generations. The politics, scheming,
devious way, inbred through generations also."[3] One of the cartoons in the effectively illustrated *Coin's Financial School* showed
a map of the world dominated by the tentacles of an octopus at the
site of the British Isles, labeled: "Rothschilds." [4] In Populist de-
monology, anti-Semitism and Anglophobia went hand in hand.

---

[1]Anti-Semitism as a kind of rhetorical flourish seems to have had
a long underground history in the United States. During the panic of
1837, when many states defaulted on their obligations, many of which
were held by foreigners, we find Governor McNutt of Mississippi defending the practice by baiting Baron Rothschild: "The blood of Judas
and Shylock flows in his veins, and he unites the qualities of both his
countrymen...." Quoted by George W. Edwards: *The Evolution of
Finance Capitalism* (New York, 1938), p. 149. Similarly we find Thaddeus Stevens assailing "the Rothschilds, Goldsmiths, and other large
money dealers" during his early appeal for greenbacks. See James A.
Woodburn, *The Life of Thaddeus Stevens* (Indianapolis, 1913), pp. 576,
579.

[2]See Oscar Handlin, "American Views of the Jews at the Opening
of the Twentieth Century," *Publications of the American Jewish Historical Society,* No. 40 (June, 1951), pp. 323–44.

[3]Harvey, *A Tale of Two Nations*, p. 289; cf. also p. 265: "Did not
our ancestors ... take whatever women of whatever race most pleased
their fancy?"

[4]Harvey, *Coin's Financial School* (Chicago, 1894), p. 124. For a
notable polemic against the Jews, see James B. Goode, *The Modern
Banker* (Chicago, 1896), chap. xii.

The note of anti-Semitism was often sounded openly in the campaign for silver. A representative of the New Jersey Grange, for instance, did not hesitate to warn the members of the Second National Silver Convention of 1892 to watch out for political candidates who represented "Wall Street, and the Jews of Europe."[5] Mary E. Lease described Grover Cleveland as "the agent for Jewish bankers and British gold."[6] Donnelly represented the leader of the governing council of plutocrats in *Caesar's Column*, one Prince Cabano, as a powerful Jew, born Jacob Isaacs. One of the triumvirate who lead the Brotherhood of Destruction is also an exiled Russian Jew, who flees from the apocalyptic carnage with a hundred million dollars which he intends to use to "revive the ancient splendors of the Jewish race, in the midst of the ruins of the world."[7] One of the more elaborate documents of the conspiracy school traced the power of the Rothschilds over America to a transaction between Hugh McCulloch, Secretary of the Treasury under Lincoln and Johnson, and Baron James Rothschild. "The most direful part of this business between Rothschild and the United States Treasury was not the loss of money, even by hundreds of millions. It was the resignation of the country itself *into the hands of England,* as England had long been resigned into the hands of *her Jews.*"[8]

---

[5] *Proceedings of the Second National Silver Convention* (Washington, 1892), p. 48.

[6] Mary E. Lease, *The Problem of Civilization Solved,* pp. 319–20; cf. p. 291.

[7] Donnelly, *op. cit.,* pp. 147, 172, 331.

[8] Gordon Clark, *op. cit.,* pp. 59–60, for the linkage between anti-Semitism and the conspiracy theme, see pp. 2, 4, 8, 39, 55–8, 102–3, 112–13, 117. There was a somewhat self-conscious and apologetic note in populistic anti-Semitism. Remarking that "the aristocracy of the world is now almost altogether of Hebrew origin," one of Donnelly's characters explains that the terrible persecutions to which the Jews had been subjected for centuries heightened the selective process among them, leaving "only the strong of body, the cunning of brain, the long-headed, the persistent . . . and now the Christian world is paying, in tears and blood, for the sufferings inflicted by their bigoted and ignorant ancestors upon a noble race. When the time came for liberty and fair play the Jew was master in the contest with the Gentile, who hated and feared him." *Caesar's Column,* p. 37. In another fanciful tale Donnelly made amends to the Jews by restoring Palestine to them and making it very prosperous. *The Golden Bottle* (New York and St. Paul, 1892), pp. 280–81.

Such rhetoric, which became common currency in the movement, later passed beyond populism into the larger stream of political protest. By the time the campaign of 1896 arrived, an Associated Press reporter noticed as "one of the striking things" about the Populist convention at St. Louis "the extraordinary hatred of the Jewish race. It is not possible to go into any hotel in the city without hearing the most bitter denunciation of the Jews as a class and of the particular Jews who happen to have prospered in the world."[9] This report may have been somewhat overdone, but the identification of the silver cause with anti-Semitism did become close enough for Bryan to have to pause in the midst of his campaign to explain to the Jewish Democrats of Chicago that in denouncing the policies of the Rothschilds he and his silver friends were "not attacking a race; we are attacking greed and avarice which know no race or religion."[10]

It would be easy to misstate the character of Populist anti-Semitism or to exaggerate its intensity. For Populist anti-Semitism was entirely verbal. It was a mode of expression, a rhetorical style, not a tactic or a program. It did not lead to exclusion laws, much less to riots or pogroms. There were, after all, relatively few Jews in the United States in the late 1880's and early 1890's, most of them remote from the area of Populist strength. It is one thing, however, to say that this prejudice did not go beyond a certain symbolic usage, quite another to say that a people's choice of symbols is of no significance. Populist anti-Semitism does have its importance—chiefly as a symptom of a certain ominous credulity in the Populist mind. It is not too much to say that the Greenback-Populist tradition activated most of what we have of modern popular anti-Semitism in the United States.[11] From Thaddeus Stevens and Coin Harvey to Father Coughlin, and from Brooks and Henry Adams to Ezra Pound, there has been a curiously persistent link-

[9] Quoted by Edward Flower, *Anti-Semitism in the Free Silver and Populist Movements and the Election of 1896* (Unpublished M.A. thesis, Columbia University, 1952), p. 27; this essay is illuminating on the development of anti-Semitism in this period and on the reaction of some of the Jewish press.

[10] William Jennings Bryan, *The First Battle* (Chicago, 1897), p. 581.

[11] I distinguish here between popular anti-Semitism, which is linked with political issues, and upper-class anti-Semitism, which is a variety of snobbery. It is characteristic of the indulgence which populism has received on this count that Carey McWilliams in his *A Mask*

age between anti-Semitism and money and credit obsessions. A full history of modern anti-Semitism in the United States would reveal, I believe, its substantial Populist lineage, but it may be sufficient to point out here that neither the informal connection between Bryan and the Klan in the twenties nor Thomas E. Watson's conduct in the Leo Frank case were altogether fortuitous.[12] And Henry Ford's notorious anti-Semitism of the 1920's, along with his hatred of "Wall Street," were the foibles of a Michigan farm boy who had been liberally exposed to Populist notions.[13]

Suggestions for Further Reading

1. Stephen Birmingham, *Our Crowd: The Great Jewish Families of New York* (New York: Harper & Row, 1967).
   Pages 143–148 contain a detailed description of the Seligman-Hilton affair.

2. Raymond J. Cunningham (ed.), *The Populists in Historical Perspective* (Boston: D. C. Heath and Company, 1968).

---

for Privilege: Anti-Semitism in America (Boston, 1948) deals with early American anti-Semitism simply as an upper-class phenomenon. In his historical account of the rise of anti-Semitism he does not mention the Greenback Populist tradition. Daniel Bell, "The Grass Roots of American Jew Hatred," *Jewish Frontier*, XI (June, 1944). 15–20, is one of the few writers who has perceived that there is any relation between latter-day anti-Semites and the earlier Populist tradition. See also Handlin, *op. cit.* Arnold Rose has pointed out that much of American anti-Semitism is intimately linked to the agrarian myth and to resentment of the ascendancy of the city. The Jew is made a symbol of both capitalism and urbanism, which are themselves too abstract to be satisfactory objects of animosity. *Commentary*, VI (October, 1948), 374–78.

[12] For the latter see Woodward, *Tom Watson, chap. xxiii.*

[13] Keith Sward: *The Legend of Henry Ford* (New York, 1943), pp. 83–84, 113–14, 119–20, 132, 143–60. Cf. especially pp. 145–46. "Ford could fuse the theory of populism and the practice of capitalism easily enough for the reason that what he carried forward from the old platforms of agrarian revolt, in the main, were the planks that were most innocent and least radical. Like many a greenbacker of an earlier day, the publisher of the *Dearborn Independent* was haunted by the will-o'-the-wisp of 'money' and the bogy of 'race.' It was these superstitions that lay at the very marrow of his political thinking." For further illustrations of the effects of the Populist tradition on a Mountain State senator, see Oscar Handlin's astute remarks on Senator Pat McCarran in "The Immigration Fight Has Only Begun," *Commentary*, XIV (July, 1952), 3–4.

This anthology contains two essays which criticize Hofstadter's thesis on populism and anti-Semitism. They are "A Critique of the Hofstadter Thesis," by Norman Pollack, and "Kansas Populism: A Case Study," by Walter T. K. Nugent.

3. Leonard Dinnerstein (ed.), *Anti-Semitism in the United States* (New York: Holt, Rinehart and Winston, 1971).

Bibliography at the end of the collection is very useful.

4. Benjamin R. Epstein and Arnold Forster, *Some of My Best Friends* (New York: Farrar, Straus and Cudahy, 1959).

Subtle forms of anti-Semitism are discussed by the famous team of Anti-Defamation League writers.

5. Abraham J. Karp (ed.), *The Jewish Experience in America,* 5 vol. (New York: American Jewish Historical Society, 1969).

6. Carey McWilliams, *Brothers Under the Skin* (Boston: Little, Brown and Company, 1951).

Chapter Nine contains a provocative discussion of the nature of anti-Semitism. One of the issues dealt with is the degree of racism embodied in anti-Semitism.

7. Gustavus Myers, *History of Bigotry in the United States* (New York: Capricorn Books, 1960).

8. Dagobert D. Runes, *The War Against the Jew* (New York: Philosophical Library, 1968).

This book is an alphabetical compendium of terms relating to anti-Semitic incidents in western Europe rather than America. However, its introduction deals with the role of the church and scripture in fostering anti-Semitic attitudes and is quite relevant for the American scene.

9. Charles Herbert Stember et al., *Jews in the Mind of America* (New York: Basic Books, 1966).

One of the many attractive features of this volume is an article by John Higham, "American Anti-Semitism Historically Reconsidered."

Chapter Eight

Other Ethnic Minorities: Immigration and Discrimination

The notion that the intense and unprecedented mixture of ethnic and religious groups in American life was soon to blend into a homogeneous end product has outlived its usefulness, and also its credibility. In the meanwhile the persisting facts of ethnicity demand attention, understanding, and accommodation. The point about the Melting Pot . . . is that it did not happen.

—NATHAN GLAZER and
DANIEL PATRICK MOYNIHAN,
Beyond the Melting Pot (1963)

There is not sufficient space in a single volume to present a complete record of racism and discrimination as they affected each of the dozens of minorities in American history. However, this chapter seeks to broaden the focus somewhat by presenting just a few samples of problems in ethnic relations that lie outside realms treated elsewhere in this book.

It would be misleading to characterize all anti-immigrant discrimination as WASP versus outgroup. There were and still are examples of important interethnic and intra-ethnic rivalries. Many ethnic rivalries are compounded with social-status rivalry or economic competition. It is not always the nativist majority which has erected barriers to those who wanted to assimilate, or which has become irritated when assimilation was shunned by the minority itself.

Older minorities, such as Italian, Polish, and Irish, have been absorbed quite well into the American mainstream, but only after considerable difficulty. But more recent arrivals have not yet fared as well, generally speaking. Recent examples of interethnic competition can be seen in black anti-Semitism and Jewish racism in New York and Mexican–black rivalries in the ghettos of the Southwest. Earlier examples are the Irish opposition to Chinese in California and the "old" versus "new" immigration. Intra-ethnic rivalries are not uncommon. Successful flights from urban ghettos create a division between middle-class and grass-roots members of a minority. Earlier in our history German Jews resented Russian Jews.

As the civil rights movement of the 1950's was transformed into the Black Power movement of the 1960's, other minorities began to register more militant forms of protest against the Majority values that were being imposed upon them, and against the discrimination they experienced as a result of being "different." By the 1970's, America was in the middle of one big human liberation movement with many aspects: gay liberation, women's liberation, Chicano and Puerto Rican liberation, Indian liberation, black liberation, and many others.

For discussion of some of these developments, see Part 5.

Ethnic Groups and the Melting Pot *

This selection contains a discussion of the importance of ethnicity in New York City and its relationship to the Melting Pot theory.

Perhaps the meaning of ethnic labels will yet be erased in America. But it has not yet worked out this way in New York. It is true that immigrants to this country were rapidly transformed, in comparison with immigrants to other countries, that they lost their languages and altered their culture. It was reasonable to believe that a new American type would emerge, a new

*Reprinted from *Beyond the Melting Pot* by Nathan Glazer and Daniel P. Moynihan by permission of The M.I.T. Press, Cambridge, Massachusetts. Copyright © 1963 by The M.I.T. Press.

nationality in which it would be a matter of indifference whether a man was of Anglo-Saxon or German or Italian or Jewish origin, and in which indeed, because of the diffusion of populations through all parts of the country and all levels of the social order, and because of the consequent close contact and intermarriage, it would be impossible to make such distinctions. This may still be the most likely result in the long run. After all, in 1960 almost half of New York City's population was still foreign-born or the children of foreign-born. Yet it is also true that it is forty years since the end of mass immigration, and new processes, scarcely visible when our chief concern was with the great masses of immigrants and the problems of their "Americanization," now emerge to surprise us. The initial notion of an American Melting Pot did not, it seems, quite grasp what would happen in America. At least it did not grasp what would happen in the short run, and since this short run encompasses at least the length of a normal lifetime, it is not something we can ignore.

It is true that language and culture are very largely lost in the first and second generations, and this makes the dream of "cultural pluralism"—of a new Italy or Germany or Ireland in America, a League of Nations established in the New World—as unlikely as the hope of a Melting Pot. But as the groups were transformed by influences in American society, stripped of their original attributes, they were recreated as something new, but still as identifiable groups. Concretely, persons think of themselves as members of that group, with that name; they are thought of by others as members of that group, with that name; and most significantly, they are linked to other members of the group by new attributes that the original immigrants would never have recognized as identifying their group, but which nevertheless serve to mark them off, by more than simply name and association, in the third generation and even beyond.

The assimilating power of American Society and culture operated on immigrant groups in different ways, to make them, it is true, something they had not been, but still something distinct and identifiable. The impact of assimilating trends on the groups is different in part because the groups are different—Catholic peasants from southern Italy were affected differently, in the same city and the same time, from urbanized Jewish workers and merchants from eastern Europe. We cannot even begin to indicate how various were the characteristics of family structure,

religion, economic experience and attitudes, educational experience and attitudes, [and] political outlook that differentiated
groups from such different backgrounds. Obviously, some American influences worked on them in common and with the same effects. But their differences meant they were open to different parts
of American experience, interpreted it in different ways, used it
for different ends. In the third generation, the descendants of the
immigrants confronted each other, and knew they were both
Americans, in the same dress, with the same language, using the
same artifacts, troubled by the same things; but they voted differently, had different ideas about education and sex, and were
still, in many essential ways, as different from one another as
their grandfathers had been.

The initial attributes of the groups provided only one reason
why their transformations did not make them all into the same
thing. There was another reason—and that was the nature of
American society itself, which could not, or did not, assimilate
the immigrant groups fully or in equal degree. Or perhaps the
nature of human society in general. It is only the experience of
the strange and foreign that teaches us how provincial we are.
A hundred thousand Negroes have been enough to change the
traditional British policy of free immigration from the colonies
and dominions. Japan finds it impossible to incorporate into the
body of its society anyone who does not look Japanese, or even the
Koreans, indistinguishable very often in appearance and language
from Japanese. And we shall test the racial attitudes of the Russians only when there are more than a few Negroes passing
through as curiosities; certainly the inability of Russians to get
over anti-Semitism does not suggest they are any different from
the rest of mankind. In any case, the word "American" was an
unambiguous reference to nationality only when it was applied
to a relatively homogeneous social body consisting of immigrants
from the British Isles, with relatively small numbers from nearby
European countries. When the numbers of those not of British
origin began to rise, the word "American" became a far more
complicated thing. Legally, it meant a citizen. Socially, it lost its
identifying power, and when you asked a man what he was (in
the United States), "American" was not the answer you were looking for. In the United States it became a slogan, a political gesture,

sometimes an evasion, but not a matter-of-course, concrete social description of a person. Just as in certain languages a word cannot stand alone but needs some particle to indicate its function, so in the United States the word "American" does not stand by itself. If it does, it bears the additional meaning of patriot, "authentic" American, critic and opponent of "foreign" ideologies.

The original Americans became "old" Americans, or "old stock," or "white Anglo-Saxon Protestants," or some other identification which indicated they were not immigrants or descendants of recent immigrants. These original Americans already had a frame in their minds, which became a frame in reality, that placed and ordered those who came after them. Those who were like them could easily join them. It was important to be white, of British origin, and Protestant. If one was all three, then even if one was an immigrant, one was really not an immigrant, or not for long.

Thus, even before it knew what an Italian or Jew or an Irishman was like, the American mind had a place for the category, high or low, depending on color, on religion, on how close the group was felt to be [to] the Anglo-Saxon center. There were peculiarities in this placing. Why, for example, were the Germans placed higher than the Irish? There was of course an interplay to some extent between what the group actually was and where it was placed, and, since the German immigrants were less impoverished than the Irish and somewhat more competent craftsmen and farmers, this undoubtedly affected the old American's image of them. Then ideology came in to emphasize the common links between Englishmen and Germans, who, even though they spoke different languages, were said to be really closer to each other than the old Americans were to the English-speaking, but Catholic and Celtic, Irish. If a group's first representatives were cultured and educated, those who came after might benefit, unless they were so numerous as to destroy the first image. Thus, German Jews who arrived in the 1840's and 1850's benefited from their own characteristics and their link with Germans, until they were overwhelmed by the large number of East European Jewish immigrants after 1880. A new wave of German Jewish immigrants, in the 1930's, could not, regardless of culture and education, escape the low position of being "Jewish."

The ethnic group in American society became not a survival from the age of mass immigration but a new social form. One could not predict from its first arrival what it might become or, indeed, whom it might contain. The group is not a purely biological phenomenon. The Irish of today do not consist of those who are descended from Irish immigrants. Were we to follow the history of the germ plasm alone—if we could—we should find that many in the group really came from other groups, and that many who should be in the group are in other groups. The Protestants among them, and those who do not bear distinctly Irish names, may now consider themselves, and be generally considered, as much "old American" as anyone else. The Irish-named offspring of German or Jewish or Italian mothers often find that willy-nilly they have become Irish. It is even harder for the Jewish-named offspring of mixed marriages to escape from the Jewish group; neither Jews nor non-Jews will let them rest in ambiguity.

Parts of the group are cut off; other elements join the group as allies. Under certain circumstances, strange as it may appear, it is an advantage to be able to take on a group name, even of a low order, if it can be made to fit, and if it gives one certain advantages. It is better in Oakland, California, to be a Mexican than an Indian, and so some of the few Indians call themselves, at certain times, for certain occasions, "Mexicans." In the forming of ethnic groups subtle distinctions are overridden; there is an advantage to belonging to a big group, even if it is looked down upon. West Indian Negroes achieve important political positions, as representatives of Negroes; Spaniards and Latin-Americans become the representatives of Puerto Ricans; German Jews rose to Congress from districts dominated by East European Jews.

Ethnic groups then, even after distinctive language, customs, and culture are lost, as they largely were in the second generation, and even more fully in the third generation, are continually recreated by new experiences in America. The mere existence of a name itself is perhaps sufficient to form group character in new situations, for the name associates an individual, who actually can be anything, with a certain past, country, race. But as a matter of fact, someone who is Irish or Jewish or Italian generally has other traits than the mere existence of the name that associates him with other people attached to the group. A man is connected to his group by ties of family and friendship. But his is also connected by ties of *interest*. The ethnic groups in New York are also *interest groups*.

This is perhaps the single most important fact about ethnic groups in New York City. When one speaks of the Negroes and Puerto Ricans, one also means unorganized and unskilled workers, who hold poorly paying jobs in the laundries, hotels, restaurants, [and] small factories or who are on relief. When one says Jews, one also means small shopkeepers, professionals, [and] better-paid skilled workers in the garment industries. When one says Italians, one also means homeowners in Staten Island, the North Bronx, Brooklyn, and Queens.

If state legislation threatens to make it more difficult to get relief, this is headline news in the Puerto Rican press—for the group is affected—and news of much less importance to the rest of the press. The interplay between rational economic interests and the other interests or attitudes that stem out of group history makes for an incredibly complex political and social situation. Consider the local laws against discrimination in housing. Certain groups that face discrimination want such laws—Negroes, Puerto Ricans, and Jews. Jews meet little discrimination in housing in New York but have an established ideological commitment to all antidiscrimination laws. Apartment-house owners are against any restriction of their freedom or anything that might affect their profits. In New York, this group is also largely Jewish, but it is inhibited in pushing strongly against such laws by its connections with the Jewish community. Private homeowners see this as a threat to their homogeneous neighborhoods. These are largely German, Irish, and Italian. The ethnic background of the homeowners links them to communities with a history of anti-Negro feelings. The Irish and Italian immigrants have both at different times competed directly with Negro labor.

In the analysis, then, of the conflict over antidiscrimination laws, "rational" economic interests and the "irrational," or at any rate noneconomic, interests and attitudes tied up with one's own group are inextricably mixed together. If the rational interests did not operate, some of the older groups would by now be much weaker than they are. The informal and formal social groupings that make up these communities are strengthened by the fact that

Jews can talk about the garment business, Irish about politics and the civil service, Italians about the state of the trucking or contracting or vegetable business.

In addition to the links of interest, family and fellow feeling bind the ethnic group. There is satisfaction in being with those who are like oneself. The ethnic group is something of an extended family or tribe. And aside from ties of feeling and interest, there are concrete ties of organization. Certain types of immigrant social organization have declined, but others have been as ingenious in remolding and recreating themselves as the group itself. The city is often spoken of as the place of anonymity, of the breakdown of some kind of preexisting social order. The ethnic group, as Oscar Handlin has pointed out, served to create a new form of order. Those who came in with some kind of disadvantage, created by a different language, a different religion, a different race, found both comfort and material support in creating various kinds of organizations. American social services grew up in large part to aid incoming immigrant groups. Many of these were limited to a single religious or ethnic group. Ethnic groups set up hospitals, old people's homes, loan funds, charitable organizations, as well as churches and cultural organizations. The initial need for a separate set of welfare and health institutions became weaker as the group became more prosperous and as the government took over these functions, but the organizations nevertheless continued. New York organizational life is in large measure lived within ethnic bounds. These organizations generally have religious names, for it is more acceptable that welfare and health institutions should cater to religious than to ethnic communities. But of course religious institutions are generally closely linked to a distinct ethnic group. The Jewish (religious) organizations are Jewish (ethnic); Catholic are generally Irish or Italian, now with the Puerto Ricans as important clients; the Protestant organizations are white Protestant—which means generally old American, with a smaller German wing—in leadership, with Negroes as their chief clients.

Thus many elements—history, family and [fellow] feeling, interest, formal organizational life—operate to keep much of New York life channeled within the bounds of the ethnic group. Obviously, the rigidity of this channeling of social life varies from group to group. For the Puerto Ricans, a recent immigrant group with a small middle class and speaking a foreign language, the ethnic group serves as the setting for almost all social life. For Negroes too, because of discrimination and poverty, most social life is limited to the group itself. Jews and Italians are still to some extent recent immigrants, and despite the growing middle-class character of the Jewish group, social life for both is generally limited to other members of the group. But what about the Irish and the Germans?

Probably, many individuals who by descent "belong" to one of these older groups go through a good part of their lives with no special consciousness of the fact. It may be only under very special circumstances that one becomes aware of the matter at all—such as if one wants to run for public office. The political realm, indeed, is least willing to consider such matters a purely private affairs. Consciousness of one's ethnic background may be intermittent. It is only on occasion that someone may think of or be reminded of his background, and perhaps become self-conscious about the pattern formed by his family, his friends, his job, his interests. Obviously, this ethnic aspect of a man's life is more important if he is part of one group than if he is part of another; if he is Negro, he can scarcely escape it, and if he is of German origin, little will remind him of it.

Conceivably the fact that one's origins can become only a memory suggests the general direction for ethnic groups in the United States—toward assimilation and absorption into a homogeneous American mass. And yet, as we suggested earlier, it is hard to see in the New York of the 1960's just how this comes about. Time alone does not dissolve the groups if they are not close to the Anglo-Saxon center. Color marks off a group, regardless of time; and perhaps more significantly, the "majority" group, to which assimilation should occur, has taken on the color of an ethnic group, too. To what does one assimilate in modern America? The "American" in abstract does not exist, though some sections of the country, such as the Far West, come closer to realizing him than does New York City. There are test cases of such assimilation in the past. The old Scotch-Irish group, an important ethnic group of the early nineteenth century, is now for the most part simply old American, "old stock." Old Dutch families have become part of the upper class of New York. But these test cases merely reveal to us how partial was the power of the old American type to assimilate—it assimilated its ethnic cousins.

Racism and Nationality*

"Discrimination was the permanent manifestation of the hostilities bred by racism." Handlin takes this theme and shows how the development of racist ideas had come to apply to other groups besides Negroes in the period between the two World Wars. As he suggests in the final sentence of this excerpt, World War II itself brought a relaxation of racial tensions within the country, as the larger national purpose of defeating a common enemy took hold.

Discrimination was the permanent manifestation of the hostilities bred by racism. It had long since limited the rights of the Negro and, with the development of racist ideas and emotions, had, by 1918, come to apply with increasing frequency to other groups as well. In the decade after the end of the war it seriously abridged the privileges of men distinguishable by their color, like the Negroes and Japanese; by their religion, like the Jews and Catholics; and by their national origins, like the Italians and Poles. Discrimination then was supported by a well-developed code of practices, by the active agitation of political movements, and by an ideology that justified the separateness and the inferiority of the underprivileged. That complex survived until the middle of the 1930's; its collapse has created the situation in which the minorities now find themselves.

By 1918 a tightly meshed pattern of discriminatory practices put substantial portions of the American population at an enormous disadvantage in almost every aspect of life. The inferiority of which such people were often accused was well on the way to being forced upon them.

Of the groups marked off by color the Negroes were most important, by virtue of their numbers, of their long history in the country, and of the tragic injustices to which they had already

---

*From *Race and Nationality in American Life* by Oscar Handlin. Reprinted by permission of Collins–Knowlton–Wing, Inc. Copyright © 1956 Oscar Handlin.

been subject. Their progress since slavery had been painfully slow. Emancipation after the Civil War had stricken from them the shackles of legal bondage, but it had not succeeded in endowing them with rights equal to those of other citizens. Once the interlude of Reconstruction had passed, the white South, redeemed, had developed a way of life that maintained and extended the actual inferiority of the blacks. In the last decade of the nineteenth century one device after another had deprived them of the ballot and of political power; their own lack of skill and of capital, as well as discrimination, had confined them to a submerged place in the economy; and the rigid etiquette of segregation made their social inferiority ever clearer. In no aspect of his life could the Negro escape awareness that he was decisively below the white, hopelessly incapable of rising to the same opportunities as his former masters. If ever he lost sight of that fact central to his existence, the ever present threat of lynching and other forms of violence reminded him of it.

Progress in ameliorating their condition down to 1917 had been too slow to kindle the flame of hope among the Negroes, and the momentary flare of enthusiasm during the war quickly subsided. Thereafter there were few sober reasons for optimism. A slowly developing middle class offered the hope of personal improvement to a tiny handful. A gradual movement to the northern cities offered an escape from the South but not an escape from the problems of discrimination; poverty, violence, and disorder dogged their heels in Chicago and Harlem as they had in Alabama or Georgia. The limited degrees of improvement were minuscule in comparison with the way that still remained to go. And when the depression struck in the 1930's, the Negroes, who were first to suffer in both the North and the South, faced a future of desperate futility.

No other group suffered the total burden of discrimination the Negro bore. Yet the Japanese and the Indians, also set off by their color, had their share of grievances. For them also the postwar period brought no confidence that a remedy was within sight.

It was the same with some groups made distinctive by religious affiliation. Catholics were widely reproached for being un-American. The hostile sentiments stirred up by the American Protective Association (the APA) in the 1890's had never died down, and during the war there had been ugly rumors that the Pope was somehow favoring the Central Powers. Was it possible that he intended ultimately to subvert American democracy? The suspicion ebbed and flowed, but never altogether receded; and stories remained current of arms stored in churches, of mysterious international emissaries, and of strange doings in convents and monasteries.

Catholicism was also a burden to its communicants. The presidential campaigns of 1924 and 1928, the savage hatreds that led numerous Democrats to desert their party, left many Catholics with the conviction that their faith was a distinct political liability. Nor were they likely to find reassurance in the efforts to outlaw parochial schools and otherwise to limit the rights of their co-religionists. In their day-to-day existence, too, boycotts of their businesses, discrimination in employment, and exclusion from important areas of social life embittered their relationships with other Americans.

The forces that generated the attacks against Catholics found another target in the Jews. From the 1800's onward a developing pattern of slights and formal barriers closed clubs and restaurants and hotels to these people and narrowed the range of their social contacts. Early in the twentieth century they began to feel the effects of discrimination in employment and of restriction in housing. After the end of the First World War they discovered also that their access to many educational institutions and to some of the professions, like medicine and engineering, was being limited.

By then, moreover, they were the victims of the full barrage of anti-Semitic accusations. The old stereotype of the Jew acquired a sinister connotation. He was the international banker, but also the inflamed radical responsible for Communist revolution in eastern Europe. Above all, he was the agent of a vast conspiracy designed to enslave America. Henry Ford's *International Jew* and the pages of his *Dearborn Independent* exposed the plot of the elders of Zion to conquer the whole world. Repercussions of the credulous acceptance of these charges poisoned the relationships of Jews with their neighbors throughout the decade.

The enemy now took the form of groups set off by their differences of national origin. In the twenty years before the First World War millions of newcomers had arrived in the United States from parts of Europe and Asia which had not theretofore produced a heavy volume of immigration. The host of aliens from Italy, from Poland, from Greece, and from Austria, disembarking in massive numbers within a very short period, evoked a reaction of shock and hostility from some Americans longer settled. All the findings of science cast doubt upon the capacity of these strange, outlandish people to adjust to the ways of American life. Totally unassimilable, they were bound to lower all national values. Beaten men from beaten stocks, they should not be entrusted with the equal rights they would, in any case, never be able to enjoy.

Possession of a Slavic or Italian name became a decisive liability. A widespread, if informal, network of discriminatory practices limited the opportunities of these people and gave subtle expression to a hostility that occasionally, as in West Frankfort, Illinois, in 1920, erupted in passionate violence.

The discriminatory practices against the minorities were supported and extended by organized movements of considerable strength aimed to make them more rigid and more consistent. The anti-Catholic APA had passed from the scene at the opening of the century. But its burden was taken up, in the South, by the followers of Tom Watson and carried by a variety of smaller groups down to the outbreak of the war. There was an interval of relaxation during the war itself while all such energies and tensions were subsumed in the more general emotions of the struggle against Germany.

*The American Irish**

Concentrating upon antipathy toward the Irish as an alien group, the author provides dramatic descriptions of violence in Philadelphia and Boston, the activities of the Nativist party, and other manifestations of anti-Irish prejudice in the mid-nineteenth century. This excerpt discusses the reactions of older elements in the eastern cities to the heightened tension which accompanied the conspicuous influx of the Irish newcomers.

The natives responded [to the Irish] in convulsive bursts of violence and prolonged withdrawals. A native mob burned a con-

---

*Reprinted with permission of The Macmillan Company from *The American Irish* by William V. Shannon. © by William V. Shannon 1963.

vent in Charlestown, Massachusetts in 1831; another mob sacked
a Catholic Church in Philadelphia in 1846; respectable ministers
and civic leaders endorsed the comic opera "disclosures" of Maria
Monk in the late 1830's; and reputable politicians flirted with organized bigotry on and off for thirty years, culminating in the
brief Know-Nothing upheaval of 1854–1858. Meanwhile, Yankee
employers everywhere in the seaboard cities published advertisements, "No Irish Need Apply." It is not easy to distinguish to
what extent the nativist crusade of these three decades was directed against Catholicism as such or against the Irish, but it
appears that the prevailing motive was an antipathy to the Irish
as an alien group. They threatened the patterns of job and trade
competition, the old values, the homogeneity of the once-small
cities. Religious sentiment was probably an available, respectable
pretext rather than the motive for action. The old community,
particularly its lower-middle class and working class, feeling
threatened, found the religious differences an easy rationale, sanc-
tioned by the anti-Catholic tradition of the colonial era. The Irish
workingman in the next block and not the Pope in Rome was the
real enemy.[1]

The raid on the Charlestown convent represented the first
démarche of the Boston workingmen against the Irish. It was also
a gesture of defiance against a darkening future. Boston in 1830
was economically a sick city; only half of the persons born there
in 1790 still dwelt in the city by 1820. Only emigration from the
farming hinterland prevented the city from suffering an absolute
shrinkage in population. The old trade with the Far East, the
glittering superstructure of the city's former maritime supremacy,
had declined. New York, even before the opening of the Erie
Canal in 1825, had pulled ahead in prosperity. The growth of factory towns along nearby rivers where electric current was cheap
provided Boston entrepreneurs with new wealth, but afforded
native craftsmen a glimpse of a dark future in which the factory
system would be triumphant.[2] Hemmed in by these pressures, the
workingmen searched for a scapegoat.

---

[1] John Higham, *Strangers in the Land: Patterns of American
Nativism 1860–1925* (1955), chap. i.

[2] Oscar Handlin, *Boston's Immigrants, 1790–1880* (1959), pp. 14–
15.

The imposing red-brick convent conducted by the Ursuline Nuns on the crest of Mount Benedict Hill in Charlestown across the Charles River from Boston was a convenient symbol. Ironically, the pupils in this convent, established in 1818, were drawn largely not from Catholic but from wealthy liberal Protestant homes. The hold of orthodox Congregationalism was breaking down under the impact of liberal Unitarian and Transcendentalist ideas about religion. A number of parents who desired a more cosmopolitan kind of education for their daughters than could be obtained in the female seminaries run by the Congregational Church entered them in the Ursuline Convent. All the hatreds born of the struggle then going on between liberal and Fundamentalist religion in Massachusetts thus became centered on the Charleston convent. "To the lower classes, with whom Congregationalism was a sacred creed, Catholics and Unitarians seemed to be combining against their religion."

On Sunday evening, August 11, 1831, after weeks of rising tension, a mob gathered before the convent. The mother superior pleaded with the crowd to go away. When her entreaties failed, she tried intimidation. "The bishop has twenty thousand Irishmen at his command in Boston," she cried.

Her threat was not only injudicious but also inaccurate (it is doubtful if there were that many Irish adults in Boston in that year). By prearranged signal, mob leaders ignited barrels of tar in a neighboring field. Fire bells began ringing. Hundreds of persons streamed up the hill to join the crowd and watch the fun. As midnight approached, a gang of forty or fifty men forced their way into the convent. The mother superior, the dozen nuns, and some sixty frightened pupils fled by the rear entrance. The gang set fire to the building and a neighboring farmhouse owned by the order. The crowd stood and cheered as the two buildings went down in flames.

Eight men were ultimately accused of arson in connection with the burning of the convent, but their trial was an orgy of anti-Catholic prejudice. All but one was swiftly acquitted, and the latter was pardoned soon after when leading Boston Catholics, in a gesture of conciliation, signed a petition asking clemency. The nuns resumed teaching a year later in another Boston suburb, but few pupils cared to risk studying with them. In 1838 the Ursulines abandoned their work in Boston and withdrew to Canada.[3]

The burning of the convent brought the smoldering fires of anti-Catholic, anti-Irish feeling to the surface of national life. Equally incendiary in its own way was the publication in 1836 of Maria Monk's *Awful Disclosures*. In this inspired work of fiction, the author told of her education in a Catholic convent in Montreal, her conversion to Catholicism, her decision to become a nun, and her subsequent shocking discoveries. The mother superior of the convent instructed her, she reported, to "obey the priests in all things," and this, she discovered, meant "to live in the practice of criminal intercourse with them." The children born of these liaisons were, she reported, baptized and immediately strangled. Nuns who refused to cooperate were murdered. Hers was a colorful picture of convent life complete with mass graves in the basement, a secret passageway to the priest's quarters, and midnight orgies. Maria explained that having become pregnant after relations with a priest, she had fled to New York to save the life of her unborn child.

Awful Disclosures, which apparently was ghosted by a professional writer, had a tremendous vogue. Maria was taken up by a sponsoring committee of Protestant clergymen and enjoyed a brief personal success. But then her mother in Montreal disclosed that Maria had never been a resident in the convent described in the book, that she had instead been in a Catholic asylum for delinquent girls, and had run away with the help of a former boyfriend, the probable father of her child. Maria's associates in the writing of the book cheated her out of most of the profits. When she gave birth to a second fatherless child, she did not bother to name him after a priest. One Protestant journal insisted her second pregnancy was arranged by crafty Jesuits to discredit her revelations, but the explanation did not catch on. Her respectable defenders deserted her, and she disappeared into obscurity. Years later she was arrested for picking the pockets of a man in a house of prostitution, and she died in prison. But the book outlived its nominal author. It went through twenty printings, sold three hun-

---

[3] Ray A. Billington, *The Protestant Crusade, 1800–1860* (1938), pp. 72–76.

dred thousand copies, and down to the Civil War served as the "Uncle Tom's Cabin" of the Know-Nothing movement.[4]

The most serious outburst of violence came in Philadelphia, the City of Brotherly Love. In 1843 Bishop Francis Kenrick persuaded the school board to permit Catholic children to read the Douai rather than the King James Version of the Bible in the public schools. Catholic children were also excused from the religious instruction that was then a customary part of the curriculum. Nativists attacked the decision as interference by a "foreign prelate" in American education. Mass meetings were held in Independence Square to denounce the change. In May, 1844, a Protestant group invaded the Philadelphia suburb of Kensington, an industrial section where the Irish predominated, to hold a protest meeting. This gesture of defiance produced street fighting in which the Irish drove off their antagonists. The nativists then called a mass meeting for the following Monday, May 6, in the same neighborhood and appealed to their supporters to turn out in force. The second meeting resulted in a far more serious melee in which one man was killed. This pitched battle touched off three days of general rioting. Protestant mobs roamed the streets of Kensington, setting blocks of houses in flames, and burning two Catholic churches.

An uneasy quiet reigned for several weeks. Then, on July 4, the holiday was converted into a testimonial to those nativist dead who had fallen in the May rioting. Seventy thousand persons paraded behind the carriages of the widows and children of these men in downtown Philadelphia. The next day street fighting broke out again. This time the focus of attack was St. Philip de Neri Church in Southwark, another suburb, where the pastor had stored guns in the basement of the church as a precautionary measure. When the rumor of the existence of this cache spread, hostile crowds gathered. Separate searches by the sheriff and by a committee of twenty drawn from members of the crowd turned up eighty-seven guns and a quantity of ammunition. When the crowd still did not disperse, the governor sent militia to pro-

---

[4] The book was again in circulation on a small scale in the presidential campaign of 1960.

tect the church. By nightfall of the second day, "a company of troops had turned the square on which the church was located into an armed fortress with barricades erected and cannon commanding the principal avenues of approach." The rioters obtained a cannon of their own and fired into the soldiers massed before the church doors. The troops returned the attack, and the sound of cannon and musket fire rang across the square for several hours.

Meanwhile, gangs roamed the streets looking for Irishmen. Priests and nuns went into hiding. Thousands of Catholics fled the city. Before these days of open civil war had passed, thirteen persons had been killed and more than fifty were wounded, most of them nativists who had engaged the militia in combat.[5]

The burning of churches and the open war in the streets in Philadelphia caused a strong backlash of public disapproval of the nativists. The middle and upper classes drew back in fear from a movement that seemed to be reenacting the horrors of the French Revolution. The diary entries of a wealthy New Yorker, George Templeton Strong, record the change in opinion in respectable circles during that tumultuous spring and early summer. On April 10 he rejoiced in the victory of the nativists in the New York municipal elections:

"Hurrah for the natives!" he wrote. "Such a blow hasn't fallen on the Hibernian race since the days of Earl Strongbow."

On May 8, when news reached New York of the first outbreak of rioting, he wrote: "Great row in Philadelphia. . . . This'll be a great thing for the natives, strengthen their hands amazingly if judiciously used."

Two months later when the fighting broke forth again, he took a darker view. "Civil war raging [in Philadelphia]," he wrote on July 8. "Mob pelting the military, not with paving stones, but with grapeshot and scrap iron out of ten-pounders; the state of things in that city is growing worse and worse every day."

"I shan't be voting for a 'native' ticket again in a hurry," he concluded.[6]

---

[5] Billington, *op. cit.*, pp. 220–31.

[6] Allan Nevins and Milton H. Thomas (eds.), *The Diary of George Templeton Strong* (1952), pp. 228, 232–33, 240.

The nativist movement rose and fell in successive waves of passion. In reaction to the episodes in Philadelphia, the movement ebbed for nearly a decade. It did not, however, go out of existence. By the 1840's a broad network of native societies, religious propaganda organizations, magazines, and newspapers was in existence. Books attacking Catholics had become staples in the publishing industry. One writer observed as early as 1835 that the abuse of Catholics "is a regular trade and the compilation of anti-Catholic books . . . has become a part of the regular industry of the country, as much as the making of nutmegs or the construction of clocks."

The last great surge of nativism came in 1854 with the emergence of the American, or Know-Nothing, party. (The party drew its name from the fact that members of the Order of the Star-Spangled Banner, a secret nativist organization, when asked about their activities said, "I know nothing.") In the elections of 1854–1855, the Know-Nothings scored unexpectedly sweeping victories. The party and its allies carried Maryland, Delaware, Kentucky, and most of New England and showed strength in other parts of the country. About seventy-five congressmen were elected, pledged to do battle against the Pope and his American adherents. The size of the victory was deceptive. In retrospect, it is clear that the Know-Nothing party was a halfway house for voters seeking a new political home. The ravaging struggle over slavery was tearing apart the dying Whig party and transforming the Democratic party. The new Republican party, pledged to halt the extension of slavery, had just been born. In this period of rapid political flux, the Know-Nothings represented an effort to divert attention away from the slavery issue to the "safer" issues of anti-Catholicism and anti-immigration about which the native community could more easily agree.

Massachusetts was the stronghold of the Know-Nothings. There they captured the governorship, all state offices, and huge majorities in both houses of the legislature. The election represented a real coming to power of the embittered lower classes of the native community. Of the 378 members of the lower house of the legislature, only 34 had ever served in office before. The great majority were "mechanics, laborers, clerks, school teachers, and ministers who understood nothing of the governmental processes and were ill-equipped to learn." The disorganized, disorderly legislative session passed little important legislation. A committee appointed to investigate convents became the butt of jokes in the newspapers. On a visit to Lowell, members of the committee charged to the state their liquor bills and also expenses incurred in their off-duty relations with a lady "answering to the name of Mrs. Patterson." The scandal became so great the legislature canceled the rest of the investigation and expelled the chairman of the committee from the legislature. Before adjourning, the members voted themselves a pay increase. At the next election, only one-sixth of the members were reelected.[7]

The fiasco in Massachusetts and the ineffectiveness of Know-Nothing legislators in other states contributed to the party's rapid decline. By 1860 it had dwindled to an inconsequential faction. Life in the cities, however, retained its violent tone. In the years just before the Civil War, a nativist mob of fifteen hundred persons rioted in the Irish districts of Lawrence, Massachusetts, burning homes and churches; in Baltimore eight men were killed in election-day battles between Know-Nothings and Democrats; and in New York, Philadelphia, and other cities violence flared sporadically.

Throughout these strife-torn decades of the 1840's and 1850's, however, each week during the spring and summer months vessels arrived in Atlantic Coast seaports carrying more Irish to America. While the battle raged intermittently in the streets between the Irish and the natives, the reinforcements poured forth from steerage. The Irish were slowly winning the battle for the city against the Protestant lower classes by sheer force of numbers.

---

[7] Billington, *op. cit.*, pp. 412–16.

Suggestions for Further Reading

1. Lenora E. Berson, *The Negroes and the Jews* (New York: Random House, 1971).

   Traces the historic alliance of two groups in their mutual struggle for equality and justice and deals with the emerging hostility of the past few decades.

2. Stewart G. Cole and Mildred Wiese Cole, *Minorities and the American Promise* (New York: Harper and Bros., 1954).

   Chapter Six discusses the Melting Pot mystique.

3. Andrew M. Greeley, *Why Can't They Be Like Us?* (New York: American Jewish Committee, 1969).

   Deals with facts and fallacies about ethnic differences and group conflicts in America.

4. Warren J. Halliburton and William Loren Katz, *American Majorities and Minorities* (New York: Arno Press, 1970).

   This comprehensive syllabus for a high school American history course covers many minority contributions. Produced under NAACP auspices.

5. Nat Hentoff (ed.), *Black Anti-Semitism and Jewish Racism* (New York: Schocken, 1970).

   Four black writers and seven Jewish writers discuss the emergence of inter-group conflict between these two minorities.

6. Michael B. Kane, *Minorities in Textbooks* (New York: Quadrangle, 1970).

   This study of forty-five junior high and senior high social studies texts shows that textbooks continue to present distorted pictures of minorities in American history.

7. Samuel F. B. Morse, *The Imminent Dangers to the Free Institutions of the United States Through Foreign Immigration* (New York: Arno Press, 1969).

   Originally published in 1835, this nativist pamphlet by the famous inventor had great impact on anti-Catholic sentiment.

8. Edward Sagarin (ed.), *The Other Minorities* (Waltham, Mass.: Xerox, 1971).

   A collection of articles on the non-ethnic or deviant minorities. Women, homosexuals, hippies, the disabled and the handicapped are among the groups discussed.

9. Thomas C. Wheeler (ed.), *The Immigrant Experience: The Anguish of Becoming American* (New York: Dial Press, 1971).

   Nine first-person accounts by Puerto Rican, Irish, Italian, Polish, English, Norwegian, Chinese, Jewish, and black writers.

10. Robert W. Winslow (ed.), *The Emergence of Deviant Minorities* (San Ramon, Ca.: Consensus Publishers, Inc., 1972).

11. Benjamin Ziegler (ed.), *Immigration: An American Dilemma* (Lexington, Mass.: D. C. Heath and Co., 1953).

    This collection of articles emphasizes ethnic attitudes and political barriers. Two articles of particular interest are Henry Pratt Fairchild's "The Melting-Pot Mistake" and Horace McKallen's "Democracy and the Melting Pot."

PART 4   BLACK TARGETS OF WHITE RACISM

Chapter Nine

Racism in the Law

The question before us is, whether the class of persons described in the plea for abatement compose a portion of this people, and are constituent members of this sovereignty? We think they are not, and that they are not included, and were not intended to be included, under the word "citizens" in the Constitution, and can therefore claim none of the rights and privileges which that instrument provides for and secures to citizens of the United States. On the contrary, they were at that time considered as a subordinate and inferior class of beings, who had been subjugated by the dominant race, and, whether emancipated or not, yet remained subject to their authority, and had no rights or privileges but such as those who held the power and the government might choose to grant them.
—CHIEF JUSTICE ROGER TANEY, opinion in the case of *Dred Scott* v. *Sandford* (1857)

In 1857 the meaning of the Dred Scott decision was trumpeted across the land: Negroes had no rights the white man was bound to respect. That was an accurate summary of the legal status of most black people prior to the Civil War.

Ten years earlier, Dred Scott had filed a suit for freedom in the Missouri courts. He argued that since he had been transported north of the 36°30′ line which the Missouri Compromise of 1820 had fixed as the northern boundary for the extension of slavery, he was being held in slavery illegally. The case reached the United States Supreme Court in the wake of the turbulent agitation about the Compromise of 1850, the Kansas-Nebraska Bill of 1854, and other explosive issues of the 1850's. The Court ruled against Dred Scott on the grounds that Negroes were never meant to be regarded as citizens with equal rights.

Discrimination against black people has received considerable authorization from federal, state, and local legislative and constitutional provisions. For example, the United States Constitution contained three clauses which revealed that from the days of the Declaration of Independence and the Constitution, black people were never intended to be included in the Melting Pot. First among the constitutional provisions respecting slavery and an inferior position for Negroes is the manner of tabulating black people for apportionment purposes. Only three out of every five would be counted. That is to say, a slave was three-fifths of a person, according to the United States Constitution. Secondly, Congress was prohibited from interfering with the slave trade for twenty years. Thirdly, fugitive slaves were to be returned to their masters in their home states. State and local laws reinforced this legal inequality.

Not until the 1860's was the Constitution amended to grant black people equal rights to freedom, due process, and voting. Yet the passage of the Thirteenth, Fourteenth, and Fifteenth Amendments did not mark the end of legal discrimination. In fact, many forms of legal discrimination arose in the postwar period. Thirty years after the Civil War, in *Plessy* v. *Ferguson,* the Supreme Court of the United States ruled that "separate but equal" school facilities were permissible. In 1896 school segregation on the basis of race was upheld as constitutional. There are many instances which support the statement that for most of his history in this country, the black man has been living under a system which is saturated with legal requirements that he be segregated.

Gradually many discriminatory laws have been overthrown. But the process was so gradual that it was 1954 before the Brown decision by the Supreme Court reversed the ruling in *Plessy* v. *Ferguson.* One hundred years after the Fourteenth Amendment, segregation remains the American way of life. The series of civil rights laws passed in the 1960's was calculated to make more explicit the fundamental guarantees of the Fourteenth Amendment. The fact that they were needed speaks for itself.

Failure to enforce earlier laws guaranteeing equal treatment created the need for additional laws which emphasized enforcement. Housing, employment, and education are three areas in which antidiscrimination laws at various governmental levels have been passed with little practical effect.

Changing the laws has taken several centuries, and the problem of enforcement of the new laws remains. Meanwhile a balanced overview must mention antimiscegenation laws which discriminate equally against black and white since they interfere with the free choice of a marriage partner on account of "race." In the early 1940's there were thirty states with antimiscegenation laws that banned black–white marriages.

A list of legal racism ought to mention, if only briefly, the covert laws which were just as effective in "keeping the Negro in his place" as the more blatant denials of the Melting Pot. Poll taxes and grandfather clauses were effective devices in preventing Negro citizens from voting, especially when punctuated by acts of terror. Voter registration drives in the 1960's were necessary in places such as Mississippi because of the heritage of legal racism. Even well organized registration drives did not completely succeed in helping all black Mississippians to overcome their fears that attempts to vote would jeopardize the security of their jobs, homes, and lives.

Other examples of the racist heritage of American law are discussed in the selections which follow.

*Legal Discrimination and Governmental Racism**

The following selection summarizes the main points covered in a very powerful book-length indictment of American legal racism.

White oppression and black resistance has been a persistent part of the American scene since the colonial period. The response of the government in its effort to suppress racial disorder has reflected the tension between the lofty ideals expressed in the documents on which constitutional government is based and the tendency of the white majority to desire summary disposition of those they regard as unpopular, unlovely, hateful, or powerless. The predilection of the white majority to suppress efforts by black people to acquire real freedom and equality in America (as black *people,* not as single individuals who may achieve some recognition of the rights), even when white repression means resorting to illegal violence and brutality, has added to that tension. Black people have not been, of course, the only oppressed group in American society—the labor movement, Mexican-Americans, Indians, Mormons, and white radicals have experienced suppression. The black experience is unique because black people have been oppressed from the day they first set foot on English-American soil. The American government and people have persistently defended the repression of blacks in the name of law and order, without admitting that the Constitution was designed and has been interpreted to maintain the racial status quo. Racism, the promotion of white nationalism, is the primary reason why black people have served as the mudsills of American society. The need to respect constitutional government has been so twisted and perverted in the name of this objective that it is no wonder that its victims see beyond the fiction and regard law and order as a mere instrument for their repression.

Racial tensions and the rationalization for the justification of suppression originated in the theory and practice of law developed before the Civil War. The constitutional history of military power, as it relates to rebellion and black–white relations in the United States, indicates that the use of troops and the threat of force have always been of major importance. In the antebellum period, the willingness to use force against blacks, in large measure, effectively prevented widespread slave revolts. The United States used the regular army to return slaves to their masters, to execute a twenty-year war against blacks and Indians in Florida, and to keep the slaves in "awe" with the strategic stationing of troops. On the other hand, the government refused to oppose the suppression of the civil liberties of antislavery activists. Dominated by southerners and "doughfaces," the executive branch of the government ignored the mobbings and beatings of abolitionists, even when state officials were among the perpetrators. The national government chose to interpret its powers in such a way as to weaken and inhibit the development of the antislavery movement and later the Black Liberation movement. This inaction was another phase of legal racism.

At the beginning of the Civil War, the behavior of the Union government reinforces the view that the emancipation of slaves was not among the Union's war aims. Troops, in fact, protected and defended slaveholders, as they had done before the war. Although the Union was forced to issue the final Emancipation Proclamation, the fact that the proclamation was only a war measure made it still uncertain whether there was a national will to end the use of military power to suppress the newly freed blacks.

Because military power was not used effectively to protect blacks and suppress white violators, even during Reconstruction, the status of black people remained in doubt. One indication of this continuing doubt was that the government was still unwilling to use force against white people for the injury or murder of blacks. However, after Reconstruction, the intentions of the government in cases of black–white confrontations and racial violence became somewhat clearer. From 1877 to 1957, federal troops or marshals were not used to prevent pre-advertised lynchings or other kinds of violence directed against black people when states refused them protection. The government's oft-asserted declaration that it lacked the power to intervene was based more on disinterest than on statutory or constitutional incapacity. Even though blacks were nominally free, the government was unsure about the extent of that status and uninterested in insuring blacks the opportunity to achieve the freedoms granted the American whites. On the other hand, the national government's pattern of inaction in cases of white violence against blacks indicated its certainty about the status of white people and its unwillingness to punish whites for murdering and assaulting blacks.

These conclusions were reinforced when, between 1957 and 1965, national power was used to enforce court orders and protect blacks from racial violence. It now became clear that the problem had not really been a constitutional one after all; the Constitution had merely been interpreted to support the disinclination of whites to regard blacks as persons. This interpretative behavior can be readily understood if one recognizes that white Americans, like people elsewhere, have historically demonstrated the human capacity to rationalize what is merely expedient into what is legally necessary.

The use of troops to suppress black riots and rebellions after 1964 was a return to the policy utilized before the Civil War. Federal force was used to defend white persons and property from blacks when state forces were inadequate or when states requested federal help. In such cases, black rioters and rebels were in the same position as slaves who attempted to revolt before 1965. They were outside the law, and federal military force has always been used to enforce the "law," whether it was the law of slavery, segregation, or disfranchisement.

The reflex action of the national government to black requests for federal action to aid in the improvement of their economic and social condition has always been token measures or assertions that no problem exists. If these tactics failed and black people persisted too vigorously, then force and suppression were used. If the slave experience is any indicator, a serious dislocation of American society might be necessary before the institutional response is changed. Also, if the failure of the economic promises of Reconstruction is relevant, satisfactory improvement in the conditions and status of blacks so as to remove the factors that give rise to riots and rebellion will be a long time in coming.

From 1789 through 1970, governmental action in response to the problem of black-white violence and black rebellion has been slow and uneven until some great cataclysm threatening white people has occurred. While white America and the government generally vacillated on the issue, black advances have been met with repression. And repression has proceeded in the guise of constitutionalism, despite the fact that the Constitution is much more flexible than those who hide behind its provisions will admit. Further, no concerted effort has been made to fully utilize its person-oriented and general welfare provisions to remove the economic and social causes of black rebellion.

Additionally, the government has demonstrated a lack of imagination in eradicating the racial prejudice which undergirds the constitutional suppression of black people. If blacks are to be a part of American society, the removal of racism should have the highest priority. Although racism may not be erased by legislation, educational techniques, even-handed justice, and black self-determination as positive government programs might prove effective. Since Americans are apparently enamored of the profit motive, perhaps a government policy for paying grants or giving tax credits to people and programs designed to end racial antagonism might be useful. Even if these ideas seem utopian, one superficial indicator of prejudice—continued racial violence—is amenable to solution. The enforcement of laws designed to make contact between whites and blacks less abrasive and a willingness on the part of the government to respond as quickly when blacks are the victims as when the persons or property of white people are at stake would be a good beginning.

This study also supports the view that the government allocates military power, as everything else, to defend those who are its friends and to injure those who are its enemies. Unfortunately, blacks in general and militants in particular have always been regarded as enemies. So long as the government possesses a virtual monopoly of military power, is unencumbered by widespread internal disorder, such as that which occurred during the Civil War, and remains able to cope with its enemies at home and abroad, white Americans apparently see no need to deal seriously with the factors which cause black rebellion. If real black revolution comes, it will result from this failure of the larger society to come quickly to an acceptable determination of the status of black people and to use the Constitution to effect needed social, economic, and political reform.

*Northern Segregation before the Civil War**

The author of this famous book traces the development of segregation in the North before the Civil War.

Segregation in complete and fully developed form did grow up contemporaneously with slavery, but not in its midst. One of the strangest things about the career of Jim Crow was that the system was born in the North and reached an advanced age before moving South in force. Without forgetting evils peculiar to the South, one might consider northern conditions with profit.

By 1830 slavery was virtually abolished by one means or another throughout the North, with only about thirty-five hundred Negroes remaining in bondage in the nominally free states. No sectional comparison of race relations should be made without full regard for this difference. The northern free Negro enjoyed obvious advantages over the southern slave. His freedom was circumscribed in many ways, as we shall see, but he could not be bought or sold, or separated from his family, or legally made to work without compensation. He was also to some extent free to agitate, organize, and petition to advance his cause and improve his lot.

For all that, the northern Negro was made painfully and constantly aware that he lived in a society dedicated to the doctrine of white supremacy and Negro inferiority. The major

---

political parties, whatever their position on slavery, vied with each other in their devotion to this doctrine, and extremely few politicians of importance dared question them. Their constituencies firmly believed that the Negroes were incapable of being assimilated politically, socially, or physically into white society. They made sure in numerous ways that the Negro understood his "place" and that he was severely confined to it. One of these ways was segregation, and with the backing of legal and extra-legal codes, the system permeated all aspects of Negro life in the free states by 1860.

Leon F. Litwack, in his authoritative account, *North of Slavery,* describes the system in full development:

> In virtually every phase of existence . . . Negroes found themselves systematically separated from whites. They were either excluded from railway cars, omnibuses, stagecoaches, and steamboats or assigned to special "Jim Crow" sections; they sat, when permitted, in secluded and remote corners of theaters and lecture halls; they could not enter most hotels, restaurants, and resorts, except as servants; they prayed in "Negro pews" in the white churches, and if partaking of the sacrament of the Lord's Supper, they waited until the whites had been served the bread and wine. Moreover, they were often educated in segregated schools, punished in segregated prisons, nursed in segregated hospitals, and buried in segregated cemeteries.

In very few instances were Negroes and other opponents of segregation able to make any progress against the system. Railroads in Massachusetts and schools in Boston eliminated Jim Crow before the Civil War. But there and elsewhere Negroes were often segregated in public accommodations and severely segregated in housing. Whites of South Boston boasted in 1847 that "not a single colored family" lived among them. Boston had her "Nigger Hill" and her "New Guinea," Cincinnati her "Little Africa," and New York and Philadelphia their comparable ghettoes—for which Richmond, Charleston, New Orleans, and St. Louis had no counterparts. A Negro leader in Boston observed in 1860 that "it is five times as hard to get a house in a good location in Boston as in Philadelphia, and it is ten times as difficult for a colored mechanic to get work here as in Charleston."

Generally speaking, the farther west the Negro went in the

free states the harsher he found the proscription and segregation. Indiana, Illinois, and Oregon incorporated in their constitutions provisions restricting the admission of Negroes to their borders, and most states carved from the old Northwest Territory either barred Negroes in some degree or required that they post bond guaranteeing good behavior. Alexis de Tocqueville was amazed at the depth of racial bias he encountered in the North. "The prejudice of race," he wrote, "appears to be stronger in the states that have abolished slavery than in those where it still exists; and nowhere is it so intolerant as in those states where servitude has never been known."

Racial discrimination in political and civil rights was the rule in the free states and any relaxation the exception. The advance of universal white manhood suffrage in the Jacksonian period had been accompanied by Negro disfranchisement. Only six percent of the northern Negroes lived in the five states— Massachusetts, New Hampshire, Vermont, Maine, and Rhode Island—that by 1860 permitted them to vote. The Negro's rights were curtailed in the courts as well as at the polls. By custom or by law Negroes were excluded from jury service throughout the North. Only in Massachusetts, and there not until 1855, were they admitted as jurors. Five western states prohibited Negro testimony in cases where a white man was a party. The ban against Negro jurors, witnesses, and judges, as well as the economic degradation of the race, help to explain the disproportionate numbers of Negroes in northern prisons and the heavy limitations on the protection of Negro life, liberty, and property.

By the eve of the Civil War the North had sharply defined its position on white supremacy, Negro subordination, and racial segregation. The political party that took control of the federal government at that time was in accord with this position, and Abraham Lincoln as its foremost spokesman was on record with repeated endorsements. He knew the feelings of "the great mass of white people" on Negroes. "A universal feeling, whether well or ill-founded, cannot be safely disregarded. We cannot, then, make them equals." In 1858 he had elaborated this view.

> I will say then that I am not, nor ever have been in favor of bringing about in any way the social and political equality of the white and black races [*applause*]—that I am not nor ever have been

in favor of making voters or jurors of negroes, nor of qualifying them to hold office, nor to intermarry with white people, and I will say in addition to this that there is a physical difference between the black and white races which I believe will forever forbid the two races living together on terms of social and political equality. And inasmuch as they cannot so live, while they do remain together there must be the position of superior and inferior, and I as much as any other man am in favor of having the superior position assigned to the white race.

It is clear that when its victory was complete and the time came, the North was not in the best possible position to instruct the South, either by precedent and example, or by force of conviction, on the implementation of what eventually became one of the professed war aims of the Union cause—racial equality.

*Legal Status after the Civil War**

The legal status of black people from Reconstruction to the present is summarized in the following selection.

In the matter of voting, even free Negroes were disfranchised throughout the South and in most of the North and West in 1860. New England, with the exception of Connecticut, permitted Negroes to vote. New York required Negroes who wished to vote to own a certain amount of property, a qualification which did not hold for whites. Wisconsin granted the suffrage to Negroes in 1849. Other northern and border states disfranchised them as follows: Delaware in 1792, Kentucky in 1799, Maryland in 1809, Connecticut in 1818, New Jersey in 1820, Virginia in 1830, Tennessee in 1834, North Carolina in 1835, and Pennsylvania in 1838. Other states in the South and West did not permit Negroes to vote.[1]

---

*From pp. 451–458 *Racial and Cultural Minorities: An Analysis of Prejudice and Discrimination* by George Eaton Simpson and J. Milton Yinger. Copyright 1953 by Harper and Brothers. Copyright © 1958 by George Eaton Simpson and J. Milton Yinger. By permission of Harper and Row, Publishers, Incorporated.

[1] C. S. Mangum, Jr., *The Legal Status of the Negro* (University of North Carolina Press, 1940), pp. 371–72.

After the adoption in 1865 of the Thirteenth Amendment abolishing slavery and involuntary servitude, except as a punishment for crime after due conviction, special restrictive legislation was enacted in the southern states. These laws, which became known as the Black Codes, virtually reintroduced the slave codes. They covered apprenticeship, labor contracts, migration, vagrancy, civil and legal rights.[2] The passage of the Black Codes brought about the adoption of the Fourteenth Amendment containing the famous statement: "No State shall make or enforce any law which shall abridge the privileges or immunities of citizens of the United States; nor shall any State deprive any person of life, liberty, or property, without due process of law; nor deny to any person within its jurisdiction the equal protection of the laws." The Fifteenth Amendment—"The right of the citizens of the United States to vote shall not be denied or abridged by the United States or by any State on account of race, color, or previous condition of servitude"—was also a reaction to the Black Codes, as was the federal Civil Rights Act of 1875. This act was declared unconstitutional in 1883, and soon thereafter the southern states began to enact segregative legislation.[3]

One of the controversial aspects of the early years of the Reconstruction period was the program carried on by the Bureau of Refugees, Freedmen, and Abandoned Lands. The Freedmen's Bureau in the War Department was created by a bill passed in 1865 and was in operation until 1872. It was criticized for the tactlessness, ineptitude, and corruptness of some of its officials. On the other hand, especially in recent years, this agency has been acclaimed for its positive accomplishments. At the time it was abolished, it had twenty-six hundred day and night schools in operation, with thirty-three hundred teachers (most of them trained by the bureau). It established Howard, Fisk, Hampton, and St. Augustine Normal School. In many parts of the South it was responsible for setting up what later became tax-supported public schools. Institutions were founded to care for the aged,

---

[2] See E. Franklin Frazier, *The Negro in the United States* (The *Macmillan Company*, 1949), pp. 126–27.

[3] Carey McWilliams, "Race Discrimination and the Law," *Science and Society* (Winter, 1945), p. 11.

the crippled, and the mentally diseased. A medical-aid program for Negroes was set up, and hospitals were established. Orphans and the destitute were furnished aid, and some thirty thousand displaced freedmen were returned to their former homes. The bureau was instructed by Congress to give every freedman forty acres and a mule. Some abandoned and confiscated land was distributed, but the bureau never had more than eight hundred thousand acres to dispose of (only two-tenths of one percent of the land of the seceding states was ever held by the bureau). Even if all these lands had been available, less than one acre could have been given to every freedman. As McWilliams indicates, most of the lands were quickly repossessed by the former owners as a result of wholesale amnesties, and Negroes who had acquired small tracts were dispossessed.[4]

Many interesting developments occurred during the Reconstruction years. In 1869 a Georgia court declared invalid a prewar statute preventing anyone with one-eighth or more Negro ancestry from holding public office. An article of the Louisiana constitution requiring racial separation in the schools was suspended in 1868, and the South Carolina public schools were opened to both races in the same year. It is reported that the University of South Carolina admitted Negro students in the first Reconstruction years, and that Richard T. Greener, a Negro graduate of Harvard, was librarian. Negroes were elected to Congress for the first time during the forty-first session (1870–1871). H. K. Revels, of Mississippi, came to fill the Senate seat of Jefferson Davis; Jefferson F. Long was a representative from Georgia. From 1870 to 1901, twenty Negroes were seated as representatives and two as senators. The largest number elected for any one Congress during these thirty years was seven (1876–1877).[5]

There is no need for us to present a detailed account of the Reconstruction period. Such a record is available in the many works dealing with the period. Most readers are more or less familiar with the martial law; the arbitrariness of some military officers and officials of the Freedmen's Bureau; the New England

---

[4] Carey McWilliams, *Brothers Under the Skin* (rev. ed.; Little, Brown and Company, 1951), pp. 357–59.

[5] Charles S. Johnson, *Patterns of Negro Segregation* (Harper & Brother, 1943), pp. 164, 342.

schoolteachers who came south; the collaboration of some Negroes, carpetbaggers, and scalawags; the waste and corruption; the positive achievements such as the new state constitutions, new laws on voting, new schools, etc.; and the disappointment and resentment of southern leaders at the loss of the war and of their cause.

The famous "Bargain of 1876" restored "white supremacy" to the South. The Republicans agreed not to oppose the election of Democrats to state office in South Carolina, Louisiana, and Florida and to withdraw troops from these states; the Democrats agreed to hand Hayes the Presidency which Tilden had won. The bargain carried with it the nullification of the Civil War amendments insofar as the Negro was concerned. From then on Negroes were to be "eliminated from politics."[6]

The important thing today, as Myrdal points out, is that the average white southerner resists the thought that Negroes should vote in the same way white men do. He needs to believe that life was unbearable when the Negro voted. The myth of "the horrors of Reconstruction" thus enables the southerner to reconcile his unwillingness to see the Negro vote on the same basis that whites do with his attachment to the Constitution.[7]

---

[6] Carey McWilliams, *Brothers Under the Skin*, p. 265. For an excellent discussion of the Reconstruction period see Paul Lewinson, *Race, Class, and Party* (Oxford University Press, 1932), chaps. ii–v. See also Gunnar Myrdal, *An American Dilemma* (Harper & Brothers, 1944), chap. xx; and E. Franklin Frazier, *op. cit.*, pp. 114–139.

[7] Gunnar Myrdal, *op. cit.*, p. 448. Moon points out that "the freedmen had neither the political know-how nor the audacity to match the corrupt practices of Huey Long of Louisiana and Theodore (The Man) Bilbo of Mississippi." According to Moon, "There is ample evidence that this propertyless class played a minor role in the corrupt practices of the postwar period in which there was nationwide relaxation of standards of political morality." More importantly, Negroes did not dominate the state governments of the South. " 'The majority of state executive offices and the most important were always filled by white men. The congressional delegations were composed of the same class of individuals. The leading men in both branches of every state legislature were representatives of the dominant race. . . .' " Every attempt was made by white southerners to assure the failure of the Reconstruction governments; the participation of Negroes in the political process was unthinkable. See H. L. Moon, *Balance of Power: The Negro Vote* (Doubleday & Company, Inc., 1948), pp. 62–64.

... To assure the permanent elimination of the Negro from political affairs in the South, various legal and nonlegal devices were invented. "Grandfather clauses" were included in a number of the disfranchising constitutions adopted by southern states in the 1890's. The Louisiana constitution of 1898 provided that one might register permanently before September 1, 1898, if he was entitled to vote in any state January 1, 1867, or if he was the son or grandson of a person so entitled and twenty-one years of age or over in 1898. North Carolina included a grandfather clause in her revised statutes of 1905.[8] These clauses excluded Negroes from voting while permitting white persons of all kinds to vote. The United States Supreme Court held these clauses to be unconstitutional in 1915.

Some southern states have disfranchised Negroes through educational qualifications for voting. Ostensibly these requirements are nondiscriminatory, and they are not limited to southern states. The Supreme Court declared in 1898 that these requirements do not violate the Fifteenth Amendment. In actual practice, they are seldom demanded of whites, but almost always of Negroes. White election officials, especially in the Deep South, have often failed to find any educationally qualified Negro voters. In most cases the "educational" test consists of reading and writing a section of the federal or state constitution in such a way that the registrar is "satisfied." At the present time there are only two states, Mississippi and Louisiana, which require, in addition to reading and writing a section of the constitution, that the prospective voter "interpret" it to the "satisfaction" of the election official. These registrars have been hard to satisfy, and reports of extraordinary rulings on the meaning of the state and federal constitutions are numerous. Ralph Bunche cites a report of an Alabama registrar who asked a Negro to recite the Constitution. The Negro eloquently recited the Gettysburg Address, and the registrar exclaimed: "That's right. You can go ahead and register."[9]

---

[8] Charles S. Johnson, *op. cit.*, p. 165.

[9] Ralph Bunche, "The Disfranchisement of the Negro," in Sterling A. Brown, Arthur P. Davis, and Ulysses Lee (eds.), *The Negro Caravan* (The Dryden Press, Inc., 1941), p. 930.

Property requirements for voting are still in effect in Alabama, Georgia, and South Carolina, but they are invoked only if an applicant cannot meet the educational requirements. They call for the ownership of forty acres of land or personal property worth three hundred to five hundred dollars, and thus provide a way out for illiterate white people. The "character" requirement for voting exists now only in Louisiana and Georgia and is used both to disfranchise Negroes and to enable whites who cannot meet the property or educational requirements to register. Myrdal reports that actually the "character" qualification is used illegally elsewhere in the South where Negroes must be vouched for by whites.[10]

Between 1889 and 1908, ten southern states (Alabama, Arkansas, Florida, Louisiana, Mississippi, North Carolina, South Carolina, Tennessee, Texas, and Virginia) through constitutional provision or statutory law adopted a poll tax requirement for voting. The effectiveness of the poll tax as a device to regulate voting was considerably enhanced in Alabama, Mississippi, Louisiana, and Virginia by the provision that there would be no proceedings to collect the tax until it was three years overdue.

The effect of the new disfranchising constitutions is seen strikingly in Louisiana. The number of registered Negro voters in 1896 was 130,344; in 1900 it was 5,320. For one reason or another, the number of Negro registrants had dropped to 1,772 in 1916. The following figures refer to (1) the twenty-one-year-old and literate Negro populations in certain states in 1920 and (2) the Negro voters at any time, 1920–1930, in those states: Alabama: 269,847 and 3,500; Georgia: 369,511 and 10,000 at most; Mississippi: 290,792 and 850; Virginia: 248,347 and 12,000 to 18,000.[11]

The poll tax has disfranchised millions of whites and seems, in some cases, to have been deliberately designed for that purpose.[12] The significance of the poll tax in reducing the white vote

---

[10] Gunnar Myrdal, *op. cit.*, pp. 483–84.

[11] Paul Lewinson, *op. cit.*, pp. 214, 218, 219, 220.

[12] Ralph Bunche, "The Negro in the Political Life of the United States," *Journal of Negro Education* (July, 1941). Reprinted in Arnold M. Rose (ed.), *Race Prejudice and Discrimination* (Alfred A. Knopf, Inc., 1951), p. 226.

is seen in these percentages: "In 1940, Oklahoma . . . had sixty percent of its adult citizenry voting compared to eighteen percent in Arkansas; North Carolina had forty-three percent compared to twenty-two percent in Virginia; and Louisiana, which has been without the poll tax only since 1934, had twenty-seven percent compared to fourteen percent in Mississippi."[13] The tight control exerted by many southern politicians over their districts was indicated also in the estimates given on the floor of the House of Representatives on July 21, 1947. "In the presidential elections of 1944, ten percent of the potential voters voted in the seven poll-tax states, as against forty-nine percent in the free-vote states. In the congressional elections of 1946, the figures are five percent for the poll-tax states as compared with thirty-three percent for the free-voting states."[14]

The final device for disfranchising Negroes by the use of law was the "white primary." Since nomination in the Democratic primary is equivalent to election in the South, exclusion from the primary election meant the removal of Negroes from participation in the democratic process. In 1923 Texas passed the first "white primary" law, in which it was stated that "in no event shall a Negro be eligible to participate in a Democratic party primary election held in the state of Texas." This law was based on the Supreme Court's declaration in *Newberry* v. *United States* (256 U.S. 232, 1921) that congressional primaries were not "elections" within the meaning of the Constitution. This statute came to the Supreme Court in 1927 in *Nixon* v. *Herndon* (273 U.S. 536), and the Court ruled that it violated the equal-protection clause of the Fourteenth Amendment. Governor Dan Moody of Texas announced that Texas would not permit Negroes to vote regardless of what the Supreme Court said. He then called a special meeting of the Texas legislature, and a new statute was passed empowering every political party in the state through its executive committee "to prescribe the qualifications of its own members" and permitting it to determine "who shall be qualified to vote or otherwise participate in such political party." The state

---

[13]Gunnar Myrdal, *op. cit.*, p. 483.

[14]President's Committee on Civil Rights, *To Secure These Rights* (Simon and Schuster, Inc., 1947), p. 39.

executive committee quickly adopted a resolution which read, "All white Democrats who are qualified under the Constitution and laws of Texas and none others are to be allowed to participate in the primary elections." By a vote of five to four the Court held the second Texas law unconstitutional (*Nixon* v. *Condon*, 286 U.S. 73, 1932). Three weeks later the state Democratic convention, instead of the state executive committee, voted to exclude all but whites from the primary. In 1935, in *Grovey* v. *Townsend* (295 U.S. 45), the Supreme Court held that a vote of the state convention of a political party to restrict participation in the primary of that party did not violate the Fourteenth and Fifteenth amendments, provided the expenses of such primaries were paid by the party and not by the state. The Court took the position that this rule was simply the action of a private group acting on its right to determine its own membership and policies.[15]

If these tactics for the disfranchisement of Negroes seem surprising to some, it should be remembered that "the actual trickery, cheating, and intimidation necessary for the smooth operation of disfranchisement need be indulged in by only a small number of persons. Most people can avoid it. Their collaboration is necessary only to the extent of preserving a public sentiment upholding and supporting the system. In most cases, a resolute registrar can himself take care of the matter. And even he does not need to act openly when it has once become generally known among the Negroes in a community that they had better keep away from all politics."[16]

Violence or the threat of violence is still used from time to time in the South to keep the Negro out of politics. In 1948 a Negro, the father of six children, was shot and killed because he had insisted on voting in Georgia's Democratic primary election.[17] However, since the elimination of the Reconstruction government by 1877, the general tendency has been to abstain from violence and to use other means of disfranchisement. It has been "easier

---

[15] See R. E. Cushman, "The Laws of the Land," *Survey Graphic* (January, 1947), pp. 14–15; and Walter White, *A Man Called White* (The Viking Press, Inc., 1948), pp. 83–88.

[16] Gunnar Myrdal, *op. cit.*, p. 449.

[17] *New York Times*, September 12, 1948.

to buy, steal, or fail to count the Negro vote or to block the Negroes voting by intricate election laws and manipulation of the election machinery."[18]

Negro voters have often been intimidated by stares, insults, and such questions as "What do you want, nigger?" Economic sanctions have been reported; they include increases in taxes, loss of jobs, and "warnings" to ministers, teachers, and others. Still other techniques have been used—telling Negroes that the registration cards have "run out"; using tricky registration cards; giving assistance to white voters but none to Negro voters; waiving some of the usual requirements for the aged or for war veterans in the white group but not for Negroes; withholding the vote from Negroes who have been convicted of a crime, but overlooking this provision for whites; informing Negroes that they have to go elsewhere to vote; and saying that a registration cannot be accepted because all members of the board are not present.[19]

Racial Distinctions in State Law

This compendium of racist laws was accurate when compiled. On June 12, 1967, the United States Supreme Court ruled that states cannot outlaw marriages between whites and nonwhites. Although some laws have been repealed, the following tables describe the legal situation only a decade ago.

TABLE 1
LAWS WHICH LIMIT INTERRACIAL SEXUAL CONTACTS
The following states have statutes which make interracial sexual contacts illegal or which impose special penalties for such contacts:

Alabama	Nevada
Arkansas	North Dakota
Florida	Tennessee
Louisiana	

TABLE 2
LAWS WHICH REQUIRE RACIAL DISTINCTIONS IN IMPRISONMENT

State	Explanation
Alabama	No chaining or sleeping together of persons of different races.

[18] Gunnar Myrdal, *op. cit.*, p. 450.

[19] *Ibid.*, pp. 485–86.

Arkansas	White convicts guarded by whites only; separate apartments, furnishings; no handcuffing together.
Florida	Separation required except where impracticable.
Georgia	Misdemeanor to chain prisoners of different races together.
Louisiana	Separation required except where impracticable.
Mississippi	Separate facilities required.
North Carolina	Separation required in eating and sleeping facilities.
South Carolina	Segregation required in all prisons and chain gangs except in state penitentiary and farms.
Tennessee	Female prisoners segregated by race.
Texas	Segregation required at prison farm.
Virginia	Separation required as far as possible.

TABLE 3

STATUTES WHICH PROHIBIT MISCEGENATION

State	*Statute*
Alabama	Marriage, adultery, fornication between white and Negro prohibited. Marriage of person of Caucasian blood to Negro, Mongolian, Malay, or Hindu void.
Arkansas	Marriage between white and Negro or mulatto illegal.
Delaware	Marriage between white and Negro or mulatto void.
Florida	Marriage between white and Negro or mulatto illegal.
Georgia	Marriage between white and person of any other race void.
Indiana	Marriage between white and Negro void.
Kentucky	Marriage between white and Negro or mulatto void.
Louisiana	Marriage between white and person of color void; marriage or habitual cohabitation between white and Negro illegal, punishable by up to five years.
Maryland	Marriage between white and Negro, Negro and Malayan, or white and Malayan illegal, punishable by up to ten years.
Mississippi	Marriage between white and Negro or Mongolian void, punishable as if incestuous; advocacy of, or publication of matter which advocates or suggests, equality of races or intermarriage illegal.
Missouri	Marriage between white and Negro or Mongolian void.
Nebraska	Marriage between white and Negro, Japanese, or Chinese void.

Nevada	Marriage between white and person of black, brown, or yellow race prohibited.
North Carolina	Marriage between Negro and white prohibited.
Oklahoma	Marriage of person of African descent to anyone who is not prohibited.
South Carolina	Marriage of white to Negro, Indian, mulatto, or mestizo void.
Tennessee	Marriage of white and Negro prohibited.
Texas	Marriage of person of Caucasian blood and person of African blood void.
Utah	Marriage between white and Negro, Malayan, mulatto, quadroon, or octoroon void.
Virginia	Marriage of white and anyone who is not white or part white and part American Indian prohibited.
West Virginia	Marriage of white and Negro prohibited.
Wyoming	Marriage of white and Negro, mulatto, Mongolian, or Malayan void.

Suggestions for Further Reading

1. Richard Bardolph (ed.), *The Civil Rights Record: Black Americans and the Law, 1849–1970* (New York: Thomas Y. Crowell Company, 1970).

   An outstanding legal documentary history with helpful interpretive introductions.

2. Albert P. Blaustein and Robert L. Zangrando, *Civil Rights and the Black American* (New York: Simon & Schuster, 1970).

3. William F. Cheek, *Black Resistance Before the Civil War* (Beverly Hills: Glencoe Press, 1970).

4. Henry Steele Commager (ed.), *The Struggle for Racial Equality* (New York: Harper & Row, 1967).

5. Leon Friedman (ed.), *The Civil Rights Reader* (New York: Walker & Company, 1967).

   This contains the basic documents of the civil rights movement in the 1950's and 1960's.

6. Joanne Grant, *Black Protest: History, Documents and Analyses, 1619 to the Present* (New York: Fawcett, 1968).

7. Winthrop D. Jordan, *White Over Black: American Attitudes Toward the Negro, 1550–1812* (Chapel Hill: University of North Carolina Press, 1968).

    A prize-winning book that traces the origin of American slavery and racist attitudes in defense of the institution of slavery.

8. Stanley I. Kutler (ed.), *The Dred Scott Decision—Law or Politics?* (Boston: Houghton Mifflin, 1967).

    This collection of primary and secondary sources contains a bibliography on pages 184–88 that provides additional suggestions for reading on the Dred Scott decision.

9. Allen Weinstein and Frank Gatell, *American Negro Slavery* (New York: Oxford University Press, 1968).

    This anthology provides insight into the origins of slavery, the slaves and masters, and the system.

10. Joel Williamson (ed.), *The Origins of Segregation* (Boston: D. C. Heath and Co., 1968).

    Fourteen articles explore various aspects of the origins of racial separation.

Chapter Ten

Extralegal Racism, Institutional and Overt

The victims of segregation do not initially desire to be segregated, they do not "prefer to be with their own people," in spite of the fact that this belief is commonly stated by those who are not themselves segregated. A most cruel and psychologically oppressive aspect and consequence of enforced segregation is that its victims can be made to accommodate to their victimized status and under certain circumstances to state that it is their desire to be set apart, or to agree that subjugation is not really detrimental but beneficial. The fact remains that exclusion, rejection, and a stigmatized status are not desired and are not voluntary states. Segregation is neither sought nor imposed by healthy or potentially healthy human beings.
—KENNETH CLARK, *Dark Ghetto* (1965)

Discrimination can assume the legal forms discussed in the preceding chapter. Laws can permit or encourage or require discrimination. Antidiscrimination laws can be ignored. But there are other forms of racism that one might refer to as "extralegal." It is quite possible that the extralegal forms of racism and discrimination shape the world of the black man more than do the legal forms.

Perhaps it is because of this extralegal racism that the legal victories pioneered by such organizations as the NAACP have not affected the basic situation of black people in significant ways.

Lunch counters can be integrated, and so can busses, but the society as a whole remains segregated. Black people, especially if they are middle-class Negroes, can find accommodations in the Disneyland Hotel, but the residents of Watts are not finding accommodations in education, housing, and employment.

One example of extralegal racism is the "whitewash and blackout" treatment of black people in most of our school textbooks. Slavery is rarely discussed from the point of view of the slave—black authors and inventors are usually ignored—and on, and on, and on—spinning the myths of black history and reinforcing the false negative stereotypes. How many American schoolchildren know about Dr. Daniel Hale Williams, the black surgeon who performed the first successful heart operation? Yet these same children are taught about far-less-significant white heroes.

The images perpetuated by Hollywood movies, the first twenty years of television, and even our language itself are thoroughly imbued with racist orientation. There may never have been any federal laws preventing the integration of sports, but it was only twenty-five years ago that Jackie Robinson had to overcome barriers of bigotry before he succeeded in breaking the color line of our national pastime.

In many areas of extralegal discrimination, very little progress toward integration is being made. Frequently, for instance, a small number of Negroes are hired as "windowdressing" to create an image of open hiring practices. The word for that kind of minimal breakdown of segregation is "tokenism."

Complete desegregation in this realm is a long way off. It is just this type of discrimination which may yet be responsible for the complete shattering of the myth of the Melting Pot. For the laws may produce a modicum of desegregation, but the segregated heart can linger for many years.

The Perpetuation of the Ghetto*

The author reveals the role of the National Association of Real Estate Boards (NAREB) as the leader of private opposition to housing desegregation. NAREB activities during the Proposition 14 campaign in California in 1964 are discussed.

The Proposition passed by a two-thirds majority of those voting and became Article I, Section 26 of California's Constitution. It was declared unconstitutional by the California Supreme Court in 1966, and the decision was upheld by the United States Supreme Court. Nevertheless, housing discrimination continues to be the dominant mode.

Neither the state nor any subdivision or agency thereof shall deny, limit, or abridge directly or indirectly the right of any person who is willing or desires to sell, lease, or rent any part or all of his real property, to decline to sell, lease, or rent such property to such person or persons as he in his absolute discretion chooses.—*From Proposition 14, now Article 1, Section 26, of the California Constitution, passed, November, 1964, general election.*

Racial segregation in South Africa is maintained by the system of laws known as *apartheid*. Although there are no such laws in America, the members of minority races find, almost without exception, that they do not have free choice of residence in any part of this nation. They discover that private groups bar their entry into all-white neighborhoods and thus force them to live in districts designated by these private groups as appropriate for minority occupancy.

For many years the National Association of Real Estate Boards (NAREB), working through state and local boards, has been the undisputed leader of these private groups. NAREB has used economic, social, political, and legal power to fashion the American style of apartheid. But since 1948, legal power has not been available to them.

In the 1948 case of *Shelley* v. *Kraemer*,[1] the United States Supreme Court withdrew from the state courts the power to enforce racial restrictions on real estate. These restrictions had been the major device used by NAREB to create segregated districts. After *Shelley*, the courts and the legislatures in many states began to fashion legal tools to enable members of minority races to break out of their ghettos. To fight this shift in legal

---

*From *Apartheid American Style* by John Denton. Copyright © 1967 Diablo Press (San Francisco: 1967).

[1] 334 U.S. 1 (1948).

power, NAREB advanced the doctrine that the law should be "neutral." This meant that the law should leave the prosegregation forces free to impose their will through economic, social, and political force. Failing in its efforts to convince the courts and legislatures, NAREB began to look for a new strategy. It found one in the legislative referendum, a device existing in some states whereby the electorate can "veto" laws passed by their state or local legislative bodies. Because of the success of the referendums in Berkeley, California in 1963, in Seattle and Tacoma, Washington in 1964, NAREB was led to try another device of popular lawmaking, the initiative.

California Initiative Proposition 14

In the 101 years since the Emancipation Proclamation in 1863, no such devious roadblock to equal treatment for all citizens had been attempted. Proposition 14, as the initiative was called, had a strange ambivalence about it; lawyers and courts could not agree on its purpose and effect. Why should anyone wanting to sell or rent property need a constitutional amendment so that he could *refuse* to sell or rent? That appeared contradictory and pointless. Yet two out of three California voters favored the proposition. Or did they?

Did the voters understand that this proposition changed the basic laws of the state and handcuffed the state legislature and all municipal councils, preventing them from taking any steps to end housing discrimination against minority citizens? This appeared to be the effect of the amendment. But the campaign for its adoption was not based on this effect. Lawyers for the California Real Estate Association (CREA) worded the amendment, but CREA's public relations specialists sold it to the public not on the basis of its wording, but on the promise that it would repeal restrictions that did not exist. CREA created a monster called "forced housing" and frightened California voters into accepting Proposition 14 as the only way to save themselves.

The "monster" was CREA's own version of California's Rumford Act. The real Rumford Act had been passed in the closing moments of the 1963 California legislative session, after a bitter struggle fomented largely by CREA. This law named for its sponsor, Assemblyman Byron Rumford, bore little resemblance to the version against which CREA mounted its repeal campaign. Almost all housing included in the Rumford Act was already covered by earlier California law or by President Kennedy's executive order of November, 1962. The principal change from previous law was that the act provided for conciliation and enforcement by the state's Fair Employment Practices Commission (FEPC). CREA's publicists distorted the function of the FEPC by claiming that it would "force" owners to accept minority buyers or renters. They also alarmed homeowners by creating the false impression that the Rumford Act greatly extended the quantity of housing covered by antidiscrimination laws.

These distortions enabled CREA to make its planned appeal to bigotry seem respectable. In the safe anonymity of the ballot booth, the realtors knew they could count on large segments of the white majority to support segregation. California initiative laws provided the means of putting before the electorate a constitutional amendment permitting owners and realtors to continue their segregation practices. All that was needed was an incident and passage of the Rumford Act was the incident that the realtors' leaders wanted. It permitted them to try out their plan to outlaw all fair housing laws. This is clearly shown by their actions in the first few months after the passage of the Rumford Act.

Immediately after the close of the 1963 legislative session, an attempt was made to collect signatures on referendum petitions for a special election to allow the voters to reject the Rumford Act. Since CREA had struggled to prevent passage of the act, the groups formed to support the referendum naturally assumed that it would lead the repeal fight. Instead, CREA officials remained aloof and strangely silent. Lacking CREA support, the proponents of the referendum failed to obtain the needed signatures. It was at this point that CREA revealed its plan for an initiative to repeal the Rumford Act.

The initiative process permits a sponsor to draft and submit directly to the electorate a proposed law or constitutional amendment. Initiative laws, which exist in more than a score of states, specify the procedures to be followed to qualify a proposition for the ballot. To qualify its proposition for the 1964 election, CREA had to submit to the secretary of state petitions containing signatures of registered voters equal to eight percent of the 1960 vote for all candidates for governor.

Adoption of initiative proposals like Proposition 14 can wipe out the effectiveness of existing antidiscrimination laws *and* freeze into state constitutions or city charters a ban on future action against housing discrimination by the legislature or city council. The outlines of a nationwide plan to thus undermine fair housing, directed by NAREB, can be seen in the initiative campaigns in the states of California and Illinois, and the cities of Detroit, Michigan and Akron, Ohio.

The real estate industry's campaign against fair housing is disguised by a sanctimonious concern with homeowners' rights. In reality it is part of a pervasive design of the industry to perpetuate ghetto housing in this country. To understand the industry's fight against fair housing laws, the reader should understand that the ghetto system means not only the concerted effort of organized real estate to maintain and strengthen segregated housing, but also the systematic exclusion of minority citizens from ownership of income-producing property, businesses, and all kinds of real estate outside the minority ghettos. The latter effect is principally accomplished by excluding minority real estate agents from membership in real estate boards and affiliated organizations controlled by NAREB and by excluding minority citizens from employment not only in the business of real estate brokerage, but also in related activities of finance, management, appraising, title insurance, escrow, and home building.

From this ghetto system many other evils flow, including the problem of *de facto* school segregation, inadequate representation of minorities in politics and government, and isolation of the minority population in the central cities where job opportunities are shrinking. Thus, seeking to understand how Proposition 14 would work to preserve the ghetto system, the courts would be faced with complicated factual and sociological problems that could not be clearly presented to them in suits testing the constitutionality of the new law. To make a legal determination about the new constitutional amendment, the courts would be required to analyze how the law would work; in brief, did the law say to segregationists "go to it" or did it say to the state government "hands off"? If the latter, was this constitutionally possible, once the state had determined that segregation was threatening the health, safety, and well-being of its citizens?

The Ghetto System and "Black" Political Power

The ghetto system enables white politicians to keep the political power of the minority voters to a minimum. The concentration of racial and ethnic minorities in a relatively small geographic area allows them to draw district boundaries to include all or most of these groups in one district, thus reducing minority political power to a fraction of what it should be. In California, the result of this bunching of minority votes has been that Negroes and Mexican-Americans are generally under-represented on city councils. Disproportionately small numbers of city jobs have been filled by members of minority racial groups. For example, in San Francisco, there were until recently no Negro firemen; and in Oakland, out of a police force of about six hundred, fewer than three percent are Negroes and fewer than one percent are Mexican-Americans.

Gerrymandering of in-city political districts combined with under-representation of urban centers in the state legislature results in a gross deprivation of political power for racial minorities in state government. The forty-member California State Senate gained its first Negro member in 1967. This, added to the five Negroes elected to the eighty-member Assembly, will bring Negro participation to a little less than five percent. But this was California's Negro population of the state well before the 1960 census.

At times in America, political power has been used to gain economic advancement, but this will be impossible for Negroes until they are free to settle where they wish. When their voting strength is spread more evenly through the general population, they can extend their power by voting as a "bloc" and thus become the crucial vote in municipal and state elections.

Many are confused about how a minority gains political power. They erroneously assume that bunching minorities into one district gives them maximum power since they are thus assured of having one representative. It is assumed that if they are spread thinly in a number of districts, the effects of their votes will be submerged in the greater effect of the majority vote. This ignores the fact that the majority is usually split between two or more candidates and that the balance of power will often rest with any small bloc of voters who have some overriding interests which unite them. To control these swing votes, parties will often choose a candidate who appeals to minority bloc voters either because he is a member of the minority group or because he expresses views consistent with their interests and in support of their needs.

This kind of appeal to the minority voter has been most evident for many years in New York City, where the major parties were often concerned with balancing their tickets with an Irish Catholic and a Jew. Today, ticket balancing in New York requires consideration of the Italian, Puerto Rican, and Negro minorities. Minority bloc voting is a legitimate and traditional American political device. When Negroes and other minority groups are prevented from settling outside designated districts, they are prevented from achieving the political power which is a necessary prerequisite to their attainment of equality with the white majority.

*The Myths of Black History**

The racist distortions and omissions, or "whitewashes" and "black-outs," are passionately exposed and condemned by the famous sociologist who was a central figure in the strike at San Francisco State College in 1968–69. Though this article may seem somewhat dated, it shows the prevailing concerns of the late 1960's.

As a boy I used to hear old folks laughing and talking about the way white folks tricked Negroes to America as slaves with stories of a land where creeks were overflowing with molasses and flapjacks grew on trees. While hardly anybody seemed really

---

*Hare, Nathan, "Brainwashing of Black Men's Minds." © 1966 by *Liberator* magazine, Vol. 6, No. 9. New York.

taken in by that myth, it did have, as most jokes have of necessity, a certain tone of truth : that the Negro in America has been everlastingly misled, tricked, and brainwashed by the ruling race of whites.

It seems certain, as recorded history bears out, that white conquerors supplemented more deadly weaponry by falling back on ideological warfare in confrontations with other races in the lands they "explored." Guns were used, as in Hawaii, for example, but not guns alone. Explorers, trailed by missionaries and other warriors, first sought to convert "natives" to the Christian religion. Then, failing to "save" the pagan chief, they merely proceeded to convert a "commoner" and provide him guns with which to overthrow the chief. This well-known tactic of divide-and-rule is proving just as efficient to this day. "Why" is still the question.

Africans in the know have finally come to realize that : "Once we had only the land. The white man came and brought us the Bible. Now we have the Bible, and they have the land." To accomplish this piracy—and retain the loot indefinitely—it was of course necessary to control the minds and bodies of the subjugated blacks. Indeed, control over the body is one basic means of manipulating thought. This was accomplished even more successfully in the case of American blacks, compared to Africans, because of the fact that brainwashing is best implemented by removing the subject from his normal setting, severing his social relations and identities ordinarily sustained only by regular interaction with family, friends, and "significant others." Communication is then restricted—in the case of the Negro slave, it was virtually destroyed—and the "stripping process," the process of self-mortification (the destruction of identity and self-esteem) is then almost a matter of course.

Not only were slaves cut off from contacts and lifelines of old, they were restricted in their social relations with one another (sold apart as well from their families on the whims of their "masters") and forbidden to congregate without the presence of a white "overseer." Even after they were permitted to enter the confines (pun intended) of Christendom, pastors of Negro churches such as First Baptist in Petersburg, Virginia, seat of a violent slave uprising, were at first typically white. Ritualistic deference (such as keeping eyes downcast in the presence of whites, addressing them as "Mr.," "Sir" or "Suh," and other means described in Bertram Doyle's *Racial Etiquette in the South*)[1] also aided in undermining the slave's self-respect and stimulating his glorification of the white man's world which in turn made him more inclined to bow down to the Great White Society.

A University of Chicago history professor, Stanley Elkins, in a book called *Slavery*,[2] has likened the practices and consequences of the slave plantation to the Nazi concentration camp. This fits in with the basic principles of brainwashing in the setting of "total institutions" (prisons, asylums, concentration and POW camps) set forth by University of California sociologist Erving Goffman in the book, *Asylum[s]*.[3] The slave plantation was a total institution in that a large number of persons were restricted against their will to an institution which demanded total loyalty and was presided over and regimented by an "all-powerful" staff and "master."

Even the language of white America has exhibited a built-in force destructive of the black man's self-image. Blacks were taught to worship a god who was always painted white, and then, to sing that they wanted to "be more and more like Jesus" who would be "riding six white horses when He comes." While the color white symbolized purity (Negroes may be found singing in church houses, even today, that they are going to be "washed white as snow in the blood of the lamb"), black stood—stands now—for evil and derogatory referents. You "blackball" a person from your club; an employee is "blacklisted"; phony magic is "black magic"; illegal commerce comprises a "black market"; you are in a "dark mood" or "blackhearted" on "Black Thursday"; especially if you are behind the eight-ball, which of course is painted black in pool. If a chartreuse cat or a polka-dot cat crosses your trail, it is no cause for alarm, but if a black cat crosses your trail, you are doomed to bad luck. We refer here only to the cat

---

[1] Bertram W. Doyle, *Etiquette of Race Relations in the South* (1968).

[2] Stanley Elkins, *Slavery* (2nd ed., 1968).

[3] Erving Goffman, *Asylums* (1961).

that purrs. Admittedly women may be in trouble when some black cats cross their trails.

It seems no accident, in any case, that a romance word for "black"—"Negro" (capitalized only in the past four decades)— was attached to a group which, owing to the white man's sexual drives and his Christian manipulation of the sexual and familial relations of his slaves, soon became a potpourri of colors and racial derivations. The word "black" was used by the English to describe a free man of color, while "Negro" was used to designate a black slave. Naturally, the word "Negro" eventually assumed a connotation of low esteem regardless of, but not exclusively independent of, the color or biological characteristics of the individual to whom the appellation was applied. This allowed some Negroes of "fair" features to "pass" (also a word for the act of death, just as a Negro who passed was called a "harp"—which he was going to play when he got to Heaven). Confusion arose requiring laws fixing a white person's race as Negro if it was known that he had even the remotest bit of white [black?] ancestry. Today's experts still stammer in their efforts to clarify the concept: *Webster's Collegiate Dictionary* finally winds up declaring a Negro anyone with "more or less Negro blood" and the 1960 Bureau of the Census instructions directed interviewers to classify as Negro any descendant of a black man, or a black man and any other race, *unless the Negro is regarded as an Indian in the community!* This was a concession to the white-Negro-Indians of the Carolinas and Oklahoma where I have known Negro women of the Aunt Jemima variety to wear a wig (long before it was the fashion), marry an Indian, fry their offsprings' hair, and send them to a white or/ and Indian school, except when the children were bounced back as a bit too black.

The standard of beauty, so essential to a group's self-image, also was derogatory to the Negro. Not only were mulatto descendants of white masters given special privileges and higher status among slaves, all beauty queens and men of power were visibly white. Even today, "Miss Washington, D.C.," where Negroes are in the majority, for example, is likely to live in the suburbs, in Fairfax, Virginia, or Silver Spring, Maryland, and, regardless of her residence, she is certain to be white.

On top of all of the foregoing, there has been a massive effort,

deliberate and persistent in speed, to keep the black man in ignorance. During the early days of slavery, it was illegal to teach,
aid, or abet a black slave to learn to read, for fear he might find
out how he was being treated. Books, newspapers, periodicals,
and other media of information have consistently been published
or controlled, in almost every case, by white men. The King James
Version of the Bible, the only book many Negroes ever read, also
plays down the black man; for example, "black but (nevertheless)
comely." Negro worshippers are exhorted to tuck in their whim-
pering tails and conform to white society by such tidbits as: "The
meek shall inherit the earth," "Thou shalt not covet [thy] neigh-
bor's goods . . . ," "We'll all be one when we get over yonder" and
"To him who hath shall be given, and to him who hath not, *even
that which he thinks he hath,* shall be taken away."

Most other books, too, including those on the Negro—especially those promoted and accepted in the United States—are not
only published but also generally written by white men. Thus
the Negro is led to depend on the white man to tell him what to
think even about himself! During Negro History Week last
February (known as "Brotherhood Week" now that we are "integrated"), I happened to notice in the lobby of Howard University's Founders Library a set of twelve books on display as "books
about the Negro." I knew, because of my special interest in
literature on the race issue, the names of eleven of the authors.
All were white. I walked over to the circulation desk and asked
the black gentlemen behind it: "How about a book about the
Negro by a Negro?" He laughed and thought the matter one
big joke.

Children (learning to read on white Dicks and Janes) inter-
nalize the hatred of black men early in life, although some black
Anglo-Saxon Negroes will claim that they never knew there was
a difference made between whites and Negroes until they were
going on seventeen or had "got grown." Only a moment ago,
even as I was writing this article, I learned that a black school-
teacher in Washington, D.C.'s summer school program got mad
at a white teacher and called her a "black Jew!" With teachers
like that, our children don't have a chance.

I once sat on a churchhouse step and watched a band of
boys about ten years old stand beside their bicycles on the side-

walk and swap black epithets for thirty minutes by the clock. "You black as tar; can't get to heaven on an electric wire." "You so black your mamma had to throw a sheet over your head so sleep could slip up on you." Thus they grow up to look down on their own kind and idolize, mimic, and conform to white standards of behavior.

Consequently, the black man's passive approval of the control of media of communication by white men in this mass society makes it virtually impossible for a black leader to emerge except through the white press. Accordingly, aspirants as well as established "spokesmen" for the Negro must slant their strategy toward capturing the spotlight of the white press.

W. E. B. DuBois, for example, had to contend in his day with white promotion of Booker T. Washington, now widely known as an Uncle Tom. DuBois sought to persuade Negroes to do half-a-century ago—though he later realized his error—what the NAACP eventually did, but, by that time, still fifty years ahead of his time and having fallen into disrepute with the white establishment, was not even invited to the NAACP's fiftieth anniversary, according to newspaper reports. Schools fail to carry his name, in spite of his legendary attributes as a scholar, just as E. Franklin Frazier, in spite of his acceptance by the white sociological establishment, has been overlooked. Instead, acceptable Negroes such as Booker T., Ralph Bunche, George Washington Carver, Charles Johnson, and Marian Anderson, along with Abraham Lincoln and Franklin D. Roosevelt, are symbols for the Nation's black schoolchildren. Although Rev. King is not a name for a school—to my knowledge yet while he lives—he eventually will join his brethren as a white-groomed Negro leader, as indicated by the plethora of prizes and honorary degrees already bestowed upon his crown.

Conversely, all the pretense of not understanding "black power" (a simple phrase) is merely an effort to whitewash the tardy awakening of black men in America and deter them from any attempt to acquire or utilize power to their own advantage.

White theorists have disseminated a number of false theories readily gobbled up and parroted by hoodwinked Negroes. One is that the Negro should not be bitter, whereas Anna Freud, in *Ego and the Mechanisms of Defense*, suggests that it is natural to be bitter in a bitter situation. For instance, if somebody sticks a pin in a portion of your anatomy and you do not yell out, then something is wrong with you or that portion of your anatomy. Another erroneous theory, geared to keeping Negroes conformist, is that Negroes are hopelessly outnumbered in America and must act to gain white sympathy, to "change white hearts and souls." This led to the assimilationist craze now increasingly apparent on the part of the Negro's "civil rights" movement before SNCC and CORE sought to put some sense into the movement. LBJ, in a recent effort to scare rioting Negroes, made a big ado about the Negro comprising only ten percent of the population (actually he comprises at least eleven percent, according to the government's own figures) but white boys never get their facts straight about the Negro. The truth is that, regardless of their numbers, white men rule—two percent in South Africa or Jamaica, forty percent in Washington, D.C. or Mississippi or ninety-nine percent in Maine or Montana. It is a mental attitude—not numbers. What excuse, then, had black men in Rhodesia (who grumbled privately when Smith took over but grinned and cowardly tucked their tails whenever a white person passed by for fear he might overhear them)? Outnumbering whites twenty-three to one, they could have taken each white man—one each grabbing a finger, ten others a toe, one the head and two whatever portion pleased them—and pulled him apart.

But, of course, black men are supposed to be nonviolent in conflict with whites, while violent in his behalf and with one another. The nonviolent hypocrisy has been perhaps the most ridiculous and appalling farce ever perpetrated upon and swallowed by a supposedly sane group of human beings. Only recently have black people begun showing signs of shedding this preposterous shackle.

It is amusing to watch the media's effort to commit the Afro-American to the Vietnam fiasco. While Afros virtually never make the daily press in a laudatory manner—not to mention the front page—they frequently find themselves turning up there now in uniform, holding up some wounded white "buddy," eating chicken, turkey, or goose on Thanksgiving Day, or saving a Bible from perspiration and harm by wearing it under the band around their helmets. It is enough to cause a man to hang his head in shame.

Even on the home front, news about the Afro is slanted and sorted to suit the white power structure's purposes. William Worthy, for example, foreign correspondent for the *Afro-American* newspaper, was gagged by white newspapers when he ran afoul of then-Attorney-General Robert Kennedy's great white liberal graces after going to Cuba, and reporting that Castro was solving the race problem exported there by United States-dominated industry. William Worthy was believed to be the first newsman to test the right to go abroad, write home the news, and come home again—and though the white press is forever crying crocodile tears over "freedom of the press"—the press fell curiously silent in this case. So much so, that some brainwashed Negro students in a class of mine, during a discussion on mass communications, insisted that the United States has a free press. Yet, when I placed the name of William Worthy on the board—at a time when his case was current—along with five multiple-choice descriptions of his identity, only six in a class of twenty-four were able to choose the correct answer.

These students were, in the full sense of the word, pathetically "miseducated," in the manner described by Carter G. Woodson, in his *The Miseducation of the Negro*. They, like most Negroes, are merely products of generations of the most efficient and gigantic system of brainwashing the world has ever known. Thus, while they once merely chanted desires of being "more and more like Jesus," they now typically long and struggle to be more and more like "whitey" as a group. No doubt their brains, at least, at last have been *"washed white as snow. . . ."*

*The Not-So-Subtle Put-Down**

The scenes described in the following pages have been experienced again and again by black victims of white racism. The cruelty of the racist system is occasionally forgotten in the mass of statistical evidence that is available. But it is much more difficult to forget the impact of personal testimony.

*Reprinted from *The Black Situation* by Addison Gayle, Jr., copyright 1970 by permission of the publisher, Horizon Press, New York.

The Negro, the world's greatest dissimulator, is unable to survive in a world where dissimulation is the norm, hypocrisy the accustomed and accepted mode of behavior. Better to be entrapped in a web of practicality where men take the word "place" as the God-ordained condition of twenty-five million people than to be enmeshed in a web where men are convinced that their manifest destiny lies in mesmerizing the natives by their spell-binding, hypnotic oratory. The first web can be cut; its strands can be severed; at the least, men never tire of attempting to rip it apart. The second web, however, is non-corporeal, having no body, no structure, no substance. It is impervious to assault, except that of the most violent nature; for the Messiah is incapable of differentiating between rhetoric and practice until such time as those who see truth in men's actions, not in their words, nail him, shamelessly and without guilt, to the cross.

It is not long before the Negro who journeys from South to North is called witness to his moment of truth. Epiphanies are almost daily occurrences. There is so much to be revealed. There are so many thousands of shapes, forms and symbols through which revelation may come. The first epiphany often occurs in the North when the Negro first faces his hoped-for-employer. Contrary to most reports, on first arriving in the North, the Southern Black is not incensed by the ghetto—this comes later—for the Northern ghetto has always held mystical, romantic connotations for him. Here it is that the tenuous tie with the North, perfected through the years by the mass exodus of his ancestors, is most secure. Few Blacks in the South have neither friends nor relatives in Northern ghettoes. Thus, neither the filth and stench of the ghetto, nor its chronic violence can rid the newcomers of that compulsion to dwell among his own in the Harlems, Wattses, Houghs and Bedford Stuyvesants of the North. . . .

Early in the morning on that dark overcast day, I checked out five jobs, all of which had surreptitiously vanished before I arrived. My sixth stop was the corner of Delancey Street and Broadway, a combination restaurant and newsstand which, according to the *New York Times*, "Wanted: a man to do light portering, some clerking." It was the "light portering" which caused me to be hopeful, for such job descriptions in the South are usually synonyms for Negroes.

I was met at the door of the shop by a dark-hued white man who, mistaking me for a customer, commented on the state of the weather. Smiling, I proceeded to point out the true nature of my business which was not to buy wares but instead to sell my labor. No sooner had I mentioned the ad than the man abruptly turned his back to me, and walked quickly to the other end of the store, informing me through a running monologue with himself that the job was taken. However, his actions, not his words, convinced me that he was lying. All morning I had been turned away from jobs, always with a smile, a sympathetic murmur of sympathy, unbelievable to be sure, yet unchallengeable on any save intuitive grounds.

This man had made it impossible for me to believe him. I left the store, went across the street to a drugstore, waited a few minutes, and dialed the number listed in the newspaper. The man himself answered the telephone. Mimicking James Mason, I asked if the job listed in the morning paper had been filled. The answer was no. I asked if I could come over to see about the job. I was told to come at once. I went to the store a second time. This time the man met me, rage breathing from every pore of his nostrils, his ugly face contorted into the most weird design.

"Yes?" he growled.

"I came for the job," I announced.

"There ain't no job!" he replied.

"I just called, and you said there was one," I answered, "You said come right over."

Briefly, a flicker of surprise came to his eyes, but he recovered quickly. "You didn't call here," he said; "that's a lie, there ain't no job." He turned on his heels and went to serve a customer who had come in.

I stared after him for a few minutes before finally walking out of the store. There was a big lump in my stomach. My hands shook noticeably. In facing him with what I knew to be the truth, in forcing him to acknowledge his own lie, I had, perhaps, scored a moral victory. Yet I was still without a job because a man who did not know me, had decided *a priori* that I should not have one. The moral victory was far less sustaining than my growing hatred.

Floyd Patterson, in his first fight with Ingemar Johanssen, was knocked to the canvas again and again, only to rise yet another time. Many were awed by the tenacious courage displayed by the champion, the refusal to stay down, to say die. I was not amazed; for I too had learned early to absorb merciless punishment, to pick myself up from the canvas of a ring in which the fight can only end in life or death.

Like the ex-heavyweight champion, I was on my feet searching for another job less than fifteen minutes after absorbing a crushing blow to my psyche. This time I intended to shape the odds nearer to my liking. I decided to buy a job.

The headquarters of the job-buying market is a narrow street at the southern tip of Manhattan, some few feet from the Hudson River. On this narrow street, occupying an entire block, is an assortment of dilapidated office buildings housing numerous agencies which legally traffic in human flesh. Sometimes as many as five agencies are in one single building. Each agency occupies a large room, two at the most, partitioned into two sections. One section, the larger, is usually, though not always, furnished with folding chairs; in the other section, beyond the partition, neat, middle-aged businessmen (white) and their assistants sit at wooden desks surrounded by telephones.

Throughout the day, from opening time at eight o'clock in the morning to closing time at five o'clock at night, people of all races come to these partitioned offices offering themselves as saleable commodities. On any given day, one will find a small number of white applicants, a large number of Puerto Rican applicants, and a great number of black applicants.

I chose one of the smaller agencies which had emptied, somewhat, at that hour of the day. A number of people were still present. Some were waiting, I suppose, for clarification of job offers. Some women were checking to see if the prospects for domestic work tomorrow were brighter than prospects today. Standing along the two walls of the agency were older Negro men, in whose faces the tragedy of a people was stenciled in bold, heavy lines. Watching each new arrival suspiciously, their ears attuned to the ring of the telephone; they smiled condescendingly each time the eyes of the agent swept their paths; for the agent was their savior, able to reward them with a half day's work, enabling them to fight off the D.T.'s, hunger, or eviction yet a little while longer.

I was met by an assistant, a charming, brownskinned girl of about twenty-one, heavily rouged, her hair in a pompadour, her false eyelashes flickering as if in amusement. We smiled at one another; and she communicated her nervousness by smoking her cigarette almost to the filter, leaving her long fingers stained a deeper brown than her skin. Like me, she too lived at a fever pitch of desperation; though she, like some omniscient spectator of Dante's Hell, watched men, women, and sometimes teenage children stacked before her eyes, no longer human, but instead objects to be auctioned away for one week's salary—the legal requirements of the agency. She had dwelled among these hollow men and women so long, these mechanical men and women of Kafka's novels, that she had become almost hollow and mechanical herself. I pitied her, even as she pitied me.

She helped me to fill out several forms, and after I had completed them, she motioned me to a folding chair, took the forms, and deposited them on the desk of a short, fat white man, whose bald head seemed a comic distraction in this place where laughter would have been an unforgivable crime.

Not too long after, I sat in a chair at the desk, staring at the man's bald head, listening to him describe a job recently referred to his agency. The job was located in a restaurant on Broadway, two blocks from City Hall. The prerequisites were for a young man who had some experience at handling a cash register, and who would not balk at long hours. I satisfied the agent that I met all the requirements, after which he brought out a number of papers upon which I scribbled my signature. The assistant gave me a card bearing the agency's letterhead and the name of the man I was to see, and smiled at me knowingly; I quickly left that little room, which smelled like something akin to death.

The restaurant was located in the basement of a large hotel which, at that time, was undergoing alteration. I passed several black workers: plasterers, hod-carriers, and porters, one of whom pointed the way to the manager at the door of the office—he, seeing me approaching, had come from behind a glass enclosure. He was young, blond, his face clean of blemishes, his body thin, athletic in appearance. His movements seemed impetuous, quick, and determined. I handed him the agent's card.

Hardly had he finished reading the card, before, without hesitation, almost as if I were not present, he blurted out: "But why did they send you? We don't hire Negroes."

We recoiled one from the other! He because he had said what he did; I because he had said it so blatantly. He was, I suppose, an honest man, and instinctively, he uttered the truth which needed no supporting rationale. I never thought for a moment that he hated me, nor that he thought much about me at all; this was not necessary to justify the irrefutable statement: "We don't hire Negroes."

It was the look of consternation on my face which made him offer me carfare, which prompted him to tell me that he was sorry. He looked after me with sympathetic eyes, as I, having spurned his offer of carfare, backed away as one fighting to sleep through some horrible nightmare. I walked away, almost in a state of shock. In this shocked state, I telephoned the agency, reported what had happened, hung up the phone, and boarded the "A" train for Brooklyn.

When finally I reached my stop in the heart of Bedford-Stuyvesant, the ghetto to which I came now for some solace, for some semblance of myself, some testament of myself as a human being, I left the subway, bypassing the bars along the way, where I would find that human misery by which to measure my own. I avoided those who knew me, even at that moment when I wanted their affection the most. I avoided them because I did not want them to see me cry. Crying is an act which one should perform only in private, for crying is a private way of groping for truth. Once inside of my apartment, I removed the phone from the hook, locked my door, fell across the bed, and cried.

On the bed, clawing and clutching at the pillows, my breath coming in quick, short gasps, my nose filled with mucus, my mouth hot, dry, I twisted, shouted, and screamed almost in convulsion; the tears gushing from my eyes; my body burning as if seared by some scorching, burning flame; with my fists I flailed the pillows; with my fingernails I tore at my hair, drew blood from my skin; like some hurt, wounded beast in orgasm. I surrendered my soul to that Faustian devil who hovers over the black male, in pain, in ecstasy, in total to complete, everlasting hatred.

In time I would come to understand that it was not only the acts of discrimination; not only the feelings of rejection; not only the soul-rending words, "We don't hire Negroes"; but, instead, the motivation for the surrender to Mephistopheles was simply that white men had made me cry, had forced me to that point where I would seek a baptism in my own tears; a baptism which would cleanse me of any sense of responsibility to them, any sense of affection for them, any sense of respect for them. The ultimate pain which any man can inflict upon another is to force him to tears.

The Boomerang of White Racism*

Black people are not the only victims of white racism against blacks. The following article shows some of the symptoms and effects on white people of their pathological racist behavior.

If you look at the racial problem from a black man's point of view, you can see the jokes as well as the injustices. Which is to say that you can then understand this: The underlying syndrome that must be attacked is much more subtle than a white policeman's nightstick. It's more like a topsy-turvy vaudeville routine in which all the funny lines come from the straight men.

A favorite comic theme among the "concerned and enlightened" elements of white society is "Let's Stamp Out Racial Hatred." Hoo boy! Hatred has very little to do with the central problem, Charlie. What is done to and withheld from black folk day by day in this country is based on neither hate nor horror. On the contrary. It is coldly impersonal. Like the brains of precocious computers.

Simply put, it seems to me that white folk are convinced, deep in their bones, that the way they run this melting pot—with black folk unmelted at the bottom—is nothing more than the natural order of things.

*From Bob Teague, "Charlie Doesn't Even Know His Daily Racism Is a Sick Joke," *New York Times Magazine*, September 15, 1968. Quoted in Robert V. Guthrie, *Being Black* (San Francisco: Canfield, 1970). © 1968 by The New York Times Company. Reprinted by permission.

What happens quite naturally for example, is that a black *bon vivant* who shows up in a clean shirt at a posh restaurant is approached by white customers who beg him to get them a good table, please. There is nothing malicious about it. They simply think of black men in clean shirts as waiters.

Similarly, a black man caught on foot near a public building lot is likely to be buttonholed by a pale proud patrician who wants his limousine fetched in a hurry.

And even the most militant white egalitarians are prone to compliment one another by saying, "That's real white of you, Edgar." Obviously, the notion that anything white is inherently superior to its black counterpart is built into the white American idiom, and thus into the white American mind.

Do you think it's accidental that the bad guys in Western movies are the ones in black sombreros?

This is not to suggest that white folk don't feel a respectable amount of guilt now and then, here and there. What the hell. They're human, too. In fact, I personally witnessed a veritable orgy of private and public breast-beating among whites early this year—that is, after they had recovered from the initial shock of learning from the President's Commission on Civil Disorders that "the main cause of black violence in the ghettos last summer was white racism."

Although I had reached a similar conclusion by the time I was ten years black, I nevertheless judged the President's commission to be somewhat crude. You shouldn't spring a thing like that on 180 million unsuspecting suspects without warning. They didn't even have time to consult their lawyers.

Fortunately for the white masses, however, before their breasts had been pounded into lily-white pulp, a nationally famous Washington ventriloquist intervened. Through a captive puppet, he delivered a one-line joke that helped to bring white America back to normal. "It would be a mistake," the straight man said, "to condemn a whole society."

The implication was clear: Perhaps only a small minority of misguided whites were the culprits.

The collective sigh of relief was still in the air when a black civic leader, a former city councilman, died in East St. Louis. Naturally, since the natural order had been restored, the Valhalla

Cemetery refused the corpse on the ground that "everybody else buried in Valhalla is white." Who said the people who run cemeteries have no sense of humor?

A popular variation of the Valhalla skit was played this summer in the Republican political arena. Bold headlines stirred up a fuss around the two leading contenders for the G.O.P. Presidential nomination because each belonged to a private club, in different states, that bars black folk from membership—as if nearly all white folk don't belong to a Society of, a Committee to, a Council for or a Convention on that maintains the same standards of purity.

I am exposed to the same basic joke almost every time I walk into an all-white apartment building to keep an appointment with a friend. I see panic in the eyes of the pale residents coming out as I go in—trying to recall whether they locked their doors. And the doorman himself seems to be trying to remember the standard procedure for What to Do Until the Cops Come.

Although it has taken me many years to reach this point of view—perhaps because I managed a get-away of sorts from the ghetto—I understand now that neither the Valhalla Cemetery nor the doorman and the rest of white America are motivated by hate. To their way of thinking, the business of keeping black folk at a comfortable distance is not a matter of racism, not a choice between right and wrong. It's like fearing the bomb, saluting the flag and sending a card on Mother's Day. It's an automatic reflex action. In other words, no emotion of any kind is necessarily involved.

Consider, for example, those magazine and newspaper advertisements for "flesh-colored" bandages. The color they mean blandly ignores the color of most flesh on this planet. Mine in particular. But the top bananas who dreamed up that bit would be sorely aggrieved if someone called them racists. Some of those chaps are probably card-carrying fellow-travelers in the N.A.A.C.P., and their wives probably sent food to the poor people's shantytown in Washington. Their "flesh-colored" bandages are merely a profitable manifestation of a common assumption among white folk: White skin is what human flesh is *supposed* to look like. Anything else—black skin, certainly—is irrelevant. Sort of a whimsical goof by Mother Nature.

How else can a black man explain those ubiquitous cosmetic ads showing a pale proud beauty using the facial lotion that promises to give her "the natural look"? The joke here is that this same beauty, and those who swear by "flesh-colored" bandages spend as much time in the sun as possible to darken their natural looks. They even buy chemical tans in bottles. And did you ever hear a commercial Goldilocks say, "Goodness gracious, my tan is much too dark"?

A spin-off joke from that particular farce is the honest pretense among whites that only their backward brothers—way down yonder in Mississippi—are hypersensitive to color. The white liberal party line says in effect that truly civilized whites regard black skin as a rather flamboyant costume for humankind, but nonetheless legitimate.

This is self-deception, of course. My experience has been that most white folk are so caught up in the seductive *mystique* of White Power that their brains are rarely brushed by the notion that the "natural order" in this country is in any way forced and unnatural.

Only last week one of my white friends—to be known here as Charlie—called my attention to one of those "flesh-colored" ads. Although Charlie is well past 35 and literate and had read similar ads over the years, he was seeing it clearly for the first time.

"Man, look at this," he said, wearing an embarrassed grin. "They even insult you in the ads, don't they?"

Charlie's insight is not yet complete, however. If it ever is, he'll say "we" instead of "they."

How could good old Charlie have missed the point of that joke for so many years and thus become an accessory to the largely unconscious white conspiracy? It was easy. Just as it is for white gossip columnists to report regularly that the sexy movie queen who appears to be nude on the screen is actually hiding the goodies in a "flesh-colored" bra. They wouldn't dream of explaining such illusions in terms of "a bra that virtually matched her skin." Those gossip columnists, by God, know "flesh color" when they see it.

All of which is to say that white folk are immersed in such a totally racist climate that—like fish born in the ocean—they have no reason to suspect for a moment that they might be all wet.

Wherever they look in this society, there are white institutions. habits, signs, symbols, myths and realities that reinforce their notion that black folk rank somewhere between King Kong and Frankenstein's monster on the scale of lower forms of life.

I recently read a best-selling novel which was not about the race problem. Yet the hero and his adversaries made the point again and again in passing that the busty blond heroine was clearly depraved and lost beyond recall since, between sexual acrobatics with the good guys, she allowed a "boogey" into her boudoir. That novel has sold more than 900,000 copies in the hard-cover editions, and more than two million more in paperback. I am not saying that its success is based in any way on its casual racial insults. The point is, it's a typical visual aid in the process of white indoctrination.

Television is even more effective in that respect. Here again, of course, white folk control both the medium and the message.

If a superintelligent visitor from another planet were to deduce, strictly from television, the nature of the 22 million black pariahs who exist in the crevices of this society, he undoubtedly would get an impression that was 99 44/100 percent pure nonsense. From the electronic evidence of omission, projected around the clock, the visitor might gather that black women are rather dull and sexless creatures. Apparently nothing known to science or Madison Avenue can help black girls to develop "the skin you love to touch." With scarcely a blond hair to call their own, they obviously are not the kind of broads who "have more fun." And without one toothbrush among them, they have no interest in the leading toothpaste that "gives your mouth sex appeal."

Black men are equally irrelevant among the fauna of the natural TV order. It is tacitly suggested, for instance, that they are socially backward—black Square Johns, so to speak. Otherwise they would be seen driving "the low-priced luxury car" to seduce more swinging chicks.

It's true that black satellites are sometimes seen in TV dramatic series, but usually as cardboard characters with virtually no lives of their own. They are perpetually in orbit around the full-blooded white supermen who perform brain surgery, fall in love, bounce children on their knees and worry about middle-aged spread.

My impression is that many white folk would like to portray black people in a more sophisticated manner. But, alas, they cannot forget all those Tarzan movies of their youth. These made it official that black folks are natural-born spear carriers, dangerous savages and beasts of the white man's burdens.

Then, too, there are all those cannibal cartoons in the slick magazines put out by and for white folks. Who wouldn't be somewhat repelled by a black gourmet whose favorite entree is fricassee of Charlie?

Such examples of how black folk are systematically misrepresented or shut out from the stuff that the American Dream is made of are virtually endless. The smiling faces on greeting cards are never black faces. Department-store manikins don't resemble anyone you are likely to meet in the ghetto. And all plastic angels who symbolize the Christmas spirit are pink.

The net effect of these deceptions is that each tailor-made reality buttresses the other in the minds of whites. This explains in large measure why so many white folk are genuinely baffled by the grumbling and violence in the ghettos. Which is the basis for the popular white joke that ends with the punch line: "What do you people want?"

When black folk bother to spell out the answer to that riddle —with expectations that can only be described as naïve—the consistent white responses add up to rather predictable pranks; another study of black frustration; another conference on brotherhood; another million-dollar crash program to tear down an old ghetto and replace it with a new ghetto.

As one of the best buffoons in the Federal Government observed after the riots last summer: "The very existence of the ghetto is un-American." But that line was much too oblique for most of white America to comprehend.

I am not suggesting that white folk don't even try. They conscientiously integrate a school here and there—even if it means doing something silly, like busing half the youngsters from A to Z and the other half vice versa. At the same time, however, they automatically prevent black families from buying or renting homes near the school in question. And they bar black folk from the jobs that pay the kind of money that would enable them to afford such a pristine neighborhood.

But getting back to how hard white people try, I witnessed one of their truly valiant efforts against insuperable odds this year. The occasion was the hint dropped by the President's Commission on Civil Disorders that the "ghetto is created by whites, maintained by white institutions and condoned by white society."

Most white folk were truly sorry about that. They rushed from their enclaves of affluence to the nearest ghetto to make amends. However, once in the wilds of Harlem and its scattered subdivisions, they simply could not resist telling corny jokes. Like the one Hitler told as he toured a concentration camp: "Jews stink."

What the Führer was smelling, of course, was Nazism. And in America the heady aroma of racism is equally confusing to the thin straight noses of the master race. Otherwise it would not be possible for those deadpan middle-class comedians to come up with such boffos as: "Why can't the black man pull himself up by his bootstraps like the other minorities have done?" While guarding the boots with bulldog tenacity day and night.

Admittedly, that is a rather large generalization. I have no doubt that some white skeptics will challenge me to prove it. My answer is this: Regard me as sort of a black J. Edgar Hoover. You didn't ask him to prove his public generalization that "Martin Luther King is one of the most notorious liars in the country."

Furthermore, I am prepared to generalize again. From my experience with white storekeepers over the years, I judge that many white merchants make a special hard-sell effort when a black customer shows up to unload whatever raunchy merchandise they have in stock.

Example: One of my soul sisters overheard a white housewife chewing out a white butcher for putting rotten meat on display. "Can't you see it's not fit to eat?" she demanded.

"Lady, this is not for you," the butcher said matter-of-factly. "It's for them. Believe me, they don't know any better. They're like pigs."

Although black folk are reluctant to admit it in this age of militant reassessment of their position, they do feel a certain amount of pity for white folk now and then. Like Sam Bowers, who resigned this year as Grand Dragon of the United Ku Klux Klans in Georgia. Sam said he wanted "to work for a united

America where black men and white men can stand shoulder to shoulder."

When I broadcast that item last spring, I couldn't help thinking: What grievous tortures poor old Sam must have suffered upon discovering the joke of white supremacy.

Another public confession was made recently at the opposite end of the spectrum by a self-declared white liberal—a Northern youth who had risked his life as a field worker in the civil-rights movement in Mississippi. Out of curiosity, he said, he took a trip on the LSD express. And the jig was up. Under the influence of the so-called mind-expanding drug, he realized for the first time that, in the Deep South of his soul, he honestly believed that black people were not now, never had been and never could be as deserving as whites. The immediate result of his insight was a nervous breakdown.

That young man was neither the first nor the last of his breed. The mass media these days are overpopulated with white liberals who portray themselves as "champions of the inarticulate masses." The sick joke here is that the masses—especially the black masses—are not at all inarticulate. They tell it like it is and like it ought to be—with precision, persistence and profanity.

But white society can't grasp the meaning of all that yammering—being too busy washing brains, their victims' and their own. They therefore have no real difficulty in maintaining their cool and the status quo in the face of massive protest and violence.

Being highly inventive jesters, white folk entertain themselves with a monologue that says, in effect, black folk are too stupid to realize that something phony is going on here. It goes like this, "It's the Communist agitators and Communist dopes who are behind all this violence."

One-liners like that are probably what killed vaudeville.

If black folk don't laugh out loud at such routines, it is because their funny bones are dulled from the same old stale material. Real comedy depends on surprises. So why should a black man chuckle over the annual Congressional Follies built around civil-rights legislation, for example? He knows in advance that the new Civil Rights Act is going to wind up like the so-called Open Housing Act of 1866—unenforced and soon forgotten.

Enforcement, he is told, would "infringe on the rights" of the white minority. That's a good one, too. But it is as familiar as, "Why does a fireman wear red suspenders?"

As for the sight gags in white society's repertoire, these too have worn thin from overexposure. How many times can an individual black man be amused by the blind cabdriver routine? After the thirty-seventh time, it no longer strikes him as suitable material for a laff-in.

Did I say "individual black man?" Actually, there is scarcely any such animal as far as white eyes can see. They recognize "the first Negro who" and "the only Negro to," but not as individuals—instead, as freaks or symbols. Which is to say that white folks have a habit of arbitrarily assigning a rather standard personality to a black man. His real self is like an iceberg, deeply submerged in a sea of white assumptions.

One of my soul brothers was recently promoted to an executive position with a giant corporation in New York City. He had earned it by bringing in more sales orders over the last five years than anyone else in his department. You can imagine how chagrined he was when several of his white colleagues dismissed his personal achievement with humorless jokes like this: "It pays to be black these days. Man, you've got it made."

Such an attitude is not founded primarily on jealousy, as it might appear on the surface. White folks are simply incapable of seeing a black man as anything beyond his blackness.

At least twice a year, for instance, I am approached for an interview by one national magazine or another. My experience as a newspaper reporter and television news broadcaster has provided me with a wealth of interesting material from face-to-face encounters with four Presidents, a half-dozen princesses, scores of prizefighters, hundreds of politicians, assorted pimps, paragons and pinup queens. But not one white interviewer ever shows the slightest interest in anything except my blackness.

"What is the role of the black newsman?" they want to know.

"The role of a black man," I tell them off the record, "is or ought to be the same as it is for everybody else in his profession; in this case, to gather the facts and report them with as much integrity, clarity and objectivity as he can muster." End of interview.

I am also rather weary of getting letters from white television fans that read like this one:

"When you first began broadcasting the news on television, I watched you every night, but I realize now, years later, that I was so conscious of the fact that you were black that I didn't hear a word you said about the news. Now, I am happy to say, I still watch you every night, but only because you are a damn good newscaster. . . ."

What I'm getting at here is that white folks are generally flabbergasted by a black man who can fly a plane, mix a martini, speak unbroken English or shoot a round of golf. Such a black man is something like the celebrated dog that could walk on its hind legs unassisted.

About the only realm of this society which seems to be perhaps one-third of the way toward the verge of catching the spirit of this thing called the free democratic society is professional sports. Even here a string of qualifying exceptions must be taken into account. To mention just a few: Boxing is obsessed by the search for a "white hope"; football is convinced that a black quarterback could not lead his team to the goal line; and baseball, like all the others, shuts out black men from the managerial and decision-making level. And besides all that, there is a great deal of friction and apartheid on the so-called integrated teams.

But baseball still deserves a better grade than white Americans generally. In the first place, black players are no longer required to be supermen like Jackie Robinson. If you watch baseball these days, you see black men fumbling routine grounders, dropping flies, striking out with the bases loaded and winding up the season with microscopic batting averages. Just like whites. And no one suggests that such derelictions are peculiar to one race or another.

Furthermore, if a white interviewer shows up in the locker room, he is full of questions about the spitball or the squeeze play that didn't quite work in the ninth. After all, why should a third baseman, even a black one, be limited to discussing racial jokes?

So how long is it going to take the rest of this country to evolve even as little as baseball? In my judgment, another 100 years at the very least, if this society manages to survive that long.

Why so much time? Well, it seems to me that while one side of those split personalities called white Americans is striving with all its might to open their minds and their society, the other side is being pulled in the opposite direction by what white Americans accept and automatically maintain as the natural order. As you can see for yourself, it is something of an unequal race.

Suggestions for Further Reading

1. Arnold Adoff (ed.), *Black on Black* (New York: Macmillan, 1968).

   The black experience in America during the twentieth century is presented through the writings of famous black Americans such as Ralph Ellison, James Baldwin, Lerone Bennett, Jr., Dick Gregory, Bill Russell, Malcolm X, Martin Luther King, Jr., LeRoi Jones, Stokely Carmichael, and others.

2. Jay David (ed.), *Growing Up Black* (New York: William Morrow and Company, 1968).

   Black adults write poignant recollections of their childhoods and what it means to grow up black in America.

3. Melvin Drimmer (ed.), *Black History: A Reappraisal* (Garden City, N.Y.: Doubleday, 1968).

4. Ruth Miller (ed.), *Blackamerican Literature* (Beverly Hills: Glencoe Press, 1971).

   This anthology of black writers has been widely acclaimed. It reveals the rich heritage that has been covered up by extra-legal discrimination.

5. Editors of *Ebony, The White Problem in America* (Chicago: Johnson Publishing Company, 1966).

   This collection of essays is the hardcover reprinting of the special *Ebony* issue of August, 1965. It looks at the white man's hang-ups through the eyes of black men who have been prominent in various fields of endeavor.

6. Lawrence J. Friedman (ed.), *The White Savage: Racial Fantasies in the Postbellum South* (Englewood Cliffs, N.J.: Prentice Hall, 1970).

7. J. Norman Heard, *The Black Frontiersmen, Adventures of Negroes among American Indians, 1528–1918* (New York: John Day Co., 1969).

8. I. A. Newby, *Jim Crow's Defense: Anti-Negro Thought in America, 1900–1930* (Baton Rouge: Louisiana State University Press, 1965).

This is a survey of the development as well as the application of racist ideology in the first three decades of this century.

9. ——— (ed.), *The Development of Segregationist Thought* (Homewood, Ill.: The Dorsey Press, 1968).

10. Irving Sloan, *The Negro in Modern American History Textbooks* (Washington: American Federation of Teachers, 1969).

Shows how racist notions are fostered and perpetuated in widely used textbooks.

11. ———, *The Treatment of Black Americans in Current Encyclopedias* (Washington: American Federation of Teachers, 1970).

Examines the treatment of black Americans in nine encyclopedias and shows how omissions and distortions contribute to racist education.

Chapter Eleven

Presidential Racism

Judged only by their written opinions on matters of race, the Presidents appear rather liberal. When measured by actual accomplishment, however, their record is for the most part one of stark failure or refusal to enforce laws involving matters of race, and extreme reluctance to champion an unreserved racial equality in the full uninhibited spirit of American democracy.

—GEORGE SINKLER, *The Racial Ideas of American Presidents: From Abraham Lincoln to Theodore Roosevelt* (1966)

At the beginning of the American Revolution, the slaveholder who was to become our first President issued an order banning Negro soldiers from the Revolutionary Army. Eventually, George Washington's order was rescinded, but only because many slaves were escaping to join the British Army in return for promises of freedom. It was a practical necessity, rather than a mellowing of racist sentiment, that permitted black soldiers to contribute as much as they did to the revolutionary cause.

George Washington may have been the first American President to accept the custom of discriminatory treatment of black people, but he was not the only one to do so. As has been indicated in previous chapters, the attitudes and actions of Andrew Jackson toward the Indians, Theodore Roosevelt toward the Japanese, and William McKinley toward the Filipinos show how much a part of American history racism and discrimination have been. Not even our Presidents have been able to disassociate themselves from the exploitations of allegedly inferior peoples. Most of our Presidents, including those whom we name as heroes, have actually encouraged racism by their words and deeds. Often by their failure to speak out or act they chose to ignore the manifestations of institutional racism.

In 1968 Eldridge Cleaver wrote in *Soul on Ice*:

> The white youth of today are coming to see, intuitively, that to escape the onus of the history their fathers made they must face and admit the moral truth concerning the works of their fathers. That such venerated figures as George Washington and Thomas Jefferson owned hundreds of black slaves, that all of the Presidents up to Lincoln presided over a slave state, and that every President since Lincoln connived politically and cynically with the issues affecting the human rights and general welfare of the broad masses of the American people—these facts weigh heavily upon the hearts of these young people.*

This chapter comes face to face with "the moral truth concerning the works of their fathers."

------

*From Eldridge Cleaver, *Soul on Ice* (New York: McGraw-Hill Inc., 1968).

Our Racist Presidents from Washington to Nixon*

The following survey of some American presidential culture-heroes shows the extent of racism in the White House.

In words as well as deed, over and over again, American Presidents have reflected the racism of the wider society from which they sprang. The victims have been white, red, brown, and yellow, as well as black.

Some argue that to condemn past Presidents for failing to combat racist practices ignores the "context" in which the Presidents function—they are truly a voice of the people. But to the generation of the 1970's that argument no longer stands up. If slavery is wrong in 1972, they say, it was wrong in 1872 and 1772. To say that a President shared the view of his contemporaries is neither to deny nor to excuse his racism.

There is a tendency to excuse the racism of American Presidents with the rationalization that they were only products of their environment. Yet that environment always included numerous opponents of racism. In George Washington's time there were many people, including some of the Founding Fathers, who advocated the abolition of slavery, and who did not try to pretend that slaves were happy.

This point of view is being expressed in increasing numbers of writings recently. For example, George Sinkler, in *The Racial Attitudes of American Presidents: From Abraham Lincoln to Theodore Roosevelt*, concluded that "If the Presidents of this period are judged only on their expressed intentions in matters of race, they make a good showing. When measured by actual accomplishment, with one or two notable exceptions, their record is one of stark failure to enforce the federal laws involving matters of race, and an extreme reluctance to champion an unreserved racial equality in the full spirit of American democracy. When it came to

---

*Adapted from Melvin Steinfield, *Our Racist Presidents from Washington to Nixon* (San Ramon, Ca.: Consensus Publishers, Inc., 1972). Reprinted by permission of Consensus Publishers, Inc.

a choice between vigorous action or inaction in matters of race the Presidents were paralyzed."[1]

Certainly such paralysis is not the result of being President or feeling that one must bow to the will of the people. American Presidents have not been paralyzed when they had a pet project to push. Kennedy's commitment to put a man on the moon, Polk's engineering of the American involvement in the Mexican War, Jefferson's purchase of Louisiana, and Nixon's sending troops into Cambodia are just a few instances of presidential power at work. Why then has this power not been used on behalf of racial minority groups? According to Schwartz and Disch, "The Presidency, the final and most absolute of the 'permission' givers, is the single office with the most influence to change attitudes. In this period [the early twentieth century] the Presidency was consistently occupied by overt racists."[2]

In the late nineteenth century, the situation was much the same. As Rayford Logan notes: "It made little difference whether a Republican or a Democrat—at least a Northern Democrat—was President. Party platforms were frankly hypocritical on the constitutional rights of Negroes. Presidents of both parties uttered pious platitudes, but said nothing and did nothing, except to give a few jobs to professional Negro officeholders."[3]

George Washington, Our First Racist President

George Washington was America's first racist President. Although he did invite black poet Phillis Wheatley, a one-time slave, to visit him at the Revolutionary Headquarters in 1776, it must not be forgotten that he was a slaveholder throughout his

[1]George Sinkler, *The Racial Attitudes of American Presidents: From Abraham Lincoln to Theodore Roosevelt* (Garden City, N.Y.: Doubleday, 1972), p. 459.

[2]Barry N. Schwartz and Robert Disch, *White Racism* (New York: Dell, 1970), p. 43.

[3]Rayford W. Logan, *The Betrayal of the Negro: From Rutherford B. Hayes to Woodrow Wilson* (New York: Collier, 1965).

adult life. While it is true that he provided in his will for the freeing of his own slaves, during his lifetime he was not above callous mistreatment of some of his slaves. For example, after one of his slaves, Tom, had run away from his plantation repeatedly, Washington sold him with the advice to the new owner that Tom be kept "handcuffed, lest he should attempt to escape."[4]

In October of 1775, General Washington issued an order banning the enlistment of Negro soldiers in the Continental Army. It was only after the British had succeeded in luring slaves to escape and fight for the King that the Revolutionary leaders were compelled to reverse their prohibition against the enlistment of black soldiers. Necessity caused Washington to reverse his racist stance on that issue.

When the Revolutionary War ended, Washington wanted to have the escaped slaves who fought for the British returned to their "owners." On April 15, 1783, Congress instructed Washington to arrange for the return of American property—a term that included slaves who had fought for the British in exchange for promises of freedom. After Washington met with a British representative on May 6, 1783, to negotiate this item, he filed a report expressing his disappointment that the British representatives refused to violate pledges made to the slaves.

In 1786 Washington wrote a letter to Robert Morris in which he expressed the conflict shared by so many slaveholders about owning slaves. A typical racist belief, the myth of the happy slave, is revealed in his letter; he thought it immoral that "happy and contented" slaves were frequently seduced by such agencies as the Society of Quakers into leaving their masters. In effect, Washington's letter shows his views to be in opposition to those of some of his distinguished non-slaveholding contemporaries, such as Benjamin Franklin. Franklin's service as President of the Pennsylvania Society, an organization devoted to abolition of slavery, stands in sharp contrast to the actions, and many of the words, of George Washington.

---

[4] William Loren Katz, *Eyewitness: The Negro in American History* (New York: Pitman Publishing Corporation, 1967), p. 25.

George Washington's words, actions, and policies during his
two terms as President of the United States did nothing to challenge institutional racism, nor did he initiate any proposals for
the reduction of overt racism. If America deserves to be called a
racist country, then there is no question about George Washington's right to be considered the father of his country. For who
can take pride in a letter written two days before the 4th of July,
1776 by George Washington:

"Sir: With this letter comes a Negro (Tom) which I beg
the favor of you to sell in any of the islands you may go to for
whatever he will fetch and bring me in return from him: One
hogshead of best molasses, one ditto of best rum. . . ." Thus, to
satisfy his desire for drink, the man destined to become the first
President of the United States sold a black man down the river.[5]

The Declaration of Independence, promulgated two days
later, obviously did not mean independence for all.

Thomas Jefferson, Egalitarian Slaveholder

"I have sworn eternal hostility against every form of tyranny
over the mind of man," wrote Thomas Jefferson (a slaveholder
throughout his adult life).

"All men are created equal," wrote Jefferson in the Declaration of Independence. But in his *Notes on Virginia*, in 1787, Jefferson refers to the ugliness of Negroes, their disagreeable odor,
their childlike mentalities, their inferiority to Indians, and numerous other alleged points of inferiority and undesirability.

"I have ever judged of the religion of others by their lives.
For it is in our lives, and not from our words, that our religion
must be read," wrote Jefferson. If Jefferson is judged by his own
standard, it is clear that he, like Washington before him, was a
racist President. Even if Jefferson were to be judged on the basis
of his words alone, the record would still be soiled. Combining his

---

[5] Richard Claxton Gregory, *No More Lies: The Myth and the Reality of American History* (New York: Harper & Row, 1971), p. 72.

words with his deeds, Jefferson emerges as a personification of the American Dilemma.[6]

Being a slaveholder took its toll of whatever humane impulses our third President might have had. Slaves, to the slaveholder, tended to become mere financial objects, mere property. As Jefferson wrote in a letter to John Taylor in 1794, "The first step toward the recovery of our lands is to find substitutes for corn and bacon, I count on potatoes, clover, and sheep. The two former to feed every animal on the farm except my negroes, and the latter to feed them, diversified with rations of salted fish and molasses, both of them wholesome, agreeable, and cheap articles of food."[7]

In *Notes on Virginia,* Jefferson mentions Phillis Wheatley in order to ridicule her poetry as proof that blacks are not smart enough to create higher forms of artistic expression. This was written eleven years after Jefferson wrote the Declaration of Independence, and thirteen years before he became President. Given this low regard for blacks, Jefferson almost inevitably ended up formulating what Professor Winthrop Jordan has called, "the most intense, extensive, and extreme formulation of anti-Negro 'thought' offered by any American in the thirty years after the Revolution."[8]

Today, historians are less willing to apologize for Jefferson's views than they used to be. Consider the following excerpts from an interview with Professor Stanley Elkins:

---

[6] This was characterized in *The American Dilemma* (1942) by social economist Gunnar Myrdal as being the plight of the white American in his interaction with the Negro, constantly torn between the dictates of his high American ideals of liberty and equality and the concerns of his baser nature (". . . personal and local interests; economic, social, and sexual jealousies; considerations of community prestige and conformity; group prejudice against particular persons or types of people. . .").

[7] Winthrop D. Jordan, *White Over Black* (Baltimore: Penguin Books, 1968), p. 430.

[8] *Ibid.,* p. 481.

One of the tragic figures in this regard in America was Jefferson. He was never really able to come to terms with slavery. He resolved his doubts by concluding that black men were so different that they could not be integrated into American society. There are some wonderful passages in his *Notes on Virginia,* in which Jefferson speculates on the character of the black man. He twists and turns, but eventually comes to the conclusion that the Negro is different. He never quite says why. . . .

Jefferson excelled at analyzing the character of society, yet when he dealt with the question of slavery, he was amazingly unimaginative. He might have encouraged manumission, or some form of sharecropping; there were all sorts of possibilities for getting around the economic problems of emancipation. He might have concocted a plan for educating the blacks. But somehow, on this subject Jefferson's social imagination was paralyzed. . . .[9]

Jefferson's views were not uncriticized, even in his own time. Gilbert Imlay, writing ten years after Jefferson, accused him of having a "warped" mind for proposing that "the African is a being between the human species and the oran-outan." Clement Clarke Moore, the author of *The Night Before Christmas,* criticized Jefferson a few years later because he "debases the Negro to an order of creatures lower than those who have fairer skin and thinner lips."

In 1791 Benjamin Banneker, a black mathematician, astronomer, almanac writer, and eventually one of the designers of the city of Washington, D.C., sent a copy of his first almanac to Thomas Jefferson, who was at that time Secretary of State. Accompanying the almanac was a letter that attacks the hypocrisy of Jefferson's egalitarian rhetoric in view of his racist actions:

This, Sir, was a time when you saw into the injustice of a state of slavery, and in which you had just apprehensions of the horror of its condition. It was now that your abhorrence thereof was so excited, that you publicly held forth this true and invaluable doctrine, which is worthy to be recorded and remembered in all succeeding ages: "We hold these truths to be self-evident, that all

---

[9] Stanley Elkins, *Interpreting American History: Conversations with Historians,* Part I, John A. Garraty (ed.) (New York: Macmillan, 1970), p. 188.

men are created equal; that they are endowed by their Creator with certain unalienable rights, and that among these are, life, liberty, and the pursuit of happiness."

Here was a time, in which your tender feelings for yourselves had engaged you thus to declare, you were then impressed with proper ideas of the great violation of liberty, and the free possession of those blessings, to which you were entitled by nature; but, Sir, how pitiable is it to reflect, that although you were so fully convinced of the benevolence of the Father of Mankind, and of his equal and impartial distribution of these rights and privileges, which he hath conferred upon them, that you should at the same time counteract his mercies, in detaining by fraud and violence so numerous a part of my brethren, under groaning captivity, and cruel oppression, that you should at the same time be found guilty of that most criminal act, which you professedly detested in others, with respect to yourselves.

I suppose that your knowledge of the situation of my brethren, is too extensive to need a recital here; neither shall I presume to prescribe methods by which they may be relieved, otherwise than by recommending to you and all others, to wean yourselves from those narrow prejudices which you have imbibed with respect to them, and as Job proposed to his friends, "put your soul in their souls' stead"; thus shall your hearts be enlarged with kindness and benevolence towards them; and thus shall you need neither the direction of myself or others, in what manner to proceed herein.

Jefferson's racism was not restricted to his actions and attitudes concerning black Americans. His view of the Indians, as stated in the Declaration of Independence, certainly excludes them from consideration as equals. King George is condemned by Jefferson in the Declaration because he excited "domestic insurrections amongst us, and has endeavoured to bring on the inhabitants of our frontiers, the merciless Indian Savages, whose known rule of warfare, is an undistinguished destruction of all ages, sexes, and conditions."

Thus, just as Washington has perpetuated the myth of the happy slave, Jefferson contributed to the myth of the savage Indian. The Declaration of Independence was undermined from the start, in more ways than one.

Abraham Lincoln, Racist Emancipator

In view of all the evidence that has been presented to the contrary, it is surprising that the myth of Lincoln as the Great Emancipator has survived so long. Still, perhaps we should not be surprised. After all, it takes more than a racist record to keep a man from becoming a popular hero.

In the case of Abraham Lincoln, many of his words and actions have gone unnoticed until recently. Now our interest in uncovering the past has led to a sharper focus on Lincoln the man in contrast to Lincoln the myth. The picture that is beginning to emerge in unmistakable outline is one of a racist President who resisted emancipation until he was pressured into it, who revoked the emancipation of some slaves in conquered territories, who would like to have seen blacks emigrate from America, who permitted differences in military pay based on race, and who for some time refused to permit blacks to fight or even perform noncombatant tasks in the Civil War. Such actions might have been expected of Lincoln when he became President. As a candidate, Lincoln had made strong statements against the idea of black equality and was criticized by a black abolitionist who viewed him as a friend of slavery.

In 1858 the campaign for the office of United States Senator from Illinois reached a high point in the Lincoln-Douglas debates. In these two excerpts from speeches he made during these debates, candidate Lincoln expresses views that are overtly racist.

> I will say then that I am not, nor ever have been, in favor of bringing about in any way the social and political equality of the white and black races; that I am not, nor ever have been, in favor of making voters or jurors of Negroes, nor of qualifying them to hold office, nor to intermarry with white people; and I will say in addition to this that there is a physical difference between the white and black races which I believe will forever forbid the two races living together on terms of social and political equality. And inasmuch as they cannot so live, while they do remain together there must be the position of superior and inferior, and I as much as any other man am in favor of having the superior position assigned to the white race. I say upon this occasion that I do not perceive that because the white man is to have the superior position

that the Negro should be denied everything. I do not understand that because I do not want a Negro woman for a slave I must necessarily want her for a wife. . . .

Anything that argues me into his [Douglas'] idea of perfect social and political equality with the Negro, is but a specious and fantastic arrangement of words, by which a man can prove a horse chestnut to be a chestnut horse. I will say here, while upon this subject, that I have no purpose directly or indirectly to interfere with the institution of slavery by the states where it exists. I believe that I have no lawful right to do so, and I have no inclination to do so. I have no purpose to introduce political and social equality between the white and black races. There is a physical difference between the two, which in my judgment will probably forever forbid their living together upon the footing of perfect equality, and inasmuch as it becomes a necessity that there must be a difference, I, as well as Judge Douglas, am in favor of the race to which I belong having the superior position. I have never said anything to the contrary, but I hold that notwithstanding all this, there is no reason in the world why the Negro is not entitled to all the natural rights enumerated in the Declaration of Independence—the right to life, liberty, and the pursuit of happiness. I hold that he is as much entitled to these as the white man. I agree with Judge Douglas he is not my equal in many respects—certainly not in color, perhaps not in moral or intellectual endowment. But in the right to eat the bread, without leave of anybody else, which his own hand earns, *he is my equal and the equal of Judge Douglas, and the equal of every living man.*

On August 19, 1862, Horace Greeley, the influential editor of the *New York Tribune,* urged Lincoln to free the slaves. In his reply to Greeley on August 22, 1862, President Lincoln showed his main concern to be preservation of the Union, rather than abolition of slavery. He was willing to free some slaves, but not others, if that were the way to keep the Union whole. That is what he actually did in the Emancipation Proclamation, which freed only those slaves who were in rebel states. The slaves in the four border states—Delaware, Kentucky, Maryland, and Missouri— were not freed by the Emancipation Proclamation.

The dubious morality of freeing some slaves but not others did not bother Lincoln as much as what he saw to be military and political necessities. In this letter to Greeley, Lincoln reveals to the public, for the first time, the possibility of partial emancipation.

EXECUTIVE MANSION, WASHINGTON
August 22, 1862

HON. HORACE GREELEY:
Dear Sir:

I have just read yours of the nineteenth, addressed to myself through the *New York Tribune*. If there be in it any statements or assumptions of fact which I may know to be erroneous, I do not now and here controvert them. If there be any inferences which I may believe to be falsely drawn, I do not now and here argue against them. If there be perceptible in it an impatient and dictatorial tone, I waive it in deference to an old friend, whose heart I have always supposed to be right.

As to the policy I "seem to be pursuing," as you say, I have not meant to leave any one in doubt.

I would save the Union. I would save it in the shortest way under the Constitution. The sooner the National authority can be restored the nearer the Union will be "the Union as it was." If there be those who would not save the Union unless they could at the same time *save* Slavery, I do not agree with them. If there be those who would not save the Union unless they could at the same time *destroy* Slavery, I do not agree with them. My paramount object in this struggle *is* to save the Union, and is *not* either to save or destroy Slavery. If I could save the Union without freeing *any* slave, I would do it; and if I could save it by freeing *all* the slaves, I would do it; and if I could do it by freeing some and leaving others alone, I would also do that. What I do about Slavery and the colored race, I do because I believe it helps to save this Union; and what I forbear, I forbear because I do *not* believe it would help to save the Union. I shall do *less* whenever I shall believe what I am doing hurts the cause, and I shall do *more* whenever I shall believe doing more will help the cause. I shall try to correct errors shown to be errors; and I shall adopt new views so fast as they shall appear to be true views.

I have here stated my purpose according to my views of *official* duty, and I intend no modification of my oft-expressed *personal* wish that all men everywhere, could be free.

Yours,
A. LINCOLN

On May 9, 1862, a Union general, David Hunter, issued an order that freed slaves in the conquered portions of South Carolina, Georgia, and Florida. Ten days later, this order was countermanded by President Lincoln. As Commander-in-Chief, Lincoln was of course constitutionally empowered to revoke the order. It is ironic, however, that the "Great Emancipator" should do so.

In interpreting Lincoln's words and actions, historians have reached conflicting conclusions. Until recent times Lincoln has been regarded without reservations as the Great Emancipator, but this view is fading fast. However, the number of apologists for his record is diminishing less quickly. Some contemporary interpretations fail to excuse his record with enthusiasm but they also fail to condemn the racist elements of that record.

Even on the basis of this small sampling of documents it becomes clear that Abraham Lincoln was more racist than emancipator. His record as President shows that, had it been left to him alone—had there not been the influence of the abolitionists and other factors, such as the pressure of military expediency—emancipation might not have occurred during his administration. Furthermore Lincoln supported or initiated discriminatory policies in the armed forces, made frequent statements in support of the right to own slaves, and, in general, helped perpetuate many forms of institutional racism in American life. His statements opposing the right of blacks to vote or serve on a jury and his pet scheme of exporting blacks are merely further extensions of this basic stance.

True, Lincoln did not do a great deal less for racial minorities than the men who preceded him. But with the opportunities and climate at the time so favorable, he could have done much more and earned the title tradition has given him.

Theodore Roosevelt, Rugged Individualist–Racist

The glorification of Theodore Roosevelt as a "rugged individualist" has contributed to his charismatic image, but it has also obscured the racist elements in his administration. The record shows that in both word and deed, Roosevelt's "square deal" was never meant to include blacks.

The following sentiment, expressed in a letter to Owen Wister, was characteristic of his attitude toward blacks:

"Now as to the Negroes; I entirely agree with you that as a race and in the mass they are altogether inferior to whites."[10]

Roosevelt's opinion of Indians was another manifestation of his racism: "I suppose I should be ashamed to say that I take the Western view of the Indian. I don't go so far as to think that the only good Indians are the dead Indians, but I believe nine out of every ten are, and I shouldn't inquire too closely into the case of the tenth. The most vicious cowboy has more moral principle than the average Indian."[11]

With overt racist attitudes such as those, it is not surprising to find that the Roosevelt record of actions as President includes a number of racist elements. Yet the popular image of Roosevelt is that he invited Booker T. Washington to a luncheon conference at the White House, and that he appointed a black postmaster and that makes him a liberal on matters of race.

White Presidential heroes lose their luster very slowly, but in the case of Theodore Roosevelt, his token actions on behalf of blacks hardly suffice to counteract the mass of evidence of his racism staring us in the face. One only needs to escape from the shackles of patriotic myth, and to keep an open mind while investigating the complete record, in order to realize that Theodore Roosevelt was an overt racist. As a recent study concluded:

> Firstly, Theodore Roosevelt did not believe in the equality of man. He pictured certain races as "inferior," one of which was the Negro. The Negro to Roosevelt was "bad enough by nature." Secondly, he believed that certain Negroes were "occasionally good" and "well-educated," but the group did not or could not attain this position. A third point in Roosevelt's philosophy was that a majority of the Negroes should not be enfranchised; in fact, only one percent should be permitted to vote. Finally, Roosevelt abandoned his fight for Negro rights—which was incidental to his political

---

[10]Barry N. Schwartz and Robert Disch, *White Racism* (New York: Dell Publishing Co., 1970), p. 42.

[11]*Ibid.*, pp. 42–43.

policy—by mid-1903 at the latest, not in 1905 or 1906 as some historians have contended.[12]

Franklin Roosevelt, Liberal Racist

Only one American President was ever elected to four terms. It seems safe to assert that Franklin Delano Roosevelt was one of America's most popular Presidents. His administration has often been praised for the improvement in the economic status of black Americans that resulted from the New Deal. However, there is substantial evidence that concern for blacks was incidental to the New Deal.

In fact, there are instances in which Roosevelt's lack of action to combat racist policies within the government is clearly revealed. One of the most severe racist policies Roosevelt allowed to continue was discrimination in various forms of the military. Although he was commander-in-chief, with the authority to eliminate by executive decree all racist discrimination in the military, and despite the fact that a top black official submitted a resignation to protest such discrimination, he took no steps in this direction.

Even among those who still revere Roosevelt, there is a growing realization that his authorization to evacuate 110,000 West Coast Japanese-Americans was an act of overt racism. Japanese in Hawaii were not rounded up and herded into concentration camps, nor were German- or Italian-Americans in this country. The story of the evacuation of the West Coast Japanese is one of the most flagrant disregard for civil liberties ever perpetrated upon a people. As Daniels and Kitano have pointed out:

> Although many factors must have entered into Roosevelt's mind as he acquiesced to the spokesmen for the military—the bad news from the war fronts, the pressures from West Coast congressmen and their allies, and the fact that failure to do anything about the "menace" of the West Coast Japanese would provide ammunition for his political enemies—it seems clear enough that the President, too, held racist convictions about the Japanese, and that the

---

[12] From Seth M. Scheiner, "President Theodore Roosevelt and the Negro," *Journal of Negro History*, 47 (July 1962) : 169–182. Copyright © by The Association for the Study of Negro Life and History, Inc.

notion that "once a Jap always a Jap" was not foreign to his thinking.[13]

Richard Nixon, Our Most Recent Racist President

We would be less than honest, Mr. President, if we did not reflect a view widely shared among a majority of the citizens we represent. That view is that the representatives of this Administration, by word and deed, have at crucial points retreated from the national commitment to make Americans of all races and cultures equal in the eyes of their government—to make equal the poor as well as the rich, urban and rural dwellers as well as those who live in the suburbs.

The above quote, taken from the statement of the Congressional Black Caucus to the President of the United States in the spring of 1971, expresses the dominant quality of Mr. Nixon's racial policies: "retreat from the national commitment." In an effort to stop the clock on the progress made during several previous administrations, the Nixon "Southern Strategy" is nothing more than a program to resist the trend toward equal rights.

The Nixon Administration has been condemned by the Civil Rights Commission for its inadequate role in enforcement of anti-discrimination laws. "Benign neglect" is what Daniel Moynihan, former Nixon advisor, advocated two years ago. That phrase is a euphemism for the same kind of do-nothing approach to enforcement of civil rights laws that characterized the Eisenhower Administration.

In addition to a policy of lax enforcement of civil rights, the Nixon Administration has proposed an acknowledged racist for the Supreme Court. In general, it has perpetuated institutional racism.

Although the Nixon Administration has participated in several attention-getting token acts of civil rights, its policy, as a whole, has effectively resisted eliminating racist practices within the government and the country at large. In this respect, it repre-

---

[13] Roger Daniels and Harry H. L. Kitano, *American Racism: Exploration of the Nature of Prejudice* (Englewood Cliffs, N.J.: Prentice-Hall, 1970).

sents a retreat from the efforts of several previous administrations. It is, however, consistent with the record of most presidential administrations since the time of George Washington.

Epilogue

There is no real way to right the wrongs that have occurred or to mend the past. What is done is done. Yet the story of the past is instructive and predictive; it holds either a warning or a promise for the future.

From George Washington to Richard Nixon, America's Presidents have failed to pursue the cause of justice for minorities with the same vigor with which they pursued other challenges of the American Dream. Slaveholders in the early years of the presidency, segregationists after the Civil War, many of the Presidents chose to mouth the rhetoric of equality and justice for all, while at the same time tolerating racist practices within their own administrations and across the country. Racism endures, prevails, and continues to haunt the conscience of America.

The fact that it is no longer fashionable to be a bigot has resulted in a paucity of overtly racist statements by recent Presidents. The fashion in behavior changes less quickly. The record of civil rights legislation is not one to which any recent President can point with pride, if one considers how long injustices have been allowed to continue, and if one considers the almost infinite patience with the system demonstrated by the vast majority of oppressed minorities in this country.

America's Presidents of the 1970's must begin to keep the American promise. The reservoir of second chances is nearly empty.

New Freedom and Old Hypocrisy*

*This selection documents the racist record of the Wilson adminis-
tration with a forthright style and abundant facts, contrasting his "New
Freedom" rhetoric with the actions of his administration. It is included
here to provide an in-depth example of the common Presidential racist
tendencies outlined in the previous selection.*

When Woodrow Wilson assumed the Presidency in 1913
many Negroes believed that he would champion their cause for
advancement. An unprecedented number of Negroes had cast
their vote for Wilson, risking ostracism or ridicule from others
of their race for so departing from the ranks of the Republican
party.[1] This deviation from the traditional line of Negro support
was nurtured by discontent with the Republican and Progressive
candidates, Taft and Roosevelt, and their platforms. It was
spurred by the stirring assurances of wholehearted support to
the Negro race by Woodrow Wilson.

Yet it was in Woodrow Wilson's administration that the
most bitter blow to Negro hopes of advancement fell: the introduction of segregation into several of the federal departments.[2]
This action raised questions of vital concern to government–race
relations, and created a sensation among nearly all elements of
the colored world as well as among some of the white.

---

*From Kathleen Wolgemuth, "Woodrow Wilson and Federal Seg-
regation," first published in *Journal of Negro History* (April, 1959),
by the Association for the Study of Negro Life and History.

[1] Statistics on Negro votes in the 1913 presidential election are
nonexistent. Of those ten northern cities with the largest colored population according to the 1910 Census, none has kept such records. However, numerous accounts in Negro newspapers (Democrat, Republican,
Independent) as well as accounts by leading Negro figures have convinced this writer that the shift in votes was indeed large. See *Bee*
(Washington, D.C.); *Planet* (Richmond, Va.); *Kelly Miller's Mono-
graphic Magazine* (May, 1913), copy in Woodrow Wilson Papers; William P. Morton, "The Future of the Negro in Politics," pamphlet and
letter to Wilson, March 14, 1913, and Morton to Wilson, November 9,
1912; Oswald Garrison Villard Paper; Alexander Walters, *My Life and
Work* (New York, 1917); W. E. B. DuBois, *Dusk of Dawn* (New York,
1940), and Interview, November 29, 1955. For a leading secondary
source, see Arthur S. Link, "The Negro as a Factor in the Election of
1912," *Journal of Negro History*, XXXII (Jan., 1947).

[2] This subject is touched upon in Arthur S. Link, *The New Freedom* (Princeton, N.J., 1956), II. See also the author's article "Woodrow
Wilson's Appointment Policy and the Negro," *Journal of Southern History*, XXIV (November, 1958), pp. 457–71.

The subject of Negro–white relationships in government was raised in a cabinet meeting, April 11, 1913, soon after the new administration had come into power. Albert Burleson, the southern-bred postmaster-general, expressed his concern to that small, closed meeting regarding certain "intolerable" conditions in the Railway Mail Service where, he said, whites not only had to work with blacks, but were forced to use the same drinking glasses, towels, and washrooms. Burleson contended that it was to the advantage of both races to be separated in their work. He announced plans to implement this philosophy of segregation in the Railway Mail Service, in a gradual way, and continuing the employment of Negroes where such "would not be objectionable." The project was aimed at only one section of the federal service, but Burleson voiced a hope that segregation could be promoted in all departments of government.[3]

If there was any dissension to Burleson's plans, it was not recorded. President Wilson was noted as saying that he desired, above all, to avoid friction in federal service posts. Later events were to show that a large measure of support for governmental segregation was given by other cabinet members, particularly William McAdoo, Secretary of the Treasury, Josephus Daniels, Secretary of the Navy, and Burleson.

Coincident with the secret cabinet talks on segregation was the formation of a nongovernmental group in Washington, D.C., the National Democratic Fair Play Association, whose purpose was the same as Burleson's. In fact, Burleson's attention had perhaps been drawn in the first instance to the Railway Mail Service's integrated organization by a letter from the Fair Play Association condemning the "low and criminal elements" employed in the Railway Mail Service, a copy of which was sent to the postmaster-general. The writer, an unidentified postal clerk working in St. Louis, Missouri, called for abolition of a mixed service because, he said, the existing setup was driving away all worthy whites.[4] The Fair Play Association was concerned not only with the Railway Mail Service. At its first mass meeting, May 1, 1913,

---

[3] Josephus Daniels *(Desk Diary in the Daniels Papers)*, April 11, 1913.

[4] *Ibid.*

the group pledged itself to fight for segregation in all government offices, and, citing figures that 24,500 of the 490,000 workers were Negro, anticipated an arduous campaign. The climate of opinion is seen in a letter, said to be written by a white woman working in the General Land Office of the Department of the Interior, which the president of the group read to the assembly. The writer complained that she had to take dictation from drunken Negroes. "I also worked for a dark-skinned, woolly-headed Negro. I then felt if a human would ever be justified in ever ending his exis-tence I would then, for I was a southern woman, my father a distinguished officer during the Civil War. . . ."[5] In the following weeks and months, the Fair Play Association employed effective Negro-baiting techniques to acquaint all who might not know of the "invidious situation" in the government. Mass meetings, peti-tions, circulars, and personal letters to high-ranking officials spread the news of white women who had to work alongside some "greasy, ill-smelling Negro man or woman." These conditions, it asserted, were "UnDemocratic, UnAmerican, and UnChris-tian."[6] President Wilson was sent copies of these letters.

Soon the fondest hopes of the Fair Play Association were being realized in several new governmental departments. Al-though the group did not know definitely of the April 11 cabinet discussion, news of segregationist activities began to leak out. Presently a whole new pattern was apparent for all to see.

The departments involved at first were those of the post office, under Burleson, and the treasury, under McAdoo. No executive orders were issued, and changes were discreet and gradual. Such respectable papers as the *New York Times* carried only a few indirect references to those activities, and the various, apparently disconnected, segregation actions found publicity largely in the Negro press alone. In June, articles began to appear asking questions about the reported screening off of Negroes in a certain office, or directing attention to separate lavatory facil-ities for Negroes in another area. The trickle of news regarding federal segregation soon became a flood. It was becoming appar-

---

[5] *New York Times,* May 4, 1913.

[6] Fair Play Association Circular, May 9, 1913, copy in Wilson Papers.

ent to white and black alike that the government's segregation policy was no accident, nor confined to a few separate offices, but was an official and widespread program, albeit enacted with no executive orders.[7]

By the end of 1913, segregation had been realized in the Bureau of Engraving and Printing, the Post Office Department, the office of the auditor for the post office, and had even begun in the city post office in Washington, D.C. This involved not only separated or screened-off working positions, but segregated lavatories and lunchrooms.[8] Segregation appeared to a lesser extent in the office of the auditor of the navy. In the navy itself, Negroes traditionally held menial posts, but segregation in the auditor's office was new. Screens set off Negroes from whites, and a separate lavatory in the cellar was provided for the colored clerks.[9]

While federal segregation was being enacted to keep Negroes and whites apart, other steps were taken to appoint Negroes only to menial posts or to prevent them from obtaining civil service jobs. Photographs were required of all candidates for civil service positions from 1914 on. This was explained as a necessary device to prevent impersonation and to enable appointing officers "to form some opinion in regard to eligibles certified."[10] But many Negroes charged that officials used the photographs for one purpose alone, that of weeding out colored applicants. Equally useful

---

[7] "The President and the Negro," *Nation*, XCVII (August 17, 1913), 114; *Crisis*, VI (June, 1913), 60–61, 79; *Crisis*, VII (November, 1913), 332, for summary of newspaper comment on segregation; "Segregation in Government Departments," *Ibid.*, pp. 343–44; "Race Discrimination at Washington," *Independent*, LXXVI (November 20, 1913), 330; O. G. Villard, "The President and Segregation at Washington," *North American*, CXCVIII (December, 1913), 800–807; McGregor, "Segregation in the Departments," *Harper's Weekly*, LIX (December 26, 1914), 620-21. The National Negro Press Association, representing 126 publications, protested to Wilson on federal segregation October 13, 1913, copy in Wilson Papers; the NAACP sent an open letter of protest to Wilson August 15, 1913, Wilson Papers, and reprinted in *New York Times*, August 18, 1913.

[8] Villard, *loc. cit.*

[9] L. J. Hayes, *Negro Federal Government Worker, 1883–1938* (Washington, 1941), p. 37.

[10] U.S. Civil Service Commission, "Minutes of Proceedings," May 27, 1914, p. 228, cited in Hayes, *op. cit.*, p. 55.

for such officials was the rule whereby appointing officers were given three names of candidates from which to choose their staff replacements. This was a civil service practice of long standing, but now Negroes asserted that such department heads as Burleson continually bypassed any Negro in the eligible group. Whatever the techniques, it is apparent that there were ample means to avoid the appointment or advancement of Negroes in the civil service. That discrimination did result is evidenced in the many accusations by Negroes against the practices.[11]

The question inevitably arose: how much did President Wilson know of the segregation policy of Burleson, McAdoo, and Daniels? When the first minor changes were performed in spring and summer, 1913, many of the persons concerned blamed only Wilson's cabinet members, particularly the three named above. Wilson, they said, perhaps was not aware of their actions.[12] There was, after all, no executive order.

But Wilson did know about the plans for racial separation in the government. He approved of them. He vigorously defended the official policy of segregation in a series of personal letters to one of his closest friends and most loyal supporters, Oswald Garrison Villard. Villard was editor of a leading liberal newspaper, the *New York Evening Post*, and had been an active worker for Wilson in the presidential campaign. Villard, the grandson of William Lloyd Garrison, was involved as well in the activities of the young National Association for the Advancement of Colored People (NAACP), the "radical" group which was challenging the more conserative group of Booker T. Washington. As a co-worker with W. E. B. DuBois and as a correspondent with DuBois' rival, Booker T. Washington, Villard was the natural person to question the President on the federal segregation.

---

[11] See *Crisis*, XV (March, 1918), 218; *Republican Campaign Text Book, 1916;* Kelly Miller to Woodrow Wilson, July 6, 1918, Wilson Papers; *Crisis*, XXXV (1928), 287–688; *Congressional Record* 70th Congress (1928) 1st Session, No. 79, pp. 10657, 6486, 7593.

[12] Villard to McAdoo, November 9, 1913; "Another Open Letter to Woodrow Wilson," *Crisis*, VI (September, 1913), 233–36; "The President and the Negro," *Nation*, XCVII (August 7, 1913), 114.

Villard asked Wilson bluntly if he were aware of the actions which had been taken in several department offices. Did Wilson realize, he wondered, the extent to which these actions had gone, and the dangers involved? Did he know that they would lead to a return of Negroes to the Republican party? He received an answer to this letter of July 21, 1913, two days later. Wilson, in reply to the "distressing letter," affirmed the presence of federal segregation, begun upon "the initiative and suggestion of the heads of departments." He knew about it, and believed it was in the interests of both races. It had been introduced, Wilson continued, "with the idea that the friction, or rather the discontent and uneasiness which had prevailed in many of the departments would thereby be removed." He expressed sorrow that Villard should so misjudge his action which, he said, was intended to render Negro federal workers "more safe in their possession of office and less likely to be discriminated against."[13]

Now that Wilson's position was clear, Villard went on to try and convince the President that it was an erroneous stand to take. He urged Wilson to accept the plans put forth earlier by the NAACP for a race commission to study scientifically the entire Negro–white situation in the United States. Wilson had indicated great interest in the idea to Villard in 1912, promising to consider it when he reached the White House, and in May, 1913, Villard had submitted the tentative plan. But in August, Wilson wrote Villard that he could not accept it in view of the sentiment of certain senators. This was a bitter setback to Villard and the NAACP which sponsored the commission plan. But more urgent was the fight against federal segregation, and Villard quickly renewed his efforts to influence Wilson against it.

Villard added strength to his arguments that Negroes were bitterly resentful of the new policy by forwarding a letter to the President from the outstanding Negro leader in the country, Booker T. Washington. Opposition was not only from the militant Negro wing. Washington wrote, in part, "I have recently spent several days in Washington, and I have never seen the

---

[13] Villard to Wilson, July 21, 1913, Villard Papers; Wilson to Villard, July 23, 1913, Wilson Papers.

colored people so discouraged and so bitter as they are at the present time." Washington asked Villard to seek a change from the "hurtful" policy before it went further.[14] Wilson was not encountering a divided Negro opinion on the segregation issue. Negroes were divided on other questions of race philosophy, but they were united in their condemnation of federal segregation.

Wilson was deeply troubled by the unexpected and violent attacks on a policy which he felt to be moderate, conciliatory, and just. But he believed that segregation was essential to the avoidance of friction. He urged Villard "to see the real situation down here," to understand that what he, as President, was trying to do "must be done, if at all, through the cooperation of those with whom I am to sit in the government." Nothing could be accomplished, he warned, if a "bitter agitation" were inaugurated. "I appeal to you most earnestly to aid in holding things at a just and cool equipoise until I can discover whether it is possible to work things out or not."[15]

In September, 1913, Wilson wrote similar sentiments to a prominent Negro minister, Reverend H. A. Bridgeman, editor of the *Congregation and Christian World*. This was the President's first public statement on federal segregation. "I would say that I do approve of the segregation that is being attempted in several of the departments," he wrote.[16] Later on in the year he promised a Negro delegation, led by the fiery young editor of the *Boston Guardian*, William Monroe Trotter, to investigate the segregation. One year later the group returned to demand the reason for continued segregation. Wilson reported to them that investigations by him and his cabinet revealed that federal segregation was necessitated by friction between Negro and white workers, and was not instituted to embarrass or harm colored workers. He admired the progress the Negro race had made and wanted to see it "continue along independent lines," but inasmuch as prejudice still remained and it would take "one hundred years to eradicate this prejudice," he said, "we must deal with it as practical men." Wilson stressed his contention that harm was

---

[14] Villard to Wilson, August 24, 1913, Villard Papers.

[15] Wilson to Villard, August 29, 1913, Villard Papers.

[16] Wilson to Bridgeman, September 4, 1914, Wilson Papers.

interjected when Negroes were told that federal segregation was a humiliation.[17]

Segregation would be continued, but Wilson told the group he would gladly investigate any specific cases of discrimination which were presented to him from time to time. He maintained that the whole question had no place in politics; it was a "human problem" not a political one.[18] The *New York Times*, which carried the story of the delegation's visit on page one under the headline, "President Resents Negro's Criticism," wrote this description of Wilson's answer to Trotter's warning that he would never again gain Negro support unless his policies were altered:[19]

> With some emotion he asserted that he was not seeking office, and that a man who sought the office of the Presidency was a fool for his pains. He spoke of the intolerable burden of the office and the things he had to do which were more than the human spirit could carry.

After labeling Trotter's words on the Negro vote as blackmail, Wilson dismissed the delegation.

From Autumn 1913 on, after Wilson's approval of federal segregation had been made public and evidence on the size and extent of the official policy mounted, Negro opposition was united, hitting hard at what was felt to be the most serious blow at Negro rights since the days of slavery. Important and little-known Negroes, important and little-known groups found common ground in demanding its abolition.

Wilson himself received letters of protest from every state in the Union, from blacks and whites. DuBois, Villard, and other officers of the NAACP sent both public appeals which were published in the NAACP news organ, *Crisis*, and private letters. Booker T. Washington expressed the concern of his group in the letter forwarded by Villard. Prominent members of the scholarly world, of which Wilson had been so recently a part, joined in the protest along with such political personages as the gover-

---

[17] *Crisis*, IX (January, 1915), 119–27.
[18] *Ibid.; New York Times*, November 13, 1914.
[19] *Ibid.*

nors of Massachusetts and Michigan. The Wilson Papers are full of letters from Negroes and whites in every walk of life.[20]

Petitions were another method of protest. Circulated in cities throughout the country and sent to the President, they varied in size from a few hundred signatures to one brought by William Monroe Trotter which was purported to contain over twenty-one thousand names. The NAACP led the drive, collecting signatures of both Negroes and whites. Several church organizations joined the crusade. The National Council of Congregational Churches of the United States registered its official resolution against federal segregation at the October, 1913 convention. The International Council of Churches added a more universal censure in a letter to Wilson, August 21, 1913.[21] Many other church groups and individual ministers of all faiths protested. No religious group appears to have written Wilson in favor of the federal segregation policy.

Another method of attack was that of mass meetings. NAACP branches held open hearings on the mounting evidence of segregation, and NAACP national officers toured through such eastern cities as Boston, New York, and Washington to arouse and inform the public. Trotter, representing the National Independent Political League, a Negro group which had been recognized by the Democratic party and had supported Wilson in the election, stood before enormous audiences in Boston and called for a united Negro front to stop the advance of "Jim Crowism" in Washington, D.C.

Villard turned to the public in October, 1913, through the medium of mass meetings after his letters and talks to Wilson convinced him that the President would not change his policies.

---

[20] E.g., Governor Woodbridge N. Ferris, Michigan to Wilson, August 1, 1913; Governor Eugene N. Foss, Massachusetts, to Wilson, October 20, 1913; Alfred Hayes, professor of law at Cornell University, to Wilson, September, 1913; George Cook, secretary and business manager of Howard University, September 19, 1913. The latter are but two of many strongly worded entreaties from educators. Private letters of protest appear in the Wilson Papers from over thirty-four states.

[21] Congregational Churches of the United States to Wilson, November 14, 1913; International Council of Churches to Wilson, August 21, 1913; Unitarian Conference of Middle States and Canada to Wilson, November, 1913, Wilson Papers.

Prior to a meeting scheduled for late October, Villard advised McAdoo what he intended to say there, and alluded to the deep sorrow he felt in opposing Wilson.

> I told the President the other day that I should have to do this, but that I should do it with complete respect both for your sincerity and for his, and I have tried to put that note into this address. It is harder for me to make this speech than you could have any idea of.[22]

McAdoo's reply was intended to correct "certain erroneous statements" in Villard's speech. There was no segregation issue in the Treasury Department, he wrote. They had planned to make the registry section an all-colored division under a Negro supervisor, he explained, and when the Negro candidate for registrar of the treasury withdrew from candidacy, the experiment was abandoned. Now there were sixty percent white and forty percent black workers in that area. Of the alleged discrimination, McAdoo stated,

> There has been an effort in the departments to remove the causes of complaint and irritation where white women have been forced unnecessarily to sit at desks with colored men. Compulsion of this sort creates friction and race prejudice. Elimination of such friction promotes good feeling and friendship.

He chastised Villard's "unjust" speech as reflecting wrong on Wilson "than whom no truer, nobler and braver soldier in the cause of humanity has appeared since the death of Lincoln."[23]

This letter from McAdoo was read to the mass meeting in Washington on October 27, 1913. It was a packed hall, and over four thousand, chiefly Negroes, had been turned away for lack of room. Villard related the outcome to McAdoo.[24] McAdoo's letter had not been received well, he said, because a great number in the audience were segregated clerks. When the sentence "There is no segregation issue in the Treasury Department" was read,

---

[22] Villard to McAdoo, October 25, 1913, Villard Papers.
[23] McAdoo to Villard, October 27, 1913, Villard Papers.
[24] Villard to McAdoo, October 28, 1913, Villard Papers.

a great derisive laugh had risen from the throng. Villard insisted that all the facts he had presented were true, based on painstaking research conducted both by the NAACP and by himself. He would continue to spread these facts.

If mass meetings, petitions, and letters were the major weapons of the antisegregationists, the press was equally important in publicizing conditions within the departments and in covering those methods of protest which were being employed to put an end to federal segregation. The major burden was assumed by the Negro newspapers and magazines. White progressive papers such as Villard's *Evening Post* added their strength, and from time to time a number of white papers of Republican or Independent leanings remarked on the changing conditions among colored government workers and questioned the merit of the change.[25]

The breadth of Negro opposition to federal segregation was suggested in the fact that colored newspapers and magazines whose policies were ordinarily opposed to each other united on this one cause. The National Negro Press Association, representing 126 newspapers at its national convention in August, 1913, sent a petition to Wilson to end the separationist policy. This group was reputed to support the policies of Booker T. Washington.[26] The *Crisis*, edited by Washington's adversary, W. E. B. DuBois, was another potent journalistic voice raised in opposition to Wilson's policies. Not the least of the services of the Negro press was to editorialize on the effects of segregation, to present the united voice of Negro opposition and its reasons for opposition.

That the protest was a large one was clear. Moreover its weapons were sharp. Its arguments were serious, thoughtful

---

[25] See footnote 7. The *New York Times* was not of this group. Its stories relating to Negroes, few in the first place, applied largely to the more optimistic pronouncements of Booker T. Washington, to aggressive, belligerent Negro meetings, or to charges made by the Fair Play Association. One *Times* editorial advocated repeal of the Fifteenth Amendment.

[26] Meier, "Booker T. Washington and the Negro Press," *Journal of Negro History*, XXXVIII (January, 1953), 57; B. F. Lee, "Negro Organization," *Annals*, CIL (September, 1931), 135.

analyses of the present and potential threat federal segregation presented.

The major Negro arguments against federal segregation were repeated in petitions, mass meetings, letters, and editorials. They began on the general theme that the present situation was unfair and unwarranted, for "never before has the federal government discriminated against the civilian employees on the ground of color."[27] The government was presenting segregation in violation of accepted policy. Conditions had not changed to justify this abandonment of a nonsegregated federal service. Negro employees had worked alongside white employees for many years, under Republican and Democratic administrations, with no apparent dissatisfaction on either side. The President wished to remove friction where friction did not even exist.

The arguments became more specific. The separate departmental facilities were said to be equal, but in reality they were not. Negroes were separated *from* whites, not the reverse. Negroes invariably were allocated the less desirable rooms, the inconveniently located lavatories, the poorly lit alcoves. Instead of lessening insults, it created an opportunity for them by presenting the Negro in an inferior position. Already Negroes were being treated as social "lepers."[28]

Furthermore, it was charged, the faith Wilson had made with Negroes before the election had been violated. The Negro policy he supported now was inconsistent with his campaign promises of "fair play" and at variance as well with his entire Christian and Democratic philosophy.[29] Despair was rising in the Negro race. Never again would it support either Wilson or the Democratic party for political office. The great gain won in splitting the solid Negro vote was lost. But even more important harm would follow, the protest continued.

Federal segregation was by far the worst blow dealt the Negro race in its years of freedom, for it signified official approval of a practice against which Negroes were fighting by

---

[27] DuBois, Villard, Storey to Wilson, August 15, 1913, Wilson Papers.

[28] NAACP Report of Segregation, August 13, 1913, Wilson Papers.

[29] Petition to Wilson from Seattle, Washington, September 8, 1913, Wilson Papers.

gradual or active means. It was an "establishment of caste in
this free Republic." Segregation invariably led to excesses and
abuses, for "injustice once started is bound to spread apace."[30]
Now that the government was entering the arena of segregationist activities, such tendencies would increase and would
operate with official sanction. The arguments Wilson gave to
explain the government's conduct were similar to those defenses
of segregation which were so familiar in the South. Perhaps
Wilson was sincere when he said segregation in the government
was in the best interests of the Negro. But regardless of his
sincerity, segregation could be and was being used by whites
to subjugate the Negro. The President said he favored segregation so that the Negro could have freedom in his own circle
to advance independently, but in practice segregation actually
was used to curtail the Negro's advancement. It did not matter
what reasons were given to support segregation. In the end, the
results were the same.[31]

Furthermore, the protesters continued, departmental segregation was inconsistent with the tenets of the New Freedom
which promised equal rights for all in every area of activity, as
well as with that philosophy upon which the United States had
been established. The President had neither moral nor legal
right to declare a political division on the ground of racial difference, no matter what his personal beliefs. The federal government had always refrained from defining social customs, yet
Wilson's administration was in essence doing that very thing.
The government did not exist "for the purpose of formulating
rules of social etiquette." Departmental segregation was undemocratic in its recognition of the aristocracy of birth. A government which was unfaithful to its own principles was, in reality,
hurting itself. Constitutional validity was also involved. Perhaps the Constitution was wrong in giving equal rights to all,
"but at least it is the law of the land and as such is not to be
nullified by any individual who happens to believe that in this
respect the Constitution is inversely drawn."[32]

[30] Calvin Chase to Wilson, August 2, 1913, Wilson Papers; *Congregational and Christian World*, October, 1913, Wilson Papers.

[31] *Crisis*, VI (November, 1913).

[32] *Courier-Citizen* (Lowell, Mass.), as cited in *Crisis*, IX (January,
1915).

Segregation in the nation's capital had special significance. Washington, D.C., although a southern city, was the center of Negro society, and the social status of the Negro there had been unequalled anywhere else in the country.[33] It had the largest Negro population of any city in the United States, 94,446 in 1910 according to the official census. Federal segregation, with its concomitants of residential and transportation segregation, was therefore a heavy burden for these Negroes who had enjoyed a measure of equality with whites for so long.

The importance of the Negro protest may be assessed in several ways. Most immediate was the impact it had upon the system it was attacking. Villard reported late in 1913 that federal segregationists had been ordered to take a back seat because of the rain of complaints.[34] A newspaper in Boston reported in December that segregation in the Post Office Department was being abandoned. The trend to remove segregation continued, and January 6, 1914, the officers of the NAACP wrote President Wilson of their joy at the reported checking of federal segregation. Two months later, a news source stated that the last vestiges of federal segregation were being destroyed under order of Assistant Secretary of the Treasury C. S. Hamlin.[35] It is improbable that integration was restored in full, but segregation as a recognized system was banished. Negro opposition had been strong, and was victorious.

It was upon Negroes themselves that the protest left a deeper mark. Federal segregation had been an issue upon which the colored population had leveled a full-scale attack, and out of this attack emerged new spokesmen and new ideas. The first decade of the twentieth century had seen the stirrings of a group of young Negroes who were dissatisfied with the moderate teachings of the accepted leader, Booker T. Washington. Of the rebels, the most outstanding was W. E. B. DuBois, the northern-born, Harvard Ph.D. who was active in the founding of the NAACP in 1910. His criticisms of Booker T. Washington had been strong,

---

[33] Interview with W. E. B. DuBois, November 21, 1955.

[34] Villard, *Fighting Years, Memoirs of a Fighting Editor* (New York, 1939), p. 241.

[35] *Boston Advertiser*, December 10, 1913; NAACP to Wilson, January 6, 1914, Wilson Papers; *Boston Advertiser*, March 7, 1914, drawn to the author's attention by Arthur S. Link in letter, September 10, 1957.

but as a member of the national board of the NAACP and as editor of its magazine, the *Crisis,* his philosophy reached a far wider audience.

The segregationist activities of the Wilson administration provided an explosive issue against which the contrasting philosophies of Washington and DuBois could be tested. Both of the men condemned the federal segregation, but their methods of protest were far different. Washington, a supporter of Taft and Roosevelt in the past, had little connection with the Democratic administration, was no longer the adviser to the President on matters which affected his race. Nor did he consult Wilson, with the exception of that letter sent through Villard. If he worked in secret against federal segregation, it was not recorded, and his public utterances were the same optimistic statements on the growth of Negro economy or the alleged decrease of lynching.[36]

In contrast, DuBois was outspoken in demanding the repeal of federal segregation. He gave voice to the growing feelings of racial solidarity. Federal segregation had intensified the Negro's sense of racial entity and convinced an increasing number of Negroes that Booker T. Washington's gradualism, while advancing the race's position in some areas of endeavor, would never answer the problems raised by white resentment and fear.

In effect, federal segregation had turned the spotlight upon the NAACP and DuBois. The *Crisis* stressed tangible and aggressive steps which must be taken to win political, economic, and social equality for the Negro race. Negroes should fight obstructions by making courts fair, seeking remedial legislation, winning national aid to education, gaining the removal of all legal discrimination based on race and color. The circle of human contact between the races should be increased, and the publication of truth about the Negro extended. Economic cooperation between the races should be increased, and the publication of truth should be promoted. The *Crisis* encouraged pride in race

---

[36] E.g., *New York Times,* January 12, 1913. An exception to his usual optimistic public statements is an article on segregation published after his death: Washington, "Segregation," *New Republic,* cited in *Crisis,* XI (February, 1916), 176.

as well, with its emphasis upon the revival of Negro art and literature, and its attempts to enlighten the Negro voter by publishing the answers of all presidential and congressional candidates to NAACP questionnaires which called for the candidates' stands on such issues as segregation and lynching laws. The Negro should continue to organize, and the NAACP was ready to extend its ranks.[37]

How successfully the NAACP appealed to the Negro may be seen in the rapid growth in membership and branches. In 1912, there were 329 members and 3 NAACP branches; by 1914, 3,000 members and 24 branches; by 1916, 8,785 members and 50 branches. From 1917 to 1920 the number jumped from 9,282 to 88,377, the branches from 80 to 356.[38] The early years of its growth, those years of activity against Wilson's program, and conditions in the country at large, were important ones for the association. They provided vital issues upon which the NAACP centered its program. The intense vigor and spirit with which this program was pursued attracted the attention of the discouraged Negro race. Although the board of directors was composed of twenty-seven whites to seven Negroes in 1910, the NAACP was essentially a Negro group, for as DuBois has recently pointed out, the lifeblood of the association was the Negro in branch membership and in financial contributions.[39] The phenomenal jump in membership is evidence of the mounting faith of Negroes in the NAACP.

Thus the Negroes weathered the first administration of Woodrow Wilson. Loss of federal offices, anti-Negro bills in Congress by the score, increases in lynching of Negroes, the introduction of segregation into federal departments—these and other actions pointed to a marked decrease in Negro status. They contrasted sharply with the idealistic phrases of Wilson's New Freedom.

---

[37] E.g., DuBois, "The Immediate Progress of the American Negro," *Crisis*, IX, 311–12.

[38] *Crisis*, XIX (March, 1920), 241.

[39] Interview with DuBois, November 21, 1955; Letter from DuBois, September 19, 1957.

Suggestions for Further Reading

1. Don E. Fehrenbacher (ed.), *Abraham Lincoln: a Documentary Portrait through His Speeches and Writings* (New York: New American Library, 1964).

2. John Hope Franklin, *The Emancipation Proclamation* (New York: Doubleday, 1963).

3. Winthrop D. Jordan (ed.), *The Negro Versus Equality, 1762–1826* (Chicago: Rand McNally and Company, 1969).

    Pages 15–36 contain excerpts of valuable original source material on the subject of Thomas Jefferson's racial views.

4. Rayford Logan, *The Betrayal of the Negro* (New York: Collier Books, 1965).

    This author traces the fortunes and misfortunes of American Negroes between 1877 and 1901, with emphasis upon national politics.

5. Louis B. Wright et al., *The Democratic Experience* (Palo Alto, Ca.: Scott, Foresman, and Company, 1963).

    A concise summary of the racist attitudes and actions of the Lincoln, Johnson, and Grant administrations is presented on pages 211–21.

6. Leslie H. Fishel, Jr., and Benjamin Quarles (eds.), *The Black American: A Documentary History* (Palo Alto, Ca.: Scott, Foresman, and Company, 1970).

7. William Loren Katz (ed.), *Eyewitness: The Negro in American History* (New York: Pitman, 1967).

8. Melvin Steinfield (ed.), *Our Racist Presidents from Washington to Nixon* (San Ramon, Ca.: Consensus Publishers, Inc., 1972).

    A documentary history of Presidential racism and discrimination.

9. Kathleen Wolgemuth, "Woodrow Wilson and Federal Segregation," *Journal of Negro History,* April 1959.

This article provides thorough documentation for the segregation policies of the Wilson administration, and shows the vigorous opposition to Wilson by anti-segregationists.

10. Arthur Zilversmit (ed.), *Lincoln on Black and White: A Documentary History* (Belmont, Ca.: Wadsworth, 1972).

Eighty-one documents focusing on Lincoln's views on race and slavery.

PART 5 **THE FUTURE OF RACISM IN AMERICA**

Chapter Twelve

Developments in the 1960's

The Negro has tried nonviolence, he has turned the other cheek, he has said "love" when the white man said "hate" and it has made no difference. Dr. King is quite an impressive man, but there is much feeling that his philosophy of nonviolence is no longer tenable. There are many Negroes, myself included, who believe that we no longer can guarantee the white man in Mississippi that we will not strike back. The white man cannot hit a Negro, or try to kill him, without expecting to be hit back or killed.

—JAMES MEREDITH, "Big Changes Are Coming," *Saturday Evening Post* (1966)

The Supreme Court decision in 1954 ordering the desegregation of schools marked the beginning of a new era in the history of the Melting Pot. The American Dilemma was at last being confronted head-on. No longer could the gap between the Dream and the reality be ignored.

For a short time there were hopes that the increasing militancy of the civil rights movement, combined with the awakening of American conscience, would result in eventual victory for the cause of "Freedom Now!" It is true that some barriers based on race did topple in the decade after the Brown decision. Bus boycotts, sit-ins, picket lines, demonstrations, freedom rides and freedom schools, and voter registration drives began to make some dents in the walls of apartheid.

By the late 1960's, however, it became increasingly apparent that racism persisted; that resistance to change was just about as high as ever; and that blacks and browns and others were not going to be welcomed into the great crucible. They were going to have to fight their way in. Earlier optimism at token victories now shifted to a mood of despair, distrust, bitterness, and rage. The climate was ripe for separation and nationalism among ethnic minorities. Although there were very early antecedents of black power, the belief that white America had failed its last chance was now so widespread that an unprecedented movement toward black consciousness, black pride, and black self-determination spread rapidly. This new radical consciousness was observed in other minorities as well, notably among Mexican-Americans and Indians.

In retrospect, we can view 1954 as the start of a ten-year effort to make the Melting Pot succeed, to reconcile the Dilemma, and to fulfill the Dream. Failure led to frustration and then to more vociferous cries for black power. The Watts riot in 1965 was an important turning point. So was the firing upon James Meredith on his march in Mississippi in 1966. The assassination of Martin Luther King in 1968 put the finishing touches on the integration movement.

America in the closing years of the decade was a nation in which deep and broad cracks were widening even though many people were reluctant to admit it.

This reluctance was shared by President Lyndon Johnson, for, while his 1965 Howard University address spoke of our failure to establish justice for Negroes as the "one huge wrong of the American nation," he continued to express faith that we were on the verge of solving this problem. At the end of the Johnson administration, in 1968, the President's National Advisory (Kerner) Commission on Civil Disorders warned of the imminent danger of America's moving toward two separate societies. Early in 1969, an independent report issued by the Urban Coalition and Urban America, Inc., entitled *One Year Later,* found virtually no progress toward ending the white racism which the Kerner report indicted. By the end of the 1960's it was clear that the myth of the Melting Pot was shattered because the last-ditch effort to keep it together had failed resoundingly. America was coming apart at the seams.

"There Is No American Dilemma"*

Four years before the Kerner report indicted America's racist record, an editor of Fortune *outlined the nature of our biggest domestic problem.*

What we are discovering, in short, is that the United States —all of it, North as well as South, West as well as East—is a racist society in a sense and to a degree that we have refused so far to admit, much less face. Twenty years ago, Gunnar Myrdal concluded that "the American Negro problem is a problem in the heart of the American," and titled his monumental study of the Negro *An American Dilemma.* Myrdal was wrong. The tragedy of race relations in the United States is that there is no American Dilemma. White Americans are not torn and tortured by the conflict between their devotion to the American creed and their actual behavior. They are upset by the current state of race relations, to be sure. But what troubles them is not that justice is being denied but that their peace is being shattered and their business interrupted.

It will take more than an appeal to the American conscience, therefore, to solve "the Negro problem," though such an appeal is long overdue. Nothing less than a radical reconstruction of American society is required if the Negro is to be able to take his rightful place in American life. And the reconstruction must begin not just in Oxford, Mississippi, or Birmingham, Alabama, but in New York, Philadelphia, Chicago and other great cities of the North as well. For when Negroes leave the South, they don't move to New York—they move to Harlem; they don't move to Chicago—they move to the South Side. Without question, Harlem is a great improvement over Birmingham—but not nearly so great as white men assume. Northern discrimination is less brutal and less personal than the southern variety, and it lacks the overt sanction of law.[1] It hurts none the less. "What makes you think you are going to Heaven?" Langston Hughes asks his

---

[1]"*De facto* segregation," James Baldwin sardonically observes, "means that Negroes are segregated but nobody did it."

folk hero, Jesse B. Simple. "Because I have already been in Harlem," Simple replies.*

The North must change for its own sake therefore. It must change for the nation's sake as well, for the South will never change—and cannot be expected to change—until the North leads the way. At the moment, the North *is* leading, but in the wrong direction. It has shown the South that Negroes can be kept "in their place" without written laws. Southern cities are rapidly learning the *de facto* technique of the North. In the spring of 1963, for example, Albany, Georgia, removed all segregation ordinances from its city code in order to balk the Negro legal attack; the city remained as Jim Crow as ever.

It isn't enough for the white North or the white South to change, however; the black North and the black South must change as well. For "the Negro problem" is not just a white man's problem, as Myrdal thought; it is a black man's problem as well, because of what white prejudice and discrimination have done to the Negro's personality and self-esteem. In a recent *New Yorker* cartoon, one overstuffed tycoon grumbled to another, "Trouble is you start treating people like equals, they begin to believe it." The converse is also true: treat people as inferiors and they begin to believe *that*, too. White men began three and a half centuries ago to treat black men as inferiors, and they haven't stopped yet. A major part of "the Negro problem" in America lies in what these three hundred fifty years have done to the Negro's personality: the self-hatred, the sense of impotence and inferiority that destroys aspiration and keeps the Negro locked in a prison we have all made. Negroes are taught to despise themselves almost from the first moments of consciousness; even without any direct experience with discrimination, they learn in earliest childhood of the stigma attached to color in the United States: "If you're white, you're right"; a Negro folk saying goes, "if you're brown, stick around; if you're black, stay back." And they do stay back.

If whites were to stop all discriminatory practices tomorrow,

---

*More of Jesse Simple can be seen in Langston Hughes, *Not Without Laughter* (New York: George Braziller, Inc., 1930); and *Simple's Uncle Sam* (New York: Hill and Wang, 1967).

this alone would not solve "the Negro problem." To be sure, an end to discrimination is a prerequisite to any solution. But too many Negroes are unable or unwilling to compete; segregation is an affliction, but for many it is a crutch as well.

The Negro will be unable to take his place in the mainstream of American life until he stops despising himself and his fellows. The Negro will be unable to compete on equal terms until he has been able to purge from his mind all sense of white superiority and black inferiority—until he really believes, with all his being, that he is a free man, and acts accordingly. In this sense, therefore, only the Negro can solve the Negro problem. For freedom and equality, like power, cannot be given or handed down as a gift. They must be taken by people unwilling to settle for anything less.

This does not mean, however, that white Americans can simply toss the ball back to their Negro compatriots, as John Fischer of *Harper's* suggested a while ago. White Americans cannot duck their responsibility by placing the burden of change on Negroes themselves. On the contrary, the doctrine Fischer propounded represented but a slightly more sophisticated version of the old racist doctrine that Negroes "aren't ready" for equality. Writing from his chair as editor-in-chief of *Harper's*, Fischer called upon Negroes to redirect their energies from the field of civil rights to that of self-improvement. Since anti-Negro prejudice "is not altogether baseless," in Fischer's view, it cannot be eliminated by lecturing whites or by enacting new legislation. On the contrary, prejudice will disappear "only when a considerable majority of whites are convinced that they have nothing to fear from close, daily association with Negroes in jobs, schools, and neighborhoods." For that to happen, Fischer argued, Negro leaders will somehow have to arrange things so that "the average Negro is willing and able to carry the full responsibilities of good citizenship." But once this happy stage is reached, Fischer assured the Negroes of the United States, they will be "surprised to see how fast white prejudice begins to melt away."

Maybe; but there is little in the history of human bigotry—nothing, certainly, in the long history of anti-Semitism—to suggest that Fischer is right. Jews are as well-behaved as any other group; yet the calculated murder of six million Jews occurred not quite twenty years ago in the country in which Jews were proudest of their assimilation. And in our own country, Dr. Ralph Bunche, with whom Fischer presumably would not be afraid to associate, can be and has been denied hotel accommodations because of his race. What Fischer fails to see is that his own sense of superiority, his arrogant assumption that "the average Negro" has not yet earned the right to full citizenship, is responsible for the behavior he deplores! *For so long as Negroes feel excluded from American society, they are not going to feel bound by its constraints.* "I can hear you say, 'What a horrible, irresponsible bastard!'" the first person narrator of Ralph Ellison's *Invisible Man*[2] declares. "And you're right. I leap to agree with you. . . . But to whom can I be responsible, and why should I be, when you refuse to see me?"

To be sure, the behavior of a good many Negroes does help perpetuate white prejudice; too many Negroes make it too easy for too many whites to rationalize their discrimination with a "they're all alike" attitude. Thus, white prejudice evokes Negro lawlessness, irresponsibility, and dependency—and these traits in turn nurture white prejudice. This is the real "American Dilemma," and [Alexis de] Tocqueville pointed it out two decades before the Civil War. "To induce whites to abandon the opinion they have conceived of the moral and intellectual inferiority of their former slaves," he wrote, "the Negroes must change; but as long as this opinion persists, they cannot change."

And so we are all, black and white together, trapped in a vicious circle from which no one seems able to escape. But we must escape, and it is up to the whites to lead the way; the guilt and the responsibility are theirs. To insist that Negroes must change before whites abandon their discriminatory practices is to deny the very essence of the Judaeo-Christian tradition: its insistence on the infinite worth of every human being. "Inasmuch as ye have done it unto one of the least of these my brethren," Jesus declared, "ye have done it unto me." "Whoever destroys a single soul," the Talmud warns, "should be considered the same as one who has destroyed a whole world."

"Divine Providence," declared Pope John XXIII in opening

---

[2] (New York: Random House, Inc., 1952).

the Ecumenical Council, "is leading us to a new order of human relations." That new order must be based on justice—and we must understand that justice is neither an abstraction, nor a sentiment, nor a relationship, but an *act*. When the Prophets of old spoke of justice, their injunction was not to *be* just but to *do* justice; it is the act that counts. There has been far too much talk, for far too long, about the need to change men's hearts, about the difficulty of legislating morality. The truth of the matter is that men's hearts follow their actions at least as often as their actions follow their hearts. An old Hasidic legend tells of a man who asks his rabbi what he should do, since he does not believe in God. "Act each day as though you believe in God," the rabbi tells him—recite all the prayers and perform all the rituals required of the believer—"and before long you will find that you *do* believe." White Americans would do well to follow the same advice. We cannot wait for time or education to erase the prejudice that is ingrained so deeply in our hearts and minds; we must act as though we really do believe in the brotherhood of man, as though we really do love our black neighbors as ourselves. The belief and the love will follow.

There is no other choice. Out of the smoke and fire on Mount Sinai came a warning which white Americans have ignored for too long: ". . . I the Lord thy God am an impassioned God, visiting the guilt of the father upon the children, upon the third and fourth generations of those who reject Me, but showing kindness to the thousandth generation of those who love Me and keep My commandments." That warning represents not a spirit of vindictiveness but a basic law of human society: that while justice may be postponed, it cannot be denied. The longer justice is postponed, the greater the penalty, the more painful the inevitable confrontation. "I tremble for my country," Thomas Jefferson wrote, "when I reflect that God is just."

And that painful, inevitable confrontation is here and now. Ours is the fourth generation since the Civil War, and the sins of the last three generations (not to mention our own), are being visited upon us. We are just beginning to see how discrimination and indifference to discrimination have corrupted the souls of white men; in the general revulsion at pictures of white policemen unleashing dogs to keep Negroes from registering to vote, of vigilantes beating lunch-counter sit-ins while a crowd of white spectators grin and cheer, we are discovering the truth of Booker T. Washington's famous remark that the white man could not hold the Negro in the gutter without getting in there himself. White Americans are also discovering, to their surprise and horror, how deep is the store of anger and hatred three and a half centuries of humiliation have built up in the American Negro, and how quickly that anger can explode into violence. The real danger, however, is not violence but something deeper and far more corrosive: a sense of permanent alienation from American society. Unless the Negro position improves very quickly, Negroes of whatever class may come to regard their separation from American life as permanent, and so consider themselves outside the constraints and allegiances of American society. The Negro district of every large city could come to constitute an American Casbah, with its own values and controls and an implacable hatred of everything white, that would poison American life.

It is not too much to say, therefore, that the plight of the Negro must become America's central concern, for he is the key to our mutual future. For one thing, the treatment of the Negro in America can affect this country's position in the world. What makes Red China loom so large a threat, for example—to the Russians as well as to us—is less its uncompromising totalitarianism than its evident desire to unite all the colored peoples of the world in holy war against the white race. It is in this context— not vague conversation about the importance of world public opinion—that what Africans and Asians think about the United States does matter. And what they think is clearly affected by Negro–white relations.

But the United States must solve "The Negro problem" out of more than political self-interest; it must accept the Negro as an equal and participating member of society because it is the only right thing, the only decent thing, to do. In the long run, the greatest threat to the United States is not political or military, but moral: the dehumanization of society that our awesome technology threatens, and that has been the central concern of theologians like Barth, Niebuhr, Buber, and Heschel, as well as of novelists and social critics.

The process is already too far advanced; man cannot deny the humanity of his fellow man without ultimately destroying his own. If we cannot learn now to reorder the relations between black and white—if we cannot allow the Negro to recover his lost identity by acknowledging his membership in America—we will never be able to handle the new problems of the age in which we find ourselves. In Camus' haunting phrase, "we are all condemned to live together." We must learn to live together in peace and in justice.

The Fires of Frustration

President Kennedy's small margin of victory over Richard Nixon in 1960 was aided by massive support from black voters. Those votes were vindicated on several occasions, as for example, when federal authority was brought to bear to guarantee James Meredith's admission to the University of Mississippi. Another example of Kennedy's role in the civil rights movement is the following address, which he made in June, 1963.

Good evening, my fellow citizens:
This afternoon, following a series of threats and defiant statements, the presence of Alabama National Guardsmen was required on the University of Alabama to carry out the final and unequivocal order of the United States District Court of the Northern District of Alabama. That order called for the admission of two clearly qualified young Alabama residents who happened to have been born Negro. That they were admitted peacefully on the campus is due in good measure to the conduct of the students of the University of Alabama who met their responsibilities in a constructive way.

I hope that every American, regardless of where he lives, will stop and examine his conscience about this and other related incidents. This nation was founded by men of many nations and backgrounds. It was founded on the principle that all men were created equal, and that the rights of every man are diminished when the rights of one man are threatened.

Today we are committed to a worldwide struggle to promote and protect the rights of all who wish to be free. And when

Americans are sent to Vietnam or West Berlin, we do not ask for whites only.

It ought to be possible, therefore, for American students of any color to attend any public institution they select without having to be backed up by troops. It ought to be possible for American consumers of any color to receive equal service in places of public accommodation, such as hotels and restaurants, and theaters and retail stores, without being forced to resort to demonstrations in the street. And it ought to be possible for American citizens of any color to register and to vote in a free election without interference or fear of reprisal.

It ought to be possible, in short, for every American to enjoy the privileges of being American without regard to his race or color. In short, every American ought to have the right to be treated as he would wish to be treated, as one would wish his children to be treated. But this is not the case.

The Negro baby born in America today, regardless of the section of the nation in which he is born, has about one-half as much chance of completing high school as a white baby born in the same place on the same day; one-third as much chance of completing college; one-third as much chance of becoming a professional man; twice as much chance of becoming unemployed; about one-seventh as much chance of earning ten thousand dollars a year; a life expectancy which is seven years shorter; and the prospects of earning only half as much.

This is not a sectional issue. Difficulties over segregation and discrimination exist in every city, in every state of the Union, producing in many cities a rising tide of discontent that threatens the public safety. Nor is this a partisan issue. In a time of domestic crisis, men of goodwill and generosity should be able to unite regardless of party or politics. This is not even a legal or legislative issue alone. It is better to settle these matters in the courts than in the streets, and new laws are needed at every level. But law alone cannot make men see right.

We are confronted primarily with a moral issue. It is as old as the Scriptures and is as clear as the American Constitution. The heart of the question is whether all Americans are to be afforded equal rights and equal opportunities; whether we are going to treat our fellow Americans as we want to be treated.

If an American, because his skin is dark, cannot eat lunch in a restaurant open to the public; if he cannot send his children to the best public school available; if he cannot vote for the public officials who represent him; if, in short, he cannot enjoy the full and free life which all of us want, then who among us would be content to have the color of his skin changed and stand in his place? Who among us would then be content with the counsels of patience and delay? One hundred years of delay have passed since President Lincoln freed the slaves, yet their heirs, their grandsons, are not fully free. They are not yet freed from the bonds of injustice; they are not yet freed from social and economic oppression. And this nation, for all its hopes and all its boasts, will not be fully free until all its citizens are free.

We preach freedom around the world, and we mean it. And we cherish our freedom here at home. But are we to say to the world—and, much more importantly, to each other—that this is the land of the free, except for the Negroes; that we have no second-class citizens, except Negroes; that we have no class or caste system, no ghettos, no master race, except with respect to Negroes?

Now the time has come for this nation to fulfill its promise. The events in Birmingham and elsewhere have so increased the cries for equality that no city or state or legislative body can prudently choose to ignore them. The fires of frustration and discord are burning in every city, North and South. Where legal remedies are not at hand, redress is sought in the streets, in demonstrations, parades, and protests which create tensions and threaten violence—and threaten lives.

We face, therefore, a moral crisis as a country and a people. It cannot be met by repressive police action. It cannot be left to increased demonstrations in the streets. It cannot be quieted by token moves or talk. It is a time to act in the Congress, in your state and local legislative body, and, above all, in all of our daily lives.

It is not enough to pin the blame on others, to say this is a problem of one section of the country or another, or deplore the facts that we face. A great change is at hand, and our task— our obligation—is to make that revolution, that change, peaceful and constructive for all. Those who do nothing are inviting

shame as well as violence. Those who act boldly are recognizing
right as well as reality.

Next week I shall ask the Congress of the United States
to act, to make a commitment it has not fully made in this century
to the proposition that race has no place in American life or law.
The federal judiciary has upheld that proposition in a series of
forthright cases. The executive branch has adopted that proposition in the conduct of its affairs, including the employment
of federal personnel, the use of federal facilities, and the sale
of federally financed housing. But there are other necessary
measures which only the Congress can provide, and they must
be provided at this session.

The old code of equity law under which we live commands
for every wrong a remedy. But in too many communities, in
too many parts of the country, wrongs are inflicted on Negro
citizens and there are no remedies in law. Unless the Congress
acts, their only remedy is the street.

I am, therefore, asking the Congress to enact legislation
giving all Americans the right to be served in facilities which
are open to the public—hotels, restaurants and theaters, retail
stores, and similar establishments. This seems to me to be an
elementary right. Its denial is an arbitrary indignity that no
American in 1963 should have to endure, but many do.

I have recently met with scores of business leaders, urging
them to take voluntary action to end this discrimination. And
I've been encouraged by their response. And in the last two
weeks, over seventy-five cities have seen progress made in the
desegregating of these kinds of facilities. But many are unwilling to act alone. And for this reason nationwide legislation is
needed, if we are to move this problem from the streets to the
courts.

I am also asking Congress to authorize the federal government to participate more fully in lawsuits designed to end segregation in public education. We have succeeded in persuading
many districts to desegregate voluntarily. Dozens have admitted
Negroes without violence. Today a Negro is attending a state-
supported institution in every one of our fifty states. But the
pace is very slow.

Too many Negro children entering segregated grade schools

at the time of the Supreme Court's decision nine years ago* will enter high schools this fall, having suffered a loss which can never be restored. The lack of an adequate education denies the Negro a chance to get a decent job. The orderly implementation of the Supreme Court decision, therefore, cannot be left solely to those who may not have the economic resources to carry their legal action or who may be subject to harassment.

Other features will also be requested, including greater protection for the right to vote. But legislation, I repeat, cannot solve this problem alone. It must be solved in the homes of every American in every community across our country.

In this respect, I want to pay tribute to those citizens, North and South, who've been working in their communities to make life better for all. They are not acting out of a sense of legal duty but out of a sense of human decency. Like our soldiers and our sailors in all parts of the world, they are meeting freedom's challenge on the firing line and I salute them for their honor— and their courage.

My fellow Americans, this is a problem which faces us all, in every city of the North as well as the South. Today there are Negroes unemployed—two or three times as many compared to whites—inadequate education; moving into the large cities, unable to find work; young people particularly out of work, without hope, denied equal rights, denied the opportunity to eat at a restaurant or a lunch counter, or go to a movie theater; denied the right to a decent education; denied, almost today, the right to attend a state university even though qualified. It seems to me that these are matters which concern us all—not merely Presidents, or congressmen, or governors, but every citizen of the United States.

This is one country. It has become one country because all of us and all the people who came here had an equal chance to develop their talents. We cannot say to ten percent of the population that "You can't have that right. Your children can't have the chance to develop whatever talents they have"; that

---

Brown v. Board of Education (1954) declared that "separate but equal" school facilities were inherently unequal and thereby unconstitutional.

the only way they're going to get their rights is to go in the street and demonstrate. I think we owe them and we owe ourselves a better country than that.

Therefore, I'm asking for your help in making it easier for us to move ahead and to provide the kind of equality of treatment which we would want ourselves—to give a chance for every child to be educated to the limit of his talent. As I've said before, not every child has an equal talent or an equal ability or equal motivation. But they should have the equal right to develop their talent and their ability and their motivation to make something of themselves.

We have a right to expect that the Negro community will be responsible, will uphold the law. But they have a right to expect that the law will be fair, that the Constitution will be color blind, as Justice Harlan said at the turn of the century. This is what we're talking about. This is a matter which concerns this country and what it stands for, and in meeting it I ask the support of all of our citizens.

Thank you very much.

*Lighting the Candle**

In the wake of the assassination of John F. Kennedy, the Johnson administration was able to rally congressional support for the passage of the Civil Rights Act of 1964. But the persistent problems of the majority of black people in America were barely affected by the legalistic reforms of the 1960's. A new phase of the struggle was beginning which required massive efforts on many fronts. President Johnson spoke in promising terms of what his administration was prepared to do in mounting the final assault upon our "one major wrong." The promises were not kept. The major assault upon white racism never materialized. The nation got bogged down in Vietnam, and the civil rights movement never recovered from it. Instead, the movement gave way to the revolution. In retrospect, President Johnson's address can be seen as the final oration of hope. Shortly after his speech, the Watts riot broke out in Los Angeles, and a new phase had begun. It was not the new phase the President had anticipated.

---

*This is the complete text of President Johnson's commencement address at Howard University, Washington, D.C., June 4, 1965.

Our earth is the home of revolution. In every corner of every continent men charged with hope contend with ancient ways in pursuit of justice. They reach for the newest of weapons to realize the oldest of dreams: that each may walk in freedom and pride, stretching his talents, enjoying the fruits of the earth.

Our enemies may occasionally seize the day of change. But it is the banner of our revolution they take. And our own future is linked to this process of swift and turbulent change in many lands. But nothing, in any country, touches us more profoundly, nothing is more freighted with meaning for our own destiny, than the revolution of the Negro American. In far too many ways American Negroes have been another nation: deprived of freedom, crippled by hatred, the doors of opportunity closed to hope.

In our time change has come to this nation too. Heroically, the American Negro—acting with impressive restraint—has peacefully protested and marched, entered the courtrooms and the seats of government, demanding a justice long denied. The voice of the Negro was the call to action. But it is a tribute to America that, once aroused, the courts and the Congress, the President, and most of the people have been the allies of progress.

Thus we have seen the high court of the country declare that discrimination based on race was repugnant to the Constitution, and therefore void. We have seen—in 1957, 1960, and again in 1964—the first civil rights legislation in almost a century. As majority leader I helped guide two of these bills through the Senate. And, as your President, I was proud to sign the third.

And soon we will have the fourth new law, guaranteeing every American the right to vote. No act of my administration will give me greater satisfaction than the day when my signature makes this bill too the law of the land. The voting rights bill will be the latest, and among the most important, in a long series of victories. But this victory—as Winston Churchill said of another triumph for freedom—"is not the end. It is not even the beginning of the end. But it is, perhaps, the end of the beginning."

That beginning is freedom; and the barriers to that freedom are tumbling. Freedom is the right to share, fully and equally, in American society—to vote, to hold a job, to enter a public place, to go to school. It is the right to be treated, in every part of our national life, as a man equal in dignity and promise to all others.

But freedom is not enough. You do not wipe away the scars of centuries by saying: Now you are free to go where you want, do as you desire, and choose the leaders you please. You do not take a man who for years has been hobbled by chains, liberate him, bring him to the starting line of a race, saying, "you are free to compete with all the others," and still justly believe you have been completely fair.

Thus it is not enough to open the gates of opportunity. All our citizens must have the ability to walk through those gates. This is the next and the more profound stage of the battle for civil rights. We seek not just freedom but opportunity—not just legal equity but human ability—not just equality as a right and a theory, but equality as a fact and a result.

For the task is to give twenty million Negroes the same chance as every other American to learn and grow—to work and share in society—to develop their abilities: physical, mental and spiritual—and to pursue their individual happiness. To this end equal opportunity is essential, but not enough. Men and women of all races are born with the same range of abilities. But ability is not just the product of birth. It is stretched or stunted by the family you live with, and the neighborhood you live in—by the school you go to, and the poverty or richness of your surroundings. It is the product of a hundred unseen forces playing upon the infant, the child, and the man.

This graduating class at Howard University is witness to the indomitable determination of the Negro American to win his way in American life. The number of Negroes in schools of high learning has almost doubled in fifteen years. The number of nonwhite professional workers has more than doubled in ten years. The median income of Negro college women now exceeds that of white college women. And there are the enormous accomplishments of distinguished individual Negroes— many of them graduates of this institution. These are proud and impressive achievements. But they only tell the story of a growing middle-class minority, steadily narrowing the gap between them and their white counterparts.

But for the great majority of Negro Americans—the poor,

the unemployed, the uprooted and dispossessed—there is a grimmer story. They still are another nation. Despite the court orders and the laws, the victories and speeches, for them the walls are rising and the gulf is widening.

Here are some of the facts of this American failure. Thirty-five years ago, the rate of unemployment for Negroes and whites was about the same. Today the Negro rate is twice as high. In 1948 the eight percent unemployment rate for Negro teen-age boys was actually less than that of whites. By last year it had grown to twenty-three percent, as against thirteen percent for whites.

Between 1949 and 1959, the income of Negro men relative to white men declined in every section of the country. From 1952 to 1963, the median income of Negro families compared to white actually dropped from fifty-seven percent to fifty-three percent. In the years 1955–57, twenty-two percent of experienced Negro workers were out of work at some time during the year. In 1961–63 that proportion had soared to twenty-nine percent.

Since 1947 the number of white families living in poverty has decreased twenty-seven percent while the number of poor nonwhite families went down only three percent. The infant mortality of nonwhites in 1940 was seventy percent greater than whites. Twenty-two years later it was ninety percent greater.

Moreover, the isolation of Negro from white communities is increasing, rather than diminishing, as Negroes crowd into the central cities—becoming a city within a city.

Of course Negro Americans as well as white Americans have shared in our rising national abundance. But the harsh fact of the matter is that in the battle for true equality too many are losing ground. We are not completely sure why this is. The causes are complex and subtle. But we do know the two broad basic reasons. And we know we have to act.

First, Negroes are trapped—as many whites are trapped—in inherited, gateless poverty. They lack training and skills. They are shut in slums, without decent medical care. Private and public poverty combine to cripple their capacities. We are attacking these evils through our poverty program, our education program, our health program, and a dozen more—aimed at the root causes of poverty. We will increase, and accelerate, and broaden this attack in years to come, until this most enduring of foes yields to our unyielding will.

But there is a *second* cause—more difficult to explain, more deeply grounded, more desperate in its force. It is the devastating heritage of long years of slavery; and a century of oppression, hatred, and injustice. For Negro poverty is not white poverty. Many of its causes and many of its cures are the same. But there are differences—deep, corrosive, obstinate differences —radiating painful roots into the community, the family, and the nature of the individual.

These differences are not racial differences. They are solely and simply the consequences of ancient brutality, past injustice, and present prejudice. They are anguishing to observe. For the Negro they are a reminder of oppression. For the white they are a reminder of guilt. But they must be faced, and dealt with, and overcome; if we are to reach the time when the only difference between Negroes and whites is the color of their skin.

Nor can we find a complete answer in the experience of other American minorities. They made a valiant, and largely successful effort to emerge from poverty and prejudice. The Negro, like these others, will have to rely mostly on his own efforts. But he cannot do it alone. For they did not have the heritage of centuries to overcome. They did not have a cultural tradition which had been twisted and battered by endless years of hatred and hopelessness. Nor were they excluded because of race or color—a feeling whose dark intensity is matched by no other prejudice in our society.

Nor can these differences be understood as isolated infirmities. They are a seamless web. They cause each other. They result from each other. They reinforce each other. Much of the Negro community is buried under a blanket of history and circumstance. It is not a lasting solution to lift just one corner. We must stand on all sides and raise the entire cover if we are to liberate our fellow citizens.

One of the differences is the increased concentration of Negroes in our cities. More than seventy-three percent of all Negroes live in urban areas compared with less than seventy percent of whites. Most of them live in slums. And most of them live together; a separated people. Men are shaped by their world. When it is a world of decay ringed by an invisible wall—when escape is arduous and uncertain, and the saving pressures of a more hopeful society are unknown—it can cripple the youth and desolate the man.

There is also the burden a dark skin can add to the search for a productive place in society. Unemployment strikes most swiftly and broadly at the Negro. This burden erodes hope. Blighted hope breeds despair. Despair brings indifference to the learning which offers a way out. And despair coupled with indifference is often the source of destructive rebellion against the fabric of society.

There is also the lacerating hurt of early collision with white hatred or prejudice, distaste or condescension. Other groups have felt similar intolerance. But success and achievement could wipe it away. They do not change the color of a man's skin. I have seen this uncomprehending pain in the eyes of young Mexican-American school children. It can be overcome. But, for many, the wounds are always open.

Perhaps most important—its influence radiating to every part of life—is the breakdown of the Negro family structure. For this, most of all, white America must accept responsibility. It flows from centuries of oppression and persecution of the Negro man. It flows from the long years of degradation and discrimination which have attacked his dignity and assaulted his ability to provide for his family. This, too, is not pleasant to look upon. But it must be faced by those whose serious intent is to improve the life of all Americans.

Only a minority—less than half—of all Negro children reach the age of eighteen having lived all their lives with both parents. At this moment, today, little less than two-thirds are living with both parents. Probably a majority of all Negro children receive federally aided public assistance during their childhood.

The family is the cornerstone of our society. More than any other source it shapes the attitudes, the hopes, the ambitions, and the values of the child. When the family collapses the child is usually damaged. When it happens on a massive scale the community itself it crippled. Unless we work to strengthen the family—to create conditions under which most parents will stay together, all the rest—schools and playgrounds, public assistance, and private concern—will not be enough to cut completely the circle of despair and deprivation.

There is no single easy answer to all these problems. Jobs are part of the answer. They bring the income which permits a man to provide for his family. Decent homes in decent surroundings and a chance to learn are part of the answer. Welfare and social programs better designed to hold families together are part of the answer. Care for the sick is part of the answer. An understanding heart by all Americans is also part of the answer. To all these fronts—and a dozen more—I will dedicate the expanding efforts of my administration.

But there are other answers still to be found. Nor do we fully understand all the problems. Therefore, this fall, I intend to call a White House conference of scholars, experts, Negro leaders, and officials at every level of government. Its theme and title: "To Fulfill These Rights." Its object: to help the American Negro fulfill the rights which—after the long time of injustice—he is finally about to secure; to move beyond opportunity to achievement; to shatter forever, not only the barriers of law and public practice, but the walls which bound the condition of man by the color of his skin; to dissolve, as best we can, the antique enmities of the heart which diminish the holder, divide the great democracy, and do wrong to the children of God. I pledge this will be a chief goal of my administration, and of my program next year, and in years to come. I hope it will be part of the program of all America.

For what is justice? It is to fulfill the fair expectations of man. Thus, American justice is a very special thing. For, from the first, this has been a land of towering expectations. It was to be a nation where each man would be ruled by the common consent of all—enshrined in law, given life by institutions, guided by men themselves subject to its rule. And all—of every station and origin—would be touched equally in obligation and in liberty.

Beyond the law lay the land. It was a rich land, glowing with more abundant promise than ever man had seen. Here, unlike any place yet known, all were to share the harvest. And beyond this was the dignity of man. Each could become whatever his qualities of mind and spirit would permit—to strive, to seek, and, if he could, to find his happiness.

This is American justice. We have pursued it faithfully to the edge of our imperfections. And we have failed to find it for the American Negro. It is the glorious opportunity of this generation to end the one huge wrong of the American nation—and in so doing to find America for ourselves, with the same immense thrill of discovery which gripped those who first began to realize that here, at last, was a home for freedom. All it will take is for all of us to understand what this country is and what it must become.

The Scripture promises: "I shall light a candle of understanding in thine heart, which shall not be put out." Together, and with millions more, we can light that candle of understanding in the heart of America. And, once lit, it will never go out.

*Red Power Meets White America**

One of the sensational events in the struggle for human liberation in this country was the seizure of the island of Alcatraz in San Francisco Bay by a group of Indians. Their claim to the island was embodied in the Proclamation that follows.

PROCLAMATION:

TO THE GREAT WHITE FATHER AND ALL HIS PEOPLE

We, the native Americans, re-claim the land known as Alcatraz Island in the name of all American Indians by right of discovery.

We wish to be fair and honorable in our dealings with the Caucasian inhabitants of this land, and hereby offer the following treaty:

We will purchase said Alcatraz Island for twenty-four dollars ($24) in glass beads and red cloth, a precedent set by the white man's purchase of a similar island about 300 years ago. We know that $24 in trade goods for these 16 acres is more than

---

*From Indians of all Tribes, *Proclamation to the Great White Father and All His People,* San Francisco, California, November, 1969.

was paid when Manhattan Island was sold, but we know that land values have risen over the years. Our offer of $1.24 per acre is greater than the 47¢ per acre that the white men are now paying the California Indians for their land.

We will give to the inhabitants of this island a portion of that land for their own, to be held in trust by the American Indian Affairs and by the bureau of Caucasian Affairs to hold in perpetuity—for as long as the sun shall rise and the rivers go down to the sea. We will further guide the inhabitants in the proper way of living. We will offer them our religion, our education, our life-ways, in order to help them achieve our level of civilization and thus raise them and all their white brothers up from their savage and unhappy state. We offer this treaty in good faith and wish to be fair and honorable in our dealings with all white men.

We feel that this so-called Alcatraz Island is more than suitable for an Indian Reservation, as determined by the white man's own standards. By this we mean that this place resembles most Indian reservations in that:

1. It is isolated from modern facilities, and without adequate means of transportation.
2. It has no fresh running water.
3. It has inadequate sanitation facilities.
4. There are no oil or mineral rights.
5. There is no industry and so unemployment is very great.
6. There are no health care faciilties.
7. The soil is rocky and non-productive; and the land does not support game.
8. There are no educational facilities.
9. The population has always exceeded the land base.
10. The population has always been held as prisoners and kept dependent upon others.

Further, it would be fitting and symbolic that ships from all over the world, entering the Golden Gate, would first see Indian land, and thus be reminded of the true history of this nation. This tiny island would be a symbol of the great lands once ruled by free and noble Indians.

*Sexism and Racism Linked**

Although some blacks have reacted against the comparisons between their plight and that of other groups that see themselves oppressed in the same way ("the student as nigger," "sexism is racism"), the comparisons continue to be made. In the following selection by an activist in the women's liberation movement, the contention is that male chauvinism is rooted in racist attitudes.

Clearly, for the liberation of women to become a reality it is necessary to destroy the ideology of male supremacy which asserts the biological and social inferiority of women in order to justify massive institutionalized oppression. Yet we all know that many women are as loud in their disavowal of this oppression as are the men who chant the litany of "a woman's place is in the home and behind her man." In fact, women are as trapped in their false consciousness as were the mass of blacks twenty years ago, and for much the same reason.

As blacks were defined and limited socially by their color, so women are defined and limited by their sex. While blacks, it was argued, were preordained by God or nature, or both, to be hewers of wood and drawers of water, so women are destined to bear and rear children, and to sustain their husbands with obedience and compassion. The Sky-God tramples through the heavens and the Earth Mother-Goddess is always flat on her back with her legs spread, putting out for one and all.

Indeed, the phenomenon of male chauvinism can only be understood when it is perceived as a form of racism based on stereotypes drawn from a deep belief in the biological inferiority of women. The so-called "black analogy" is no analogy at all; it is the same social process that is at work, a process which both justifies and helps perpetuate the exploitation of one group of human beings by another.

The very stereotypes that express the society's belief in the biological inferiority of women recall the images used to justify the oppression of blacks. The nature of women, like that of slaves, is depicted as dependent, incapable of reasoned thought, childlike

---

*From Marlene Dixon, "Why Women's Liberation," in *Divided We Stand* (San Francisco: Canfield Press, 1970).

in its simplicity and warmth, martyred in the role of mother, and mystical in the role of sexual partner. In its benevolent form, the inferior position of women results in paternalism; in its malevolent form, a domestic tyranny which can be unbelievably brutal.

It has taken over fifty years to discredit the scientific and social "proof" which once gave legitimacy to the myths of black racial inferiority. Today most people can see that the theory of the genetic inferiority of blacks is absurd. Yet few are shocked by the fact that scientists are still busy "proving" the biological inferiority of women.

In recent years, in which blacks have led the struggle for liberation, the emphasis on racism has focused only upon racism against blacks. The fact that "racism" has been practiced against many groups other than blacks has been pushed into the background. Indeed, a less forceful but more accurate term for the phenomenon would be "social Darwinism." It was the opinion of the social Darwinists that in the natural course of things the "fit" succeed (i.e. oppress) and the "unfit" (i.e. the biologically inferior) sink to the bottom. According to this view, the very fact of a group's oppression proves its inferiority and the inevitable correctness of its low position. In this way each successive immigrant group coming to America was decked out in the garments of "racial" or biological inferiority until the group was sufficiently assimilated, whereupon Anglo-Saxon venom would turn on a new group filling up the space at the bottom. Now two groups remain, neither of which has been assimilated according to the classic American pattern: the "visibles"—blacks and women. It is equally true for both: "it won't wear off."

Yet the greatest obstacle facing those who would organize women remains women's belief in their own inferiority. Just as all subject populations are controlled by their acceptanec of the rightness of their own states, so women remain subject because they believe in the rightness of their own oppression. This dilemma is not a fortuitous one, for the entire society is geared to socialize women to believe in and adopt as immutable necessity their traditional and inferior role. From earliest training to the grave, women are constrained and propagandized. Spend an evening at the movies or watching television, and you will see a grotesque figure called woman presented in a hundred variations upon the themes of "children, church, kitchen" or "the chick sex-pot."

For those who believe in the "rights of mankind," the "dignity of man," consider that to make a woman a person, a human being in her own right, you would have to change her sex: imagine Stokely Carmichael "prone and silent"; imagine Mark Rudd as a Laugh-In girl; picture Rennie Davis as Miss America. Such contradictions as these show how prevasive and deep-rooted is the cultural contempt for women, how difficult it is to imagine a woman as a serious human being, or conversely, how empty and degrading is the image of woman that floods the culture.

Countless studies have shown that black acceptance of white stereotypes leads to mutilated identity, to alienation, to rage and self-hatred. Human beings cannot bear in their own hearts the contradictions of those who hold them in contempt. The ideology of male supremacy and its effect upon women merits as serious study as has been given to the effects of prejudice upon Jews, blacks, and immigrant groups.

It is customary to shame those who would draw the parallel between women and blacks by a great show of concern and chest beating over the suffering of black people. Yet this response itself reveals a refined combination of white middle class guilt and male chauvinism, for it overlooks several essential facts. For example, the most oppressed group within the feminine population is made up of black women, many of whom take a dim view of the black male intellectual's adoption of white male attitudes of sexual superiority (an irony too cruel to require comment). Neither are those who make this pious objection to the racial parallel addressing themselves very adequately to the millions of white working class women living at the poverty level, who are not likely to be moved by this middle class guilt-ridden one-upmanship while having to deal with the boss, the factory, or the welfare worker day after day. They are already dangerously resentful of the gains made by blacks, and much of their "racist backlash" stems from the fact that they have been forgotten in the push for social change. Emphasis on the real mechanisms of oppression—on the commonality of the process—is essential lest groups such as these, which should work in alliance, become divided against one another.

White middle class males already struggling with the acknowledgment of their own racism do not relish an added burden of recognition: that to white guilt must soon be added "male." It is therefore understandable that they should refuse to see the harshness of the lives of most women—to honestly face the facts of massive institutionalized discrimination against women. Witness the performance to date: "Take her down off the platform and give her a good fuck," "Petty Bourgeois Revisionist Running Dogs," or in the classic words of a Berkeley male "leader," "Let them eat cock."

Among whites, women remain the most oppressed—and the most unorganized—group. Although they constitute a potential mass base for the radical movement, in terms of movement priorities they are ignored; indeed they might as well be invisible. Far from being an accident, this omission is a direct outgrowth of the solid male supremist beliefs of white radical and left-liberal men. Even now, faced with both fact and agitation, leftist men find the idea of placing any serious priority upon women so outrageous, such a degrading notion, that they respond with a virulence far out of proportion to the modest request of movement women. This only shows that women must stop wasting their time worrying about the chauvinism of men in the movement and focus instead on their real priority: organizing women.

*The Black Panthers**

One of the important manifestations of the Black Power movement in the last part of the 1960's was the development of the Black Panther Party. For many whites, the Party represented the new "bogeyman" in the civil rights movement (replacing the assassinated Malcolm X), but as the decade drew toward a close it became apparent that the Black Panthers enjoyed much wider popular support than was at first supposed. The Black Panthers continued the tradition of Malcolm X in "telling it like it is," and that may account for much of their appeal, and for the appeal of writers like Eldridge Cleaver.

These were new voices from Black America, and White America was starting to listen to them.

1. *We want freedom. We want power to determine the destiny of our Black Community.*

---

*From the October 1966 Black Panther Party Platform and Program.

We believe that black people will not be free until we are able to determine our destiny.

2. *We want full employment for our people.*

We believe that the federal government is responsible and obligated to give every man employment or a guaranteed income. We believe that if the white American businessmen will not give full employment, then the means of production should be taken from the businessmen and placed in the community so that the people of the community can organize and employ all of its people and give a high standard of living.

3. *We want an end to the robbery by the white man of our Black Community.*

We believe that this racist government has robbed us and now we are demanding the overdue debt of forty acres and two mules. Forty acres and two mules was promised 100 years ago as restitution for slave labor and mass murder of black people. We will accept the payment in currency which will be distributed to our many communities. The Germans are now aiding the Jews in Israel for the genocide of the Jewish people. The Germans murdered six million Jews. The American racist has taken part in the slaughter of over fifty million black people; therefore, we feel that this is a modest demand that we make.

4. *We want decent housing, fit for shelter of human beings.*

We believe that if the white landlords will not give decent housing to our black community, then the housing and the land should be made into cooperatives so that our community, with government aid, can build and make decent housing for its people.

5. *We want education for our people that exposes the true nature of this decadent American society. We want education that teaches us our true history and our role in the present-day society.*

We believe in an educational system that will give to our people a knowledge of self. If a man does not have knowledge of himself and his position in society and the world, then he has little chance to relate to anything else.

6. *We want all black men to be exempt from military service.*

We believe that Black people should not be forced to fight in the military service to defend a racist government that does not protect us. We will not fight and kill other people of color in the world who, like black people, are being victimized by the white racist government of America. We will protect ourselves from the force and violence of the racist police and the racist military, by whatever means necessary.

7. *We want an immediate end to POLICE BRUTALITY and MURDER of black people.*

We believe we can end police brutality in our black community by organizing black self-defense groups that are dedicated to defending our black community from racist police oppression and brutality. The Second Amendment to the Constitution of the United States gives a right to bear arms. We therefore believe that all black people should arm themselves for self-defense.

8. *We want freedom for all black men held in federal, state, county and city prisons and jails.*

We believe that all black people should be released from the many jails and prisons because they have not received a fair and impartial trial.

9. *We want all black people when brought to trial to be tried in court by a jury of their peer group or people from their black communities, as defined by the Constitution of the United States.*

We believe that the courts should follow the United States Constitution so that black people will receive fair trials. The Fourteenth Amendment of the U.S. Constitution gives a man a right to be tried by his peer group. A peer is a person from a similar economic, social, religious, geographical, environmental, historical and racial background. To do this the court will be forced to select a jury from the black community from which the black defendant came. We have been, and are being tried by all-white juries that have no understanding of the "average reasoning man" of the black community.

10. *We want land, bread, housing, education, clothing, justice and peace. And as our major political objective, a United Nations-supervised plebiscite to be held throughout the black colony in which only black colonial subjects will be allowed to participate, for the purpose of determining the will of black people as to their national destiny.*

When, in the course of human events, it becomes necessary for one people to dissolve the political bands which have connected them with another, and to assume, among the powers of the earth, the separate and equal station to which the laws of nature and nature's God entile them, a decent respect to the opinions of mankind requires that they should declare the causes which impel them to the separation.

We hold these truths to be self-evident, that all men are created equal; that they are endowed by their Creator with certain unalienable rights; that among these are life, liberty, and the pursuit of happiness. *That, to secure these rights, governments are instituted among men, deriving their just powers from the consent of the governed; that, whenever any form of government becomes destructive of these ends, it is the right of the people to alter or to abolish it, and to institute a new government, laying its foundation on such principles, and organizing its powers in such form, as to them shall seem most likely to effect their safety and happiness.* Prudence, indeed, will dictate that governments long established should not be changed for light and transient causes; and, accordingly, all experience hath shown, that mankind are more disposed to suffer, while evils are sufferable, than to right themselves by abolishing the forms to which they are accustomed. *But, when a long train of abuses and usurpations, pursuing invariably the same object, evinces a design to reduce them under absolute despotism, it is their right, it is their duty, to throw off such government, and to provide new guards for their future security.*

*The Young Lords**

The Puerto Rican victims of American expansion and racism are no exception to the growing number of minority groups organized to resist oppressors. One of the better-known groups is the Young Lords, modeled somewhat after the Black Panthers and the Brown Bèrets, but concentrating on issues of concern to the Puerto Rican communities in America.

1. *We want self-detemination for Puerto Ricans, liberation on the island and inside the united states.*

---

*From the Young Lords 13-Point Program and Platform, originally written in October of 1969 and revised in May 1970.

For 500 years, first spain and then the united states have colonized our country. Billions of dollars in profits leave our country for the united states every year. In every way we are slaves of the gringo. We want liberation and the Power in the hands of the People, not Puerto Rican exploiters. *Que viva Puerto Rico libre!*

2. *We want self-determination for all Latinos.*

Our Latin Brothers and Sisters, inside and outside the united states, are oppressed by amerikkkan [*sic*] business. The Chicano people built the Southwest, and we support their right to control their lives and their land. The people of Santo Domingo continue to fight against gringo domination and its puppet generals. The armed liberation struggles in Latin America are part of the war of Latinos against imperialism. *Que viva La Raza!*

3. *We want liberation of all Third World people.*

Just as Latins first slaved under spain and the yanquis, Black people, Indians, and Asians slaved to build the wealth of this country. For 400 years they have fought for freedom and dignity against racist Babylon. Third World people have led the fight for freedom. All the colored and oppressed peoples of the world are one nation under oppression. *No Puerto Rican is free until all people are free!*

4. *We are revolutionary nationalists and oppose racism.*

The Latin, Black, Indian and Asian people inside the u.s. are colonies fighting for liberation. We know that washington, wall street, and city hall will try to make our nationalism into racism; but Puerto Ricans are of all colors and we resist racism. Millions of poor white people are rising up to demand freedom and we support them. These are the ones in the u.s. that are stepped on by the rulers and the government. We each organize our people, but our fights are the same against oppression and we will defeat it together. *Power to all oppressed people!*

5. *We want equality for women. Down with machismo and male chauvinism.*

Under capitalism, women have been oppressed by both society and our men. The doctrine of machismo has been used by men to take out their frustrations on wives, sisters, mothers, and children. Men must fight along with sisters in the struggle for economic and social equality and must recognize that sisters make up over half of the revolutionary army: sisters and brothers are equals fighting for our people. *Forward sisters in the struggle!*

6. *We want community control of our institutions and land.*

We want control of our communities by our people and programs to guarantee that all institutions serve the needs of our people. People's control of police, health services, churches, schools, housing, transportation and welfare are needed. We want an end to attacks on our land by urban renewal, highway destruction, and university corporations. *Land belongs to all the people!*

7. *We want a true education of our Afro-Indio culture and Spanish language.*

We must learn our long history of fighting against cultural, as well as economic genocide by the spaniards and now the yanquis. Revolutionary culture, culture of our people, is the only true teaching. *Jibaro si, yanqui no!*

8. *We oppose capitalists and alliances with traitors.*

Puerto Rican rulers, or puppets of the oppressor, do not help our people. They are paid by the system to lead our people down blind alleys, just like the thousands of poverty pimps who keep our communities peaceful for business, or the street workers who keep gangs divided and blowing each other away. We want a society where the people socialistically control their labor. *Venceremos!*

9. *We oppose the amerikkkan [sic] military.*

We demand immediate withdrawal of all u.s. military forces and bases from Puerto Rico, VietNam, and all oppressed communities inside and outside the u.s. No Puerto Rican should serve in the u.s. army against his Brothers and Sisters, for the only true army of oppressed people is the People's Liberation Army to fight all rulers. *u.s. out of Vietnam, free Puerto Rico now!*

10. *We want freedom for all political prisoners and prisoners of war.*

No Puerto Rican should be in jail or prison, first because we are a nation, and amerikkka [sic] has no claims on us; second, because we have not been tried by our own people (peers). We also want all freedom fighters out of jail, since they are prisoners of the war for liberation. *Free all political prisoners and prisoners of war!*

11. *We are internationalists.*

Our people are brainwashed by television, radio, newspapers, schools and books to oppose people in other countries fighting for their freedom. No longer will be believe these lies, because we have learned who the real enemy is and who our real friends are. We will defend our sisters and brothers around the world who fight for justice and are against the rulers of this country. *Que viva Ché Guevara!*

12. *We believe armed self-defense and armed struggle are the only means of liberation.*

We are opposed to violence—the violence of hungry children, illiterate adults, diseased old people, and the violence of poverty and profit. We have asked, petitioned, gone to courts, demonstrated peacefully, and voted for politicians full of empty promises. But we still ain't free. The time has come to defend the lives of our people against repression and for revolutionary war against the businessmen, politicians, and police. When a government oppresses the people, we have the right to abolish it and create a new one. *Arm ourselves to defend ourselves!*

13. *We want a socialist society.*

We want liberation, clothing, free food, education, health care, transportation, full employment and peace. We want a society where the needs of the people come first, and where we give solidarity and aid to the people of the world, not oppression and racism. *Hasta la victoria siempre!*

Suggestions for Further Reading

1. Stokely Carmichael and Charles Hamilton, *Black Power: The Politics of Liberation in America* (New York: Vintage Books, 1967).

   A brilliant and perceptive analysis of the need for black power to combat white racism.

2. Eldridge Cleaver, *Soul on Ice* (New York: McGraw-Hill, 1968).

   This highly acclaimed book was written while Cleaver was serving a prison term.

3. ———, *Post Prison Writings* (New York: Random House, 1969).

4. Frantz Fanon, *The Wretched of the Earth* (New York: Grove Press, 1968).

   This important book has become a handbook for revolutionary leaders of the Third World.

5. Philip S. Foner (ed.), *The Black Panthers Speak* (Philadelphia: Lippincott, 1970).

   An anthology of articles and essays by Huey Newton, Bobby Seale, Eldridge Cleaver, David Hilliard, Fred Hampton, and others.

6. Malcolm X, *The Autobiography of Malcolm X* (New York: Grove Press, 1966).

   Essential reading for an understanding of black nationalism in the 1960's.

7. August Meier and Elliott Rudwick (eds.), *Black Protest in the Sixties* (Chicago: Quadrangle, 1970).

8. Jack Olsen, *The Black Athlete—A Shameful Story* (New York: Time-Life Books, 1968).

   Exposes the myth of integration in American sports and illustrates the revolt of black athletes in the late 1960's.

9. Julian Samora (ed.), *La Raza: Forgotten Americans* (Notre Dame: University of Notre Dame Press, 1966).

10. *Urban America, Inc. and the Urban Coalition, One Year Later* (New York: Praeger, 1969).

    An assessment of the nation's response to the 1968 Kerner Report.

11. Nathan Wright, Jr., *Black Power and Urban Unrest* (New York: Hawthorn Books, 1967).

Chapter Thirteen

The 1970's and Beyond

> *Black power activism—thrust by default temporarily at the head of a powerful movement—is a conception that contributes in a significant way to the strength and unity of that movement but is unable to provide the mature vision for the mighty works ahead. It will pass and leave black people in this country prouder, stronger, more determined, but in need of grander princes with clearer vision. We believe that the black masses will rise with a simple and eloquent demand to which new leaders must give tongue. They will say to America simply: "GET OFF OUR BACKS!"*
> —WILLIAM H. GRIER and PRICE M. COBBS,
> *Black Rage* (1968)

The Melting Pot is obsolete. It had long ago outlived its usefulness, but it is manifestly obsolete today. Aroused members of ethnic minorities are seeking equality under the law and non-discrimination in society; but they are also attempting to preserve the many elements of their individual cultures without having to conform to the cultural dictates of the majority. They regard Anglo-Saxon culture less than lovingly, and they know that they were never fully accepted by WASP society anyway, even when they wanted to assimilate.

The historical record shows that the Melting Pot was one of

those ideas that just hasn't worked out. Racism and discrimination are part and parcel of American life, and are likely to remain so in the years to come. It would be unjustifiable optimism and frivolous irresponsibility to delude ourselves into believing that there are significant trends away from racism. For every white like Father James Groppi of Milwaukee, who led marches through the streets in favor of open housing in 1968, there are hundreds of whites who take their stand among those who would preserve the sacred right of the homeowner to discriminate.

If it is difficult to emerge from the decade of the 1960's with any type of optimism about the future of American ethnic relations, it is virtually impossible to imagine that the resurrection of the Melting Pot can ever take place in the foreseeable future. The decade of the 1970's promised more conflict and confrontation.

Black Rage*

The two black psychiatrists who authored this important work have formulated a powerful conclusion to their best-selling book. It is an articulate prediction of the future which agrees with the analyses of Eldridge Cleaver and Stokely Carmichael.

Depression and grief are hatred turned on the self. It is instructive to pursue the relevance of this truth to the condition of black America.

Black people have shown a genius for surviving under the most deadly circumstances. They have survived because of their close attention to reality. A black dreamer would have a short life in Mississippi. They are of necessity bound to reality, chained to the facts of the times; historically the penalty for misjudging a situation involving white men has been death. The preoccupation with religion has been a willing adoption of fantasy to prod an otherwise reluctant mind to face another day.

We will even play tricks on ourselves if it helps us stay alive.

---

*From Chapter X of *Black Rage* by William H. Grier and Price M. Cobbs, © 1968 by William H. Grier and Price M. Cobbs, Basic Books, Inc., Publishers, New York.

The psychological devices used to survive are reminiscent of the years of slavery, and it is no coincidence. The same devices are used because black men face the same danger now as then.

The grief and depression caused by the condition of black men in America is an unpopular reality to the sufferers. They would rather see themselves in a more heroic posture and chide a disconsolate brother. They would like to point to their achievements (which in fact have been staggering); they would rather point to virtue (which has been shown in magnificent form by some blacks); they would point to bravery, fidelity, prudence, brilliance, creativity, all of which dark men have shown in abundance. But the overriding experience of the black American has been grief and sorrow and no man can change that fact.

His grief has been realistic and appropriate. What people have so earned a period of mourning?

We want to emphasize yet again the depth of the grief for slain sons and ravished daughters, how deep and lingering it is.

If the depth of his sorrow is felt, we can then consider what can be made of this emotion.

As grief lifts and the sufferer moves toward health, the hatred he had turned on himself is redirected toward his tormentors, and the fury of his attack on the one who caused him pain is in direct proportion to the depth of his grief. When the mourner lashes out in anger, it is a relief to those who love him, for they know he has now returned to health.

Observe that the amount of rage the oppressed turns on his tormentor is a direct function of the depth of his grief, and consider the intensity of black men's grief.

Slip for a moment into the soul of a black girl whose womanhood is blighted, not because she is ugly, but because she is black and by definition all blacks are ugly.

Become for a moment a black citizen of Birmingham, Alabama, and try to understand his grief and dismay when innocent children are slain while they worship, for no other reason than they are black.

Imagine how an impoverished mother feels as she watches

328

the light of creativity snuffed out in her children by schools which dull the mind and environs which rot the soul.

For a moment make yourself the black father whose son went innocently to war and there was slain—for whom, for what?

For a moment be any black person, anywhere, and you will feel the waves of hopelessness that engulfed black men and women when Martin Luther King was murdered. All black people understood the tide of anarchy that followed his death.

It is the transformation of *this* quantum of grief into aggression of which we now speak. As a sapling bent low stores energy for a violent backswing, blacks bent double by oppression have stored energy which will be released in the form of rage—black rage, apocalyptic and final.

White Americans have developed a high skill in the art of misunderstanding black people. It must have seemed to slave-holders that slavery would last through all eternity, for surely their misunderstanding of black bondsmen suggested it. If the slaves were eventually to be released from bondage, what could be the purpose of creating the fiction of their subhumanity?

It must have seemed to white men during the period 1865 to 1945 that black men would always be a passive, compliant lot. If not, why would they have stoked the flames of hatred with such deliberately barbarous treatment?

White Americans today deal with "racial incidents" from summer to summer as if such minor turbulence will always remain minor and one need only keep the blacks busy till fall to have made it through another troubled season.

Today it is the young men who are fighting the battles, and, for now, their elders, though they have given their approval, have not joined in. The time seems near, however, for the full range of the black masses to put down the broom and buckle on the sword. And it grows nearer day by day. Now we see skirmishes, sputtering erratically, evidence if you will that the young men are in a warlike mood. But evidence as well that the elders are watching closely and may soon join the battle.

Even these minor flurries have alarmed the country and have resulted in a spate of generally senseless programs designed to give *temporary summer jobs!* More interesting in its long-range prospects has been the apparent eagerness to draft black men for military service. If in fact this is a deliberate design to place black men in uniform in order to get them off the street, it may be the most curious "instant cure" for a serious disease this nation has yet attempted. Young black men are learning the most modern techniques for killing—techniques which may be used against *any* enemy.

But it is all speculation. The issue finally rests with the black masses. When the servile men and women stand up, we had all better duck.

We should ask what is likely to galvanize the masses into aggression against the whites.

—Will it be some grotesque atrocity against black people which at last causes one-tenth of the nation to rise up in indignation and crush the monstrosity?

—Will it be the example of black people outside the United States who have gained dignity through their own liberation movement?

—Will it be by the heroic action of a small group of blacks which by its wisdom and courage commands action in a way that cannot be denied?

—Or will it be by blacks, finally and in an unpredictable way, simply getting fed up with the bumbling stupid racism of this country? Fired not so much by any one incident as by the gradual accretion of stupidity into fixtures of national policy.

All are possible, or any one, or something yet unthought. It seems certain only that on the course the nation now is headed it will happen.

One might consider the possibility that, if the national direction remains unchanged, such a conflagration simply might *not* come about. Might not black people remain where they are, as they did for a hundred years during slavery?

Such seems truly inconceivable. Not because blacks are so naturally warlike or rebellious, but because they are filled with such grief, such sorrow, such bitterness, and such hatred. It seems now delicately poised, not yet risen to the flash point, but rising rapidly nonetheless. No matter what repressive measures are invoked against the blacks, they will never swallow their rage and go back to blind hopelessness.

If existing oppressions and humiliating disenfranchise-
ments are to be lifted, they will have to be lifted most speedily,
or catastrophe will follow.

For there are no more psychological tricks blacks can play
upon themselves to make it possible to exist in dreadful circumstances. No more lies can they tell themselves. No more
dreams to fix on. No more opiates to dull the pain. No more
patience. No more thought. No more reason. Only a welling
tide risen out of all those terrible years of grief, now a tidal
wave of fury and rage, and all black, black as night.

*Brown Power**

*In June, 1967, Reies Lopez Tijerina and some of his followers tried
to make a citizen's arrest of the district attorney in Tierra Amarilla, New
Mexico. Tijerina charged the official with violating the people's constitutional right to free assembly. The group had been barred from holding
a meeting two days earlier. The incident at the courthouse led to charges
of kidnapping and other capital crimes. In early 1969, Tijerina was
acquitted of all charges against him stemming from that incident.*

*As the author points out, poverty and discrimination invariably lead
to revolution. The activities of Tijerina and La Alianza are portents of what
the future holds in store for America.*

In 1846 the Mexican population rose in armed insurrection against the American incubus. The insurgents gained control of northern New Mexico and succeeded in killing the first
Anglo-American governor of the territory, Charles Bent, before
the United States troops crushed the revolt. These insurgent
leaders still linger as folk-heroes in the minds of many Mexican-
Americans in New Mexico. Recently, in the very same region,
a group of Mexican-Americans—La Alianza Federal de Mercedes
led by Reies Lopez Tijerina—allegedly staged a guerrilla attack
on Rio Arriba's county courthouse in Tierra Amarilla. As a
sequel to the recent activities of La Alianza, the threat of an
armed insurrection by the Mexican-American population of
northern New Mexico is again thrust into the forefront of the
"land of enchantment."

---

*Reprinted from Armando Valdez, "Insurrection in New Mexico—
the Land of Enchantment," *El Grito* (Fall, 1967).

For the past four years, La Alianza has struggled to bring its claim on vast acreages of land throughout New Mexico and Colorado to the attention of state and federal officials. In July of 1966, Alianzistas staged a sixty-two mile protest march from Albuquerque to Santa Fe. In October of the same year, Alianzistas closed off to public use for five days, the five hundred thousand acre Carson National Forest. Two forest rangers were arrested for trespassing Alianzista-held territory and later released. On June 5, 1967, Alianzistas allegedly shot up the county courthouse in Tierra Amarilla, a northern New Mexico townlet. This incident at Tierra Amarilla, as described in the news media, had overtones of guerrilla warfare—attacking a village courthouse, seizing hostages, and fleeing into surrounding hills—all guerrilla tactics. The facts regarding the alleged attack on Tierra Amarilla are obscured by contradictory and sensationally written news reports. However, it is significant that state officials felt that the situation warranted the mobilization of the National Guard—complete with tanks. Generally, the National Guard is mobilized only to meet emergencies arising from natural disasters or massive civil disorder. Therefore, it is evident, judging from this desperate reaction, that New Mexico officials felt an eminent threat of insurrection by the Mexican-American population.

Ethnic Denominator

Before considering the basis of the current conflict in New Mexico, the ethnic designation for the Hispanic population of New Mexico must be clarified. Though the term "Spanish-American" is commonly used in New Mexico to denote persons of Hispanic heritage, the ethnic designation "Mexican-American" is more appropriate. It must be acknowledged that some residents of relatively isolated New Mexican villages are the direct descendants of Spanish colonists. However, to designate such persons as Spanish, either culturally or linguistically, is to negate the influences of Mexican and Indian elements which blended over the centuries with Spanish elements so that today a uniquely heterogeneous culture totally distinct from Spanish culture prevails in these regions. In essence, the adoption of

the term, Spanish-American, gained prominence in New Mexico
during the 1920's as a reaction to the great influx of Mexican
immigrants into the United States during that decade. The
"earlier" residents sought to dissociate themselves from the
unskilled, uneducated "aliens." A similar identity transformation occurred in Texas during the same period and the term
"Latin-American" made its debut.[1] This phenomenon of self-
reclassification is not without parallels in the history of European immigration to the United States, especially among the
northern and western European immigrants of the late nineteenth century. An implicit factor in this phenomenon of self-
reclassification is a dichotomy between the cultured (i.e.
established, wealthy) and the non-cultured (i.e. foreign, poor).
Therefore, to designate the Spanish-surname, Spanish-speaking
population of New Mexico as "Spanish-American" is not only
grossly contradictory to historical fact but is a vacuous ethnic
taxonomy.

Insurrection

The question of an impending armed insurrection in New
Mexico may best be examined by considering the current conflict in its historical context. Since insurrection is the product
of a long period of ferment, [a] historical perspective is imperative if causation is to be established.

La Alianza's struggle stems from an effort to regain lands
annexed to the United States by the Treaty of Guadalupe-
Hidalgo in 1848. This treaty guarantees the protection of the
civil and property rights of the residents of the annexed territories.[2] However, it is [a] historical fact that these rights—
though guaranteed by treaty—were never meant to be taken
seriously by the United States government. In fact, the Treaty
of Guadalupe-Hidalgo was a treaty of conquest dictated by the
United States upon a defeated Mexican government. The

---

[1] Carey McWilliams, *North from Mexico* (Philadelphia: Lippincott,
1949), pp. 78–79, et. al.

[2] Ex. doc. No. 50 (House of Representatives) 30th Cong., 2nd Sess.
and Ex. doc. No. 52 (Senate) 30th Cong., 1st Sess.

Mexican residents in annexed territories were accorded the treatment of a conquered people. Moreover, the annexed territories (greater in area than Germany and France combined, and representing about one-half of the territory then held by Mexico) were dealt with as spoils of war. These formerly Mexican, American citizens have been assigned the role of a subordinate citizen since their conquest.

The conduct of General Stephen W. Kearny, commander of the United States military expedition through New Mexico and eventually California, attests to the fact that the newly absorbed American citizens were considered and correspondingly treated as a conquered people. Kearny was the first United States official to declare to the people of New Mexico that their rights "of person and property" would be held inviolable. Simultaneously, Kearny was under orders to declare the residents of this territory citizens of the United States and to *demand their allegiance*. Kearny's sanguine chauvinism is forcefully conveyed by Phillip St. George Cooke in his narrative, *The Conquest of New Mexico and California*, in the following description of addresses by Kearny to the villagers of Tecolote and San Miguel, New Mexico, respectively:

> ... the general and suit were conducted by the alcalde to his house and there, through his interpreter, General Kearny, addressed him and the village notables, informing them of the annexation and its great advantages to them. *He required the alcalde to take the oath of allegiance.*[3]
> ... the general and his staff, the alcalde and a priest, and a few others ascended a flat housetop overlooking the plaza; the general, through his interpreter, delivered his address with the advantage of its success at Tecolote, but whether the priests' influence, the crowds', or his own peculiar firmness, the alcalde positively refused to take the oath. The general then enlarged upon the perfect freedom of religion under our government, mentioning that his chief of staff, then present, was a Roman Catholic. All persuasion failed, and at last *the old man was forced to go through the form and semblance of swearing allegiance.*[4]

---

[3] Phillip St. George Cooke, *The Conquest of New Mexico and California*, p. 18. Emphasis my own.

[4] Cooke, *op. cit.*, p. 20. Emphasis my own.

This attitude displayed by Kearny is merely an example of the subsequent attitudes and behavior of *gringos* toward the incipient wards of the United States—Mexican-Americans. It established a precedence of Anglo domination, both political and cultural. This arrogance of the conquering nation has resulted in the loss to Mexican-Americans of over two million acres of public land and seventeen hundred thousand acres of communal lands in New Mexico since 1854. Eighteen hundred thousand acres of these lands are now in the possession of the United States federal government. These and other equally significant land losses have occurred in violation of Articles VIII and IX of the Treaty of Guadalupe-Hidalgo which guarantees the security of "property of every kind to Mexicans in the acquired territory." Only six years after the Treaty of Guadalupe-Hidalgo, Congress enacted a law reserving congressional prerogative to pass upon private land claims in New Mexico by direct legislative enactment, an action diametrically opposed to the treaty. Provisions for adverse proceedings or for surveying the boundaries of tracts were completely excluded from this act.[5] Since the [n]otion of Manifest Destiny characterized the United States during the mid-nineteenth century, it should come as no surprise that Congress enacted such a law. During this period Americans were convinced that they were the legitimate heirs of *all* North America and viewed their struggle with Mexico as a struggle for their heritage; their manifest destiny was to rule North America from Atlantic to Pacific. The armies of Fremont, Taylor, and Kearny realized this "American Dream."

Anglo Law

A major factor in the transfer of land from Mexican to Anglo propriety was the change in legal jurisdiction. The manner in which the Anglo legal system was introduced into this territory and its impact on the indigenous population is histor-

---

[5] Clark S. Knowlton, *Causes of Land Loss Among the Spanish-Americans in Northern New Mexico* (Mimeographed paper, Texas Western College, n.d.), p. 6.

ically paralleled only by the introduction of Christianity into this same region several centuries earlier. Both of these doctrines were equally unsolicited and equally forced upon their unsuspecting beneficiaries by equally fervent "missionaries" of a conquering political order. Both doctrines were employed as instruments for exploiting and dominating their conquered subjects.

Within the Mexican legal system, land ownership was based primarily upon traditional and recognized rights of occupancy. Grant lands were immune from taxation since the financial needs of the Mexican and, formerly, Spanish governments were met by taxes upon harvests and livestock increases. Accordingly, the concept of property taxation was totally remote and a system of land survey was unknown to the Mexican landowner. Land boundaries were vague and imprecise, and land titles were generally unregistered. Conversely, the Anglo concept of property taxation as the economic base of county government demanded an authoritative system of land survey and concomitant registration of land titles. Therefore, the mandatory transposition of largely antithetical legal systems experienced by the Mexican-American residents of the acquired territory placed their land ownership in a very precarious position. Under the jurisdiction of the Anglo legal system, property owned by Mexican-Americans became subject to property taxes, precise delineation of boundaries, and registration of land titles. Herein lies a major causal factor in the demise of Mexican-American land ownership.

Avaricious Anglos employed their legal system as an instrument of intimidation, fraud, and deceit. Obscure and unregistered land titles held by Mexican-Americans were challenged in Anglo courts by lawyers, surveyors, land recorders, as well as by no lesser personages than governors, state supreme court justices, state and national politicians. Anglo lawyers, particularly, saw the vulnerability of Mexican-American land ownership and proceeded with great enterprise (i.e. Yankee ingenuity) to defraud Mexican-Americans of their land. One very common practice, for example, involved legal partners jointly conspiring to obtain these lands. One legal partner would file suit against an unregistered parcel of land while his associate would offer his services for the defense of the land title, *agreeing to accept land as retribution for his services.* Regardless of the outcome of the case, both lawyers would win; the Mexican-American landowner would be the sole loser. Indicating the prevalence of this fraudulent practice is the fact that *one out of every ten* Anglos in New Mexico in the 1880's was a lawyer.[6]

The policies of the federal government further contributed to the land losses of Mexican-Americans in New Mexico resulting from unregistered and obscure land titles. The Homestead Laws opened up *over one million acres* of these lands to Anglo settlers.

Anglo Taxes

Prior to 1848, property taxes were totally absent from the socio-political system of the annexed territory. However, the advent of Anglo law was accompanied by the practice of land taxation. Accordingly, land taxation provided yet another source of facile land gain for Anglos. Tax-delinquent properties multiplied during the period immediately succeeding the Treaty of Guadalupe-Hidalgo. The extent of the property losses that ensued is exemplified by the subsequent demise of the Anton Chico grant near El Cerrito, New Mexico. By 1860, the property had become chronically tax delinquent and large parcels of the two hundred seventy thousand acres were sold to meet the taxes levied. In 1926, the New Mexico legislature passed a statute declaring that lands delinquent in taxes for three years would be sold for the cost of the delinquent taxes. A decade later, in 1939, only eighty-five thousand of the original two hundred seventy thousand acres remained under Mexican-American ownership. Moreover, twenty-two thousand acres of these remaining lands were under lease.[7]

The most vicious form of deceit employed by Anglos was the practice of differential tax assessments. In an effort to dispossess Mexican-Americans of their property, tax assessments

---

[6]Knowlton, *op. cit., p.* 5.

[7] McWilliams, *op. cit.*, p. 78.

levied against them were greater than those levied against
Anglos. Once the property was transferred to Anglo ownership, the tax assessment was reduced. In *North from Mexico*,
Carey McWilliams cites incidences in which taxes of $1.50 per
acre levied against grazing lands owned by Mexican-Americans
were reduced to thirty and forty cents per acre when transferred to Anglo ownership.[8]

Federal land reclamation projects, irrigation projects, and
the establishment of forest reserves all directly contributed to
the losses of vast expanses of Mexican-American properties.
Though the land owners received retribution for their confiscated property, the severity of the losses assumed subtle forms.
The enormous amount of land required for these projects greatly
increased the competition for agri-land. Powerful land corporations (generally Anglo-owned) seeking to expand their operations, incessantly strove to force out smaller landowners,
frequently Mexican-Americans, by some strange coincidence.
Moreover, increased conservation and water-use costs heightened the pressures directed against these smaller landowners,
who frequently were forced to sell at a great financial loss.
Land losses due to these factors still occur today in the Albuquerque region and in the Mesilla Valley in the vicinity of Las
Cruces, New Mexico.

The terms of the Treaty of Guadalupe-Hidalgo, ratified by
Mexico and the United States on May 30, 1848, have been
flagrantly violated by the United States. Anglo law served not
to protect the rights of the Mexican-Americans but conversely
served to intimidate and exploit them. The historical accounts
of the duplicity and intimidation employed to defraud Mexican-
Americans of their land endure as testimony of Anglo disregard for the property rights of the Mexicans residing within
the territory annexed to the United States, particularly in New
Mexico. Consequently, Mexican-Americans in New Mexico were
from the onset disenfranchised of their rights and concomitant
opportunities. Today the situation has not changed; Mexican-
Americans largely occupy a subordinate position as citizens of
New Mexico and are, in every sense of the word, a minority

---

[8] McWilliams, *op. cit.*, p. 77.

group. Moreover, the demarcation between Mexican-Americans and Anglos is not only socio-economic but geographic as well. The population of the six northern counties of New Mexico is approximately seventy percent Mexican-American, and these counties are generally referred to as "the Spanish-American counties." In contrast to an urban ghetto, northern New Mexico constitutes a regional ghetto which extends over six counties and encompasses several hundred square miles. This entire region is plagued by chronic poverty, economic decline, high mortality rates, and a growing out-migration rate. The 1961 per capita income in these northern counties ranged from $662 to $818 as compared to a range of $2,000 to $3,000 for the remaining counties of New Mexico. Unemployment rates for the northern counties compared to the remaining areas of the state are 16 percent and 5.1 percent, respectively. Fifty-nine percent of the state's draftees are drawn from the Mexican-American population which comprises only thirty percent of the state's population. Approximately thirteen percent of the state's population resides in the six northern counties, yet this region comprises thirty percent of the state's welfare expenditures.[9] Essentially, the Mexican-American population of northern New Mexico is living in abject poverty. For these persons, the prospects for the future look increasingly dismal.

In this setting of chronic poverty, complemented by a long history of suppression and exploitation, the query of armed insurrection becomes a superfluous one. Poverty and exploitation have historically been the prime ingredients of revolution. Today, both of these elements are present in northern New Mexico as they were prior to the 1846 insurrection. The recent activities of La Alianza symbolize the discontentment of an exploited, impoverished people—a discontent that may once again provide the impetus for insurrection in New Mexico.

---

[9] The depressed state of the northern counties correlates land losses and welfare cases. Under the welfare statutes, welfare assistance cannot be extended to families who own land; the depressed economy affords meager economic gains from lands, especially smaller plots, and in this sense, encourages the sale of land at drastic losses for the sole purpose of becoming eligible to receive welfare assistance.

*The New Order**

Revenge and retribution are the natural outcomes of the rage which has been pent up for centuries, according to Julius Lester, an articulate spokesman for the black power position.

It is clear that America as it now exists must be destroyed. There is no other way. It is impossible to live within this country and not become a thief or a murderer. Young blacks and young whites are beginning to say no to thievery and murder. Black power confronts white power openly, and as the SNCC poet Worth Long cried: "We have found you out, false-faced America. We have found you out!"

Having "found you out," we will destroy you or die in the act of destroying. That much seems inevitable. To those who fearfully wonder if America has come to the point of a race war, the answer is not certain. However, all signs would seem to say yes. Perhaps the only way that it might be avoided would be through the ability of young white radicals to convince blacks, through their actions, that they are ready to do whatever is necessary to change America.

The race war, if it comes, will come partly from the necessity for revenge. You can't do what has been done to blacks and not expect retribution. The very act of retribution is liberating, and perhaps it is no accident that the symbolism of Christianity speaks of being washed in blood as an act of purification. Psychologically, blacks have always found an outlet for their revenge whenever planes have fallen, autos have collided, or just every day when white folks die. One old black woman in Atlanta, Georgia, calmly reads through her paper each day counting the number of white people killed the previous day in wrecks, storms, and by natural causes. When the three astronauts were killed in February, 1967, black people did not join the nation in mourning. They were white and were spending money that blacks needed. White folks trying to get to

---

the moon, 'cause it's there. Poverty's here! Now get to that! Malcolm X spoke for all black people when a plane full of Georgians crashed in France: "Allah has blessed us. He has destroyed twenty-two of our enemies."

It is clearly written that the victim must become the executioner. The executioner preordains it when all attempts to stop the continual executions fail. To those who point to numbers and say that black people are only ten percent, it must be said as Brother Malcolm said: "It only takes a spark to light the fuse. We are that spark."

Black power is not an isolated phenomenon. It is only another manifestation of what is transpiring in Latin America, Asia, and Africa. People are reclaiming their lives on those three continents, and blacks in America are reclaiming theirs. These liberation movements are not saying give us a share; they are saying we want it all! The existence of the present system in the United States depends upon the United States taking all. This system is threatened more and more each day by the refusal of those in the Third World to be exploited. They are colonial people outside the United States; blacks are a colonial people within. Thus, we have a common enemy. As the black power movement becomes more politically conscious, the spiritual coalition that exists between blacks in America and the Third World will become more evident. The spiritual coalition is not new. When Italy invaded Ethiopia in 1938, blacks in Harlem held large demonstrations protesting this. During World War II, many blacks were rooting for the Japanese. Blacks cannot overlook the fact that it was the Japanese who were the guinea pigs for the atomic bomb, not the Germans. They know, too, that if the United States were fighting a European country, it would not use napalm phosphorus and steel-pellet bombs, just as they know that if there had been over one hundred thousand blacks massed before the Pentagon on October 21, 1967, they would not have been met by soldiers with unloaded guns. In fact, they know they would never have been allowed to even reach the Pentagon.

The struggle of blacks in America is inseparable from the struggle of the Third World. This is a natural coalition—a coalition of those who know that they are dispossessed. Whites in America are dispossessed also, but the difference is that they will not recognize the fact as yet. Until they do, it will not be possible to have coalitions with them, even the most radical. They must recognize the nature and character of their own oppression. At present, too many of them recognize only that they are white and identify with whites, not with the oppressed, the dispossessed. They react against being called "honky" and thereby establish the fact that they are. It is absolutely necessary for blacks to identify as blacks to win liberation. It is not necessary for whites. White radicals must learn to non-identify as whites. White is not in the color of the skin. It is a condition of the mind: a condition that will be destroyed. It should be possible for any white radical to yell "honky" as loud as a black radical. "Honky" is a beautiful word that destroys the mystique surrounding whiteness. It is like throwing mud on a sheet. Whiteness has been used as an instrument of oppression; no white radical can identify himself by the color of his skin and expect to fight alongside blacks. Black power liberates whites also, but they have refused to recognize this, preferring to defend their whiteness.

Black power is not anti white people, but is anti anything and everything that serves to oppress. If whites align themselves on the side of oppression, then black power must be antiwhite. That, however, is not the decision of black power.

For blacks, black power is the microscope and telescope through which they look at themselves and the world. It has enabled them to focus their energies while preparing for the day of reckoning. That day of reckoning is anticipated with eagerness by many, because it is on that day that they will truly come alive. The concept of the black man as a nation, which is only being talked about now, will become reality when violence comes. Out of the violence will come the new nation (if the violence is successful) and the new man. Franz Fanon wrote that "For the colonized people this violence, because it constitutes their only work, invests their characters with positive and creative qualities. The practice of violence binds them together as a whole, since each individual forms a violent link in the great chain, a part of the great organism of violence which has surged upwards in reaction to the settler's violence in the beginning. The groups recognize each other and the future nation is already indivisible. The armed struggle mobilizes the people; that is to say, it throws them in one way and in one direction."[1]

It is obvious, of course, that white power will not allow black power to evolve without trying to first subvert it. This is being attempted. . . . This attempt will fail and white power will have no choice but to attempt to physically crush black power. This is being prepared for, with intensive riot-control training for the National Guard, chemicals for the control of large crowds, and concentration camps. It is to be expected that eventually black communities across the country will be cordoned off and a South African passbook system introduced to control the comings and goings of blacks.

At the moment, though (but, oh, how short a moment is), the tactic is one of subversion. Particular attention and energy is being given toward the subversion of SNCC. An inordinate number of SNCC men have received draft notices since January of 1967. Another tactic has been the calling of court cases to trial that have lain dormant for two or three years—cases that in many instances had been forgotten by SNCC. The most sophisticated tactic has been the legal maneuvers the government has used to keep SNCC's chairman, H. Rap Brown, confined to Manhattan Island, thus preventing him from traveling around the country and speaking. Having accomplished that, the government now seems content to take its own good time about bringing Brown's cases up for trial.

Black power, however, will not be denied. America's time is not long and the odds are on our side.

Black power seeks to destroy what now is, but what does it offer in replacement? Black power is a highly moral point of view, but its morality is one that sees that a way of life flows from the economic and political realities of life. It is these that must be changed. Mrs. Ida Mae Lawrence of Rosedale, Mississippi, put it beautifully when she said, "You know, we ain't dumb, even if we are poor. We need jobs. We need houses. But even with the poverty programs we ain't got nothin' but needs. . . . We is ignored by the government. The thing about

---

[1] Franz Fanon, *The Wretched of the Earth* (New York: Grove Press, 1965), p. 73.

property upset them, but the things about poor people don't.
So there's no way out, but to begin your own beginning, whatever way you can. So far as I'm concerned, that's all I got to
say about the past. We're beginning a new future."

In his 1966 Berkeley speech, Stokely Carmichael put it
another way.

> ...Our vision is not merely of a society in which all black men
> have enough to buy the good things of life. When we urge that
> black money go into black pockets, we mean the communal pocket.
> We want to see money go back into the community and used to
> benefit it. We want to see the cooperative concept applied in busi-
> ness and banking.... The society we seek to build among black
> people is not a capitalistic one. It is a society in which the spirit
> of community and humanistic love prevail. The word love is sus-
> pect; black expectations of what it might produce have been be-
> trayed too often. But those were expectations of a response from
> the white community, which failed us. The love we seek to encour-
> age is within the black community, the only American community
> where men call each other "brother" when they meet. We can
> build a community of love only where we have the ability and power
> to do so; among blacks.

Those whites who have a similar vision and want to be
a part of this new world must cast down their bucket where
they are. If this kind of a world is as important and as necessary for them as it is for us, they must evolve an approach
to their own communities. We must organize around blackness,
because it is with the fact of our blackness that we have been
clubbed. We therefore turn our blackness into a club. When
this new world is as totally necessary for whites as it is for
blacks, then maybe we can come together and work on some
things side by side. However, we will always want to preserve
our ethnicity, our community. We are a distinct cultural group,
proud of our culture and our institutions, and simply want to
be left alone to lead our good, black lives. In the new world,
as in this one, I want to be known, not as a man who happens
to be black, but as a black man. With that knowledge I can visit
the graves of my slave foreparents and say, "I didn't forget
about you ... those hot days you worked in the fields, those
beatings, all that shit you took and just grew stronger on. I'm
still singing those songs you sang and telling those tales and

passing them on to the young ones so they will know you, also.
We will never forget, for your lives were lived on a spider web
stretched over the mouth of hell and yet, you walked that walk
and talked that talk and told it like it is. You can rest easy
now. Everything's up-tight."

The old order passes away. Like the black riderless horse,
boots turned the wrong way in the stirrups, following the coffin
down the boulevard, it passes away. But there are no crowds
to watch as it passes. There are no crowds, to mourn, to weep.
No eulogies to read and no eternal flame is lit over the grave.
There is no time, for there are streets to be cleaned, houses
painted, and clothes washed. Everything must be scoured clean.
Trash has to be thrown out. Garbage dumped and everything
unfit, burned.

The new order is coming, child.

The old is passing away.

*Future Trends**

*This review of seven books is a brilliant and perceptive statement
of emerging trends among black writers. Eleanor Norton is Assistant
Legal Director of the American Civil Liberties Union.*

> In silence, we have spent our years watching the ofays[1], try-
> ing to understand them, on the principle that you have a better
> chance coping with the known than with the unknown. Some of us
> have been, and some still are, interested in learning whether it is
> *ultimately* possible to live in the same territory with people who
> seem so disagreeable to live with; still others want to get as far
> away from ofays as possible. What we share in common is the de-
> sire to break the ofays' power over us.
>
> —ELDRIDGE CLEAVER, *Soul on Ice.*

What can only be described as a new genre of American
Negro writing appears to be emerging from the works of black
writers over the past year or so. Theirs is a departure from
the writing of perceptive analysts of the mid-sixties, whites such
as Charles Silberman (*Crisis in Black and White*, 1964) and

---

*Eleanor Holmes Norton, "New Black Directions: A Reappraisal,"
in *Civil Liberties* (December, 1968).

[1]"Ofay" is pig latin for "foe" and is commonly used by blacks to
refer generally to whites.

even blacks such as Kenneth Clark (*Dark Ghetto*, 1965). These are black writers with a new and pronounced sense of the mission of racial discovery.

Among them only Martin Luther King, Jr. (whose last work, *Where Do We Go from Here: Chaos or Community*, is reviewed here principally for contrast) places any priority on integration as encouraged by black and white liberals in the thirties, forties, fifties, and sixties. While not necessarily separatists, the others are concerned less with reconciling the races than with reconciling the black man with himself. Harold Cruse in *The Crisis of the Negro Intellectual* shows that he has gone this dissenting course since the 1940's. The others, however, despite the differences among them, all are indebted to the recent prophet, Malcolm X—not for his specific philosophy and program but for the direction toward self-discovery he alone beaconed.

. . . The revelation of the meaning of one's blackness for a people who have suffered so singularly because of color bears explanation. The black man's negative sense of self is quite different from the self-hatred often attributed to minority groups. Originally separated from his tribesmen and then from his family to lessen the inevitable urge toward revolt, the black man could pass on to his descendants nothing of the cultural cohesion that might have aided self-knowledge and made American racism more bearable. Worse than self-hatred, slavery and racism produced a people whose fate in this country seemed unexplained by any positive *raison d'être*, any ancient collective mission, any historical cultural source. The result was that generations of black people lived their lives with no possibility of discovering who they were.

That quest is what black writers now are pursuing with angered purpose. Black people labored in the past to find a solution to the whole racial dilemma (a purpose which should have fallen equally to white Americans but only recently pursued by them in any numbers, lamentably propelled, it would seem, by the instinct for self-preservation). Today they are breaking down the problem into its component parts. The new perspective has revealed some commanding new priorities. For many blacks it now seems that before they can come to terms with white people, they must come to terms with themselves and with other black people. The discovery of the meaning of blackness in America—put off for so many generations—is now assuming urgency.

Martin King, alone among the writers here, attached equal priority to the general problem and the specific one—the racial dilemma confronting the country and the personal quest for self-discovery by black people. Yet he was unable to marshal in behalf of the latter the brilliance and inspiration he brought to the former. It is not that he failed to appreciate the importance of self-knowledge for black people. On the contrary, "Every man must ultimately confront the question 'Who am I?' and seek to answer it honestly," he wrote in *Where Do We Go from Here.* But the other writers would find fault in his other conclusion— that today Negroes "have reached the stage of organized strength and independence to work securely in alliances."

What the other books are ultimately about, indeed, is the prematurity of this conclusion. If, as King claimed, the "Negro–white alliance . . . can attain the strength to alter basic institutions by democratic means," by what steps can such strength be attained? Have blacks ever been more than supplicants in the "Negro–white alliance?" What except morality, a principle too often lacking sanctions, has ever assured the existence of the alliance? Does not the "Negro–white alliance" lack the component of mutual power out of which alliances are generally forged? If so, can such an alliance in turn bring results in the face of steadfast opposition buttressed by real power? For Cleaver, Carmichael, Hamilton, Cruse, Cobbs, Grier, and the rest, these questions have come up for answer now.

. . . King's rejection of black power was directly traceable to the circumstances under which the call was first put forth, as he made clear in *Where Do We Go from Here.* Coming as it did in the militant anger of the 1966 march following the shooting of James Meredith, the slogan, King felt, threatened his entire philosophy of nonviolence. Perhaps the greatest mistake of his brilliant career was that he conceded too much to that feature of black power which he thought carried an "unconscious and often conscious call for retaliatory violence." When the black power slogan was first raised by the youthful Stokely Carmichael, King was too dismayed to give the concept the mature leadership he had exerted in the past. Unlike Whitney Young, who has recently supported black power and defined it creatively and positively, King responded to what he thought was an inherent threat in a cry raised by youthful militants whose patience could no longer absorb the failures of integration.

In retrospect, it is possible to see a distinct flaw in King's singular moral approach to a problem that had withstood the constraints of decency for three centuries. Against entrenched racist power he threw up nonviolent activism, a majestic weapon which had worked against proper targets in the past but which four years of street rebellions had largely repudiated. His approach could have incorporated, not the possibility for violence, but a greater emphasis on the "call for black people in this country to unite, to recognize their heritage, to build a sense of community," as Carmichael and Hamilton *(Black Power)* would have it. Then the frustration that led to violence might have been turned instead to constructive community building, albeit for a transition period during which Negroes might have addressed their problems in black communion instead of dealing with race relations in gross. The result might have been a nonviolent but truly revolutionary search of the kind revealed in the other books.

The other writers are part of the struggle through which the black man's psyche (though not his objective situation) is today undergoing revolutionary change. Eschewing the disinterestedness of scholarship, these writers pursue a mission they feel called to as a small elite in possession of the intellectual tools of change.

. . . Thus, psychiatrists William Grier and Price Cobbs dedicate *Black Rage* to "our intrepid black brothers: keep on keeping on." Amidst the amazing case studies that reveal the link between racial oppression and mental illness, there emerges a theory of psychotherapy adapted specifically to the problems of black people. The usual psychiatric goal of changing one's self in order to adapt to the "world outside" is not recommended for black people. Rather, say the doctors, "A black man's soul can live only if it is oriented toward a change of the social order." Further, some distortion in the black personality—"cultural paranoia"—is ironically the way to mental health, Doctors Grier and Cobbs have discovered from their treatment of black patients. For the survival of his psyche, the black man "must maintain a high degree of suspicion toward the motives of every white man and at the same time never allow this suspicion to impair his grasp of reality. It is a demanding requirement and not everyone can manage it with grace." Nor is the black therapist free to stand on the sidelines as he treats black patients, adhering to the objectivity, even passivity, associated with the psychiatrist–patient relationship. For therapists faced with patients whose pain has been accentuated by the reality of racism, "the essential ingredient is the capacity of the therapist to love his patient. . . . If you must weep, I'll wipe your tears. . . . I will, in fact, do *anything* to help you be what you can be—my love for you is of such an order." It is fair to suppose that only therapists focused specially on blacks and deliberately rejecting the more objective considerations of orthodox integrationists, and for that matter, of their profession, could adhere to such a theory of psychotherapy, in the face of its general unfashionability. Nevertheless, its effectiveness is demonstrated in the analysis of suffering black patients described in *Black Rage*.

William Styron's Nat Turner: Ten Black Writers Respond is more an exercise in personal redemption. To a man, these ten writers reject Styron's southern white liberal vision of Nat Turner as a complex black Hamlet-like figure. For them Turner is a revolutionary hero, an example to his people, the father of the black revolutionary tradition obscured and falsified by generations of self-serving white racist historians and novelists. Their Nat makes a wooden literary figure, but it is more important that he be, as John Killens the novelist and essayist sees him, a man of "epic and heroic proportions." Charles Hamilton, the political scientist, is compelled to grant that Styron "is entitled to his literary license, but black people today cannot afford the luxury of having their leaders manipulated and toyed with." The historian Vincent Harding speaks for them all when he complains, "You've Taken My Nat and Gone."

. . . This intolerance of the artistic imagination that is so embedded in the liberal Western tradition seems strangely discordant. Ernest Kaiser, the Schomburg (Afro-American) Collection curator, for example, decries the "unspeakable arrogance of this young southern writer daring to set down his own personal view of Nat's life as from inside Nat Turner in slavery!" Often in these essays, it is as if these writers are unaware of the high importance of individual expression, however mistaken, in a free society.

But the passion of these ten points up precisely how little blacks have partaken of the personal freedom properly valued by the white liberal tradition. For these writers, historical distortion—and Styron has changed many of the known and salient facts of Turner's life—is a luxury blacks cannot shoulder at a time when the long-delayed search for identity has become so urgent. These writers are experiencing conflicts and taking on responsibilities they feel called to by history and by their special roles. Theirs is a mission analogous to that Grier and Cobbs feel in their special field.

No scholar of libertarian values can fail to see the possibilities for danger and misdirection here. But if he believes these values truly worthy he may be able to summon the faith that any dispensation of them among Negroes now is a temporary result of the black crisis of our times.

The evidence is now compelling that black intellectuals are only one group within Negro society which is experiencing a revolutionary reevaluation of themselves and their people. The characteristics of such a revolutionary vision are well-known. When intolerable conditions have been sustained so long that revolutionary rejection must be summoned to end them, a concentrated attack on the perceived evil normally takes priority over other important values. Sometimes disastrous consequences have resulted—especially in political life, as when oppressive regimes have given way to other oppressive, albeit revolutionary regimes. There is reason to believe, however, that the psychic revolution now in progress among blacks will be spared awful and repressive features precisely because it openly incorporates humanist principles and is bottomed on a cry as old as the Enlightenment—a cry for the recognition of the humanity of a group of people heretofore virtually excluded from the human family.

... Though the ten are diligently subjective in their response to Styron's novel, there is nevertheless historical evidence that their special vision has unearthed a worthwhile criticism. The ten writers here are not flailing at the wind. Styron's changes do make Nat a more interesting literary character, but they distort his historic personality, and they hurt most decidedly. Especially for black males, for whom the legacy of slavery and the experience of racism have been particularly brutal, they are hard to bear. Against the historical evidence of a black wife and black parents, Styron's Nat is a single man whose virtues are attributed to the kindness of his slave masters, who is obsessed with white women (again, no evidence) and whose single sexual episode is homosexual. Not surprisingly, the popular historian Lerone Bennett, Jr. interprets this in the context of "a pattern of emasculation" no one can deny pervades America's treatment of black males. Bennett's essay—the best of the ten for historic refutation—points up also the relish with which Styron exploits the theme of self-hatred and "reverence for whiteness." Who can expect black people caught in today's currents to appreciate this passage from Styron:

> In a twinkling I became white—white as clabber cheese, white, stark white, white as a Marble Episcopalian. . . . I was no longer the grinning black boy in velvet pantaloons; for a fleeting moment instead I owned all, and so exercised the privilege of ownership by unlacing my fly and pissing loudly on the same worn stone where dainty tiptoeing feet had gained the veranda steps a short three years before. What a strange, demented ecstasy! How white I was! What wicked joy!

Perhaps objective scholars will marvel at its syntax and imagery (I don't). One can only hope that the effects of racism will soon disappear from America so that black people can view such passages with disinterest.

. . . Throughout the ten anti-Styron essays appears the manhood theme compellingly developed also by Eldridge Cleaver in *Soul on Ice.* But unlike the essayists, Cleaver accepts the existence of the stereotypic Negro in order to make a start toward his redemption: Cleaver is of the streets and the jails of America and thus has been too close to the depravity produced by racism to wish to deny its existence. He is closer to the spirit of the angry street blacks, who in creating themselves anew, feel compelled to acknowledge the past in order to repudiate it. Cleaver's final essay, "To All Black Women, From All Black Men," is a painfully honest acceptance of responsibility for the failing of black men beyond all factual justification for such a confession. It is as if in reclaiming his manhood (and that of all black men), Cleaver cannot share objectively with whites the responsibility for the failures of earlier generations. The subjective vision that causes the ten essayists to diffuse responsibility acts here to coalesce it and assign it regally if unfairly to black men alone.

Thus, Cleaver accepts the harshest version of black history, in order that he may emerge strong and free of it. Of the general events that absorb the ten essayists he writes:

> Instead of inciting Slaves to rebellion with eloquent oratory, I soothed their hurt and eloquently sang the Blues! . . . When Nat Turner sought to free me from my Fear, my Fear delivered him up unto the Butcher—a martyred monument of my emasculation. My spirit was unwilling and my flesh was weak. Ah, eternal ignominy!

This rebel's approach to the repair of the black psyche should hearten those who think they see a monolith in the current black mood. Indeed, Cleaver's intellectual development is mirrored so well in this book that it should be read closely for a key to complexities of black responses in this period.

Joanne Grant's *Black Protest* is an important collection of documents of the widest variety ("The Emancipation Proclamation" by John Hope Franklin; "Revolution in Mississippi" by Tom Hayden; *United States* versus *Wood,* 5th Cir., 1961; "Negroes with Guns" by Robert F. Williams, etc.). Beyond its convenient reference function it succeeds in giving a sense of the continuity of the struggle from 1619 to the present. Especially those who are bewildered by the minor manifestations of extremism apparent in the black community today need to read closely this evidence of seemingly endless peaceful petition.

The directions the new black writers have taken can only gratify the most mature of them, Harold Cruse, a free-lance writer obscure until recently. *The Crisis of the Black Intellectual* is a life's work based on a lifetime of dissent from what Cruse sees as the distractions of integrationists and other black and white would-be curers of the black man's ills. Although Cruse is a cultural nationalist, his critique is ultimately a political repudiation of virtually every tendency—including the most militant—that has come forth in the Negro struggle since the turn of the century. This richly documented book, though marred by wordiness (it could have been cut in half) and frequent self-indulgent lapses, is the most important of the new black-authored books of this period.

... Here is the first intellectual history of black Americans and the first thorough-going critique of its course. Cruse's chief lament is that "cultural integration" has been so readily accepted by blacks because of the disadvantages of ethnic identity. He documents this development and contrasts it to periods when "the black world was rich in the pristine artistic essentials for new forms in music, dance, song, theatre, and even language." He traces the influence and resulting deterioration of the all-black style and approach to the Communist Party, the integrationists, the socialists, and even the black nationalists, none of whom escape his condemnation. The case for an ethnic cultural and political orientation is forcefully put in the context of a historical analysis that is often convincing. The breadth and imagination of the book establish Cruse as the leader of the new self-centered black scholarship and writing of this period.

It is too early to evaluate the trends now beginning to show among black people and especially among black intellectuals. But it is not too early to appreciate the direction of these books. If the period is troubling, so must be its literature. From such steadfastly earnest searches for identity, the black man may emerge whole. If that happens this confusing time will surely be seen as a second Negro renaissance.

Ironically, the *Report of the National Advisory Commission on Civil Disorders* could herald a new era of self-centered white scholarship and analysis of the source of white racism.

Should the black man emerge whole and should the white man discover his role, then Americans may at last be able to face one another as psychological equals. Though pain will ensue, if pain will excoriate racism, it is devoutly to be wished.

*Which Way to Attack Racism?**

Some of the most difficult decisions in the struggle against racism during the 1970's involve a choice between two conflicting courses of action. As the complexities of combatting racism have become more illuminated, divisions over the best strategy have developed among all minority groups.

The following article describes a tragic conflict within the Chicano community of Los Angeles.

Some prominent Chicanos have expressed strong positions on both sides of a new state law barring the hiring of illegal aliens, but the majority of Mexican-Americans are maintaining a cautious middle ground.

Their reasons are both complex and poignant.

There is sympathy, on the one hand, for fellow Latin Americans who come north seeking economic betterment.

Yet they also must face the fact that those same aliens adversely affect employment opportunities for Mexican-Americans, lowering their wages by competing for work if not taking potential jobs outright.

There is probably no Mexican-American in any barrio who is not familiar with people in both positions—the illegal alien and the unemployed young Chicano. Often he may be related to one or the other.

At the forefront of camps which hold opposing views on the Arnett Act, which would impose fines on employers who knowingly hire illegal aliens, are two veteran activists who have often been allied in the past—farm union leader Cesar Chavez and community organizer Bert Corona.

Chavez, 45, head of the United Farmworkers Union and the nation's most widely known Chicano, has supported the Arnett Act wholeheartedly.

He said he has seen too many farm workers' strikes broken by growers who bring in Mexican laborers to gather crops at struck farms—often paying them the low wages that the striking workers refused to accept.

---

*From Frank del Olmo, "Chicanos Divided by Sympathy for Aliens, Fear for Own Jobs," *Los Angeles Times,* March 25, 1972. Copyright, 1972, *Los Angeles Times.* Reprinted by permission.

Corona, 52, while not as widely known among Anglos as Chavez, is highly respected among Mexican-Americans for years of labor organizing and work with the Mexican-American Political Association.

Currently he is helping organize a community-based service center, Casa Hermandad—Brotherhood House—to counsel illegal aliens and provide social services for them.

Corona says he has led opposition to the law for varied reasons. He has charged that it hurts Mexican-Americans who are fired or laid off because they cannot prove citizenship to wary employers. Such claims have not been proved to the satisfaction of the act's proponents.

Corona and other opponents also charge that the law has imposed an added hardship on illegal aliens, some married and supporting families, who cannot establish the legitimacy of their status because of stringent (Corona says discriminatory) U.S. immigration laws.

Many in the anti-Arnett Act forces concur with an opinion summarized by Corona recently before an Assembly committee considering the Arnett Act.

"There is no such thing as an illegal alien," he said.

Proponents of this view claim both legal and moral justification.

They refer to the Treaty of Guadalupe Hidalgo, which ended the U.S.-Mexican War. They claim it gave Mexicans free access to the conquered portions of Mexico, including Alta California.

They also quote papal encyclicals and statements by religious leaders which defend the right of individuals to emigrate to improve their personal situation, whether their hardships are caused by natural disaster or economic forces.

An increasing number of Mexican-Americans also believe that the U.S.-Mexico border is an artificial line arbitrarily imposed by a conquering nation in 1848.

Corona charges that the Arnett Act causes "human suffering" by depriving hard-working, honest people of financial support for themselves and their families.

Chavez says the Arnett Act would alleviate human suffering by depriving large farmers of a cheap labor force, thus pressuring them to pay the higher wages necessary to employ U.S. citizens as farm workers.

Both men express sympathy with the views of the opposite group but insist their own concerns are more vital.

Chavez: "We know our Mexican brothers face great problems, but so do farm workers and other working men in this country. Look at who supports the aliens. It's not the working people, but those whose jobs aren't threatened by the illegals."

Corona: "Rural workers need legal protection against agribusiness and the methods it uses to exploit Chicanos by using Mexicans against them.

"But this law hurts the Chicano in the city by putting the burden of proof on the worker, an added burden on a community already burdened by discrimination."

Chicano activists and average citizens see merit on both sides, but decline to ally themselves with either side although both men command great loyalty.

The result, according to at least one well-informed community leader, is the potential for "the most serious split the Chicano community has ever faced."

Most other activists are not as blunt. They insist a common ground can be found to protect the interests of both Mexican-Americans and job-seeking aliens.

Many suggest the Arnett Act requires some revision or carefully monitored enforcement to prevent its abuse by discriminatory employers.

Significantly, all insist that much more must eventually be done to adequately deal with the constant influx of poor Latin Americans into the nation's job market.

It is in the Chicano manpower programs, those efforts designed to alleviate Mexican-American unemployment, that the effects of alien job competition are most acutely visible.

Men like Esteban Torres of the East Los Angeles Community Union and Phil Soto of Operation SER say the Mexican-Americans who come to their programs for job training and placement services tend to accept the fact that illegal aliens hurt their chances of finding work.

Any hostility, however, is still tempered with empathy for the aliens' plight, according to Soto.

"They almost accept it (competition from illegals) as a fact of life," he said. "Many are favorable to the law because they see it providing a possible break in their favor."

The personal anguish that can result from the controversy, and personal knowledge of the difficulties on both sides, was summarized by Torres, a union man with deep roots in the Mexican-American community.

"I'm torn because the whole thing is so damned complex," he said. "I know the economics involved, that illegals deplete the labor market and hurt wages. But I know there's sympathy here for those who come up here trying to better themselves."

Dionicio Morales, director of the Mexican-American Opportunity Foundation, objects to the Arnett Act because it "lacks teeth" and "lets the employer off the hook."

"We've talked to lawyers for big companies," he said, "and they feel they can circumvent the term 'knowingly'."

Should that prove to be the case, Morales warns, the law will be "just another vehicle through which our people can be molested."

As of now, he contends, "this situation pits a poor Chicano against a poverty stricken Mexican and between the two of us our struggle makes someone else rich."

"The employers are the real culprits," Morales said, "those people who are willing to use Mexicans at low occupational levels and with low pay."

Morales, who has traveled privately to Mexico on occasion to ask Foreign Ministry officials to cooperate in stemming the flow of illegals across the border, also summarized a point of view common to all Mexican-Americans queried about the Arnett Act controversy—that the issue is too much for one state to solve.

"Both governments (the U.S. and Mexico)," Morales said, "will have to get together on this eventually. It's too big and complex for anyone else. It's an entangled international situation with tangled economic and social repercussions."

A Symbol of Black Resistance in the 1970's*

Angela Davis became famous when she was banned from teaching at the University of California at Los Angeles because of her political beliefs (she is an avowed Communist), and (some say) because she represented a threat to the Establishment. Her fame and notoriety increased when she was accused of complicity in the courthouse shootout to free the Soledad Brothers. In the following statement, she indicts the judicial and political system for oppressing her and other blacks, especially those who defy their racist oppressors.

As a preface to my brief remarks I now declare publicly before the court, before the people of this country that I am innocent of all charges which have been leveled against me by the State of California. I am innocent and therefore maintain that my presence in this courtroom today is unrelated to any criminal act.

I stand before this court as a target of a political frameup which, far from pointing to my culpability, implicates the State of California as an agent of political repression. Indeed the State reveals its own role by introducing as evidence against me my participation in the struggles of my people—Black people—against the many injustices of society. Specifically my involvement with the "Soledad Brothers Defense Committee." The American people have been led to believe that such involvement is constitutionally protected.

In order to insure that these political questions are not obscured, I feel compelled to play an active role in my own defense as the defendant, as a Black woman and as a Communist. It is my duty to assist all those directly involved in the proceedings as well as the people of this State and the American people in general to thoroughly comprehend the substantive issues at stake in my case. These have to do with my political beliefs, affiliations, and my day-to-day efforts to fight all the conditions which have economically and politically paralyzed Black America.

---

*From Angela Y. Davis, "Statement to the Court," Marin County Courthouse, California, January 5, 1971.

No one can better represent my political beliefs and activities than I. A system of justice which virtually condemns to silence the one person who stands to lose most would seem to be self-defeating.

It is particularly crucial to Black people to combat this contradiction inherent in the judicial system, for we have accumulated a wealth of historical experience which confirms our belief that the scales of American justice are out of balance.

In order to enhance the possibility of being granted a fair trial, of which at present I am extremely doubtful, it is imperative that I be allowed to represent myself. I might add that my request is not without legal precedent.

If this court denies our motion to include me as co-counsel in this case it will be aligning itself with the forces of racism and reaction which threaten to push this country into the throes of fascism and the many people who have become increasingly disillusioned with the court system in this country will have a further reason to solidify their contention that it is no longer possible to get a fair trial in America.

The Awakening of Chinatown*

A young Chinese-American reveals the barely-below-surface tensions of activist, youth-oriented Chinese-Americans in Chinatown, San Francisco. The explosive potential for the 1970's is high.

While the history of the Chinese in the United States may be compared to that of the other immigrant populations who faced discrimination, anti-employment legislation, and the social stigma of being colored in a white society, no other group has resisted assimilation as ferociously as the Chinese. Behind bland smiles and reassurances from Chinese spokesmen active in the causes of anticommunism and law and order, the Chinese have been left to their own affairs, encouraged to manage themselves for as long as they have been in this country. Only recently have Americans begun to question ghettos like Chinatown.

---

*From Jeffrey Paul Chan, "Let 100 Flowers Bloom," *Los Angeles Times, West Magazine,* January 4, 1970. Reprinted by permission of the author.

The immigrants who continue to settle in Chinatown seek refuge. For these people Chinatown has not changed since the good ship *Libertad* arrived on July 19, 1854, from Hong Kong with a consignment of 500 coolies (100 of them dead), contracted labor for the railroads, the laundries, the gold mines, the delta swamps. To save themselves from the contempt of bigots, to hide the self-contempt they feel for the menial work forced on them, the Chinese built a wall of ignorance and fear around themselves.

To maintain *face*, dignity, they allowed themselves to be governed by representatives they had no power to select, who spoke for Chinatown through the family associations, district associations, the tongs and the Chinese Six Companies. These organizations now help to maintain the so-called Chinese ways and meanwhile have acquired millions of dollars worth of real estate and made Chinatown the most over-organized ghetto in the United States.

The power held by the Chinese Associations rests largely on the fear Chinatown residents have for the institutions of racial discrimination peculiar to this country. The protective, insulating barriers set up by the Associations insure a social life and opportunities for a limited survival. But there are no checks, no boundaries to their authority.

The lesson that is being taught to the Chinese now by other ethnic groups in the United States is very clear. To become an American, the Chinese must recognize the fact that he is colored. And to be colored is to be taken for a black man, a chicano, to be a *chink*.

Most Chinese in Chinatown freely admit to themselves that corruption and a spiritual decay are loose in the community; but add that, at least, it's Chinese. While liberal elements within the Chinese community are ready to open Chinatown to the rest of the nation, the conservative associations need only point to the black man's experience and stay convincingly aloof.

Even if a Chinese-American should escape from the ghetto, as about 35,000 who live in the greater Bay Area have, he still remains infected with the same insularity.

There are Chinese dentists and doctors, lawyers, bankers, insurance salesmen, retail florists and, of course, laundrymen, restaurant owners, teachers and even a State Assemblywoman, March Fong, famous for her fight against pay toilets. Most of these so-called assimilated Chinese refuse to acknowledge Chinatown and its problems. They would rather not remind their neighbors that Chinatown used to be synonymous with tong wars, opium dens, prostitution and gambling. They don't want society to see that corruption still exists.

Denying the stereotype of the inscrutable facade, and publicly declaring war on the miseries of Chinatown are the young. Young people concerned with Chinatown these days come in three varieties, with hair: They may be students, attending the University of California at Berkeley or San Francisco State College; they may be dropouts who have lived most of their lives in Chinatown, who may have had run-ins with the juvenile authorities in the past, who see themselves as hip, hard-core casualties in the War on Poverty; or they may be fresh off the boat from Hong Kong, speaking very little English, with a life-style and sense of survival learned in the streets of a British colony, and unable to get a job. These widely different groups of young people have come together, sharing the view that the problems of Chinatown mirror the complexities of any ghetto community, and the understanding that Chinatown is as American a phenomenon as Watts.

To be a young Chinese-American living in Chinatown means that you attended an all-Chinese elementary school and that your first encounter with racially integrated education came at the high school level. The young Chinese-American comes of age when he enters Galileo High School, where most of the students who are not Chinese are black. The pride of his being Chinese in an all-Chinese society suffers a bone-shaking, unsettling shock. His racial consciousness is born, painfully. The experience is humiliating in the extreme, but it is a necessary rite of passage for any member of a minority in this country.

Coming of age in Chinatown today is much easier than it was twenty years ago. For all their bowing and scraping, the Chinese establishment has consolidated second-class citizenship. But that is not enough for the Chinese youth. In a time when the blacks and chicanos are establishing their rights to full-time participation in political and economic life, young Chinese-Americans are following that lead by trying to gain a foothold in the power structure that governs their community.

Several coalitions to attack the many problems of Chinatown were organized by the young, especially in the last two years.

While they have not been entirely effective, while they are working with a borrowed vocabulary of social protest, they have gone a long way toward defining the ills of the Chinese community.

But some of them underestimated the complexities and difficulties of community politics as well as the power of corrupting institutions to corrupt.

Students from [San Francisco] State and Berkeley have established community projects in Chinatown as part of their program of ethnic studies and are receiving minimal support from the State of California at this writing. Their programs include a tutorial program designed to help students who have problems with English and a program to recruit students for admissions to other state colleges and universities.

The answer to the many Chinatown problems will not be forthcoming while the generation gap between Chinese-American young people and their elders who control the Association remains. The young have refused to learn their native dialects, their parents say; they do not appreciate the Chinese way of solving problems, so they must learn before they have the right to question our authority. They must be Chinese, first.

In a very real sense, the generation gap we speak of is simply a metaphor for the ignorance and naïvete each generation imposes on itself for the sake of coherence, stability and justification. The only practical argument against the institutions employed for survival, like the ghetto, like the tongs, is one that would criticize that institution's effectiveness. We have survived, say the Chinatown Establishment, we have survived as Chinese people.

Without answering, the young people are hopeful that confrontations and embarrassing exposures of the Chinatown living conditions will force necessary, humanitarian changes for the immigrants, for the elderly and for the young growing up in the ghetto. But what they represent in American culture today goes begging.

Chinese-Americans living in the United States are descended from a generation of immigrants who took it for granted that they were "sojourners," here for a moment in time to return to China after mining their "Mountain of Gold."

Frank Chin, novelist and film-maker, has begun to sketch an outline of the problem in letters, articles and lectures delivered at colleges and community meetings in the San Francisco area.

He writes:

> We're schizoid. The myth of the Chinese family says that we
> are patriarchal. In the America of the Depression, the men of the
> family took jobs as live-in cooks, houseboys and manservants or
> worked in the steward service of the railroads. Daddy Chinaman
> was out of town. Again, the myth of the Chinese family says that
> when we're not patriarchal, we're matriarchal; we're crazy about
> obeying and respecting our elders and preserving all that good
> Chinese culture. The two Chinese-American autobiographies sup-
> port the widespread belief that all us Chinamen want nothing to do
> but work our chopsticks, burn a little joss stick and build great
> walls. And we've learned it from the movies and never realized that
> Hollywood had confused Chinese-Americans with Chinese in China.
> This confusion was partly due to the only instance of the Chinese
> effectively using the media to speak for themselves. The tongs,
> acknowledged as the spokesmen of Chinatown, convinced the press
> that Chinatown was a foreign country, a cartoon foreign country
> inhabited by cartoon creatures, Bambis and Thumpers. And what
> of the real Chinese-American, he's not interested in cultural-his-
> torical pride. That's strictly for export.

In his bitterness and disillusionment, Chin strikes at the
center of the problem that divides the young and old in Chinatown.
The young would ask, who are we? And the old would answer,
we are exiles who have survived.

For the moment, the Chinese-American is the last voice to be
heard in the struggle for recognition by the minorities. Well
behaved, parochial, discreet, seemingly exotic, he has watched
three major wars in Asia. He watched the Japanese being sent to
detention camps. He has rallied to the cause of law and order,
anticommunism, Chiang Kaishek, free enterprise and the YMCA.
I think he knows as little about Chinese culture as he accuses his
son of knowing. I suspect that after 150 years of residency in the
United States, no Chinese-American can know too much more.
They never wanted to be pioneers . . . .

A Ray of Hope in a Modest Dimension?*

From all that has been presented in this chapter thus far, the evidence points to continued conflict and resistance because of our society's failure to resolve the problems of racism. This final selection presents a small ray of hope that, after the confrontations, changes—small ones—do occur eventually. Will the changes come before it is too late?

Madison Avenue copywriters, who long ago learned to walk on eggs when it came to Jewish and Negro sensitivities, are learning the hard way that Mexican-Americans, too, have sharp antennae for ethnic slurs.

The media market is now being assailed by organized protests against printed ads and television commercials that:

—Exploit the fictional Frito Bandito in pushing a line of corn chips.

—Romanticize Elgin as the watch "Zapata would kill for," contending that the Mexican revolutionary hero, Emiliano Zapata, were he alive today, would be "stealing Elgins" as fast as the company could make them.

—Depict fictional but unnamed fat Mexican men at arms on behalf of Granny Goose potato chips.

—Portray Mexicans as lacking in perseverance (L & M cigarettes), sleepy (Camels), sleepy again (Philco TV), so far behind the times that when they break into a home they marvel at the freezer (Frigidaire), raucous party-makers forever borrowing ice cubes (Whirlpool), easily intimidated when a single "gringo" points a gun at a bunch of them (Buick), and, as the ultimate test of a deodorant, suggesting that if the product will work for a Mexican, it will work for anyone (Mum).

Runners-up as "fall guys" for Madison Avenue in recent years have been the American Indians, who until a decade ago were truly the silent Americans. They went on the warpath in 1965 when a Calvert distiller ad showed a Sioux brave in a war bonnet holding a slug of the company's new booze.

---

*From "Madison Avenue Minds Its P's and Q's," *San Diego Union*, August 30, 1970. By permission of the North American Newspaper Alliance.

The caption read: "If the Sioux had soft whiskey, they never would have called it firewater. The Indians didn't call whiskey 'firewater' for nothing. (Why do you think they were yelping all the time?)"

Quick as an arrow, the Association of American Indian Affairs shot off a volley of telegrams to Calvert, the New York City Commission on Human Rights, and to Doyle Dane Bernbach, the red-faced agency that created the horror. Within one week after the ads broke nationally in 300 newspapers, outdoor postings and magazines, Calvert killed the campaign and about $600,000 went up in smoke.

The Indian association went into action the next year, too, complaining to Pillsbury that the company's "Funny Face" drink mix wrappers carried caricatures that "hold up to ridicule some 550,000 American Indian citizens and 700,000 American citizens of oriental descent."

The mixes were Injun Juice, which showed a cross-eyed, grinning Indian, and Chinese Cherry, depicting a buck-toothed oriental. The products were promptly renamed Jolly Ollie Orange and Choo-Choo Cherry and the funny faces came off.

Ironically, Madison Avenue has coordinated and consulted so long and carefully with the Negro and Jewish communities that it can now play up their ethnic qualities without fear of a backlash. Yiddishims—in speech and manner—are old hat now in the ad game (El Al helped lead the way with its Jewish mother proclaiming the virtues of "my son the pilot"). And now Sea & Ski has black comedian Flip Wilson selling a product to whites: "If you think brown is beautiful and you weren't born that way, like some folks we know, get Sea & Ski."

Every so often, of course, somebody still makes a boo-boo, like the newspaper ad run by TEC Cash Register Corporation in 1967. It showed an elderly gentleman wearing a yamulkah (skull cap) and holding a cash register, remarking "oy vay!" Jewish leaders thought the ad portrayed Jews as overly money-oriented.

The fact is that nobody is insultable these days unless he consents to being insulted. One agency man, who prefers not to be identified, says you can still get away with maligning Gypsies ("they don't seem to care what you say—or at least they don't have an anti-defamation group yet"). And James Reilly, of Foote,

Cone & Belding (the ad agency that handles the controversial Frito Bandito commercial) says, "actually, I suppose you could insult the good old WASP (White Anglo-Saxon Protestant). He's the man you can probably most safely offend."

The Mexican-American Anti-Defamation Committee is making its voice heard on "the mad avenue." It got the Elgin Company to apologize, and to promise not to repeat the Zapata ad. And Foote, Cone & Belding have yielded on the personal appearance of Frito Bandito. Whereas he first appeared two years ago as a slovenly gun-slinger, he soon became clean-shaven and neat. Following the assassination of Sen. Robert Kennedy, he cut out the gun play.

Still there were protests, and last Christmas Bill R. Jones, Frito-Lay national advertising manager, rose to Bandito's defense, describing him as "amusing, likable, cute and lovable." He discounted the complaints by citing a survey of 1,600 Mexican-Americans in Los Angeles and San Jose which showed that "85 percent interviewed had no hangup on the Bandito whatsoever, 8 percent did have a hangup and 7 percent couldn't care less."

Nevertheless, four months ago the company announced it planned to dump Frito Bandito.

Suggestions for Further Reading

1. Angela Y. Davis et al., *If They Come in the Morning: Voices of Resistance* (New York: New American Library, 1971).

     A collection of powerful writings on the theme of black liberation from an oppressive system.

2. Mervyn M. Dymally (ed.), *The Black Politician: His Struggle For Power* (Belmont, Ca.: Duxbury, 1971).

     The challenge of black politics is viewed by practitioners such as Julian Bond, Carl Stokes, Richard Hatcher, Shirley Chisholm, Charles Evers, and others.

3. LeRoi Jones and Larry Neal (eds.), *Black Fire* (New York: William Morrow, 1968).

     This anthology contains writings by today's newest generation of Black Power advocates and artists.

4. Seymour Matin Lipset, "Anti-Semitism from the Left," *Los Angeles Times*, January 3, 1971.

     The revival of anti-Semitism is cited in this perceptive article.

5. Robert J. Minton, Jr., *Inside Prison American Style* (New York: Random House, 1971).

     As the struggle for reducing racism spreads to all segments of society, prisons become the focal point of observations and proposals. This anthology of inmate writings reveals the extent of the problem.

6. *Time Magazine,* Special Issue, "Black America 1970," April 6, 1970.

INDEX

A

Abernathy, Ralph, 24

Aguinaldo, Emilio, 106, 120

Alcatraz, 53, 311–312

Allotment Act of 1887, *see*
   Dawes Act

American Creed, xx

American Dilemma, xx, 45, 291,
   292, 293, 296
     See also Myrdal, Gunnar

"American Dream," xx, 269, 291,
   292, 334

Anglo, xxi, 334–338

Anglo-Americans, *see* Anglo

Anglo-Saxon, 85, 108, 118, 129,
   154, 165, 177, 183, 325
     mission, 30, 80
     superiority, 80, 107, 108, 109,
   115, 116, 117, 165
     See also WASP

Apartheid, xiv, 8, 23–24, 223

"Asiatic coolieism," *see* Coolie
   labor

Assimilation, xix, xxiv, 25, 51, 112,
   129, 130, 177, 183, 184, 194, 296,
   325

B

Baldwin, James, 251

"Ban the Japs," 140, 143

"Bargain of 1876," 212

"Benign neglect," 268

"Black apes," 12

Black Caucus, 268

Black Codes, 210
     South Carolina, 28

Black Panthers, 30, 316 ff.

Black power, 16, 233, 316, 339–342,
   366

Bond, Julian, 366

"Braceros," 102

Brown Berets, 30, 319

Brown brothers, *see* "Our little
   brown brothers"

Brown, H. Rap, 342

Bureau of Indian Affairs, 68, 75

Burgess, John, 108–110

C

Calhoun, John C., 83

Carmichael, Stokely, 251, 315, 326,
   343, 346

Caste system, 5, 6, 19
Chamberlain, Houston Stewart,
    18, 165
Chargin, Gerald, 32
Chavez, Cesar, 82, 102, 353 ff.
Cherokee Indians, 53, 62–64
    removal, xxii, 61–65, 105
Chicano, xxi, 82, 94, 102, 176, 353,
    355
    See also Grape strikers
Chisholm, Shirley, 366
Clark, Kenneth, 221, 345
Cleaver, Eldridge, 316, 326, 345,
    350–351
Cobbs, Price, 346
Congress of Racial Equality,
    see CORE
Coolie labor, 36–37, 129, 359
CORE, 234
Corona, Bert, 253 ff.
Coughlin, Father Charles E., 162,
    168
Crèvecoeur, J. Hector St. John de,
    xix
Crusade for Justice, 82
Cruse, Harold, 345, 346, 351, 352

D

Davis, Angela, 357
Dawes Act, 73
Dearborn Independent, 161–162,
    163, 167, 186
De Tocqueville, Alexis, 71–72, 296
Douglas, Stephen, 35, 262, 263
Douglass, Frederick, 31, 38
Dred Scott decision, 35, 199
DuBois, W. E. B., 233, 274, 277 ff.

E

Ellison, Ralph, 251, 296
Emancipation Proclamation, 263

Ethnocentrism, xxii, 16–17, 19–21,
    52
Evers, Charles, 366

F

"Fifty-four Forty or Fight," 79
Fiske, John, 108–110
Ford, Henry, 161–163, 167, 173,
    186
Foreign Miners' Tax, 90–94
Frank, Leo, 161
Frito Bandito, 363, 365

G

Genocide, 3, 33, 51, 52, 317
Gentlemen's Agreement of 1907,
    130, 136, 141
"GI babies," 11
Gobineau, Count de, 18, 165
Gong Lum v. *Rice* (1927), 130
Gonzalez, Rodolfo "Corky," 82
Goolagong, Evonne, 24
Grant, Madison, 165
Grant, Ulysses, 158, 159
Grape strikers, 81
Greeley, Horace, 263 ff.
Gregory, Dick, 251
Grier, William, 346 ff.
Groppi, Father James, 326
Guadalupe-Hidalgo, Treaty of, 81,
    86, 332, 334–337, 354
Guevara, Che, 322

H

Hamilton, Charles, 346 ff.
Hatcher, Richard, 366
Hickel, Walter, 53
Hilton, Henry, 160
    See also Seligman-Hilton
    Affair

Hippies, xxi
"Honky," 341
Humphrey, Hubert, xiii

I

Indian Bureau, *see* Bureau of
    Indian Affairs
Indian Removal Act, 62
    See also Cherokee Indians,
        removal

J

Jackson, Andrew, 52, 61, 62, 63,
    71, 117, 118, 253
Jefferson Thomas, 20, 21, 35, 118,
    256, 258 ff.
"Jim Crow," 45, 206, 294
Johnson, Lyndon B., 234, 292, 304

K

Kearney, Denis, 132
Kearny, Stephen W., 333–334
Kennedy, John F., 256, 299, 304
Kennedy, Robert F., 67, 68, 235,
    365
Kerner Report, xv, 29, 242, 292,
    293, 352
King, Martin Luther, xx, 247, 251,
    291, 328, 345–347
KKK, *see* Ku Klux Klan
Know-Nothing Party, 188, 191,
    193, 194
Korematsu v. *United States*, 151
Ku Klux Klan, 42, 161, 165, 167

L

La Alianza, 330 ff.
*Letters from an American
    Farmer, see* Crèvecoeur

Lincoln, Abraham, 35, 81, 119, 159,
    208, 209, 233, 262 ff., 301
Lynching, xxiv, 40–42, 203

M

Malcolm X, 251, 316, 340, 345
Manifest Destiny, 30, 80, 109, 111,
    334
March on Washington, xx
Marshall, John, 61, 64, 71
McKinley, William, 106, 118, 120,
    121
MECHA, 82
Meredith, James, 291, 292, 299,
    346
Monk, Maria, 190–191
Montagu, Ashley, xxiii
My Lai, 30
Myrdal, Gunnar, xx, xxi, 293
    See also American Dilemma

N

NAACP, 221, 233, 243, 274, 275,
    277 ff.
National Advisory Commission
    on Civil Disorders
    See Kerner Report
Nativism, 89, 187, 193, 194
"Niggers," 41, 42, 44, 217
Nixon, Richard, xi, 66, 256, 268 ff.,
    299

O

"One year later," 292
"Our little brown brothers," 105,
    119, 125
"Our worst wartime mistake," 139
"Overseas Chinese," 6

P

People v. *Hall* (1854), 130
Plessy v. *Ferguson* (1896), 200
Police brutality, 318
Powell, Enoch, 3
Protocols of the Elders of Zion,
    148, 162, 163, 166–167

R

"Red power," 15, 53
Relocation camps, 130, 135–140
Report of the National Advisory
    Commission on Civil Disorders,
    see Kerner Report
Robinson, Jackie, 37, 222
Roosevelt, Franklin, 137, 149,
    267 ff.
Roosevelt, Theodore, xix, 18, 21,
    105, 113, 136, 141, 265 ff., 270
Russell, Bill, 251

S

"Salad bowl," xiii
Salazar, Ruben, 82
Schlesinger, Arthur M., xx
Schultz, Alfred P., 165
Schurz, Carl, 112–113
Scott, Dred, *see* Dred Scott
    decision
Seligman-Hilton affair, 173
Seligman, Joseph, 160–161
Shelley v. *Kraemer* (1948), 223
Silberman, Charles, 344
SNCC, 234, 339, 342
Social Darwinism, 20, 22, 106, 314
Soledad Brothers, 357
Stokes, Carl, 366
Strong, Josiah, 108, 109–110

T

Taney, Roger, Chief Justice, 35,
    199

Thoreau, Henry, 81
Tijerina, Reies Lopez, 330 ff.
Tio Taco, 53
Tocqueville, *see* De Tocqueville
"Trail of Tears," 61
    See also Cherokee Indians
Trotter, William Monroe, 276-278

U

"Uncle Tom," 53
"Uncle Tomahawk," 53
Untouchables, *see* Caste system

V

Villard, Oswald Garrison, 274 ff.

W

Waldheim, Kurt, 23
Washington, Booker T., 233, 246,
    274, 275 ff., 298
Washington, George, 253, 256,
    269
WASP, xxi, 129, 175, 179, 325, 365
Watts Riot (1965), 292, 304
"White Man's Burden," 106
Williams, Bert, 43
Williams, Dr. Daniel Hale, 222
Williams, Robert F., 14, 351
Wilson, Flip, 364
Wilson, Woodrow, 166, 270 ff.
Wounded Knee, 30

Y

"Yellow Peril," 130
Yippies, xxi
Young, Whitney, 347
Young Lords, xiii, 125, 319 ff.

Z

Zangwill, Israel, xix
Zapata, Emiliano, 363
Zoot-suit riots, 81, 102